EXPERTISE IN REGULATION AND LAW

Expertise in Regulation and Law

Edited by

GARY EDMOND
University of New South Wales, Australia

ASHGATE

Published by
Ashgate Publishing Limited
Gower House
Croft Road
Aldershot
Hants GU11 3HR
England

Ashgate Publishing Company
Suite 420
101 Cherry Street
Burlington, VT 05401-4405
USA

Ashgate website: http://www.ashgate.com

British Library Cataloguing in Publication Data
Law's Experts Conference (2002 : Canberra, A.C.T.)
 Expertise in regulation and law. - (Applied legal
 philosophy)
 1.Evidence, Expert - Congresses
 I.Title II.Edmond, Gary
 347'.067

Library of Congress Cataloging-in-Publication Data
Expertise in regulation and law / edited by Gary Edmond.
      p. cm. -- (Applied legal philosophy)
   Includes bibliographical references and index.
   ISBN 0-7546-2401-3
    1. Administrative law--United States. 2. Evidence, Expert--United States. I. Edmond,
Gary. II. Series.

 KF5422.E97 2004
 342.73'06--dc22

ISBN 0 7546 2401 3

2004057370

Printed in Great Britain by Antony Rowe Ltd, Chippenham, Wiltshire

Contents

Contributors

John Abraham is Professor of Sociology and Director of the Centre for Research in Health and Medicine (CRHaM) at the University of Sussex. His previous authored books include *Science, Politics and the Pharmaceutical Industry* (UCL/St Martins Press, 1995); *The Therapeutic Nightmare: The battle over the world's most controversial sleeping pill* (Earthscan, 1999); and *Regulating Medicines in Europe* (Routledge, 2000). He is also editor of *Regulation of the Pharmaceutical Industry* (PalgraveMacmillan, 2003). Address: Dept of Sociology, School of Social Sciences & Cultural Studies, Arts E Building, University of Sussex, Falmer, Brighton BN1 9SN, UK. email: J.W.Abraham@sussex.ac.uk

David S. Caudill is Professor of Law and Alumni Faculty Fellow at Washington and Lee University, where he teaches property, contracts, and legal ethics. His books include *Lacan and the Subject of Law* (Prometheus Books, 1997) and *Disclosing tilt: Law, belief, and criticism* (Free University Press, 1989), and he is co-editor of a volume of essays entitled *Radical Philosophy of Law* (Humanities Press 1994). He has published numerous journal articles in the fields of law and religion, psychoanalytic theory, law and literature, and professional ethics; his recent works are studies of scientific expertise in the courtroom. Address: School of Law — Lewis Hall, Washington and Lee University, Lexington, Virginia 24450, USA. email: CaudillD@wlu.edu

Simon A. Cole is Assistant Professor of Criminology, Law and Society at the University of California, Irvine. He received his AB in History from Princeton University and his PhD in Science and Technology Studies from Cornell University. He specializes in the historical and sociological study of the interaction between science, technology, law and criminal justice. He is the author of *Suspect Identities: A History of Fingerprinting and Criminal Identification* (Harvard University Press, 2001), which was awarded the 2003 Rachel Carson Prize by the Society for Social Studies of Science. Address: Department of Criminology, Law and Society, School of Social Ecology, 2357 Social Ecology II, University of California, Irvine CA 92697-7080, USA. email: scole@uci.edu

Gary Edmond is a Senior Lecturer in the Faculty of Law at the University of New South Wales. His research interests focus on expert evidence, the public understanding of law and the relations between law and science. He is particularly interested in mass torts, miscarriages of justice and the legal use of social science and humanities research. He originally trained in the history and philosophy of science and subsequently received a law degree from the University of Sydney and a PhD in law from the University of Cambridge. Address: Faculty of Law,

The University of New South Wales, Sydney 2052, Australia.
email: g.edmond@unsw.edu.au

Marc A. Eisner is Professor of Government in the Government Department at Wesleyan University. He is the author of several books on regulation, political economy, and American political development. His major publications include *Antitrust and the Triumph of Economics* (University of North Carolina Press, 1991), *Regulatory Politics in Transition* (Johns Hopkins University Press, 1993, second edition 2000), *The State in the American Political Economy* (Prentice Hall, 1995), *Contemporary Regulatory Policy* (co-author with Jeff Worsham, Evan J. Ringquist and Lynne Rienner, 2000) and *From Warfare State to Welfare State* (Pennsylvania State University Press, 2000). His current research examines corporate environmental policy and the implications for regulatory reform. Address: Department of Government, John E. Andrus Public Affairs Center, Wesleyan University, Middletown, CT 06459, USA.
email: meisner@wesleyan.edu

Alan Irwin is Professor of Sociology at Brunel University, West London. He is the author of *Risk and the Control of Technology* (Manchester University Press, 1985), *Citizen Science* (Routledge, 1995) and *Sociology and the Environment* (Polity, 2001). He is co-author (with Mike Michael) of *Science, Social Theory and Public Knowledge* (Open University Press, 2003). With Brian Wynne, he co-edited *Misunderstanding Science?* (Cambridge University Press, 1996). Alan Irwin's research interests include sociology of the environment, scientific governance and science-public relations. He is currently studying the relationship between risk understanding and social exclusion. He is also part of a thematic network exploring 'Science, Technology and Governance in Europe' (STAGE). Address: Department of Human Sciences, Brunel University, Uxridge UB8 3PH, UK.
email: Alan.Irwin@brunel.ac.uk

Michael Lynch is Professor in the Department of Science and Technology Studies at Cornell University. He has a background in sociology, and specializes in studies of the organization of day-to-day laboratory practices. He has also studied the organization of courtroom testimony, and is currently studying the intersection of law and science in criminal investigations involving DNA profiling. His publications include *Scientific Practice and Ordinary Action* (Cambridge University Press, 1993), which reviews and critically examines social constructionism in social studies of science, and (with David Bogen), *The Spectacle of History: Speech, Text, and Memory at the Iran-Contra Hearings* (Duke University Press, 1996). Address: Department of Science and Technology Studies, Cornell University, 632 Clark Hall, Ithaca, NY 14853-2401 USA.
email: mel27@cornell.edu

David Mercer is a Senior Lecturer in the Science, Technology and Society program at the University of Wollongong, Australia. His research interests include

the interaction of law and science, and public understanding of science and technology. Current projects include an analysis of the 'vertical integration of expertise' in controversial areas of science, discourses of 'risk' in the EMF and mobile telephone debates, and the social history of communication technology. Address: Science, Technology and Society, School of Social Science Media and Communication, University of Wollongong, NSW 2522, Australia.
email: david_mercer@uow.edu.au

David Turnbull is a fellow at Deakin, Melbourne, Monash and Lancaster Universities. His itinerant scholarship is concerned with knowledge and space, indigenous knowledge and databases, weather knowledge, and narratives of prehistory. Address: 591 Canning St, Nth Carlton, Vic 3054, Australia.
email turnbull@deakin.edu.au

Preface

The essays in this volume emerged from a conference on expertise sponsored by the ANU and held in Canberra in August 2002. The speakers were invited and each maintains a longstanding research interest in the area. After the conference the papers were reviewed and revised for publication in this collection.

I would like to thank all of those who participated in the *Law's Experts* Conference whether as speakers, respondents, attendees, organizers or sponsors. The following participants presented challenging papers, comments and ideas which helped to refine and clarify some of the issues at the heart of this collection: John Abraham, Rachel Ankeny, John Braithwaite, Chris Bryant, David Caudill, Simon Cole, Tony Connolly, Angus Corbett, Susan Dodds, Marc Eisner, Ian Freckelton, Jeremy Gans, Jane Goodman-Delehunty, Stephen Healy, Keith Houghton, Alan Irwin, Andrew Ligertwood, Mike Lynch, Leighton McDonald, David Mercer, Rosemary Robins, Tim Rowse, Colin Scott, Hugh Selby, Margaret Somerville, Jane Stapleton, David Turnbull and Judy Wajcman.

The international depth of this collection reflects the very generous contribution toward the costs of the Conference provided by the ANU, in particular from the National Institute of Government and Law (NIGL), the Law Program in the Research School of Social Sciences (RSSS) and RegNet. Later, the Faculty of Law at the University of New South Wales provided financial assistance for the final preparation of the manuscript. This enabled Janice Beavan, albeit late in the day, to provide invaluable editorial assistance.

The success of the Conference was in no small part the result of the planning, logistical support and enthusiasm provided by Chris Treadwell, Bronwyn Stuart and Chris Debono.

I would also like to express my special thanks to Jane Stapleton, Peter Cane and John Braithwaite. The Law Program in the Research School of Social Science at the Australian National University provided tremendous stimulation and hospitality during my year in Canberra. Finally, I thank Tom Campbell and Ashgate/Dartmouth.

Gary Edmond

Abbreviations

AAAS	American Association for the Advancement of Science
ADR	adverse drug reaction
AEBC	Agriculture and Environment Biotechnology Commission (UK)
ALF	Atlantic Legal Foundation
AMA	American Medical Association
BSE	bovine spongiform encephalopathy ('mad cow' disease)
CMR	Centre for Medicines Research
CNS	central nervous system
COMAR	Committee on Man and Radiation
DNA	deoxyribonucleic acid
EBM	evidence-based medicine
EMF	electric and magnetic fields
EMS	environmental management systems
EPA	Environmental Protection Agency (US)
EWG	expert working group
FDA	Food and Drug Administration (US)
FOIA	Freedom of Information Act (US)
FRE	Federal Rules of Evidence (US)
FSE	farm scale evaluations
GM	genetically modified or genetic modification
HPS	history and philosophy of science
ICH	International Conference of Technical Requirements for Registration of Pharmaceuticals for Human Use
ICNIRP	International Committee for Non-Ionising Radiation Protection
IEEE	Institute of Electrical and Electronics Engineers Inc.
IFAR	International Foundation for Art Research
IFPMA	International Federation of Pharmaceutical Manufacturers Associations
IoM	Institute of Medicine
JPMA	Japanese Pharmaceutical Manufacturers' Association
LCGIS	London Centre for Governance Innovation and Science
LEO	Legal Ethics Opinions
MLP	multi-locus probe
NAAQS	National Ambient Air Quality Standards (US)
NAS	National Academy of Sciences (US)
NDA	new drug application
NEPT	National Environmental Performance Track (US)
NGO	non-governmental organization
NRC	National Research Council (US)
OMB	Office of Management and Budget (US)

OMB-OIRA	Office of Management and Budget's Office of Information and Regulatory Affairs (US)
PCDB	Public Consultation on Developments in the Biosciences (UK)
PCR	polymerase chain reaction
PDAC	Psychopharmacological Advisory Committee (US)
PUS	public understanding of science
QC/QA	quality control/quality assurance
RCEP	Royal Commission on Environmental Pollution (UK)
RIA	regulatory impact assessments
RF	radiofrequency radiation
SLP	single-locus probe
SPS	Shirley Primary School Trustees
SRS	spontaneous reporting system
SSK	sociology of scientific knowledge
STR	short-tandem repeat
STS	science and technology studies or science, technology and society
VNTR	variable number tandem repeat
WHO	World Health Organization

Cases

Chapter 1

Experts and Expertise in Legal and Regulatory Settings

Gary Edmond and David Mercer

Introduction

Who is an expert? How is expertise authorized? How are the opinions of one expert to be weighed against those of another? Can experts be trusted? What are the responsibilities of an expert? Are the legal and regulatory demands placed on experts distorting expert practice? How should courts and regulators deal with new technological processes and knowledge claims? What processes or institutional designs will produce the most appropriate forms of expertise? How do we prevent experts from becoming advocates or 'hired guns'? How do our visions of society shape our responses to expertise (and vice versa)? While many of these questions are not new, what binds the contributions to this book is an empirical orientation explicitly sensitive to changing discourses about science and expertise and the emergence of new institutional forms and procedures.

Most of the chapters have been shaped by recent and intense debate over the nature of expertise (see, for example, Turner 2001; Collins and Evans 2002). Renewed interest in expertise seems to have been prompted by a series of crises, public controversies and litigation clusters, many of which are ongoing. 'Mad cow' disease, genetically modified organisms, environmental pollution, the regulation of domestic economies, the efficacy and distribution of pharmaceuticals, recognition of indigenous knowledges, changes in forensic science, institutional reform and the ethical dimensions of expertise have brought expertise to the forefront of contemporary politics, law and regulation. As the subject matter for this collection, these examples provide a clear indication of the continuing significance of experts and expertise in public life. Protracted controversies, unimaginative proposals for reform, the prevalence of polemical concepts such as 'junk science' and impediments to public participation all point toward limitations in much contemporary theory and practice.

Most commentators treat the concepts of *expert* and *expertise* as non-problematic. The concepts are presented as predetermined, temporally and spatially stable, quite often obvious, and even natural. Typically, 'experts' from specific fields, occupations or with special skills—perceived or represented as relevant— are identified and their 'expertise'—whether skills, opinions, authority and so on— invoked, evaluated or criticized. *Problems* tend to arise when experts stray beyond their *proper* sphere, *misrepresent* their knowledge or experience, *exaggerate* degrees of certitude and *disregard* the standards (or norms) of their field or profession. In contrast, the essays in this text encourage the reader to dispense with some of these commitments in order to direct attention to the roles played by experts and expertise in real world situations.

Questions around what counts as expertise and who is an expert need to be examined in *context*. What ought to be considered as 'context', along with its perceived significance, will vary. It will depend on the stakes involved, the issues being considered, the resources available, the strength of institutional traditions, rules and procedures, the position of institutions in the particular legal or regulatory hierarchy, the audiences, and the interests of experts and those engaging them. What we can suggest is that *expertise has no natural condition*. Definitions of expertise, like the development, mobilization, appropriation and representation of expertise, are always situated, always purposive. That some experts and some forms of expertise appear mundane, institutionally appropriate or uncontroversial should not disguise the historical emergence of different kinds of expertise, the roles of legal and regulatory institutions in the social legitimation of specific kinds of expertise, competition between individual experts or entire fields, and continuing professional and institutional dynamics.[1] Attention to context extends the analytical focus *beyond* the technical content of expertise.

The following essays provide a challenging response to much of the existing literature on expertise in legal and regulatory settings. Each of the studies problematizes the ostensibly orderly operation of legal and regulatory institutions, especially in relation to the roles played by experts and expert knowledge. Each, in its own way, could be read to suggest that attempts to design (or reform) institutions and procedures to produce (non-problematized forms of) *objective*, *neutral*, *impartial* or *reliable* knowledge might be incorrigible. None of the contributors makes recourse to such simplistic images of expertise, accepts expert rhetorics at 'face value' or adverts to the need for, or possibility of, acquiring more *objective* knowledge. To suggest that expertise, whether in courts or regulatory agencies, can be reduced to impersonal formulaic expressions trivializes or excludes the social, institutional and political dimensions which underlay the production, management and representation of all expert knowledge. Instead, these essays illustrate the complexity intrinsic to the production and use of expert knowledge during the transition from specialist to other domains—particularly policy formation, regulatory standard-setting and litigation. Consequently, our understanding of the production and use of specialized knowledges and skills is infused at every stage with potential socio-political significance.

The essays might also be read in a way that suggests the need for caution. There may be a need to temper the expectations we place on institutions, procedures, experts and decision-makers. The contributions, therefore, raise important and enduring questions about the shapes of our legal, regulatory and political institutions and the nature and roles of expertise in contemporary democratic societies (see Albury 1983; Ezrahi 1990).

Knowledge in context: Sociological approaches to experts and expertise

From here this essay is divided into two parts. Part one offers several themes for approaching the study of expertise in legal, regulatory and political settings. Insights from recent empirical studies of science and technology suggest fresh sites and issues for investigation. They direct attention to areas which have often escaped investigation because they were not perceived as significant or to have serious social and epistemological implications. They expand our analytical scope beyond poorly theorized or empirically implausible images of expertise and unreflective aspersions directed at the technical competence of lawyers, judges and other publics. The second part offers two interpretations of the influential *Daubert v Merrell Dow Pharmaceuticals, Inc.* decision.[2] These divergent interpretations illustrate how theories of expertise may generate very different impressions of the operation of our legal and regulatory systems as well as the social and political implications of procedures and decision-making.

Context shapes contests over expertise and the emergence of specific forms of expertise

Expertise is not mono-dimensional. Expert knowledge, authority and opinions are regularly contested, and contested in ways which are sensitive to the standing and credibility of individuals (Shapin 1994, 1995), the organization of the discipline, field or profession (Gieryn 1998; Abbott 1988), the particular (institutional) context (Wootten 2003; Glass 2003), and pervasive public registers of science and expertise (Irwin and Wynne 1996).

Expertise is designed (or adapted) for particular settings and to fulfil particular purposes within those, usually institutional, settings. Usually this requires active processes of selection, emphasis and omission. It may also involve misrepresentation, exaggeration and, particularly in legal settings, degrees of simplification (Hilgartner 1990). Contests around the meaning of technical and specialized knowledges unavoidably, and sometimes strategically, 'spill over' into debates about rules, procedures, public technical literacy, public safety, the economic consequences of decision-making, the significance and reliability of instruments, the meanings of standards and guidelines, and even arcane debates about the philosophy of science. Because regulatory institutions, courts and public inquiries have established rules, procedures and traditions—usually reflecting entrenched politico-legal values such as procedural fairness, degrees of transparency and burdens of proof—the use and assessment of expert knowledge is difficult to extricate from its specific institutional incarnations. Controversies, therefore, routinely extend beyond the technical dimensions associated with 'battles' between experts and are not adequately captured by the concept of legal or regulatory *distortion* (Hand 1901; Goldberg 1994).

Extending our analytical focus beyond narrow technical debates or knowledge claims reveals how experts are simultaneously required to balance a range of expectations and obligations which may be in tension. For example, an expert may need to provide expertise tailored to the needs of an employer, and attend to their professional and ethical responsibilities, while adhering to particular institutional requirements and rules (Caudill in this volume).[3] In many legal and regulatory contexts being (perceived as) a *competent* expert requires training, a performance and reputation which extends beyond the provision of detail or demonstrations of technical prowess. Some experts are chameleon-like in their ability to adapt to or manipulate legal or administrative processes. As the essay by Mercer (in this volume) suggests, many experts are entrepreneurial: able to deftly traverse a variety of settings and perform in a variety of capacities. To designate experts with positions in international organizations responsible for negotiating health standards, such as the World Health Organization, *and* who hold professional consultancies to large corporations or trade groups, *and* undertake research, *and* possess considerable experience as advisers and witnesses—including some with legal qualifications—simply as 'experts' is to eliminate some of the complexity associated with, and stimulated by, modern legal and regulatory practice. It excludes—or suggests the possibility of excluding—the disciplinary constraints, social character, institutional dimensions and valencies of what is presented and recognized as expertise.

Recognizing social, disciplinary and institutional dimensions, and their interactions, is important for understanding expertise. Many areas of specialization, such as the forensic sciences, patent and intellectual property law, and certain areas of psychology, psychiatry, epidemiology and social work, possess something of a *hybridized* legal or regulatory character which reflects their historical emergence *in tandem* with particular legal and regulatory cultures (Wynne 1989a; Cambrosio et al. 1990; King and Kaganas 1998).[4] The peculiar history of adversarial trial procedures (Langbein 1977, 2003; Damaska 1997) and the more recent creation of regulatory agencies has generated a range of institutional forms which bolstered their own legitimacy through the use of experts and expertise. Courts and agencies continue to play an important role in the *recognition*, *legitimation* and *status* of different forms of expertise (Jasanoff 1990).

Furthermore, the contextualization of expertise frequently shifts agency, and consequently the analytical focus, from the evidence (which once purportedly 'spoke for itself') to experts, decision-makers, institutions, traditions and the procedures associated with the situated production, representation and assessment of expertise. Even where specific types of expertise are privileged or predominate, we should remain alert to the conditions in which particular forms of expertise emerge (or have emerged), flourish and decline (e.g. Mnookin 1998; Haflon 1998; Golan 2004).

Institutions, rules and procedures confer advantages and disadvantages

The institutions and processes designed to deal with experts and expertise are inherently and unavoidably political, conferring (dis)advantages and opening the possibility for strategic action both in particular settings and beyond (Abraham and Eisner in this volume).

In the US, the last two decades have witnessed intense debate around the most *appropriate*—in this context a politically loaded—standard for the admissibility of expert evidence in federal courts. Large corporations have been among the most active participants in campaigns for reform. Manufacturers and insurers—in Galanter's (1974) terminology, the highly experienced, attentive and well-resourced 'repeat players'—have orchestrated high profile campaigns designed to raise the standards governing the admission of expert evidence *as well as* tighten substantial tort and product liability doctrine (Edmond and Mercer 2004). That is, institutional rules and procedures and legal standards, *as well as* individual proffers of evidence, have been subjected to protracted scrutiny, critique and revision.

The contest around admissibility standards represents an important site in the struggle over the volume of civil litigation. If the standards for the admission of expert evidence are raised it confers advantages upon civil defendants, particularly serial defendants (i.e. the 'repeat players'). Higher admissibility standards may also have chilling effects which radiate beyond the courts. More onerous admissibility standards may prevent recourse to litigation as a response to a perceived grievance. They make it harder for plaintiffs to succeed and tend to reduce the amount of litigation. Potential litigants may either 'lump it' or pursue alternative 'solutions'. If, by contrast, admissibility standards were lowered it may become easier for plaintiffs (and their lawyers) to find *relevant* experts, to litigate and negotiate settlements. These conditions may encourage more plaintiffs and greater recourse to law as a remedy for perceived social ills. Judges, legislatures, regulators, lawyers, manufacturers, insurers, labor and consumer organizations are all acutely aware of these implications.

In addition to localized struggles and protracted contests over rules and procedures there are other ways in which legal and regulatory forms of life may shape proceedings and outcomes. Some types of 'expertise' may be discounted or excluded by the terms of reference or the traditions and values which govern an institution. In a well-known study of the Windscale Inquiry into nuclear power, Brian Wynne (1982) examined the way in which Justice Parker delimited the *legitimate* scope of his inquiry. While the Inquiry held serious implications for the future of British policy on nuclear power, the proceedings assumed a form which effectively excluded discussion of energy policy. Questions on these topics were raised predominantly by environmental groups, whose assembled expertise did not always neatly conform with the fairly conventional legal categories imposed by the Inquiry. Under Justice Parker, the Inquiry preferred evidence which could be quantified, such as 'scientific risk estimates', presented by experts with more legally familiar credentials. These particular framing choices, shaped by Parker's legal training and judicial experience, tended to favor industry groups. Parker routinely preferred evidence derived from more 'recognisable' forms of expertise, such as engineering and physics, particularly from those experts with industrial experience with nuclear power (see also Yearley 1989).

Expertise rarely stands alone

Expert knowledge is usually combined with other types of knowledge and values, frequently in novel (factual and/or institutional) situations. These combinations can make assessments quite complicated.

It is rare for courts or regulators to be confronted with a single type of evidence. And, even rarer to be confronted with a single type of 'unequivocal' evidence. Consequently, decision-makers are often required to choose between or evaluate a range of different types of evidence and opinions. How, for example, should epidemiological evidence be weighed against apparently inconsistent *in vivo, in vitro* and chemical structure evidence? Even where there are long traditions associated with the use of particular types of evidence and established preferences, these may be qualified by the existence of other types of evidence, controversy around the value of the preferred evidence or (apparent) inconsistencies between different types of evidence.

This kind of issue may be particularly acute in trials where the evidence of experts is combined with the testimony of lay people; whether victims, witnesses or defendants. The combinations may require considerable finesse and creativity as common law judges and lay juries seek to evaluate contradictory claims from a variety of different sources. How should incriminating DNA evidence be compared with the inconsistent recollections of a distressed witness (Lynch and McNally 2003)? These types of assessments can become acute. In indigenous land claims and heritage protection litigation the evidence of historians, sociologists, anthropologists, archaeologists and linguists is regularly evaluated in conjunction with indigenous oral history, art, dance and mythology, and occasionally disparate Aboriginal voices (Goodrich 1990; Turnbull in this volume) by judges entrenched in, what Twining (1990: 32–91) has described as, 'the rationalist tradition of evidence scholarship'. Sensitivity to these 'traditions', like the framing choices enacted by Justice Parker, is important for understanding the treatment of expert evidence as well as judicial rationalizations of decision-making.

Specific contests may be part of a larger controversy

Often, individual trials, submissions to a regulatory agency and appeals can be meaningfully interpreted as *episodes* in ongoing *campaigns*.

In mass tort litigation and miscarriage of justice cases there are a range of options available to the parties. Contests may extend beyond the specific legal or regulatory *context*. The 'innocent' may pursue their case through the media and corporations may lobby congress for revised tort standards or rules of evidence because of the amount of allegedly spurious litigation and its detrimental commercial implications. However, even in specific legal and regulatory settings the parties may embark upon highly strategic action which anticipates responses and recognizes the possibility of (judicial) review, future litigation or continuing relations (e.g. Macaulay 1963; Rabin 1992).

If we consider mass tort litigation, for example, the first case to be litigated on a subject can be extremely influential. The first trial is particularly significant where the suit may—as in problems attributed to a faulty pharmaceutical or therapeutic product—apply to hundreds or even thousands of potential plaintiffs. Corporations are confronted with choices when a plaintiff alleges harm or loss caused by the corporation's products or negligence. The corporation can seek to settle quietly, requiring the plaintiff and lawyers to remain silent about the terms of any settlement. This has the benefit of limiting adverse publicity and the terms of settlement may prevent 'informed' lawyers from pursuing related cases. Alternatively, the corporation might endeavor to defend the allegation. The decision to defend, the associated publicity and the possibility of losing the litigation may stimulate additional suits. Early trials may operate as test cases, with potentially serious implications for future litigation and settlement negotiations, and possibly even the viability of corporations.

Litigants, especially 'repeat players' and experienced plaintiff and defence lawyers, are attentive to the implications (and value) of their tactical decisions, especially on future litigation. In mass tort litigation experts, lawyers, parties and judges refine their tactics and responses diachronically. In the case of the anti-morning sickness drug Bendectin, the manufacturer (Merrell Dow) defended itself in individual trials and simultaneously undertook comprehensive settlement negotiations. Merrell Dow actively challenged the plaintiffs' expert evidence and pursued litigation 'losses' through the courts of appeal. Across the course of a decade of litigation the lawyers for both sides modified their strategies and the kinds of evidence and expert witnesses used (Sanders 1993; Schuck 1986). For example, initially the defendant called the authors of epidemiological and *in vivo* studies to personally testify about their research. In response to critical cross-examination, which attributed 'limitations' in the studies to personal deficiencies of the authors, in later trials the defendant replaced the authors with authoritative generalists. These witnesses were credible experts in the field, apparently unaffiliated to the manufacturer and able to, with an imputed independent authority, excuse or qualify any defects in studies which tended to identify only weak or negligible associations between Bendectin and birth defects.

In large scale litigation individual cases may dramatically influence future litigation. Defendant successes may reduce the number of suits filed or litigated and reduce the value of settlement. Plaintiff successes may encourage the use of administrative solutions. Judicial responses may impose onerous requirements or force individual plaintiffs to become part of a larger 'congregation'. Different *stages* in legal and regulatory processes may shape the selection, presentation and assessment of evidence. From a methodological perspective, the breadth of inquiry and the 'stage(s)' examined will structure how expertise and its treatment is understood. Focusing upon particular stages or cases in isolation may conceal a much richer realm of strategic moves and responses. In consequence, *the trial* or *the case* may not always be the appropriate unit for analysis (Forrester 1996).

Contests involving expertise may continue across multiple arenas

Contests around expertise and procedures for handling expertise may extend beyond the local legal or regulatory context into other settings, such as policy fora and the popular media.

Expertise may be contested in specific legal or regulatory settings according to local rules or contested in other ways. It may be subjected to sustained challenge across many different social spaces. Interventions by litigants and those regulated are not restricted to legal and regulatory forums or specific hearings. Judges and regulators are not insensitive to the institutional, social and political implications of their decision-making, or broader social discourses. Consequently, responses to expertise may be influenced by normative visions of law and regulation and perceptions of the social world (Edmond 2001, 2002c).

Factors, usually conceived as extrinsic to the production and use of expert knowledge, often mediate its treatment and our understanding of it. In recent decades, anxieties about the growth in litigation (Huber 1991, Olson 1991, 2003), an increase in the number of professional expert witnesses allegedly willing to testify in favor of any proposition (Weinstein 1986), increased institutional economic accountability, more active case management (Resnik 1982), the uncertainty associated with many risks (Beck 1992), changes to institutional rules and procedures (Yeazell 1994; Molot 1998; Berger 2001), intense media interest in 'pathological' litigation (Bogus 2001; Chase 1995; Bailis and MacCoun 1996; Garber 1998), concerns about the competence of the (civil) jury, the deleterious social and economic consequences attributed to spurious litigation and excessive regulation (Galanter 1998), have featured prominently in legal and regulatory discourses. Notably, pervasive, though empirically contentious, beliefs about excessive litigation and the prevalence of unreliable expert witnesses appear to have influenced the reception and treatment of expert evidence.[5]

'Objectivity' can assume many forms

The idea of *objectivity* may be useful as a rhetorical (or justificatory) resource but it is inadequate as a description of expert practice or characterization of knowledge. In legal and regulatory settings 'objectivity' is frequently taken to mean different things. Epistemological and moral nuances, notions of intention and effect are mixed and matched. 'Objectivity' can refer to impartiality, emotional detachment, indifference to outcome, truth to Nature and capacity for critical reflection (Albury 1983; Daston and Galison 1992). What is taken as 'objective', in a particular setting, will be linked to networks of ancillary considerations such as conformity with routine practices, formal standards of conduct, and whether expertise is received in an environment of trust, scepticism or conflict (Nelkin 1979; Smith and Wynne 1989).

Notwithstanding the multivalent nature of 'objectivity' and its unreflexive use in much analysis of legal and regulatory practice, several commentators have identified a trend in the way appeals to specific forms of objectivity have changed over time. Theodore Porter (1995), for example, has traced a shift in the way expertise has been legitimated in public life. Porter describes the process as a turn from *disciplinary* to *mechanical* objectivity. 'Disciplinary' objectivity emphasizes tacit learning, experience, social relations and trust, insight, and the need to link solutions to their specific contexts. 'Mechanical' objectivity, in contrast, involves attempts to control individual opinions and biases through reliance on quantification, formal rules and a fixation with methodological review.[6]

In a study of the emergence of evidence-based medicine and standardization in health care, Timmermans and Berg (2003: 132) found that while 'objective' standards may assume an appearance consistent with 'mechanical' objectivity, their practical meaning is unavoidably determined by the context of use. When Dutch insurance physicians were provided with a new 'objective' standard for assessing compensatable health complaints, the criteria, amongst other things, suggested that complaints should be 'objectively medically determinable ... observable in a controllable and reproducible manner ... through means generally accepted in health care'. Despite the formalization of standards, the final part of the 'objective' criteria—'generally accepted in health care'—enabled the physicians to maintain (*subjective*) discretion and professional judgment while apparently adhering to a broader register resonating with Porter's characterization of mechanical objectivity. This example indicates flexibility in the use of *objectivity* and suggests the need to be cautious about embracing the concept as an adequate or unambiguous description of expertise in legal and regulatory practice. Ostensibly *mechanical* or *epistemological* solutions to perceived problems with expertise may simply elide or 'backstage' the more tacit, contingent and discretionary dimensions of expert knowledge and practice (Goffman 1959; Hilgartner 2000). For our purposes, the widespread support for more 'mechanical' means of managing expertise might be understood, on the basis of the attendant justifications, as a self-conscious *epistemological turn*.

Evidence of an 'epistemological turn' can be · found in the emerging expectation, in mass tort and product liability litigation that, in addition to the testimony of a personal physician, an injured plaintiff will adduce quantitative epidemiological evidence (Edmond and Mercer 2000). Here, 'particularist inquiries into individual case histories' have been replaced by concerns about collective efficiency, risk mitigation and simplified criteria for compensation (Jasanoff 2002: 42), legitimated by appeals to the authority of images of science-in-general (Michael 1992). Over the past two decades an 'epistemological turn', incorporating a more overt commitment to 'truth', has been prominent in evidence jurisprudence, law reform and legal decision-making across the common law world (see 'Reading *Daubert*' below). Confronted with more experts, greater specialization, increasing complexity and the *potential* for exogenous criticism, judges and regulators have demonstrated a tendency to embrace (what are presented as) more *epistemologically* focused—for Porter (1995) more *mechanistic*, for Jasanoff (2002) more *regulatory*, and for Lynch (in this volume) more *administrative*—means of organizing and assessing expertise.

Lawyers, judges and regulators have been reluctant to engage with specialized literatures on science and expertise

An endemic, if understandable, reluctance, among regulators, judges, law reformers and lawyers, to systematically engage with research or findings from the humanities and social sciences has led them to embrace popular, but empirically tendentious, images of expertise (e.g. Freckelton, Reddy and Selby 1999; compare Edmond 2004b). The perpetuation of such models—exemplified by 'junk science' and unexplicated images of 'objectivity'—has meant that legal discourse, accounts of social problems and proposed solutions tend to be simplistic, usually empirically misconceived and, by way of understatement, optimistic.

Some of the images regularly invoked in and around legal and regulatory practice appear to be loosely based on heavily criticized and arguably outdated philosophical models of the sciences such as those developed by Karl Popper and Thomas Kuhn (see Fuller 2003). The broad appeal of a few influential, or 'pop', philosophers and bowdlerized, or 'folk', versions of their work should not be underestimated when attempting to understand contemporary approaches to law, regulation and expertise.

One conspicuous example of an under-theorized and impressionistic response to expertise is the customary use of the term 'junk science' in legal and regulatory discourse. Conceptually, 'junk science' is more of a polemical tool than an analytical one. Despite its rhetorical value, definitional imprecision and theoretical superficiality render it unsuited to practically demarcating or assessing expert knowledges. Those who use the term may not experience difficulty identifying what *they believe* to be examples of 'junk science', but they do encounter difficulties when it comes to credibly distinguishing 'junk science' from so-called authentic or proper scientific knowledge on the basis of consistent application of their preferred demarcation criteria. The process of classification (or demarcation) inevitably seems to incorporate overt ideological dimensions (Bowker and Star 1999). These tend to be predicated upon *a priori* commitments which are rarely linked to practical or technical distinctions and almost never engage with specialist literatures (Edmond and Mercer 1998a).

Perhaps it is no coincidence that those alarmed by the purported abundance and pernicious influence of 'junk science' are often proponents of institutional and procedural reform. Their reforms usually advance the need for a more overtly epistemological focus, often including the use of technically skilled decision-makers and/or the need for, and possibility of, attaining *objective* expertise. In England (in 1998) and Australia (between 1999 and 2004) legal reforms were enacted with the aim of reducing partisanship and making litigation more efficient—at least for judges (Woolf 1996; Abadee 2000; compare Edmond 2003). New rules encourage a reduction in the number of expert witnesses appearing in courts in order to reduce the amount of expert disagreement. They also place renewed emphasis on experts' paramount duty to the court, (literally) encourage experts to achieve consensus away from the courtroom, and perpetuate longstanding legal commitment to pragmatically elusive ideals of objectivity. The complexity of institutional reform and the implications of specific changes are often obscured by the range of models of science and expertise promoted as *proper, reliable* and *objective*.

Despite the appeals to various forms of *objectivity*, and the adoption of more explicitly *mechanical* criteria for handling expertise, generally legal and regulatory standards are rationalized through a non-reflexive reliance on syncretic mixtures of scholarly writing, popular impressions of science and expertise, alongside earlier decisions (and authority). Images of science and expertise are routinely tailored to the specifics of a case, drawing from the many *key* features of science and expertise (and exceptions to these features) which litter our cultural landscapes (Edmond 2000, 2001). Judges, legal commentators and regulators often create 'purpose-built' models of science and expertise for specific legal and regulatory needs (e.g. Odgers and Richardson 1995; Freckelton 1994; Foster and Huber 1998; Ruse 1988).

Few commentators seem to be aware of the potential difficulties involved in translating the models of science authorized by universalist epistemological assumptions—characteristic of the 'epistemological turn'—to diverse legal and regulatory arenas. While subjecting knowledge claims to testing and peer review may be an integral, but contested (see Abraham in this volume) part of the culture of pharmaceutical regulation, these types of requirements have not traditionally played a significant role in the practice of many of the forensic sciences. The imposition of *universal* standards or the appropriation of standards developed for other contexts may raise new administrative and justificatory obstacles even for established fields (see Cole and Lynch in this volume).

For common law judges, the potential benefits conferred by engaging with the work of historians, sociologists, anthropologists and philosophers are not always immediately obvious. For an outsider, the social sciences and humanities may appear inconsistent, even incoherent. Indeed, methodological and theoretical pluralism and the proliferation of different 'schools'—whether versions of feminism, law and economics or the sociology of scientific knowledge—may make engagement difficult and appear opportunistic or capricious. These appearances may have been exacerbated by the more epistemologically radical work of postmodern and post-structural theorists (consider Farber 1997; Gross and Levitt 1997). The need to select among the profusion of methods, theories and approaches may actually compromise, or appear to compromise, legal practice— especially legalistic appeals to judicial objectivity.

The suggestion that judges and regulators exhibit little inclination and have few incentives to engage with the history, philosophy or sociology of science is not intended to suggest that they should, or could, embrace such perspectives. Rather, the terms of successful *intervention* in legal and regulatory practice, along with the production of tractable forms of analysis, are areas which require further attention from social scientists and humanities scholars. We need to consider how professionals in the social sciences and humanities might develop and present their knowledge and fields in ways that are both *representative* and *practically useful*. These terms, along with the issue of *reliability*, are not without their difficulties. The most productive interventions may be in the areas of law reform and policy debate around rules and procedures rather than merely attempting to intervene with the provision and assessment of evidence in individual cases. The last essay in this collection suggests that even eminent social scientists exert limited control over how their 'advice' will be used in legal and regulatory contexts and that as a generalization sociologists (and social scientists and humanists) may be more enamored by the courts than vice versa.

At this point it is important to recognize that common law judges, like regulators, are not engaged in the sociology (or philosophy or anthropology or ...) of science or expertise. Any apparent correspondence between legal practice and the reflexive, symmetrical deconstruction often promoted by sociologists of science is largely coincidental (see Lynch 1998). Notwithstanding claims by a few sociologists (e.g. Jasanoff 1995: 211–18), courts do not provide particularly fertile spaces for the systematic *deconstruction* of expert evidence or broader *civic education*. 'Legal deconstruction'—the 'pulling apart' of evidence to expose social contingency, usually during cross-examination—is an analyst's category. Few actors or observers leave the courtroom having learned a sociological 'lesson' about the nature of expertise (Edmond 1998: 391–400). Peculiar rules and procedures and highly strategic action often prevent comprehensive or balanced assessments of evidence in courts and regulatory institutions. Paper trials, consensus regulation and regulatory capture may all accentuate these limitations. The uneven distribution of burdens of proof, power and resources, media reporting, and degrees of evidentiary indeterminacy, allow judges and well-resourced litigants (such as large corporations) to 'teach' many of the lessons.

Even if sustained engagement is unlikely and intervention proves difficult, erratic or indecisive, the case study below demonstrates the immediate value of adopting more explicitly sociological theories of expertise for understanding legal practice, the political dimensions of judicial and regulatory decision-making and the constraints on intervention.

Expertise is not homogenous and lay–expert relations are contextually 'thick'

The interaction between lay and expert knowledge and understanding is an important dimension in legal and regulatory practice, particularly in relation to juries and public participation (Irwin in this volume).

Many accounts of expertise trade upon the existence of a sharp division between lay people and experts. Historically, studies of expertise have approached the relationship between lay and expert perspectives rather broadly. Sociological accounts have responded to increasing specialization in Western society and dependence, in daily life, on new forms of scientifically predicated expertise. For convenience we will label such approaches as 'technocracy theories'. Generally, technocracy theories monitor changes in the significance of expertise. They trace the salience of expertise across different forms of social organization; from industrial, to post-industrial, to information society, and so on. Technocracy theorists can be roughly divided into two 'strands'. The first strand is technologically optimistic. The other is more cautionary and pessimistic. Both strands are concerned with shifts in knowledge–power relationships, public accountability and the relations between experts and lay people as new elites linked with, or composed of, experts assume more powerful roles in modern societies.

In the more optimistic strand of technocracy theories, lay–expert relations have occasionally manifested as a preoccupation with enhancing the scientific and technical literacy of the lay public in order to improve their responsiveness to expert advice and enhance participation in civil society (Wildavsky 1995; National Science Foundation 1991). Within this frame the expansion of expertise is the inevitable by-product of the proliferation of theoretical knowledge and the skills attained for its mastery (Bell 1973). The expansion of expertise is generally conceived as beneficial even though it requires active management and more effective communication between experts (and experts) and lay people.

'Optimistic' technocratic models tend to frame public participation as desirable—to the extent that it addresses normative questions—and interpret expert disagreement as deviance or evidence of political interference. They also tend to endorse simple realist, or 'folk', epistemologies of science. These models have, or so it would seem, gained tacit acceptance in many legal and regulatory cultures, notably those which have restricted the power of lay juries and encouraged the use of court-appointed experts, expert panels and public inquiries, to insulate the public from expert disagreement.

Within the more pessimistic tradition, technocracy theorists have expressed alarm at the redefinition of humanistic questions of knowledge and practice as technical issues amenable to expert judgment. Anxiety at what is presented as the improper extension of expertise into social domains has been taken in a range of directions with different political nuances (Habermas 1971; Illich 1973; Elliot and Elliot 1976; Sclove 1995). What tends to unite the 'pessimistic' theorists, however, is a shared desire to restrict the general power of experts, to enhance public participation, and nurture 'a public sphere' with the potential for clear communication about social and political objectives (Woodhouse et al. 2002). While this more critical strand of technocratic theorizing moves part of the way toward examining the links between expertise, institutions and political organization, it shares with its more optimistic counterpart a tendency to reify and homogenize expertise. Expertise remains an identifiable 'entity' (Barnes 1985). The symbolic value of such homogenous images of expertise (as both *saviour* and *threat*) is where theories of technocracy are most salient in legal and regulatory debates.

In contrast, the following chapters avoid such reified and normatively charged models of expertise. They dedicate more attention to context: to the local constitution of expertise. The boundaries between lay and expert knowledge and experience and between different expert and lay groups are presented as more fluid and open to (re)negotiation. In light of this fluidity, attempts to delimit the role of lay juries or public participation in political decision-making can become quite complex. They extend beyond merely establishing boundaries according to pre-conceptions of knowledge and ignorance. As Collins and Evans (2002) suggest, there is a need to nuance the lay–expert divide according to the experiences held by particular groups or individuals. Aggregate political effects, shaped by experts aligning with political elites, or experts becoming elites in their own right, become empirical questions which cannot be answered by invoking universal theories of expertise or static models of understanding and ignorance.

So, acknowledging that public exposure to scientific and technical forms of expertise may create certain difficulties, recent work on the public understanding of science (PUS) tends to destabilize rigid attributions of (in)competence, ignorance and (mis)understanding and sometimes blurs lay/expert boundaries (Irwin and Wynne 1996). Studies by sociologists and anthropologists suggest that public responses to complex and technical knowledges are multifaceted. Reactions to technical and scientific knowledge claims vary widely across highly variegated publics. Without wanting to simply valorize the technical competence of lay people, studies remind us that many areas of technical knowledge are embraced by enthusiastic 'amateurs'. Examples include ornithology, plant taxonomy and astronomy (Wynne 1991, 1995). Sometimes lay individuals or groups will have strong incentives for acquiring specialized knowledge. Members of environmental groups and those confronted with illnesses provide obvious examples (Irwin 1995; Epstein 1996). On other occasions, apparent public disenchantment, apathy or ignorance may represent considered, even reasonable, responses to particular circumstances. Public responses to experts and expert knowledge may be shaped by impressions of the reliability of the source. Those, for example, who live close to an industrial plant may be sceptical about the safety pronouncements made by industry scientists. To cast this rejection as ignorance may fail to capture more subtle valencies around the safety history, relations between the factory and the local residents, or broader social perceptions about the nature of 'reliable' expertise. Furthermore, the use of concepts such as 'understanding' and 'competence' often fails to capture the complexity involved in translating and simplifying technical knowledge, or allow for the variety of understandings (in the plural) among those who would normally be considered technically competent (Collins 1999).

To impose a stark dichotomy between competence and incompetence, between experts on one hand and judges, lawyers, juries and administrators on the other, would draw the line sharply and peremptorily. In legal and regulatory practice sharp divisions are often compromised. Regulators often possess technical skills. Judges and lawyers may acquire familiarity and understanding through formal training and experience. Juries may follow the evidence, take their responsibility very seriously and possess a wide range of opinions, experiences and skills (Edmond and Mercer 1997b). Even experts must respond to rules, procedures and legal definitions (e.g. 'insanity' or 'beyond reasonable doubt'), the conflicting opinions of other experts and a range of objectives in legal and regulatory proceedings.

The theories of expertise used in public institutions have important political and participatory implications

How we interpret expertise, and the ways in which we incorporate different types of expertise into our legal, political and regulatory institutions have important social, procedural and participatory implications (Irwin in this volume).

Once the epistemological privilege attributed to expert knowledge and expertise is compromised—but certainly not annulled—as we recognize social, procedural and institutional influences on the production of expertise, then representations and the use of expertise become more susceptible to political interpretation. If method discourses, professional norms and ethical precepts do not operate in the *mechanical* (or *epistemological*) capacity routinely suggested, then attempts at understanding decisions associated with the use of expertise may not be assisted by recourse to abstract images of *method, norms, objectivity* or claims about *distortion*. These insights not only have the potential to change how we understand the roles played by experts and expertise, but in opening-up and politicizing expertise—the production, mobilization, representation and assessment of knowledge and skills as well as the institutional arrangements—some of the dominant approaches to evidence and decision-making may require reconceptualization. Legal and regulatory practice may be in need of critique and, more importantly, innovative reform.

Reading *Daubert*: Beyond the 'epistemological turn'

In order to demonstrate the analytical benefits conferred through the adoption of more sociological orientations to expertise we now provide two interpretations of the seminal *Daubert v Merrell Dow Pharmaceuticals, Inc.* (1993) judgment. *Daubert* was a Supreme Court decision which established the admissibility standard for scientific evidence in US federal courts. The judgment has dominated evidence jurisprudence and law–science commentary throughout the common law world and is one of the most important and enduring symbols of recent preoccupation with expertise. In *Daubert,* and the cases that followed, senior US judges purported to turn their traditional interest in an expert's relevance, qualifications, and the degree of 'acceptance' of a position in a particular specialized 'field' to a more explicit concern with 'epistemological' registers and 'truth'. This evidence 'revolution' was, for the most part, rationalized by naïve–positivist philosophies of science and expertise.

Reading 1 is drawn from a recent text on law and science. In this example *Daubert* is presented as an epistemological solution to the problems attributed to expert evidence. Exemplifying the use of fairly conventional registers of expertise it provides an indication of their limitations. *Reading 2* provides a more detailed and sociologically informed response to the images of expertise in *Daubert*. This second reading shows how problematizing expertise has the potential to transform representations of science and expertise into purposive political interventions, and demonstrates how representations and the use of expertise are inextricably linked to institutional sensitivities, legal traditions and textual interpretations, as well as broader questions of institutional legitimacy and social order.

Reading 1: Dominant Dauberts

The following extract is taken from a prominent text on law and science written by a leading American evidence and constitutional law scholar six years after the *Daubert* judgment.

> Prior to *Daubert*, most courts, both federal and state, applied the "general acceptance" test, which was articulated in its modern form in the 1923 case of *Frye v. United States*. The general acceptance or *Frye* test called on judges to assess the degree of acceptance of a novel scientific technique in the field in which it belonged. The central premise of *Daubert*, in contrast, is that judges must assume the responsibility of conducting the evaluation of the scientific merit of expert testimony. Under a general acceptance test, the judge need not understand any of the science; he or she must merely identify the pertinent field in which the science falls and survey the opinions of scientists in the field. This nose-counting approach had

the virtue of permitting judges to survey specialists who presumably knew the most about the science. It had the vice, however, of surveying the very people who had an interest in the outcome of the admissibility decision. Not surprisingly, if judges ask handwriting identification analysts whether their specialty of identifying handwriting is generally accepted, the answer is yes. This is not unlike asking tea-leaf readers whether tea-leaf reading is generally accepted. The general acceptance test thus depends on the scientific integrity of the field surveyed. Whereas particle physicists accept findings only after considerable rigorous research has been completed, many other ostensibly scientific fields accept findings more readily. This insight is the key to understanding *Daubert*.

   Daubert requires judges to adopt a rigorous scientific mindset for evaluating the validity of the scientific research that supports expert testimony. The basic rule the Court adopted is that trial judges must assess the scientific foundation of expert testimony and be convinced that the science is more likely than not valid. In order to assist judges in this task, the Court suggested four factors that could be used, with others, to make the validity determination. These factors are whether (1) the hypothesis is testable and has been tested; (2) the error rate associated with the use of the science is not too great; (3) the basic research has been published in a peer-reviewed journal, and (4) the science supporting the expert opinion is generally accepted in the scientific community. In effect, the *Daubert* holding calls on judges to assess scientific research in much the same way scientists might. It incorporates the essential values of the scientific culture. Yet judges are not, nor should they be, as rigorous as particle physicists in evaluating research. At the same time, judges should be more rigorous than many scientists who, until now, have been permitted to testify routinely. Therefore, in practice, *Daubert* will be more liberal and lead to the admission of more expert testimony when it comes from fields with a long tradition of rigorous testing; but it should also be more conservative and lead to the exclusion of expert testimony when it is based on fields that do not have a tradition of rigor.

   ...

   After *Daubert*, a critical issue that arose concerned the scope of the gatekeeping function. Since *Daubert* involved scientific expert testimony, many experts with less than exemplary scientific credentials or data began to renounce the science label and call themselves "specialists". For forensic "scientists" and others with little or no research to support their claims to expertise, the key to continued admission appeared to be to claim that *Daubert* did not apply to them.

   ...

   In a unanimous decision, the Supreme Court in 1999 put an end to this debate. Using the Eleventh Circuit case of *Kumho*, the Court held unequivocally that all expert testimony falls within the purview of *Daubert's* gatekeeping requirement for federal trial courts: "We conclude the *Daubert's* general holding—setting forth the trial judge's general 'gatekeeping' obligation—applies not only to testimony based on scientific knowledge, but also to testimony based on 'technical' and 'other specialized knowledge'". Significantly, the Court rejected the distinction lower courts had drawn between "scientific" and "non-scientific," with the former getting close scrutiny and the latter getting a free ride. (Faigman, *Legal Alchemy* (1999: 62–63, 79–80 references omitted)

   These extracts from *Legal Alchemy* draw upon and exploit questionable images of science and expertise. According to Faigman, *Daubert* more or less captures the essence of scientific practice. The Supreme Court's decision is presented as *the appropriate* response to admissibility *difficulties*. Significantly, the four *Daubert* criteria are rehearsed without critical commentary. Implicitly, they provide a practical and scientifically rigorous means for determining 'scientific validity'. For Faigman, *Daubert* 'incorporates the *essential values of the scientific culture*' and 'requires judges to adopt a rigorous scientific mindset'. In effect, the criteria enable judges to assess evidence 'in much the same way scientists might'. Faigman's account conflates the images of science promulgated in *Daubert* with actual scientific practice. Lack of historical and sociological sophistication seem to prevent him from recognizing the highly idiosyncratic images of science collocated in the *Daubert* decision. Faigman accepts the *Daubert* decision and the models of science at face value. In this account, that acceptance transforms the decision into an appropriate response to 'unreliable' expertise.

According to Faigman, the approach to admissibility adopted by the majority in *Daubert* has the potential to alleviate the problems he attributes to the earlier 'general acceptance' standard derived from *US v Frye*.[7] Judges are no longer required to 'count noses'. Instead, we are told, judges are to 'assume the responsibility of conducting the evaluation of the scientific merit of expert testimony' based on an understanding of the science. The fact that the *Frye* rule, like almost all admissibility standards (including *Daubert*), could be interpreted more or less strictly passes without comment (Gianelli 1980). This is significant because the contest over admissibility standards in the federal courts was highly politicized. While *Frye* was not without difficulties, having been interpreted and applied inconsistently between 1923 and 1993, simply substituting *Frye* with *Daubert* prevents analysis of the procedural difficulties and implications associated with both *Frye* and *Daubert*.

In the extract from *Legal Alchemy* the *Frye* standard is characterized as inadequate because it allowed self-credentialing groups, like tea-leaf readers, to potentially testify in court. (In practice, few tea-leaf readers ever testified.) Faigman devotes little attention to the variety of ways *Frye* was used in practice, including the difficulties trial judges might have encountered if they had actually endeavored to 'survey the opinions of scientists in that field.' While Faigman's identification of the limits of general acceptance are presented as 'the key to understanding the impact of *Daubert*', other dimensions of Supreme Court jurisprudence tend to be omitted or sanitized. The implications of replacing the 'liberal' *Frye* standard emerge incidentally or indirectly, if at all. The inability (or unwillingness) to question the images of science promulgated in *Daubert* or consider a broad range of potential alternatives prevents a more critical, reflexive interpretation of *Daubert,* and later the *Kumho Tire Co. v Carmichael* (1999) judgment.[8]

Concern with rigor and reliable scientific knowledge obscures analysis of *Daubert's* exclusionary effects and the circumstances motivating them. It makes the Supreme Court's newfound concern with *gatekeeping*, replacing admissibility decision-making and the earlier 'screening' metaphor, appear natural and necessary. The extension of the *Daubert* approach to non-scientific expert evidence in the subsequent *Kumho* appeal emerges as the proper response to the need to define the 'scope of the gatekeeping function'. Whereas we would suggest that boundaries around 'good' and 'bad' science and between 'science' and 'non-science' are strategically erected, potentially malleable, and frequently contested, Faigman seems to accept the propriety of extending *Daubert's* 'essential values of the scientific culture' to non-scientific form of expertise (also Faigman 1999: 79). A reluctance to acknowledge that images of science, including those articulated in *Daubert*, are flexible, contestable and impregnated with implications leads Faigman, and many others, to deprecate the efforts of lawyers, experts and judges who endeavored—an implicitly *improper* attempt—to circumvent the remit of *Daubert*.

Lurking behind and motivating Faigman's interpretation of US admissibility jurisprudence is a concern with unreliable forms of expertise and the reprehensible practices attributed to many experts and lawyers. *Daubert* and *Kumho* are presented as necessary responses to the threats posed by unscrupulous experts— those 'with less than exemplary scientific credentials' or 'no research to support their claims'. The existence and dangers posed by unreliable forms of expertise are simply assumed and perpetuated. The purportedly science-based *Daubert* regime offers a powerful corrective to perceptions of socio-legal disorder. While *Daubert* does not, according to Faigman, require judges to be quite as scrupulous as particle physicists, it does require the adoption of a more rigorous approach to admissibility decision-making: 'judges should be more rigorous than many scientists who, until now, have been permitted to testify routinely'. Faigman is confident that the new standard will transform the routine admission of expertise, effectively preventing scientists (and nonscientists) who are not 'rigorous'—which becomes a synonym for 'reliability'—from continuing to testify. For Faigman, *Daubert* means that the pernicious 'free ride' is over.

Faigman's account subtly, and somewhat asymmetrically, assigns interests and motives to experts (and lawyers) while presenting judges and judicial practice as largely uncontroversial. In explaining the weaknesses inherent in *Frye* we are told that it surveyed 'the very people who had an interest in the outcome of the admissibility decision'. Faigman's model of judicial practice is sociologically thin. While 'unreliable' experts may hold professional and personal interests in the legal status of their expertise, judges (and 'competent' experts) also have personal and professional interests in the management of trials and assessments of expertise. Commitment to the correctness of the images of science (and non-science) deployed in *Daubert* and *Kumho*, affords Faigman little scope to consider the possibility that particular standards were pragmatic responses to perceptions of socio-legal change.

We agree that *Kumho* has contributed to the tightening of admissibility standards, effectively reinforcing an exclusionary ethos manifested, if not entirely inaugurated, in *Daubert*. For us, however, these developments are not the result of the Supreme Court *properly* constructing the *Federal Rules of Evidence* or locating the essence of *real science* and adapting it to legal practice. Rather, the selection and endorsement of *sui generis* and potentially onerous admissibility criteria provided resources and encouragement for trial and appellate judges to (continue to) raise the standards of admissibility across the federal circuits. *Daubert* and

Kumho represent a concerted response to the perceived threats posed by unreliable forms of expertise, specifically 'junk science'. These distinctions are not insignificant. Faigman's reading of changes in evidence jurisprudence are politically benign. For Faigman, the Supreme Court's *Daubert* and *Kumho* jurisprudence represent an implicitly obvious, or proper, response to perceived problems with expert evidence. The question of why, after hundreds of years of expert opinion testimony, the Supreme Court only decided to embrace the *proper* criteria in 1993 passes almost without comment. Faigman's account obscures decades of judicial persistence with (modifications of) *Frye*.

In the work of Faigman and many others, empirically contentious *problems* with expertise are, like the image of science and reliability championed in *Daubert*, uncritically perpetuated. Faigman's orientation and limited sociological interest restricts his interpretation of the *Daubert* decision to literal exegesis. His ambivalence about the liberal and conservative implications of recent judgments is the result of an inability to distinguish the Supreme Court's rhetoric of liberalization from its practice of exclusion. For Faigman, *Daubert* and *Kumho* represent a scientifically informed, and therefore appropriate, response to suspicious forms of expertise.

This, as we hope to demonstrate, is a politically superficial reading of '*Daubert* and its progeny'.

Reading 2: Re-reading Daubert

It is now our intention to attempt a more sociologically sensitive, and somewhat more detailed interpretation of *Daubert* and *Kumho*.

The *Daubert* appeal was part of mass tort litigation around the teratogenic effects of the morning sickness drug Bendectin (Debendox in the UK and Australia). Highly publicized, the litigation had been running for more than a decade in state and federal courts by the time the Supreme Court agreed to hear the appeal in the cases of Jason Daubert and Eric Schuller. Indeed, by that stage, in what Sanders (1992) described as the 'Bendectin cycle', the suits, which had been almost entirely unsuccessful, were almost at an end. Several federal appellate courts had, by the second half of the 1980s, already refused to allow further litigation unless the plaintiffs produced new epidemiological studies demonstrating statistically significant associations between Bendectin and specific types of birth defect (Edmond and Mercer 2000).

Most legal accounts suggest that the Supreme Court agreed to hear the *Daubert* appeal to determine the standard for the admission of scientific evidence under Rule 702 of the *Federal Rules of Evidence* (1975, hereafter the FRE). While inconsistent application of the FRE in the federal circuits may have stimulated the Court's interest, *Daubert* is probably better understood as a deliberate intervention into debates around perceived problems with expert evidence and its social consequences. The FRE may have established the parameters for the decision—conforming to traditional legal practice the judges were obliged to refer to its text—but the *Rules* could hardly be considered to have *determined* the outcomes in *Daubert* or *Kumho*.

In the *Daubert* judgment, as Faigman explains, the entire Court found the previously influential common law 'general acceptance' (or *Frye*) standard to be inconsistent with the *Federal Rules*. However, the Court was divided over what standard or approach to scientific evidence should replace general acceptance. *US v Frye* (1923) had been decided long before the FRE had come into effect in 1975. In *Daubert*, *guided* by the FRE, the majority erected a new admissibility platform. Justice Blackmun, the author of the majority judgment, explained that the *Federal Rules* imposed conditions upon admissibility: expert evidence should be both *relevant* and *reliable*. This meant that for scientific evidence: 'The subject of an expert's testimony must be "scientific ... knowledge"', that is, 'an inference or assertion must be derived by the scientific method' (*Daubert* 1993: 589–90). Blackmun was so confident about the power of 'the scientific method' that he dispelled the need to worry about an expert's conclusions, providing the methodology was reliable: 'The focus, of course, must be solely on principles and methodology, not on the conclusions they generate' (*Daubert* 1993: 595).

In order to determine whether proffered evidence is 'scientific knowledge' that 'will assist the trier of fact [usually the jury] to understand or determine a fact in issue', the majority provided a list of four factors (hereafter the *Daubert* criteria) to assist the trial judge's decision-making.

[1]   Ordinarily, a key question to be answered in determining whether a theory or technique is scientific knowledge that will assist the trier of fact will be whether it can be (and has been) tested. "Scientific methodology today is based on generating hypotheses and testing them to see if they can be falsified; indeed, this methodology is what distinguishes science from other fields of human inquiry." Green 645. See also C. Hempel, *Philosophy of Natural Science* 49 (1966) ("[T]he statements constituting a scientific explanation must be capable of empirical test"); K. Popper, *Conjectures and Refutations: The Growth of Scientific Knowledge* 37 (5th ed. 1989) ("[T]he criterion of the scientific status of a theory is its falsifiability, or refutability, or testability") (emphasis deleted).

[2]   Another pertinent consideration is whether the theory or technique has been subjected to peer review and publication. Publication (which is but one element of peer review) is not a *sine qua non* of admissibility; it does not necessarily correlate with reliability, see S. Jasanoff, *The Fifth Branch: Science Advisors as Policymakers* 61-76 (1990) ...

[3]   Additionally, in the case of a particular scientific technique, the court ordinarily should consider the known or potential rate of error ...

[4]   Finally, "general acceptance" can yet have a bearing on the inquiry. (*Daubert* 1993: 593–94, emphasis added)

Notwithstanding the provision of specific criteria, the majority explained that any inquiry should be 'flexible' (*Daubert* 1993: 594). In consequence, these factors were characterized as indicative rather than 'a definitive checklist or test' (*Daubert* 1993: 593).

Two members of the Court did not support the majority's approach. According to Chief Justice Rehnquist and Justice Stevens, 'the unusual subject matter' and variety of non-legal authority—emboldened in the previous extract—submitted in relation to the appeal 'should cause us to proceed with great caution in deciding more than we have to, because our reach can so easily exceed our grasp' (*Daubert* 1993: 599). While affirming their confidence in federal judges the dissentients indicated that the *Daubert* criteria, especially falsification, might produce practical difficulties: 'I am at a loss to know what is meant when it is said that the status of a theory depends on its "falsifiability," and I suspect some of them will be, too' (*Daubert* 1993: 600). The dissenting judgment does not seem to suggest that the majority had defined science incorrectly, but rather expresses concern that the definition might not meet the practical needs of federal judges. Interestingly, both of the judgments in *Daubert* seem to suggest that falsification captures the scientific mindset: that is, what it is *to do science*.

The *Daubert* judgment purports to present a fairly conventional model of science. However, for those conversant with professional history, philosophy or sociology of science, the judgment combines a range of philosophical and sociological approaches which are normally understood as distinctive and potentially inconsistent (Haack 2001). This point is raised, and perhaps recognized, by few lawyers, judges or legal commentators.[9] The curious collocation of approaches is not restricted to Popper and Hempel. We might be as surprised to find reference to a leading social constructivist, like Sheila Jasanoff, adjacent to the work of Popper and Hempel (see the final chapter in this volume).

Drawing from research in the history, philosophy and sociology of science, initially we might be intrigued by the particular—in the sense of idiosyncratic— images of science and expertise advanced by the judges in *Daubert* and consolidated and expanded in *Kumho*. However, rather than simply endorse the model—à la Faigman—or endeavor to determine whether the Supreme Court got the model of science (or expertise) correct, we are inclined to ask: Why were these particular models of science advanced? and Why were they extended to non-scientific forms of expertise? These questions bring concerns about the implications of different models of expertise and the motivations of proponents of particular models to the forefront of any analysis. These questions emerge before we even begin to consider how the models were understood, applied and contested.

The Supreme Court was effectively compelled to develop its admissibility standard for expert opinion evidence around the text of Rule 702 of the FRE:

> Rule 702. Testimony by Experts. If scientific, technical, or other specialized knowledge will assist the trier of fact to understand the evidence or to determine a fact in issue, a witness qualified as an expert by knowledge, skill, experience, training, or education, may testify thereto in the form of an opinion or otherwise.

We can observe from a casual inspection of its text that Rule 702 does not obviously dictate the particular choices embedded in *Daubert*, particularly the criteria ([1] – [4]). Similarly, the images of science depicted in *Daubert* were not obviously prefigured in pre-*Daubert* evidence jurisprudence. Arguably, there are no earlier decisions which resemble *Daubert* or incorporate all of the 'key' determinants proposed by the majority. There are no earlier references to Popper and Jasanoff in federal jurisprudence. The images of science in *Daubert*, particularly the combination and emphasis on a strong distinction between method and conclusion, the gatekeeping responsibility and the four criteria are idiosyncratic and original. It is perhaps less surprising, given the Supreme Court's position in the federal legal hierarchy, to find that after the judgment was 'handed down' *Daubert* became a surrogate for understanding, describing and assessing scientific expertise both in courts and beyond.

Once we recognize that the image(s) of science promoted in *Daubert* were not self-evident, were not derived from earlier jurisprudence (that is, precedent) and do not find widespread support in specialist science and expertise literatures, then their selection might begin to appear intriguing, and perhaps revealing. Consequently, unlike Faigman, we are left to wonder why the Supreme Court decided to repeatedly intervene in evidence jurisprudence in the 1990s and in doing so decided to draw on the *authority* of Popper and others. That is, why was a version of Popper's philosophy of falsification suddenly introduced into US evidence jurisprudence in 1993, after it had experienced several decades of sustained, and mostly critical, specialist commentary? If Popper's philosophy of science described how science is actually practised then this might not have been noteworthy.[10] However, the fact that falsification is merely one model, among many different models, of scientific practice opens its enrolment and use to more critical examination.

Conventionally, Popper (1902–94) is regarded as a politically conservative philosopher.[11] He enjoyed his widest intellectual prestige in the Cold War Anglophone world of the 1950s and 1960s where he exerted a longstanding influence at the London School of Economics. Popper promoted falsification as a means of exposing the scientific pretensions of Marxist social theory and various psychological theories, especially those influenced by Freud and Adler. While, in these contexts, Popper stridently presented falsification as a clear and simple scientific demarcation criterion, in other contexts he modified falsification so that it became the ideal methodology and attitude that scientists should aspire toward. In response to mounting philosophical criticism Popper conceded that falsification was not a simple guide that could be mechanically applied to the routine practice of science. These more complex valencies of Popper's philosophy, along with his exposure to sustained criticism from historians, philosophers and sociologists, tend to be missing from Popper's legal incarnation.

If Popper's theory of falsification does not adequately describe or prescribe scientific practice—what scientists actually do or should do—then the Supreme Court's recourse to falsification may be significant for understanding federal evidence jurisprudence. Here, we return to the question of why the Supreme Court cited Popper, for the first time, in 1993. There appear to be two main reasons. First, notwithstanding sustained specialist criticism of his work, Popper's approach to science is widely considered to be a practically demanding standard. Popper's authority and/or reference to falsification are often invoked in pedagogical settings and public controversies where the rhetorical value of rigor, and the potential for exclusion, have appeal (Ruse 1988; Gieryn, Bevins and Zehr 1985). The second reason also draws on popular impressions of Popper and falsification in public discourse, especially around the demarcation problem. Falsification, or testing, was widely promoted in the large number of *amicus curiae* briefs submitted to the Supreme Court *Daubert* appeal in support of the revision of admissibility standards for scientific evidence. Numerous briefs, prepared by peak bodies and prestigious organizations with considerable social authority, such as the American Medical Association, the National Academy of Sciences (NAS), the American Association for the Advancement of Science (AAAS), the Carnegie Commission, the National Association of Manufacturers and Business Roundtable, referred to Popperian falsification in the context of developing a new legal admissibility standard. Interestingly, many of these briefs tended to characterize falsification as the defining feature, and for some the essential method, of all modern scientific practice.

While not strictly (or legally) necessary, the Supreme Court reference to non-legal authority such as Popper, Hempel and Jasanoff, eased the revision of admissibility standards. References to authorities (in the plural) from the history, philosophy and sociology of science conferred social legitimacy on the majority's characterization of science. Apparent indifference to the diverse range of approaches to science and expertise embraced in the majority decision implied widespread consensus over the implicitly unitary nature of science. The standing and social authority of the US Supreme Court is such that few among those cited in the judgment, including Jasanoff (1996a), were particularly censorious about the use of their work. The credibility conferred through the assembly of a diverse collection of authorities is important, but we should not underestimate the popular appeal and conservative dimensions of falsification. Similarly, we should not exaggerate judicial interest in accommodating, or reconciling differences between, historians, philosophers, sociologists and scientists. The name of Popper, in particular, conferred both authority and an approach to expertise that could—despite the dissentients' worries—be simplified and operationalized in practice.

While the Supreme Court cited Popper and referred to falsification, in their own practice and in the judgments of subordinate courts Popper is rarely cited and his philosophy of science is typically transformed into a simplified or 'folk' theory of 'testing'. Perhaps understandably, neither the Supreme Court judges nor the federal judiciary seem to be particularly interested in philosophical engagement. The transformation of testing and the other criteria into legal categories allows judges to routinely *apply* them, without having to address their philosophical (in)adequacy. Post-*Daubert* legal practice has effectively converted the social authority conferred by Blackmun's reference to the work of Popper (and Hempel and others) into a legally tractable exclusionary tool. Rather than engage with the history and philosophy of science federal judges can now simply inquire whether a knowledge claim has been 'tested'. In this way social scientific 'authority' has been subordinated to legal practice and quickly displaced from evidence jurisprudence.

If legal versions of Popper's doctrine of falsification make it harder to adduce expert evidence in federal courts, then we should not underestimate the impact caused by the philosophically questionable combination of 'testing' with the other criteria ([2], [3] and [4]). According to the *Daubert* and *Kumho* judgments, trial judges are to flexibly adapt the *Daubert* criteria, and possibly others, to the particular expert evidence before them. In practice, however, the *Daubert* criteria are frequently applied as an inflexible checklist. The few qualifications in *Daubert*, including the qualification attributed to Jasanoff [2], are invariably ignored. In its *Kumho* judgment the Supreme Court exemplified this tendency by applying all of the *Daubert* criteria to exclude the plaintiffs' expert evidence. The judges exemplified a willingness to actively exclude expert evidence. This practice adds a range of exclusionary criteria—peer review and publication [2], error rates [3] and general acceptance [4]—to an already onerous standard [1]. In this way, the *Daubert* decision provides a set of resources which tend to be more demanding than even the most onerous versions of 'general acceptance' standing alone. These new admissibility standards have been felt most acutely by plaintiffs, who bear the burden of proof in civil litigation. Significantly, the *Daubert* criteria have not been applied as strictly to state-produced forensic scientific evidence.

Our reading of the exclusionary impact of *Daubert* is supported by recent empirical investigation. Two surveys, in particular, are instructive for obtaining some sense of civil litigation trends in the federal courts. The first, conducted for the Rand Corporation by Dixon and Gill, provides quantitative support for *Daubert's* exclusionary impact (Dixon and Gill 2001: 19–20). This survey compared approximately four hundred pre- and post-*Daubert* opinions (between January 1980 and June 1999) from federal cases involving expert evidence. Dixon and Gill reported that after *Daubert* expert evidence was more regularly contested and more frequently excluded. After *Daubert* 'general acceptance' persisted as an important barrier to admission, but judges incorporated additional admissibility criteria which included the consideration of theories, methods and the qualifications of experts (Dixon and Gill 2001: xiii; Bernstein 1996, 2001).

These findings are consistent with a survey conducted for the Federal Judicial Center by Krafka, Dunn, Johnson, Cecil and Miletich (2002). Krafka et al. compared three surveys—two of federal judges in 1991 and 1998, and a survey of attorneys in 1999. According to the authors, the surveys suggest that judges were more likely to scrutinize, limit and exclude expert testimony before trial in 1998 than in 1991. Before *Daubert* (1993) judges reported that they had excluded or limited some of the expert testimony in twenty-five per cent of cases. This figure rose to forty-one per cent by 1998. Krafka et al. explain that this finding may understate the exclusionary effect of *Daubert* as the survey did not include cases where all expert testimony was ruled inadmissible (Krafka et al. 2002: 15). Another difference between 1991 and 1998 was the prevalence of pre-trial hearings (now called *Daubert* hearings) on the admissibility of expert evidence. In 1991 only fifty-one per cent of judges reported using pre-trial hearings, and thirteen per cent of these were limited to cases with complicated scientific or technical evidence. By 1998, in contrast, seventy-seven per cent of judges reported using pre-trial admissibility hearings (Krafka et al. 2002: 20). Most attorneys reported that they had altered their post-*Daubert* practices: forty-eight per cent scrutinized their own experts more carefully; forty-one per cent said they were more likely to object to the admissibility of opposing expert testimony at trial; and, twenty-four per cent made more motions for summary judgment (Krafka et al. 2002: 23).

At this point, because we are able to suggest that the effects produced by the incorporation of 'testing' and the other criteria were not neutral, we might also infer that their inclusion and widespread uptake was not coincidental. It is our contention that through the quite deliberate emphasis on 'testing', in conjunction with the other criteria, the Supreme Court sought to encourage a more onerous and more predictable approach to admissibility decision-making among federal judges.

While it is our contention that *Daubert* has exerted a considerable exclusionary impact, we are reluctant to accord a fixed or determinate set of implications to judicial responses to *Daubert*. The large number of cases are too diverse to permit such a straightforward reading. What we do propose is that the images of science in *Daubert*, particularly the criteria, provided useful resources for judicial decision-making, especially for the exclusion of evidence. The apparent philosophical incoherence of *Daubert* has not prevented the images of science and criteria being mobilized—that is being made to 'work'—to explain admissibility decision-making by federal judges (Mulkay and Gilbert 1981). Typically, the criteria are invoked to exclude (plaintiffs') evidence.

If admissibility standards are being raised and if judges are excluding more expert evidence then we might want to ask: Why have judges interpreted *Daubert* and their gatekeeping responsibility restrictively? That is, why have federal judges raised the bar? While the Supreme Court's example is one immediate explanation, a more comprehensive answer will require attention to judicial practice and institutional values. We can suggest that an answer will not be based entirely on the text of the FRE or previous evidence jurisprudence. Indeed, the elaboration and consolidation of novel admissibility standards suggests new influences, or pre-occupations. In trying to explain trends in evidence jurisprudence, judicial impressions of the legal system and concerns about the prevalence of unreliable expertise seem to be revelatory. Impressions of the litigation landscape, like admissibility standards, have been actively contested both inside and outside American courtrooms. Impressions of the operation of the legal system and admissibility standards are often correlated. Those alarmed by their perception of a litigation 'explosion' linked to the prevalence of 'junk science' tend to be proponents of tort reform and raised admissibility standards. Those less concerned about the state of adversarial legal systems, tend to advocate (what are presented as) 'traditional' models of legal practice and characterize judge-led reform as improper activism.

In endeavoring to understand judicial responses to proffers of expertise, the FRE and *Daubert* we would, unlike Faigman, attempt to incorporate the social and institutional concerns maintained by judges. In adversarial jurisdictions, many judges and commentators seem to believe that their legal system is in some sort of serious trouble. Some of these 'troubles' are attributed to expert evidence (Freckelton, Reddy and Selby 1999). There are several reasons for this tendency. Media reporting of tort and products liability litigation tends to focus on mass torts and unusual cases, especially those with complex evidence and massive damage awards. Unrepresentative, and apparently pathological episodes, are over-represented. Popular impressions of litigation tend to be mediated by images displaced from the realities of ordinary legal practice (Galanter 1998, 2002; Bogus

2001). Legal, media and political commentators, lobby groups and think-tanks play important roles in the ongoing contest around images and definitions of the legal landscape, particularly perceptions of the extent of serious social problems (Gusfield 1981), the prevalence of 'junk science' and the need for evidence and procedural reform (Edmond and Mercer 2004). Judges are acutely sensitive to the social and policy implication of their decision-making, social problem discourses and public criticism of legal institutions. Consequently, in response to the widespread perception of a litigation 'crisis', increasing budgetary pressures and social criticism, in recent decades many judges have become more active gatekeepers.

Galanter suggests that in trying to understand contemporary perspectives on the civil justice system we should not underestimate the privileged social position and ideological proclivities of the federal judiciary. Federal judges are members of a small social elite, sharing considerable ideological space with their political and corporate peers (Galanter 1998, 2002). In addition to concerns about the legitimacy of legal institutions, shared 'ideological space' may help to explain why the practical experience of legal practitioners and judges does not seem to have insulated them from the meta-framing of popular, media and corporate discourses. Interestingly, the approach to expertise adopted by the Supreme Court in *Kumho*, even more explicitly than in *Daubert*, converged with the positions promoted in *amicus curiae* briefs submitted by many large corporations and peak organizations (Edmond 2002c). Along with the Supreme Court, these institutions were keen to extend *Daubert* and the gatekeeping ethos to non-scientific forms of expertise lest Rule 702 be 'eviscerated' and an exception developed 'that could be exploited so mercilessly and so frequently that … [it] would easily swallow the rule'.[12]

Perhaps most revealing, from our perspective, is how the political and ideological implications of *Daubert* and Supreme Court jurisprudence tend to be obscured by the widespread failure to recognize the 'epistemological turn' and its implications. Once the suitability of falsification is questioned, or the political implications and criticisms of even 'pop' versions of Popper's work are incorporated into the analysis, then the decision to embrace (a legally tractable version of) falsification becomes informative. There is a lot of interpretative space between the words of Rule 702, the images of science promoted in *Daubert* and the consolidated response by judges across the federal circuits.

Provisioned with critical understandings of expertise and sensitive to a range of institutional concerns, we are capable of identifying apparently inconsistent aspects of the *Daubert* judgment and extending our analysis into judicial practice. Interestingly, all of the judges in *Daubert* (1993: 588) expressed commitment to the '"liberal thrust" of the *Federal Rules*' and 'relaxing the traditional barriers to "opinion evidence"', which had motivated those who drafted and enacted them. The majority went even further, reiterating its confidence in the civil jury, adversarial trial processes and even the potential admissibility of 'shaky' evidence.

> In this regard respondent [Merrell Dow] seems to us to be overly pessimistic about the capabilities of the jury and of the adversary system generally. Vigorous cross-examination, presentation of contrary evidence, and careful instruction on the

burden of proof are the traditional and appropriate means of attacking shaky but admissible evidence. ... the court remains free to direct a judgment ... and likewise to grant summary judgment. (*Daubert* 1993: 596)

Our reading of *Daubert* questions these representations, or makes them appear somewhat ironic. On the one hand, we could endeavor to 'rescue' the Supreme Court judges by claiming that the majority were not entirely clear about the potential implications of *Daubert* and thought, like Faigman, that the new admissibility standard reflected the 'essence of the scientific culture' with the potential to liberalize the expert evidence entering federal courts. However, we find it difficult to interpret the criteria enlisted and combined in *Daubert* as merely coincidental. Even if we could accept such an interpretation of *Daubert*, the subsequent cases of *General Electric Co. v Joiner* and *Kumho* are more difficult to reconcile with that interpretation.[13] Together, they represent a concerted shift, replacing appeals to expert consensus with appeals to 'reliability' and 'truth'. Furthermore, this interpretation is supported by the responses to *Daubert* in the federal circuits. On the whole, the *Daubert* decision has been understood by federal judges as an exclusionary intervention.

In *Kumho* (1999), the Supreme Court extended the *Daubert* criteria to non-scientific forms of expert evidence. Six years after *Daubert* had materially contributed to the tightening of admissibility decision-making in the Federal Courts, the Supreme Court judges applied all of the *Daubert* criteria in their assessment of the evidence before them.[14] The Court inflexibly applied the *Daubert* criteria to exclude the testimony of the plaintiffs' expert. Rather than invoking the liberal aspirations behind the FRE or embracing their earlier enthusiasm for adversarialism and confidence in the lay jury, in *Kumho* the Supreme Court emphasized the need for gatekeeping to protect the jury from unreliable (actually *fausse*) expertise. In *Daubert* gatekeeping was described as a responsibility. In *Kumho*, gatekeeping became an obligation. If the Supreme Court judges did not fully appreciate the potential impact of the *Daubert* (1993) judgment *at the time*, once its exclusionary implications were recognized they were neither discussed nor tempered. In line with corporate aspirations, in *Kumho* the *Daubert* criteria were extended to all forms of expertise. If there were lingering doubts about the implications of *Daubert* and its progeny the appeal in *Weisgram v Marley* (2000) appears to resolve them conclusively.[15] There, the Supreme Court characterized the impact of the admissibility jurisprudence in the following terms: 'Since *Daubert*, moreover, parties relying on expert evidence have had notice of the exacting standards of reliability such evidence must meet' (*Weisgram* 2000: 1021).

Sociological approaches to science and expertise allow us to comment, albeit speculatively, on judicial rhetoric and practice. Legalism, including the possibility of uncontroversially identifying precedent and applying rules of law and procedure, has been on the wane since the American Legal Realists in the 1930s. More recent analyses, often inspired by new approaches to law embracing feminist and race theory, critical legal studies as well as the use of more traditional sociological and psychological tools (such as those provided by the Law and

Society movement) have consolidated or extended many of the earlier criticisms or concerns. Our analysis supports some of these approaches to legal practice. While judicial practice appears highly conventional and constrained, the unveiling of judicial ideology around the strategic deployment of images of science and expertise confirms that conventions might not always be as constraining as judges and some commentators suggest. The 'guidance' provided to the Court by the text of—or intentions behind—the FRE is not only quite limited, but apparently subservient to the ideological and institutional factors motivating the exclusionary orientation.

In making these claims it is important to recognize that the judgment is a rationalization, a work in persuasion, predicated upon and reinforcing particular realities. This study suggests that traditions of practice, institutional values and a range of loose ideological affinities have combined to shape the development and rationalization of an exclusionary ethos in recent US evidence jurisprudence. At no stage did the rules or traditions of practice require the Court to pursue such an exclusionary course. Concerted, but not necessarily conspiratorial, action across the judiciary can be explained in ideological, institutional and professional terms (Rubin and Feeley 1999). Judges are acutely sensitive to some of the potential implications of litigation and the public legitimacy of legal institutions. The reform of admissibility standards constitutes an attempt to prevent litigation and limit the number of cases going to the jury. While we wonder about the genuineness of the majority's commitment to the traditional adversarial trial in *Daubert*, it is possible that the final form of the judgment was a negotiated settlement among the majority as well as an attempt to improve the accuracy of decision-making. Degrees of inconsistency and rhetorical deference to traditional aspects of the adversarial trial may have been the price of settlement. Perceptions of the social world, in conjunction with earlier decisions, the FRE, ongoing inconsistency in the federal circuits and an active public debate about expertise and civil litigation, shaped the *Daubert* and *Kumho* decisions and the way they were subsequently understood by the federal judiciary. In the absence of perceived threats to socio-legal order, it is questionable whether judges would have selected the particular criteria or interpreted them so aggressively. Unconstrained by highly normative and empirically untenable models of expertise, the sociology of expertise opens these aspects of judicial practice to new forms of critical scrutiny.

Reading *Daubert* in conjunction with *Kumho* and their reception in the federal circuits allows us to suggest that notwithstanding the rhetorical commitment to constitutionally sanctioned features of the adversarial trial, most conspicuously the civil jury, the Supreme Court appears to have been more concerned with managing the (perceived) threats posed by unreliable expertise. In this way, images of expertise incorporated into mundane interpretations of the FRE might be understood to have substantially modified evidence jurisprudence and the reach of constitutional guarantees. It would have been extremely controversial for the Supreme Court to have raised admissibility standards for the avowed purposed of limiting the number of civil suits or to ease the burden on scientifically 'incompetent' lay juries. The *epistemological* focus encouraged by *Daubert* and *Kumho* enabled the judges to contribute to these outcomes surreptitiously.

Historically, courts have been interested in 'truth', or the accuracy of fact finding, subject to legal constraints. Appeals to rules, processes and fairness often mediated their access to evidence. Not every piece of relevant evidence is admissible in court. Now we can observe a subtle rhetorical shift in the Supreme Court's admissibility jurisprudence around 'truth' between *Frye, Daubert* and *Kumho,* which is consistent with the 'epistemological turn'. Those courts which embraced the *Frye* standard were generally concerned, even if only rhetorically, with the expert's account of the field and whether the particular approach was generally accepted. Few judges are resourced or possess the inclination to inquire about the boundaries of particular fields or what actually transpires in practice. In *Daubert,* and even more explicitly in *Joiner* and *Kumho,* general acceptance was subordinated to a range of criteria with a conspicuously 'epistemological' orientation.

In *Daubert,* Blackmun referred to the different purposes of 'law' and 'science':

> There are important differences between the quest for truth in the courtroom and the quest for truth in the laboratory. ... [the] Rules of Evidence [are] designed not for the exhaustive search for *cosmic understanding* but for the particularized resolution of legal dispute. (*Daubert* 1993: 600, italics added)

That Blackmun emphasized differences between 'law' and 'science' should not compel us to overlook the fact that he actually articulated criteria which purported to have an epistemological focus. Further, *Daubert* was presented as a substantial departure from the more socially oriented general acceptance approach to admissibility jurisprudence, which apparently relied upon trust, consensus, forms of accreditation and social recognition. If, for Blackmun, the law's quest for 'truth' was not the equivalent of 'cosmic understanding', the *Daubert* criteria were, nevertheless intended to get the law close—certainly closer than *Frye.* Such a reading is consistent with the more explicit concern with 'truth' in the *Joiner* and *Kumho* judgments.

In *Joiner,* acknowledging offers of assistance from peak scientific and medical organizations, such as the AAAS, NAS and the New England Journal of Medicine, Justice Breyer explained that:

> Given the various Rules-authorized methods for facilitating the courts' task, it seems to me that *Daubert's* gatekeeping requirements will not prove inordinately difficult to implement, and that it will help secure the basic objectives of the Federal Rules of Evidence, which are, to repeat, the ascertainment of *truth* and the just determination of proceedings. (*Joiner* 1997: 521, italics added)

The FRE required not only the just determination of suits, but that 'the truth may be ascertained' (*Joiner* 1997: 520, 521; *Kumho* 1999: 1176). A more *efficient* and socially *legitimate* legal system requires judges to make factually accurate decisions. In *Joiner* and *Kumho,* in the general approach advocated by Breyer, concern with scientific truth was characterized as an overriding purpose of the FRE. *Truth,* rather than merely *Law's truth,* was to be obtained through the application of the *Daubert* criteria. Here a particular version of *truth* masquerades as universal *Truth*. Interestingly, this more restrictive approach to evidence and proof converges with the espoused aspirations of corporations, industry and many peak professional organizations. The approach is succinctly delineated in the words of a highly influential corporate-sponsored proponent of evidence and tort reform. According to Peter Huber: 'The rule of law is indeed a grand thing, but not half so grand as the rule of fact' (Huber 1991: 225).

Notes

1   Legal and regulatory settings, particularly Anglo-American adversarial processes and regulatory sites, are conventionally (studied as) sites of expert disagreement (see Lynch in this volume). Institutional processes, different types of evidence, established rules of evidence and proof—including the possibility of cross-examination and the use of non-specialized fact finders—facilitate and shape the forms of contestation. Stakes and interests provide the incentives.

2   *Daubert v Merrell Dow Pharmaceuticals, Inc.* 509 US 579, 125 L.Ed.2d 469, 113 S. Ct. 2786 (1993).

3   Professional debates and controversies are rarely restricted to exclusively 'technical' issues (see Latour 1983b; Rudwick 1985; Collins and Pinch 1993).

4   Any attempt to study the forensic sciences, for example, without reference to specialization and professionalization, law enforcement priorities and budgets, the operation of the wider criminal justice system or sensitivity to individual legal rights, rules and procedures would be deficient. Similarly, evaluations of the performance of experts employed by government and regulatory agencies without considering regulatory cultures (Brickman, Ilgen and Jasanoff 1985), relations with government and industry (Gillespie, Eva and Johnston 1979), the increasing use of negotiation and self-regulation and even career structures will provide a very partial account (Robbins and Johnston 1976).

5   Compare the use of similar metaphors in legal philosophy, see Pound (1908).

6   Empirical studies of litigation trends and damage awards frequently cast doubt on common perceptions of rapid growth in litigation rates or grossly inflated damage awards. Appellate reversals or reductions in damage awards rarely attract the coverage received by judgments at first instance. These empirical findings, which might strike many readers as counter-intuitive, tend to have limited influence on judicial practice, policy debate or law reform (Hensler 1989, 1998; Saks 1992; Bogus 2001).

7   *US v Frye* 293 F 1013 (D.C. Cir. 1923)

8   *Kumho Tire Co. v Carmichael* 526 US 137, 143 L.Ed.2d 238, 119 S. Ct. 137 (1999).

9   Exceptions include Cooper Dreyfuss (1995), Leiter (1997), Farrell (1994), Schwartz (1997), Edmond and Mercer (1997a).

10   There might be debate about whether 'scientific' standards should apply to legal and regulatory practice.

11   Although recently Fuller (2003) has attempted a sophisticated reconstruction, explaining the more complex normative valencies of Popper's general vision for the relationship between science and society.

12   Brief of Petitioners (*Kumho*), Brief for the American Automobile Manufacturers Association and the Association of International Automobile Manufacturers, Inc. (*Kumho*); Brief of Rubber Manufacturers Association (*Kumho*).

13   *General Electric Co. v Joiner* 522 US 136, L.Ed.2d 508, 118 S. Ct. 512 (1997).

14   Whereas in *Daubert* the case was remanded to the Ninth Circuit Court of Appeals. That decision is reported as *Daubert v Merrell Dow Pharmaceuticals, Inc.* 43 F.3d 1311 (9th Cir. 1995).

15   *Weisgram v Marley* 528 US 440, 120 S. Ct. 1011, 145 L.Ed.2d 958 (2000).

Chapter 2

Expertise and Experience in the Governance of Science: What is Public Participation for?

Alan Irwin

Introduction

One international response to expressed public concerns over the direction of technical change (especially in controversial areas such as stem cell research and genetically modified food) has been to call for a 'new partnership' between science and society. As the European Commissioner for Research presents this: 'In a knowledge-based society, democratic governance must ensure that citizens are able to make an informed choice from the options made available to them by responsible scientific and technological progress' (European Commission 2002: 3). However, and as I will explore in this chapter, the move towards enhanced public participation in technical decision-making raises significant questions concerning the *form* of such 'partnership' and the *assumptions* upon which this is to be based. Does 'partnership' imply an active or a passive role for citizens? Should it operate in a top-down or bottom-up fashion? Should there be *limits* to participation?

As I will argue, a partial and usually implicit set of answers to these questions can be identified within current engagement initiatives. At the heart of these answers there lies a generally latent but important debate over the particular contribution that 'citizens' can make to scientific governance and, indeed, over the very meaning of 'citizenship' in this context. Put succinctly, what is public participation *for*? Amidst the many calls for increased 'partnership' and 'engagement', it is noteworthy that very little is generally said about the aims, purposes and intentions of a closer relationship between scientific institutions and wider society.

While these questions have wide sociological significance—and indeed a very long philosophical pedigree—I will suggest that they are also of practical importance for the conduct of scientific governance. In particular, I will argue that the question of 'what public participation is for' is bound up with issues of the status of expertise and the validity of different kinds of experience. What counts as 'knowledge' and who can claim to know best about the direction of technical change? How should public (and other forms of) experience be taken into account and to what purpose? As I will also argue, these questions cannot be separated from the wider climate of social and technical change. At a time when 'partnership' is being presented as a remedy for public scepticism and concern over certain technologies, it is important to consider what the basis of this relationship has been and, indeed, should be.

A convenient entry point to this discussion is the deliberately polemical contribution made in 2002 by Harry Collins and Robert Evans. Putting these broad questions in academic context, they argue that '[t]echnical decision-making in the public domain is where the pigeons of much recent social science are coming home to roost' (Collins and Evans 2002: 235). Restating a familiar theme within science policy and science studies (see, notably, Nelkin 1975), Collins and Evans focus on the potential dichotomy between democratic openness and technical expertise. In making decisions, should we *open up* the process as widely as possible to citizens (on the grounds that they may be directly affected by the outcome and so deserve a significant influence) or *restrict* input to those with specific technical expertise (since experts can be expected to 'know best')? The implication is that democracy and expertise, if not exactly incompatible, are certainly in tension with one another. Citizen participation can be justified on democratic grounds but giving greater emphasis to 'lay' involvement will typically downgrade the influence of technical experts. Reliance on expert advisory committees and the like may help ensure that decisions are technically informed but will also serve to exclude the wider publics. For Collins and Evans, the starting point for any discussion of public participation in technical decision-making must be a clear epistemological distinction between 'experience' and 'expertise'. Each is important, but the two should not be confused.

Reflecting on the development of science and technology studies (STS)—and especially of STS explorations of science-public relations—Collins and Evans divide the field into three 'waves'. In the first wave during the 1950s and 1960s, there existed a 'golden age' before the 'expertise problem' raised its head. Scientists could speak with authority. It was 'inconceivable' that technical decisions could be made in any other way than 'top-down'. The positivist view of scientific knowledge was largely uncontested: science could be relied upon to provide an objective and unchallenged base for decision-making.

In the second wave from the early 1970s, the 'constructivist' approach within the social sciences challenged the status of scientific knowledge and its presumed separation from social and political matters—an approach exemplified by the new 'sociology of scientific knowledge' (SSK). At this point for Collins and Evans, the distinctiveness of 'technical expertise' began to be clouded amidst the sociological enthusiasm for extolling the virtues of 'lay expertise' (in other words, the knowledges and understandings possessed by 'non-expert' groups: see Irwin 1995). Rather than viewing scientific knowledge as context-free, homogeneous or objective, SSK emphasized the political, institutional and economic influences on science (Barnes and Edge 1982; Latour and Woolgar 1979; Mulkay 1991). In these largely empirical studies (often based on the detailed exploration of particular case histories), 'expertise' emerges as a contested and multi-dimensional category, open to many interpretations and challenges—and no longer distinct from wider forms of experience and understanding. As Collins and Evans portray developments within the 'second wave', sociologists became uncertain about what makes scientific knowledge 'different' from other forms of knowledge and understanding. In stressing that what counts as 'knowledge' is a social and institutional judgment—an *outcome* of social processes rather than an *input*—social scientists have lost the ability to separate 'expertise' from 'experience'. For Collins and Evans, members of the public may have relevant experience to offer decision-making—but this is not the same as the possession of knowledge or expertise.

Looking forward to a third wave of science studies, Collins and Evans call for the 'oxymoron' of 'lay expertise' to be abandoned. Instead, the scientific and technical input to decision-making should be separated from the political input. Pockets of expertise do exist among the citizenry and these should be recognized and built upon. Ultimately, however, the roles of expertise and democratic rights are separate. This separation would in turn have major implications for the design and operation of engagement initiatives: whatever public participation would now be for, it would generally *not* be for the acquisition of knowledge.

> Lay people as lay people ... have nothing to contribute to the scientific and technical content of debate. Even specific sets of lay people... have a special contribution to make to science and technology only where it can first be shown that their special experience has a bearing on the scientific and technical matters in dispute. (Collins and Evans 2002: 281)

For Collins and Evans, it is important to identify both where public groups have expertise to offer and where participation could be usefully *decreased*. Thus, they observe that what is often presented as 'local knowledge' can be very partial. The local population in the case of mineral extraction or waste disposal will tend to have a disproportionate understanding of the disadvantages of development but it is likely that only 'planning specialists' will be able to understand the advantages. As the authors acknowledge, political considerations and technical considerations can get mixed up in such situations, but it is still both 'possible and useful' (Collins and Evans 2002: 267) to separate them.

In terms of this chapter's discussion of the purposes of public participation, Collins and Evans therefore offer a very categorical response. While citizens may at times have relevant expertise to offer, this should not undermine the significance of scientific understanding within decision-making. To return to the European Commission's call for partnership, it will be important not to confuse the 'political' and the 'technical' aspects of science-society relations. Just as in the above quotation from the European Commission, the implication is that, even if 'experience' may be brought into technical decision-making, the underlying questions should be framed by the best available expertise. Equally, calls for participation should not confuse democratic rights and expert judgment.

As might be anticipated, there has been a robust critical response to Collins and Evans. Jasanoff, for example, has indicated that the very distinction upon which they build their case is open to question:

To label some aspects of society's response to uncertainty 'political' and some others 'scientific' makes little sense when the very contours of what is certain or uncertain in policy domains get established through intense and intimate science-society negotiations. (Jasanoff 2003: 394)

Jasanoff also argues that Collins and Evans present a false dichotomy since '[w]e need both strong democracy and good expertise to manage the demands of modernity' (Jasanoff 2003: 398). Meanwhile, Wynne has noted that Collins and Evans's account of decision-making pays little account to the broader culture of science in society and especially ignores the manner in which technical decisions are made within 'dominant, often scientistic, frames of public meaning' (Wynne 2003: 413). Thus, decision-making cannot be reduced to a series of discrete questions but should instead be seen as part of a wider framework of authority. For Wynne, the manner in which the questions for discussion are framed in the first place represents a significant political process—and one in which 'politics' and 'science' are not so easily separable. The task for science and technology studies is not to 'surrender' to the 'authoritarian idiom, in which public meanings (and identities) are ... presumed and imposed' (Wynne 2003: 404). Instead, STS should 'try to articulate what a more inclusive social debate over knowledge and its proper grounds and purposes should be' (Wynne 2003: 408).

Other criticisms could be made of Collins and Evans's 'three wave' formulation and the assumptions upon which it is built (see also Rip 2003; Collins and Evans 2003). Was there really a 'golden age' of universal deference to science and scientific institutions? The authors themselves admit this to be an outrageous simplification (see also Welsh 2001). Is it necessarily the case that constructivist analysis undermines the 'special' status of scientific knowledge? SSK could reasonably be construed as doing the very opposite. Is 'local' knowledge inevitably more restricted than 'expert' assessment? The latter can certainly also be partial—focusing, for example, on the advantages rather than disadvantages of a particular development and ignoring the social dynamics of policy enactment (Irwin 1995). However, in this chapter I have a more specific purpose: to explore the implications of this 'expertise/experience' (or 'science/politics') distinction for discussions over public engagement in scientific governance (in other words, for the 'debate over debate').

As noted above, this is not merely a matter of academic discussion. Collins and Evans's argument that democracy and expertise should not be confused resonates strongly with official reports and institutional initiatives since the late 1990s concerning public participation in scientific policy-making. At the start of this century, the requirement for citizen engagement in science has indeed become a mantra within many national and international institutions. However, and just as Collins and Evans seek to maintain an epistemological divide between democratic engagement and technical expertise, so also do many policy initiatives construct a firewall between the 'ethical' (or 'social' or 'perceptual') and 'scientific' aspects of policy-making. To take one prominent example of this, the UK Royal Commission on Environmental Pollution (RCEP) anticipated many of Collins and Evans's points in its ground-breaking 1998 report on *Setting Environmental Standards*. The

RCEP report argued that people's environmental and social values should be incorporated within environmental standard-setting and that the public should be given substantial opportunity to exert an influence at 'every stage' in environmental management. However, the RCEP stressed that '[I]n setting an environmental standard, the starting-point must be scientific understanding of the cause of the problem or potential problem under consideration' (RCEP 1998: 131). The report also established the same epistemological distinction as Collins and Evans: 'A clear dividing line should be drawn between analysis of scientific evidence and consideration of ethical and social issues which are outside the scope of a scientific assessment' (RCEP 1998: 28).

In what follows, I will argue that the current enthusiasm for public engagement characteristically operates within a highly restricted model of the scope and purposes of such 'dialogue'—especially when compared with the larger negotiation over 'public meaning' called for by Wynne. Drawing often implicitly upon the same epistemological divide developed very explicitly by Collins and Evans, policy statements and consultation initiatives typically claim a degree of openness and flexibility in the face of public concerns which is not in practice realized. In exploring what public participation is *for*, we are therefore also considering the institutional framing of controversial socio-technical issues such as genetically modified (GM) food and the epistemological and cultural assumptions embedded within these frameworks. The realist conception as advocated by both Collins and Evans and by many scientific institutions suggests that there is a neutral or context-free manner of establishing the issues for discussion. At the same time, it argues that the 'social' and the 'scientific' elements of dialogue are analytically (and practically) separable. Experience of recent initiatives in biotechnology suggests that these are not justifiable or defensible assumptions.

Rather than treating this discussion as an entirely philosophical matter or making analytical judgments in advance, it becomes important to investigate where the 'epistemological line' is drawn within specific engagement exercises (and related statements) and the implications of this for public debate. Accordingly, we can begin to explore in more open and empirical terms the relationship between experience and expertise in practice and, very importantly, the manner in which such categorical judgments are made. In this way, we can also draw attention to the policy contexts in which 'public opinion' is constructed and consider the influence of these contexts on the form and conduct of public participation and consultation.

In order to pursue these questions of experience and expertise and, more broadly, of the purposes of public participation in scientific governance, I will consider two public engagement initiatives within the UK—both dealing in questions of biotechnology and the biosciences. The Public Consultation on Developments in the Biosciences (PCDB), which took place between 1997 and 1999, explicitly attempted an open and two-way dialogue between government and citizens over the direction of technical change. Covering a range of issues—including xenotransplantation, animal and human cloning, genetic testing and the genetic modification (GM) of food—it was, at least in British terms, a highly significant and path-breaking exercise. The 2003 'GM Nation?' initiative was in its turn the most sophisticated British attempt at encouraging a national debate over biotechnology issues: specifically, over the commercial growing of GM crops in the UK. Both these activities represented significant attempts to bring just the kind of partnership envisaged by the European Commission into action. The two initiatives also follow directly from one another since the body that oversaw the second exercise was established as a direct consequence of the first. In that way, these two examples offer a unique vantage point to study UK activities in the especially sensitive area of biotechnology. As I will explain, both raise questions about just what public participation is *for*, and about the relationship between knowledge and experience within social controversies.

Consulting the biosciences

The late 1990s were a critical period for science-public relations in the UK. Although the official investigation into the Government's handling of mad cow disease (BSE) had not yet been published (Phillips et al. 2000), there was a growing feeling among science policymakers and senior politicians that relations with the wider public had in that case been badly managed. A previous food scare over salmonella poisoning had left its political mark—with public mistrust in science and innovation seen as a growing issue. The incoming Labour Government also brought a commitment to greater openness and responsiveness to the electorate (accompanied by much media mockery of 'government by focus group'). Meanwhile, ethical and political concerns over biotechnology were beginning to rumble (see for example Grove-White et al. 1997) and by 1999 the controversy over GM food had broken out in many European countries. The British Prime Minister faced particular accusations over Monsanto's export of GM soya to Europe and the Government's general handling of 'Frankenstein foods'. In these circumstances, and in keeping with the new climate of science-public relations, it was not (at least in retrospect) surprising that the Minister for Science announced in November 1997 his intention to hold a public consultation over bioscience issues. As the (soon to be replaced) Minister expressed it to a meeting of interested parties in early 1998, the main purpose of the exercise was to identify and explore public hopes and concerns, and to feed these into the policy process.

Two general issues about this planned initiative are especially important for the current discussion of scientific governance. First of all, there is the *practical construction* of such an exercise: what specific form should it take? It is very likely (based on subsequent interviews) that when the Minister initially announced his intention to 'go public' little thought had been given as to *how* this would be carried out. Public consultation can take many forms: from a national referendum to a questionnaire survey and from a series of focus groups to an internet debate. The adoption of these different frameworks can have important consequences for the conduct of the engagement exercise. For example, does the engagement allow full opportunity for debate and reflection? Does it encourage a sustained relationship with the issues or assume that people carry pre-formed attitudes and opinions? Are citizens defined as individualized agents or as part of larger social networks? This institutional construction of consultation will in turn draw upon generally implicit understandings of the best relationship between policy-making and the wider public. Are citizens seen as a significant input to the policy process or else as a target for officially sanctioned information? In the current political climate within many European countries, the danger is that the latter approach will be seen as merely tokenistic and legitimatory.

Secondly, and in keeping with Wynne's arguments above, the *questions selected for discussion* can in themselves prefigure and constrain what is to follow. In particular, there is a key judgment to be made within consultation exercises concerning *who* gets to define the issues and according to *what* sets of assumptions. For example, official institutions may view it as entirely appropriate to narrow the range of discussion to matters that are seen to be of short-term practical value in terms of current operational requirements. In this way, broad and potentially difficult issues can be transformed into highly focused and definable concerns with which intelligent bureaucrats can efficiently deal. Members of the public meanwhile may have a much broader grasp of what needs to be discussed so that, for example, issues of scientific innovation are bound up with larger questions of social empowerment, trust in institutions and the quality of life (Irwin, Simmons and Walker 1999). From this public perspective, apparently specific issues of technical decision-making can become inseparable from larger cultural and political concerns: for example, over the need for rapid technological change or the potential imbalance of social and economic benefits. Of course, science from this larger perspective may not be given unique status but seen instead as yet another representation and projection of larger social patterns and processes.

These broad questions (crudely, of *how?*, *who?*, and *what?*) relate closely to the relationship between 'expertise and experience'. Thus, nationally randomized social research procedures appear an inappropriate means of tapping into groups that have been defined as 'knowledgeable' (for example, consumer organisations, medical self-help associations, those with personal experience of xenotransplantation) for whom deliberate selection will be required. It is certainly not typical for scientific experts to be approached in such an indirect fashion. The questions selected for discussion may also relate to the expertise–experience relationship. Are they framed according to the understandings, concerns and priorities of citizens or do they link most closely to the needs of scientific institutions? Do the questions begin with a 'technical' framing of the issues (emphasizing a 'science-centred' worldview) or are they open to alternative experiences and understandings? Thus, prior assumptions about the legitimacy and relevance of different forms of knowledge and expertise can be expected to frame any consultation exercise. Such assumptions typically become taken for granted (and hidden from view) as the exercise progresses.

In this particular case, the consultation took shape as a combination of qualitative discussion groups (two sessions for each group of participants, held one week apart) and a larger quantitative survey (essentially, an individual questionnaire). As the House of Lords Select Committee subsequently noted: 'we see this exercise as closer to market research than to public consultation' (House of Lords 2000). Certainly, the construction of the initiative as a relatively sophisticated social research exercise meant that it was very much under the control of its organizers—with little opportunity for exchange between government and the wider publics (and then only through the researchers hired for this purpose).

Meanwhile, the questions for discussion were established by the incoming Minister in October 1998 and are worth citing in full:

- What is the level and nature of people's awareness of technological advances in the biosciences?
- What issues do people see arising from these developments in the biosciences and how important are these compared to other major scientific issues?
- What is the extent of people's knowledge of the oversight and regulatory process in the United Kingdom and Europe?
- What issues do people believe should be taken into account in any oversight of developments in the biosciences?
- What information should be made available to the general public from the regulatory system and about advances in the biosciences?

As the new Minister put it: 'The consultation sets the challenging task of seeking the public's views and promoting informed debate. Our long-term aim is to encourage public confidence in the Government's use of scientific information and know-how' (Lord Sainsbury quoted in LCGIS 1998: 17).

Reviewing these questions and the quotation from the Minister, it is clear that they suggest a very particular and institutionally derived framework for the issues at hand. Thus, the ministerial statement makes it quite explicit that it is for the Government to employ 'scientific know-how' and for the public to have confidence in this. There is no suggestion here of a loss of certainty concerning the boundaries around expertise nor any hint that citizens might have expertise of their own to contribute. In Collins and Evans's terms, the epistemological divide between expertise and experience appears intact and unchallenged. On this evidence also, there is little indication of a 'second wave' in Government thinking within which the distinction between scientifically-based 'expertise' and public 'experience' has become blurred or undermined. Instead, it would appear that official philosophy remains—despite previous experience of science-public relations—firmly rooted in the first wave 'golden age'.

A similar impression is gained from Lord Sainsbury's set of questions. Information is potentially being 'made available' to the 'general public' rather than received, exchanged or challenged. Where 'knowledge' figures in this list it relates to the public's grasp of governmental and regulatory processes rather than any form of 'lay expertise'. In general, the questions suggest a very particular—and particularly restricted—framework within which, for example, the public criticism and scrutiny of institutional procedures and operational assumptions are deemed irrelevant. To offer one illustration of this institutional framing, it is questionable whether members of the public would make *any* comparison between the 'biosciences' and 'other major scientific issues'. Such a comparison would be of specific interest to the government body that was running this exercise but its relevance to members of the public cannot simply be assumed. Even the term 'biosciences' is both unfamiliar and problematic, bringing together a range of 'food' and 'health' concerns. Instead, it could hypothetically be argued that the 'red' and 'green' forms of biotechnology might be given different social assessments combining as they do different patterns of risk, need and benefit. It would appear that 'the biosciences' were selected as the focus of consultation in order to avoid an inter-departmental squabble over which branch of government 'owned' the consultation (as would have occurred if, for example, the 'health' or 'food' dimensions of the issue had been prioritized).

In further illustration of the concern to maintain a barrier between 'experience' and 'expertise', considerable debate took place within the advisory group concerning the technical objectivity of the materials presented to the qualitative discussion groups. It was seen to be essential that information on the biosciences made available to members of the public (in the form of handouts between the two sessions) should be of unimpeachable scientific authority. In that way, public discussion could be properly 'informed' and consultation could centre on scientifically defined issues. However, when one considers the actual materials used within the qualitative phase of the exercise to stimulate discussion, it is very clear that this science/ethics (or experience/expertise) dichotomy is impossible to maintain in practice. To offer two examples of stimulus materials from the exercise:

- *Are genes good or bad?* 'Genes are present in all living organisms. They do not have moral characteristics. They are merely chemical components.'
- *Is it natural?* 'In a natural world, human beings would not fly in airplanes, send rockets to the moon, eat Pot Noodle ... have governments, or live until they were 70, 80 or 90. So what is natural?'

It is no criticism of the consultation to point out that these statements are not 'neutral' but deliberately offer social and cultural propositions for discussion and challenge. What is noteworthy here is that a different approach to neutrality was practised according to whether the issues were seen to be 'factual' (and therefore beyond public debate) or 'open for discussion' (i.e. relating to the world of experience). Once again, an epistemological distinction was maintained according to which facts could be separated from matters of judgment or opinion. Within the exercise, 'facts' were not opened up to debate or scrutiny.

However, the 'facts' within an area of considerable technical as well as social uncertainty may not be separable in this fashion—creating a major problem for the exercise in question but also for the wider epistemological assumption on which it was based. To offer one illustration of this, the environmental and health consequences of GM crops are not simply a matter of scientific appraisal but will unavoidably depend upon essentially *social* predictions about the practical implementation and enactment of agricultural systems. Thus, the risk of GM crops is unavoidably bound up with levels (and types) of pesticide application: will farmers reduce pesticide levels (as has generally been claimed by the agrochemical industry), maintain them or even increase pesticide usage as a form of insurance against a novel and potentially unpredictable situation? Evidence from the United States suggests that GM crops may actually have led to increased levels of pesticide use (Vidal 2004)—thus undermining many of the environmental claims made on behalf of the new agricultural products.

As a second example of socio-technical interaction—and hence of the difficulty of separating 'experience' from 'expertise'—one considerable issue for the risk assessment of GM crops concerns 'bioconfinement'. That is, the practicality of avoiding cross-contamination between GM and non-GM materials. It is in the very nature of agricultural practice that seeds can be misplaced, dropped or wrongly sown and that materials may be mixed, incorrectly administered or stolen. Significant uncertainties therefore emerge as one moves from tightly controlled experimental conditions to the messiness and uncontrollability of the 'real world' (see also Irwin 2001). In illustration of this, one gene-altered crop did contaminate the US food supply—leading to the recall of grocery products such as taco shells. While such examples may be consigned to 'human error', it appears more appropriate to view them as an inherent characteristic of complex socio-technical systems—in Perrow's (1984) terminology 'normal accidents'.

Rather than presenting such 'social' responses as quite separate from the 'scientific' factors, it can reasonably be argued that 'scientific' assessments unavoidably depend upon prior assumptions about social and behavioral responses to technological change—what Wynne (1989b) has termed 'naïve sociology'. One practical problem with current approaches to public consultation is that they offer a very restricted definition of expertise which excludes any explicit questioning of such embedded assumptions. In this way also, the 'technological' and the 'social' dimensions are presented as separate rather than—as these examples suggest—mutually embedded. Meanwhile, risk assessments often downplay such social uncertainties and so suggest a possibly spurious level of technical capability and competence. Equally, those with direct experience of the social conditions of practical enactment and implementation are excluded from 'expert' status.

The final report on the consultation appeared in May 1999. Prepared by the market research organization that had conducted the exercise, its key findings were:

- the public believe advances in human health represent the biggest benefit to arise from scientific developments;
- the vast majority of people (97 per cent) believe it is important that there are rules and regulations to control biological developments and scientific research;
- the main issues people say should be taken into account when determining whether a biological development is right or wrong are whether people will benefit from it and whether it is safe to use;

- the thing that people most want in relation to the biosciences is more information on the rules and regulations. (MORI 1999)

In May 1999, the Minister for the Cabinet Office presented the main results (three volumes with the third consisting of 145 quantitative tables) and at the same time announced a new regulatory structure for biotechnology—a structure which created the Agriculture and Environment Biotechnology Commission (AEBC) which will feature in the next section. As an exercise in public engagement—and despite the stated reservations of the advisory group—it had broken new ground and demonstrated that consultation was not simply a political aspiration but could be bureaucratically achieved. However, and as I have suggested in this section, the maintenance of a division between 'information giving' and 'consultation' constrained the exercise in many important ways—and not least by limiting the possibilities for public groups to set the issues for discussion themselves or to challenge the 'science-centred' culture of government. One notable manifestation of this was that the exercise effectively gave no space for respondents to *oppose* (or even contest) developments in the biosciences. Instead, the whole premise of the exercise was that development would occur and that the only issue for public discussion related to the form of regulatory oversight.

It can be observed also that this exercise effectively turned the initial Ministerial call for consultation into a social research project. We are presented here with a 'technology' of consultation operating within strictly defined parameters (see also Rose 1999): a technology that did little to engage with wider issues of governance. The discussion group and questionnaire phases of the exercise were professionally conducted—often under huge time pressures (the final report in particular was produced at great speed). However, the possibilities for 'engagement' were severely restricted by this methodology. Instead, government could keep its distance from members of the public. Of course, this meant that the pre-defined agenda for consultation was efficiently and effectively pursued. At the same time, it dictated that the possibilities for revisiting the agenda or opening up the culture of governance to wider scrutiny were severely restricted. Instead, any direct encounter between a member of the advisory group and members of the public would have been seen as a form of data contamination.

In political terms, the 1997–9 biosciences consultation raises many questions about the character of 'scientific citizenship' in contemporary society. Succinctly put, this was a very attenuated form of democratic engagement. The analytical point which I also wish to establish is that the *form* of this exercise was inextricably linked with its operational *assumptions*. The quantitative phase of the initiative in particular took for granted that public attitudes could be kept apart from matters of expertise and 'fact'. In this way, the epistemological and the institutional assumptions within the exercise worked very much together. However, and as was suggested by the discussion of GM crops, such an approach serves to exclude potentially important questions of the prior framing of these questions and of the forms of knowledge which might help illuminate socio-technical uncertainties. In broader terms, the attempt to insulate institutional assumptions from wider scrutiny suggests a governance culture far from at ease with the possible range and diversity of public concerns over technical change.

Debating GM

As noted already, the UK Government announced in 1999 the main findings of the biosciences consultation alongside the creation of a new regulatory structure for biotechnology. One important aspect of this structure was the establishment of an innovative institutional form, the Agriculture and Environment Biotechnology Commission (AEBC). In that way, and even though the precise relationship between the actual consultation exercise and the ministerial announcement of new bodies was never quite explicit, the biosciences consultation had a more significant legacy than one hurriedly prepared report. The AEBC was set up in June 2000 with twenty members from a range of backgrounds including non-governmental organizations (NGOs) and academia, scientific organizations and agriculture, consumer organizations and industry. The very constitution of this body, therefore, represented a novel (at least for the UK) experiment in public engagement and participation. As the AEBC described itself, it was 'a new and distinctive kind of body' (AEBC 2001: 6). The Commission's remit included advising government about the social and ethical implications, and also public acceptability, of developments in biotechnology. One central question for discussion in this section concerns the relationship between this innovative institution and the wider culture of scientific governance in the UK.

At its first meeting in July 2000, the AEBC noted that the UK Government's Farm Scale Evaluations (FSEs) of genetically modified herbicide-tolerant crops were causing considerable controversy. As one illustration of this, 28 Greenpeace members had been brought to court in April 2000 charged with criminal damage following the partial cutting down and removal of a field of GM maize (see Greenpeace undated). As the AEBC observed in its 2001 report, *Crops on Trial*, the public interest and concern caused by these field trials seemed to have 'puzzled and surprised' government, industry and scientists. In a detailed discussion of the trials and the criticisms that had been generated, the AEBC argued that 'robust public policies and regulatory frameworks for GM crops need to expose, respect and embrace the differences of view which exist, rather than bury them' (AEBC 2001: 12). On that basis, the AEBC recommended:

> We believe that the Government must now encourage comprehensive public discussion of the ecological and ethical—including socio-economic—issues which have arisen. Time is needed for people to overcome differences of language and explore the extent of their shared understandings, and above all there is a need to include those who have felt themselves to be excluded and hence to have no control over events. We have initiated such a discussion, and we look forward to continuing it. (AEBC 2001: 12)

In its response to the *Crops on Trial* report, in January 2002 the Government endorsed the notion of a public debate and requested further advice about how and when to hold a discussion over the commercialization of the GM crops involved in the field trials. That advice duly followed and in July 2002, the Government announced the creation of a steering board—to be led by the AEBC chair—which would manage the debate. The eventual exercise—'GM Nation? The public debate'—was held between 3 June and 18 July 2003. The debate's findings were published on the 24 September 2003. As the final report stressed, this was intended to be a 'different kind of debate'. Drawing implicitly on the lessons of the biosciences consultation, the AEBC called for 'the public to guide the way in which the issue was debated, rather than respond to an agenda set by others' (GM Nation? 2003: 10). Equally, it was intended that the exercise would not offer a simple 'yes' or 'no' but instead 'establish the nature and full spectrum of the public's views on GM and the possible commercialisation of GM crops, and any conditions it might want to impose on this' (GM Nation? 2003: 10).

The GM Nation? exercise was certainly very different in quality and scale to the previous biosciences consultation—suggesting a considerably more ambitious and sophisticated approach. An estimated 675 public meetings were held and the web-site received over 2.9 million hits. Around 37,000 feedback forms were returned. As noted in the final report (GM Nation? 2003: 11–12), the debate's steering board had four main principles in mind:

- the debate 'should give people new and effective opportunities to deliberate on the issues, with access to the information people may want and need in order to do so';
- the public should 'as far as possible frame the issues and questions for debate';
- to 'try and involve people in debate activities ... who had not previously expressed a view on GM issues';
- to 'throw light on whether the open debate activities had been "captured" by special interests, as some feared might happen'.

In practical terms, these principles took shape as a series of regional meetings followed by a large number of county-level and local sessions. Additionally, and in order to access members of the public who had not been actively involved in discussing GM issues, a series of deliberative workshops were convened: the so-called 'narrow-but-deep' sessions. It is also important to note that the public debate was simply one strand in the Government review. Alongside this strand were two others: the 'science' and 'economic' reviews. In addition, the outcome of the FSEs would inform the eventual Government decision over commercialization.

The main conclusions of the final report on the public debate can be summarized as: people are generally uneasy about GM; the more people engage in GM issues, the harder their attitudes and the more intense their concerns; there is little support for early commercialization; there is widespread mistrust of government and multi-national companies. Simply put, the report characterizes public opinion over the commercialization of GM as 'not yet—if ever'.

Given that this was a novel exercise in UK terms, it is entirely predictable that subsequent criticism and debate over the report would occur. At the time of writing, the 'debate over the debate' is still very much alive, thereby raising some interesting questions (to which we will return) over whether this represented the— soon to subside—'high water mark' for such consultation exercises in the UK or an indication that public engagement was now an established part of government decision-making. In this, of course, the GM Nation? debate has implications not just for biotechnology but also for other emergent domains of socio-technical change—with nanotechnology a prominent area where public concerns are being actively anticipated (Wood et al. 2003).

In its report on the exercise, a House of Commons committee noted that: 'The public debate was an imaginative initiative, but nonetheless represents an opportunity missed' (House of Commons 2003: 18). The Commons committee blamed two principal problems for this: the tight deadline set for completion and the 'paltry resources' allocated by the Government. In fact, both these matters had been the subject of lively discussion during the exercise, with the steering board having some success in putting the debate commencement back to July 2003 and doubling the original budget to the eventual level of £500,000. For the Commons committee, the deadline nevertheless meant that data from the economics and science strands were not available to debate participants. As the committee concluded: 'The Government ... must allay the suspicion that, having agreed to undertake a public debate, it did as little as it could to make it work' (House of Commons 2003: 18).

Although the Commons report drew the main lesson from the consultation that future exercises should be 'adequately resourced and must be given enough time to be conducted properly' (House of Commons 2003: 20), discussion in this chapter suggests that there are wider lessons to be learnt. Once again, it can be argued that the form of the exercise and its underlying assumptions fit closely together—and indeed reinforce one another. These assumptions embrace the questions of experience and expertise with which this chapter is specifically concerned but also address the wider culture of technical decision-making in the UK and elsewhere. This is not to suggest that the GM consultation was 'merely' an exercise in legitimation or that it failed to engage with public opinion. In both respects, the 2003 exercise represented a substantial step forward from its 1997–9 counterpart (even if it was still possible for most citizens to be wholly unaware that a public debate was taking place). Nevertheless, it is important to note that specific initiatives such as this cannot be separated from the larger governance culture in which they operate. In that sense, even the most imaginative and well-resourced consultation cannot succeed within a political setting that serves to undermine the very conditions of success.

Specifically, the separation of the GM review into 'factual' and 'public' strands represents an obvious manifestation of the expertise/experience dichotomy as challenged in the previous section. As noted above, the GM Nation? debate ran in parallel with a separate review of the science behind GM and an economic assessment of the costs and benefits of GM crops. The economic report was published seven days before the end of debate, the science review appeared three days *after* the debate's conclusion. Meanwhile, public discussion was concluded before publication of the main field trials of genetic crops. It would appear that the construction of public debate, economic and scientific reviews as three separate but parallel strands inhibits the possibility of transparent public engagement in 'technical' analysis or of public discussion openly reflecting upon technical issues raised by the other streams (a point made also by debate participants). However, this should not be presented as simply a matter of time and resources (although the level of support offered by government may indicate the relative priority being given to public consultation) but rather raises more basic questions of the relationship between such exercises and the routine operation of government.

It is important to stress that there was opportunity *within* the debate for 'expertise' to be discussed and challenged—even if the absence of two-way dialogue meant that points were simply raised, recorded and left for the organizers to sift and sort. Thus, a carefully prepared booklet set out the 'Debating Zone' and attempted a balanced summary of the views on 'both sides of the debate'. The booklet covered issues such as: What is GM? Are chemicals involved? Is GM good for me? Are GM foods safe? Will it harm the environment? Is GM ethical? Intriguingly, one of the issues raised is: Can we get unbiased information? In each case, both 'views for' and 'views against' are summarized. The questions asked and the structure of the whole booklet suggest a willingness to raise fundamental issues of both an 'expert' and an 'experiential' kind. Nevertheless, the separation of this 'public' element from the two 'technical' strands denied the possibility of more direct engagement or responsiveness. This does not primarily suggest a failure of the consultation itself but rather indicates the wider problem of conducting such exercises within a governance culture that maintains an arm's length relationship between 'expertise' and 'experience' (and indeed an arm's length between government ministers and public consultation—Government was keen to stress the 'independence' of this exercise). In general, there was an unwillingness in this case to allow the 'public' and 'technical' strands to confront one another directly. Public challenges to expert knowledge could be made but within this structure no direct answers were available. Equally, and as was pointed out in the previous section, social assumptions within the 'technical' assessments were removed from challenge.

The separation of experience and expertise contrasts with two 'GM juries' being conducted by a Newcastle University team at approximately the same time as the GM Nation? debate (PEALS 2003). The establishment of two separate juries, each meeting ten times, allowed in that case a direct examination of several witnesses and the preparation of much more detailed reports than was possible within the GM Nation? format. These reports explicitly mixed 'social' and 'technical' arguments—for example, in expressed concerns that 'Government communication and media coverage does not give sufficient weight to the importance and complexity of the GM issue' (PEALS 2003: 2). In the case of the GM juries also, greater ownership and empowerment were assumed by involved citizens—far beyond what was possible within the much more constrained (and much larger) national GM debate. Instead, juries were relatively free to pursue issues of their own choosing. Linked to that point, one other noteworthy feature of this jury approach is that it allowed two separate groups to reach slightly different conclusions—even if there was substantial agreement with regard to the call for a halt on the sale of GM foods.

While the national GM debate was concerned to establish a broad consensual position as an input to government decision-making, more local exercises such as the GM jury permit a diversity of expression and a significantly more intense engagement. On the specific question of expertise and experience, the Newcastle University report on the juries stressed that the point was not to denigrate expert views but instead to create 'democratic spaces' where different claims to expertise could be properly scrutinized:

> While few would wish to suggest that we do not need a variety [of] experts in society, each bringing valuable specialist knowledge, action inquiry methods such as juries are necessary ways of allowing other citizens—who may themselves be experts in some areas relevant to the subject—the space to assess the broad validity and applicability of such knowledge. We believe that the development of such democratic spaces ... [is] essential if [the] public is to recover its trust in policies made around science and technology. (PEALS 2003: 28)

The modernist culture of scientific governance dictates not simply that 'expertise' and 'experience' belong to separate strands of the decision-making process but also that (perhaps more importantly) the possibilities for cross-examination and mutual scrutiny between these strands are severely restricted. In this regard, specific limitations in the design of the GM Nation? debate, although significant in themselves, may be less crucial than the constraints imposed by the broader framework of governance and priority-setting. In this situation, there is a particular danger that exercises such as the 2003 GM consultation represent temporary—and very partial—experiments in 'open' governance which in themselves do little to challenge the underlying framework of science-centred innovation and restricted accountability. Put differently, the maintenance of a clear division between expertise and experience serves to remove 'technical' matters from public scrutiny—and in so doing imposes great limitations on even the most well-resourced debate.

In discussing this second case of public engagement, it has become important to consider the relationship between 'expertise and experience' not simply *within* a specific initiative (as in the previous biosciences consultation) but also as it operates *across* what has been termed the 'larger culture of governance'. In this section, we have observed that one important limitation of exercises such as GM Nation? relates to the restricted opportunity for *cross-engagement* between the 'expert' and 'experiential' strands. The characteristic separation of 'factual' and 'public' issues detracts from even the possibility that it is legitimate and valid for citizens to interrogate apparently 'technical' assumptions. In illustration of this point, one of the GM juries was keen to raise issues of the privatization of research and to call for more independent and government-funded research so that 'public interest must not lose out to corporate interests in this area. We have a right to ask for fair scientific research in all our interests' (PEALS 2003: 14). The separation of 'technical' and 'public' strands within scientific governance is not simply an *epistemological* distinction but also a means of insulating policy-making from such fundamental questions of research direction and control. It also follows that even the very best-designed consultation initiative will be of limited value if it is marginalized by the prevailing policy culture.

One important test of initiatives such as 'GM Nation?' will be whether they continue to exist as marginal exercises or instead serve to open up and challenge institutional processes of scientific governance—and thus facilitate a wider consideration of science-public relations. A sceptical account of the two 'experiments' considered in this chapter would suggest that they are likely to have only limited impact on a culture of governance which places over-riding emphasis on a restricted notion of 'best expertise' and a broad commitment to international competitiveness through science-led innovation. Given the potential economic significance of, for example, biotechnology, is it reasonable to expect a meaningful social and political debate over the desirability of particular forms of technical change? A more 'optimistic' viewpoint would point out that even the limited initiatives discussed above represent a move towards wider discussion of the social and ethical implications of technical change in a manner that would have been unthinkable in (say) early 1990s Britain (and certainly during the 1980s). Now that the principle of consultation has become established with regard to biotechnology, can it be avoided in other actual or potential areas of social controversy?

In the end, these are empirical questions to be tested out in institutional and political practice. Developments over the next decades will determine whether this was indeed the 'high water mark' for public consultation or an early indication of a larger institutional and cultural change. Of course, this is a matter that must also be understood in *global* terms: scientific and technological innovation is an internationally-driven phenomenon and individual nations cannot generally act alone. Given the potential significance of areas such as biotechnology, nanotechnology and information technology, this is an issue of considerable intellectual, political and practical importance.

Conclusion

We began this chapter with a discussion of what public participation is *for*. In asking that question, we especially highlighted the relationship between 'experience' and 'expertise'. In the course of examining two recent initiatives in public engagement, a number of specific points have emerged:

> The manner in which 'expertise' and 'experience' cannot stand alone but unavoidably draw upon one another—not least in terms of social assumptions about the 'real world' of risk enactment and implementation. In the case of GM crops, we observed that risk models partly build upon social and organisational predictions about the practical implementation of

agricultural regimes (predictions, one might add, which require—but are not generally given—robust social 'testing'). We also noted that members of the public may wish to ask questions about the sponsorship of scientific research and the direction of technical change. In both these areas, it is reasonable to argue that 'non-experts' may have a legitimate (and important) contribution to make within matters that are conventionally presented as 'expert' in character;

The realist assumption that expertise and experience can be separated operates not simply as an epistemological dividing line but also serves to insulate institutions from further-reaching questions about their social commitments—not least to economic development through certain forms of technological innovation. In that way, the expert/experience distinction is not simply a philosophical nicety but is also culturally and politically loaded.

In examining two biotechnology consultations, we noted that it is important to explore both the specific construction of scientific citizens *within* the individual exercises but also the relationship *between* such activities and the wider culture of scientific governance. Certainly, it is difficult to imagine an effective role for public participation within policy cultures that characteristically serve to screen out larger questions over the direction of technical change and reduce complex issues of life quality to merely 'technical' decisions over specific risks.

We also observed the manner in which the framing of public consultation (the 'how?, who?, and what?' of such exercises) can have a substantial impact upon the conduct of what follows. Once again, the assumption that such frameworks can be unproblematically defined in scientific terms (often in terms of 'risk') acts as a hindrance to full democratic engagement.

None of these points should be interpreted as undermining the legitimacy or importance of 'expertise'. Rather than denying the existence of 'expertise', the point has been to establish the *variety* of expertises that may be applicable within apparently technical situations but also the necessity of operating clear and open *processes* for the scrutiny of and (as necessary) challenge to expert statements. One difficulty with the insistence on an epistemological expert/public divide is that it obfuscates such issues of oversight and accountability.

It follows that the claimed distinction between experience and expertise fails to capture much of the reality of contested areas of social and scientific policy as considered in this chapter. Instead, the attempt to build a barrier between 'public' and 'expert' assessments (whether on the part of sociologists or policymakers) represents a turning away from the complexities of decision-making under conditions of social and technical uncertainty. Rather than offering a way of resolving current difficulties in scientific governance or a fresh perspective on challenging issues, rigid insistence on this distinction seems to offer nostalgia for a 'golden age' which may not have existed even in the 1950s and has little relevance at the start of the new millennium.

What then is public participation for? In this chapter, we have suggested a number of answers to this question: a means of stifling public objections, a well-intentioned effort at gauging opinion, a complement to expert advice, an exploration of bureaucratic agenda, an attempt to 'educate' citizens about science, an input to decision-making, a first step towards cultural and institutional change. In reality, these (and other) motivations will co-exist and jostle within any participation exercise. There is no single logic in operation here nor will actors necessarily agree. The complexity of the modern world dictates that governance is not even under the control of national governments and the unitary portrayal of institutions such as 'science', 'industry', 'government' and 'the public' must give way to more heterogeneous and dynamic understandings (Irwin and Michael 2003). In these circumstances, public participation might best be seen as an extended form of intelligence gathering and a testing of the changing conditions for socio-technical development (see also Funtowicz and Ravetz 1993). Far from limiting ourselves to the old categories of 'experience and expertise', we need to develop fresh ways of considering, and acting upon, the already close—but often unchallenged—relationship between technical change, democracy and contemporary culture. If experiments in public participation can stimulate that discussion, then they will indeed have been successful.

Acknowledgements

I would like to thank the following people for their particular support and encouragement: Rob Hagendijk, Peter Healey, Tom Horlick-Jones, Maja Horst, Kevin Jones, Tim O'Riordan and Nick Pidgeon.

Chapter 3

Scientific Expertise and Regulatory Decision-making: Standards, Evidential Interpretation and Social Interests in the Pharmaceutical Sector

John Abraham

Introduction

Commentators on public policy and regulatory policy often discuss the legislative framework within which policy-making should take place and/or the institutional relations which ought to guide regulation. Within such discussions, the implicit assumption seems to be that the scientists involved can be left to themselves to determine technical assessments while politics operates at the more general level of enabling legislation for regulators or legal sanctions against those who violate regulations. This assumption is especially problematic in areas of regulation where the input of scientific expertise is very pervasive, such as environmental chemicals, food additives and pharmaceuticals.

The conventional split between science and politics within many governmental regulatory systems operates on the following logic:

- politicians in the legislature determine laws requiring regulations and regulators for their enforcement—e.g. that only safe and effective new prescription drugs may be approved for marketing;
- to enforce the law, regulators develop regulatory standards, which are science-based, that is, derived from existing scientific knowledge;
- scientists in, or advising, regulatory agencies apply these standards in assessing individual cases—e.g. risk–benefit assessments of particular new drug products;
- scientists in, or advising, regulatory agencies recommend a decision or a policy regarding whether the risks associated with the new technological product are 'acceptable';
- politicians in the executive arm of government either 'rubber-stamp' or reject the recommendations of the regulatory agency.

In capitalist societies the legal framework for regulation is also conventionally related to citizenship rights. Historically, citizens of a nation state were declared as having rights to liberty, property and security with the law adjudicating between these rights when they came into conflict (Halfmann 1998; Turner 1990). Regarding rights to security, social science has often concentrated attention on rights of access to the welfare state (Mann 1987; Marshall 1981; Richardson 1998; Walby 1994). However, when considering the regulation of technological products, one may be confronted with an array of potentially conflicting citizenship rights, namely, industry's rights to private property attained from the legal right to market their products following regulatory approval by the state, on the one hand, and consumers', patients' and/or workers' rights to security in health via protection from exposure to unsafe and/or ineffective products following regulatory denial of the market legality of the product (Abraham and Lewis 2002).

Hence, the nature of the relationships between scientific expertise and regulatory decision-making raises questions about citizenship. For example, technological risk–benefit assessments can be of major social and political importance when they lead to one governmental regulatory outcome or another as thousands or even millions of consumers, patients or workers may be affected (Abraham and Lawton Smith 2003; Lawton Smith 2002). In recent times, sociological and policy analyses of scientific expertise and regulation have challenged the conventional split between regulatory policy-making and scientific knowledge (Abraham 1995; Jasanoff 1990). The scientific knowledge involved in regulatory policy-making is better conceptualized as 'regulatory science', whose production is influenced by social and technical factors (Abraham and Reed 2002). Those factors deserve to be empirically investigated because they may shape intellectual decisions about 'the legitimate and relevant dimensions of a risk problem; the preferred paradigms of analysis; the criteria for certifying and interpreting evidence; and the ways in which different types of uncertainty are recognized, engaged with and represented' (Van Zwanenberg and Millstone 2000). In this way, social analysts of science and technology can learn more about the depth and scope of socio-political influence on regulatory science, and can make a major contribution to assessing the claims of scientificity made by regulatory policymakers.

By drawing on two major case studies—the risk–benefit assessment of the 'sleeping pill', Halcion, and the standard-setting at the International Conference of Technical Requirements for Registration of Pharmaceuticals for Human Use (ICH)—I shall argue that politics relating to social interests are involved in both how evidence is interpreted by scientists by reference to existing standards in individual cases, and how standards are developed by expert scientists within regulatory settings. Yet such processes are presented by industry and government protagonists as the business of technical scientists and apparently accepted as such by official political discourse. Consequently, they are protected from questions that are typically asked of political processes about accountability, democracy, power relations and social interests.

The theoretical importance of this investigation is to demonstrate that the nature of regulatory science and scientific expertise can be related to fairly stable and enduring social interests, which are in turn related to citizenship. Thus, I presuppose that pharmaceutical companies have significant and enduring structural interests in marketing their drugs profitably, and that it is in the interests of patients that the benefit-to-risk ratio of the drugs they take is as high as possible in relation to their illness. These interests are related to citizenship rights, to private property and to public health, respectively. The extent to which regulatory decisions derived from scientific expertise protect and/or advance the interests of public health informs about how well regulatory science and the regulatory state express citizenship rights to security in health. Moreover, gaps between the interests of public health and regulatory practices help us to understand why non-state actors, such as public health advocacy groups or other civil society organizations may be justified in greater involvement in advancing such citizenship rights.

I am not suggesting that these interests are necessarily in conflict or mutually exclusive. In particular, it may be in the interests of both patients and a pharmaceutical company that a new drug with a high benefit-to-risk ratio receives marketing approval quickly. On the other hand, these interests may diverge, or even conflict, if a new drug, posing serious risks, offers little benefit over alternative treatments, including placebo. In this scenario, it may be in the interests of patients and public health that the drug is denied approval or withdrawn from the market, contrary to the commercial interests of its manufacturer. Hence, such research is empirically important because it documents precisely which interests are positively or negatively related to the regulatory outcomes. Equally important, it also explains how the production of regulatory science is influenced by particular interests and points the way to possible reform and improvement in relation to citizenship.

The first case study scrutinizes the interpretation of evidence by two expert scientific bodies in the US. By comparing how evidence is interpreted in different contexts, it is demonstrated how the safety and efficacy of a drug within regulatory science is established consistently in favor of one set of interests, but without any credible scientistic justification of technical consistency. The second case study complements the first by examining the construction of standards themselves in regulatory science. This case reveals how regulatory science is pushed along a particular direction to comply with particular interests, but again in a way which cannot be justified by any superior technical merit.

Case study 1: Evidential interpretation

Triazolam (Halcion), is a 'sleeping pill' (hypnotic benzodiazepine). The safety of any drug can only be sensibly considered in relation to its effectiveness to treat illness. Notably, there is no known population for which triazolam is uniquely effective compared with other hypnotics. In 1988, the manufacturers, Upjohn, reduced the recommended starting dose for American adults from 0.5 mg/day to 0.25 mg/day. Accordingly, the recommended starting dose for the elderly was reduced to half this, 0.125 mg/day. However, the US drug regulatory authority, the Food and Drug Administration (FDA), did not require the company to prove the efficacy of the lower dosages at that time. Almost four years later the FDA sought to do this by convening its expert science advisers on the Psychopharmacological Advisory Committee (PDAC) to examine the drug's safety and efficacy.

The PDAC risk–benefit assessment

On 18 May 1992, the FDA presented two of a number of placebo-controlled clinical trials showing efficacy of the 0.25 mg dose for insomniacs (PDAC 1992: 70–85). There were just two studies of the efficacy of the 0.125 mg dose for the elderly—both 17-day placebo-controlled with geriatric insomniacs. In one triazolam was found to have no significant therapeutic effect, while in the other it was effective in increasing total sleep time and in shortening sleep onset, but did not help in reducing patients' number of awakenings (PDAC 1992: 95). One member of the PDAC, Regina Casper, Professor of Psychiatry at the University of Chicago, was 'not convinced' that sufficient data had been presented to address the effectiveness of the 0.125 mg dose in the elderly (PDAC 1992: 266–8). Another, Dr Larry Ereshefsky, Director of Psychiatric Pharmacy at the University of Texas Health Center, concluded that the sample sizes (of 4 and 44 patients) were too small to meet the standards of a New Drug Application (NDA) (PDAC 1992: 271).

Despite these limitations, most members of the PDAC were willing to conclude that the 0.125 mg dose was effective *by extrapolating beyond the controlled clinical trial data to clinical experience of use of the drug* (PDAC 1992: 309, 312). For example, David Dunner, Professor of Psychiatry at the University of Washington Medical Center, reasoned:

> I think that if these were a new NDA, looking at the dose ranges being described, I think there would be an inadequate number of patients to support efficacy. But I think that, given the clinical use of this drug, the efficacy is supported. (PDAC 1992: 283–4)

Similarly, Ereshefsky surmised:

> I think many of us have the *sense* that we are dealing with an effective drug, but the data that we are looking at isn't satisfying ... I think there's enough data to at least begin to address that issue ... my sense is that there's enough data out there to suggest that the blood levels achieved in most people at the doses being used is sufficient for sedation. (PDAC 1992: 315)

Two main types of safety data were considered: controlled clinical trials and postmarketing spontaneous reports of adverse drug reactions (ADRs) in clinical practice, which the FDA stores in its Spontaneous Reporting System (SRS) database. The latter demonstrated that triazolam was associated with far more reports of adverse central nervous system (CNS) effects per prescription than another benzodiazepine hypnotic, temazepam (Restoril)—about 40 times as many seizures, 26 times as many cases of amnesia, 23 times as many cases of hostility, 13 times as many cases of dependence and over 10 times as many cases of psychosis, even after adjusting for secular trends in reporting. Robert Temple, the FDA's Director of New Drug Evaluation, characterized some of these adverse events as 'scary' (PDAC 1992: 268). As the incidence of triazolam ADR reports increased with dosage and the *large risk ratios remained* despite adjusting for many factors, including publicity, time of entry into the market, manufacturers' reporting practices and secular trends in overall reporting rates, (PDAC 1992: 105–11, 119–20; Tsong 1992), FDA's epidemiologists concluded that triazolam's high reporting rate ratios for amnesia, dependence, hostility, psychosis and seizures appeared to 'reflect actual differences in risk of neuro-psychiatric adverse effect causation', and that triazolam appeared to 'have *greater intrinsic capacity* to provoke these adverse effects' (Graham 1992: 6–7).

Table 3.1 Drop-out analysis sorted by dose

Patient Groups	Per Cent Drop-out		Risk Ratio
	Triazolam	Flurazepam	Tr/Fl
Any Adverse Event			
Low Dose	19/272 (7.0%)	3/71 (4.2%)	1.7
High Dose	126/896 (14.1%)	55/536 (10.3%)	1.4*
Anxiety			
Low Dose	8/272 (2.9%)	0/71 (0.0%)	>>
High Dose	36/896 (4.0%)	9/536 (1.7%)	2.4*
Memory Impairment			
Low Dose	0/272 (0.0%)	0/71 (0.0%)	---
High Dose	8/896 (0.9%)	0/596 (0.0%)	>>
All Psychiatric Adverse Events			
Low Dose	9/272 (3.3%)	0/71 (0.0%)	>>
High Dose	54/896 (6.0%)	15/536 (2.8%)	2.1*

Key: * = statistically significant ($p<0.05$, 1-sided p-value, Fisher's exact test)
>> = 'infinitely large' and hence 'significant'.
Low Dose = 0.125, 0.125–0.25, 0.25 mg Halcion; 15 mg Dalmane
High Dose = 0.25–0.5, 0.5, 0.6 mg Halcion; 15–30, 30 mg Dalmane.
Source: Laughren, T. and Lee, H. (1992) 'Review of adverse event data in Upjohn-sponsored clinical studies of Halcion' FDA submission to PDAC, 1 May, table 6.25a.

The FDA's presentation of safety data from controlled clinical trials analysed 25 Upjohn-sponsored studies with insomniacs of at least one-week duration, comparing triazolam with flurazepam (Dalmane) or placebo. These 25 studies involved 1168 patients on triazolam, 607 on flurazepam and 566 on placebo, comparing 0.5 mg triazolam with 30 mg flurazepam ('high' doses) and/or 0.125/0.25 mg triazolam with 15 mg flurazepam ('low' doses). That is, they assumed that 30 mg flurazepam was 'equipotent' to 0.5 mg triazolam and 15 mg flurazepam was 'equipotent' to 0.25 mg triazolam. There was a statistically significantly higher risk of patients dropping out of trials due to adverse reactions when taking 0.5 mg triazolam than when on 30 mg flurazepam, and that that relative risk increased, when considering solely 'psychiatric' adverse effects (Table 3.1). These differences were not statistically significant at the lower doses.

The findings in Table 3.1 supported the trends identified in the SRS data, albeit at much lower levels. However, FDA scientists also presented an alternative analysis in which they accepted Upjohn's argument that 30 mg flurazepam was equipotent to just 0.25 mg triazolam, even though the trials themselves were based on protocols defining 30 mg flurazepam as equipotent to 0.5 mg triazolam (PDAC 1992: 147). Given that the adverse effects of triazolam are generally dose-related, an acceptance that 30 mg flurazepam was equipotent with just 0.25 mg triazolam was guaranteed to lower the recorded risk of triazolam relative to flurazepam. Such an acceptance, therefore, would be to opt retrospectively for a test (trial protocol) of the drug that would be less likely to detect damage to patients.

Table 3.2 Sample size and duration of use features for 'appropriately dosed' subgroups

Subgroup Features	Triazolam	Flurazepam
Sample Size	285 patients	423 patients
Median Duration	7 days	14 days

Source: Laughren, T and Lee, H (1992) 'Review of adverse event data in Upjohn-sponsored clinical studies of Halcion' FDA submission to PDAC, 1 May, unnumbered table.

FDA scientists constructed 'appropriately dosed' patient groups in which 'low' dose triazolam was compared with 'high' dose flurazepam. As the clinical trials were not designed in this way, the length of time 'appropriately dosed' patients had taken the two drugs was very different and the sample dropped to about a quarter of its original size (Table 3.2). Specifically, the relatively small sample ensured that the analysis lacked the power to translate differences into statistical significance, and secondly, patients were dosed for much longer on flurazepam, thus skewing analysis in favor of triazolam (PDAC 1992: 148, 322). Taking all the adverse effects together, the 'appropriately dosed' analysis implied a disappearance of any difference in risk for drop-out between triazolam and flurazepam (PDAC 1992: 157), but a greater risk remained for triazolam psychiatric adverse effects, albeit without statistical significance (Table 3.3).

Seven out of eight committee members voted that Halcion was safe and effective at the doses of 0.125 mg and 0.25 mg as recommended in the labelling

(PDAC 1992: 363). They prioritized the safety data from controlled clinical trials in spite of the robustness of the SRS data, as Ereshefsky noted:

> The spontaneous reporting data was the most bothersome of all the data, this apparently large signal sticking out there, and the agency has done a good job of trying to explain it away and control for variables, and it's still there. (PDAC 1992: 315)

Even in the closing minutes of the meeting, another of these seven members said: 'I don't believe that there is not safety—I fail to believe that there is safety' (PDAC 1992: 362).

Table 3.3 Summary drop-out analysis for 'appropriately dosed' patients

Adverse Event Term	Number of Drop-out Events		Risk Ratio Tr/Fl
	Triazolam (N=285)	Flurazepam (N=423)	
Any adverse event	20 (7.0%)	31 (7.3%)	1.0
All 'psychiatric'	8 (2.8%)	7 (1.7%)	1.7
Anxiety	8 (2.8%)	4 (0.9%)	3.0
Memory impairment	0	0	----

Source: Laughren, T and Lee, H (1992) 'Review of adverse event data in Upjohn-sponsored clinical studies of Halcion' FDA submission to PDAC, 1 May, tables 6.26 & 6.26a.

The IoM risk–benefit assessment

Following the PDAC's majority verdict the FDA permitted the 0.125 and 0.25 mg doses of triazolam to stay on the American market. Nevertheless, as controversy over the drug's safety continued, the FDA contracted the Institute of Medicine (IoM) to conduct a separate assessment in 1997. According to the Institute's reanalysis of Upjohn's clinical trials, compared with placebo, 0.25 mg triazolam was effective in reducing time to fall asleep, increasing total sleep time and reducing nocturnal awakenings. For elderly patients, the 0.125 mg dose was also significantly better at improving sleep, except that it did not reduce their number of awakenings. While this evidence supported triazolam's effectiveness at the geriatric dose, it was based on just two studies (IoM 1997: 22–9, 34–9).

The IoM was unable to find any sleep laboratory studies of the 0.125 mg dose conducted by Upjohn, but did reanalyse three such studies of the 0.25 mg dose. One was inconclusive and one showed loss of efficacy after the first few nights. The third and most substantial indicated that triazolam was significantly more effective than placebo at reducing time to sleep onset, but not at increasing total sleep time or reducing number of awakenings (IoM 1997: 32–3). Yet, with remarkable generosity to triazolam, the IoM deduced that 'despite small sample sizes and few studies, the [laboratory] findings are supportive of the questionnaire findings [from clinical trials] that sleep latency and total sleep time are affected by the 0.25 mg Halcion dose'.

The institute reviewed four placebo-controlled clinical trials from the published medical literature. One substantial study, in 1997, with 335 elderly subjects for four weeks found that 0.125 mg triazolam did not significantly improve sleep. In 1994, the larger of two clinical trials studying the effects of 0.25 mg triazolam in 1,507 non-elderly subjects produced no significant response compared with placebo. In the other one, in 1997, involving 357 patients, triazolam was found to be effective. The fourth study, in 1993, involving 221 elderly patients taking 0.25 mg triazolam for three weeks also showed that the drug was significantly better than placebo (IoM 1997: 39–43).

The IoM summarized this evidence as follows:

> Thus, two of the three studies provide support for the efficacy of Halcion at 0.25 mg in the general population, including elderly subjects. Halcion was not significantly better than placebo in the third study at 0.25 mg. The one study with elderly patients with a 0.125 mg dose does not support efficacy in that population. (IoM 1997: 39–43)

This interpretation was extremely generous to triazolam because it did not mention that the 0.25 mg dose is double the recommended dose for the elderly. An alternative summary might have said that the published clinical trials did not support the effectiveness of 0.125 mg triazolam in the elderly at all, while effectiveness was supported in the less substantial of the two trials of the 0.25 mg with the non-elderly.

To complete its assessment of efficacy, the IoM reviewed the sleep laboratory studies of triazolam published in the literature. This comprised five studies at 0.25 mg in the non-elderly, two studies at 0.25 mg in geriatrics, one at 0.125 mg in the non-elderly and two at 0.125 mg in geriatric insomniacs. In three of the 0.25 mg studies triazolam did not significantly improve sleep on most or all efficacy criteria, in three it did, and in the other one it produced significant improvement only on decreasing number of awakenings. Of the three 0.125 mg studies, one showed significant improvement in sleep, one showed improvement in total sleep time and the other showed a lack of effectiveness after three nights together with rebound insomnia. The IoM chose to represent these findings with the comment that 'in all but one study of subjects with insomnia, triazolam significantly improved various objective parameters of sleep on the first three nights' (IoM 1997: 39–43).

The IoM concluded that the evidence supported the effectiveness of 0.125 and 0.25 mg doses, but noted that the support for the 0.125 mg dose was 'weak' (IoM 1997: 46). They took the view that the published literature 'generally supports the claim that the drug is efficacious' (IoM 1997: 46). However, these conclusions are not a good representation of the institute's own analysis. At the very least, it should be added that neither the published clinical trials nor the unpublished sleep laboratory studies that were reviewed supported the efficacy of the drug at 0.125 mg in elderly patients.

To assess the safety of the 0.125 and 0.25 mg doses of triazolam, the IoM reanalysed SRS data and the drop-outs from the 25 clinical trials which the FDA had evaluated before the PDAC in 1992. They found no significant differences between 0.25 mg triazolam and 30 mg flurazepam in the total number of adverse effects reported in clinical trials, but they did find a significantly increased incidence of memory impairment with increased duration of triazolam use and more drop-outs due to anxiety and memory impairment among patients taking triazolam than for those taking flurazepam. The institute also reviewed a large postmarketing safety study by Upjohn, during which more of the 8,000 subjects taking triazolam dropped out than did subjects on temazepam (IoM 1997: 73). Regarding the FDA's SRS data, the institute's report reads:

> The IoM committee is left with what seems to be strongly suggestive evidence from SRS data that, among users of Halcion, there is some group of patients who, by personal characteristics, prescription pattern, or medication use, do experience CNS-related adverse events not seen at the same rates as those seen in patients taking comparator drugs. The rates of these adverse events in the Halcion group or among the various groups taking other drugs must be so small as to escape detection statistically in any of the variety of controlled studies mounted so far. (IoM 1997: 82)

The IoM further noted that at least some adverse effects associated with Halcion in spontaneous reports were 'similar to those that had been reported in some of the early clinical trials with higher doses of triazolam and with longer duration of use' (IoM 1997: 94). They were also aware of the surveys showing that many people use hypnotics for longer and at higher doses than recommended. Nevertheless, the IoM set aside the implications of these issues, preferring instead to give priority to the safety data derived from clinical trials, and to conclude that triazolam is safe and effective as recommended for use on the label.

Both the FDA and the PDAC endorsed the findings of the IoM at a public hearing on 4 December 1997. Indeed, Robert Temple, Chief of the FDA's Office of Drug Evaluation, was motivated to declare:

> We don't believe that there is a clear distinction between this drug [triazolam] and others in the class [of benzodiazepine hypnotics]. (IoM 1997, cited in Ault 1997)

Discussion

Scholars concerned with environmental risk are particularly familiar with the precautionary principle. Simply stated, it means that a technology should not be released, or continue to be released, into the environment until there is compelling evidence that it will not cause harm. According to this principle, the burden of proof falls on those who would like to introduce, or maintain, the technology to show that it does not inflict serious short-term or long-term damage on the environment (Mayer and Clegg 1998). As a corollary to this, within a technology-testing process, the precautionary principle often implies that the test options most sensitive to hazards and damage are selected, so that potential adverse effects to the environment can be detected during testing (Calow 1998). By opposition, a permissive principle implies that the benefits of a technology are assumed to outweigh its risks unless there is compelling evidence that serious harm is being done. Within the technology-testing process, it also often implies that the test options selected are likely to highlight the benefits of the technology and limit the detection of hazard and damage to the environment. The application of the permissive principle means that the burden of proof falls on those who believe that the technology is unsafe.

The triazolam case shows how the permissive, rather than the precautionary, principle can function in medical risk assessments. When the permissive principle applies, the benefit of the scientific doubt is awarded to the technology's efficacy and its manufacturers. This has occurred *consistently* in the risk–benefit assessments of triazolam by the PDAC and the IoM, despite reservations expressed by some individual members of the PDAC. There was insufficient controlled clinical trial data to support the efficacy of the 0.125 mg dose, yet most members of the PDAC persuaded themselves that the lower doses were effective because of *anecdotal evidence from the widespread use of triazolam while on the market.* Even by 1997, the IoM could find only weak evidence to support the efficacy of the 0.125 mg dose. On safety, the anecdotal SRS evidence from triazolam in use suggested that the drug was associated with much greater risks than comparator drugs in 1992 and 1997, but the controlled clinical trial did not. In this instance, *anecdotal evidence of safety-in-use was set aside by the PDAC and the IoM in favor of the controlled trial results.*

Thus, the PDAC gave priority to *anecdotal evidence* about triazolam in use, when assessing *efficacy*, but to *controlled clinical trial data*, when assessing *safety*. In each instance the types of data which favored triazolam were given priority over those which threatened its viability. While a lack of compelling evidence of efficacy from clinical trials was regarded as insufficient to undermine the drug's capacity to deliver therapeutic benefit, compelling evidence from clinical trials was required to confirm signals of lack of safety.

Furthermore, in relation to public health, the triazolam case illustrates the importance of making the conceptual distinction between 'experimental' drug safety and the safety of patients in 'the real world'. For example, the FDA's construction of 'appropriately dosed' patients, which influenced both the PDAC and the IoM, demonstrated a concern for *drug* safety without attention to the safety of *patients*. For if it took the manufacturers of the drug over twenty years to 'appropriately dose' a small sample of patients in clinical trials, how realistic could it be to expect prescribing doctors to achieve extensive 'appropriate dosing' in the general population of patients? But the IoM and the PDAC avoided this problem of patient safety in 'the real world' by limiting their conclusions to the safety of the drug under the conditions of use recommended on the label. Yet in 1989, de Tullio et al. published startling results that the average length of triazolam therapy among a sample of 72 patients was 6.2 months, rather than the 10 days recommended (de Tullio, Kirking, Zacardellie and Kwee 1989).

This case study illustrates how the selection and interpretation of evidence crucially affects risk–benefit assessments which have implications for various social interests involved. In this case, the social interests of the manufacturers and scientific enterprise of drug development were prioritized over the wider interests of public health. Many of the expert scientists on the PDAC and IoM were themselves involved in clinical trials with drugs and drug development. They identified with the goal of bringing new drugs to the market. It is clear, however, that on many occasions different evidence could have been selected and/or interpreted differently with at least as much rationality as the PDAC and the IoM, and with a different outcome in terms of risk–benefit assessment. The challenge for regulatory settings is how to construct a system of risk–benefit assessment which can accommodate the inevitably socio-political nature of such judgements.

Case study 2: The construction of regulatory standards

The transnational pharmaceutical industry has sought to persuade the major regulatory agencies around the world to harmonize their regulatory standards for drug testing (Abraham and Lewis 2000). As the Director of Regulatory Affairs at Schering-Plough put it, 'the industry tends to look optimistically at anything which will reduce development time for its products, such as reductions in toxicity testing'.[1] In order to achieve this, in 1990 the International Federation of Pharmaceutical Manufacturers Associations (IFPMA) organized the creation of ICH, whose key participants are the three pharmaceutical industry associations and three government drug regulatory agencies of the EU, Japan and the US (Nakajima 1996: 32). In the context of increasing pressure of state funding for regulatory agencies, international harmonization also promised the possibility of reducing wasteful duplication of regulatory effort across borders.

Over the last thirty years, government regulatory agencies have required pharmaceutical companies to test their new drug products for cancer-inducing potential before seeking marketing approval. Due to the long latency period of cancer, and the fact that most cancer risks multiply with ageing, carcinogenicity testing involves lifespan studies in animals in order to assess the carcinogenic risk of new drugs before they are taken long-term by patients (Maugh 1978). Typically, rodents are fed the test drug over their lifespan, usually between 18 and 24 months, and at the end of the study, the incidence and nature of the tumors found among the rodents given the test drug are compared with 'control' animals which do not receive the drug, but are treated identically otherwise (World Health Organization 1974).

A major challenge for carcinogenic risk assessment is the uncertainty involved in extrapolating the results from tests in rodents to risks for humans. For this reason in 1969 the World Health Organization (WHO) recommended that lifespan carcinogenicity testing should be conducted in *at least two species* (typically mice and rats) (WHO 1969). By the late 1970s, the regulatory agencies in North America, Western Europe and Japan accepted this view (Contrera 1996). Hence, in 1990, the international regulatory standards for such testing were much the same.

Despite this, the first ICH meeting agreed that 'there should be a re-examination of the need for using two rodent species to detect carcinogenicity' (Van Oosterhout et al. 1997: 6–7). Although the remit of the ICH was initially to harmonize inconsistent regulatory standards, in this aspect of carcinogenicity testing, its concerns included a (harmonized) *reduction* in testing requirements. Indeed, the editorial background to 'carcinogenicity studies' at the third ICH meeting acknowledged: 'It is hoped that consensus on the sensitive question of, in effect, reducing requirements for carcinogenicity studies may be reached at ICH3' (ICH Expert Working Group on Safety 1996: 259).

Under the auspices of ICH, between 1992 and 1996, a retrospective survey of databases on pharmaceuticals tested in both mice and rats, and positive in at least one, was conducted. The four databases were provided and analysed by German and Dutch regulators, the Japanese Pharmaceutical Manufacturers' Association (JPMA), the Centre for Medicines Research (CMR) and the FDA. It is clear that this exercise aimed to provide a 'techno-scientific' rationalization for a reduced regulatory standard requiring one carcinogenicity test solely in the rat because, as early as 1992, the ICH Expert Working Group on Safety (EWG) declared that lifespan carcinogenicity testing in mice should be jettisoned (Emmerson 1992; Hayashi 1994). The questions guiding the analysis were established accordingly, as Van Oosterhout et al., who conducted the ICH review of the German and Dutch regulatory databases, explained:

> The necessity of the mouse bioassay for risk assessment of pharmaceuticals can be indicated in two ways: (1) the degree to which mouse tumour findings gave rise to regulatory decisions against pharmaceuticals submitted for registration [i.e. marketing approval]; (2) the degree to which mouse studies were needed for the interpretation of positive rat studies. (Van Oosterhout et al. 1997: 8)

In their review of the Dutch and German regulatory databases, the ICH experts found that 13 pharmaceuticals generated tumors in mice, but not rats, out of a total of 181, which had been tested in both species. For only one of these compounds (8 per cent) did the positive mouse findings lead to regulatory action. In all other cases, the regulators judged that 'the findings *appeared* to be species-specific, not occurring in rats, and therefore *probably* [emphases added] not relevant to humans' (Van Oosterhout et al. 1997: 10). The overall conclusion reported to ICH regarding these Dutch and German regulatory databases was that 'the relevance of the carcinogenicity study in mice was low' (Van Oosterhout et al. 1997:16), and that 'one carcinogenicity study in the most appropriate species, preferably the rat, will suffice' (Van der Laan 1996: 271).

According to the JPMA analysis of 99 pharmaceuticals in their database, 12 produced positive tumor findings solely in mice. Apparently, these had little effect on the drugs' development because eight were marketed, three were still in development at the time of analysis, and one was terminated due to problems in early clinical trials (Usui et al. 1996: 280). Similarly, the UK industry-funded CMR reported that, of the 79 pharmaceuticals in their database, 15 produced tumors in mice only, and that for only one (7 per cent) of those 15 compounds did the mouse tumors contribute to a decision to terminate drug development. Consequently, the JPMA and the CMR concluded that 'mouse carcinogenicity studies contribute very little, if anything, to the overall risk assessment of new medicines' and recommended that the ICH should endorse a reduction in carcinogenicity testing from two rodent species to one, the rat (Usui et al. 1996: 283).

Representatives of the FDA also presented a retrospective analysis of their database. They found that, out of 125 pharmaceuticals causing tumors in at least one rodent species, 52 (42 per cent) produced tumors in both mice and rats, 45 (36 per cent) produced them solely in rats, and 28 (22 per cent) solely in mice. On their analysis, approximately 78 per cent of all pharmaceuticals with positive findings in rat and mouse carcinogenicity studies would have been identified by a rat study alone, whereas 64 per cent would have been identified by a mouse study alone. Hence, the FDA's review of its database for ICH implied that without the mouse study nearly a quarter of the carcinogenic effects from new drugs in their files would not have been detected (Contrera et al. 1997).

While thirteen (25 per cent) of the 52 trans-species rodent carcinogens and 12 (27 per cent) of the 45 rat-only carcinogens were not approved for marketing in the US, as many as five (18 per cent) of the 28 mouse-only carcinogens were also not approved. Evidently, the regulatory risk assessment of FDA scientists was also influenced by tumor findings solely in mice (Contrera et al. 1997: 139). Furthermore, during the discussion at the third ICH meeting, Joseph DeGeorge, the Associate Director of Toxicology at the FDA, explained that his regulatory agency had used carcinogenicity data in mice as part of the weight of risk–benefit evidence to require manufacturers to conduct additional testing which indicated 'that compounds were acting through a mechanism which may be relevant to humans', or 'even in recommending non-approval of certain agents' (DeGeorge 1996a: 300). Significantly, he also noted that he could not say in advance for any given pharmaceutical whether it would be more appropriate to require a single lifespan carcinogenicity study in rats instead of mice or vice versa, and urged against dismissing carcinogenic effects in mice, as follows:

> We need to look at the data and make an honest, scientific judgement from the information we have about the relevance of a tumour, but you can't just automatically say "tumours are irrelevant because they are in the mouse or the rat". (DeGeorge 1996a: 299)

The ICH's drive to abolish the second lifespan carcinogenicity study of new drugs in mice was inconsistent with the fact that the FDA representatives at the ICH declared that they believed one could not stipulate in advance, for any given pharmaceutical, whether a single lifespan carcinogenicity study in rats would be more appropriate than one in mice. The thrust of the argument by industry and European regulators at ICH was that regulatory standards should be reduced from two rodent lifespan carcinogenicity tests to a single lifespan study in rats—and that this could be done without losing important regulatory information which might compromise safety because testing in the mouse was either unnecessary or irrelevant for human carcinogenic risk assessment. However, the implication of the FDA's position was that this reduction could *not* be done without losing important regulatory information which might compromise safety because testing in the mouse *was sometimes, and unpredictably, relevant* to human carcinogenic risk assessment. The FDA's report to the ICH not only directly challenged the predominant ICH conviction that the lifespan mouse study should be abolished, but also threatened to undermine the entire ICH project to reduce rodent lifespan carcinogenicity testing requirements from two studies to one because there was even less scientific justification for jettisoning the lifespan carcinogenicity test in rats than for abolishing the mouse test.

Nevertheless, those committed to the abolition of lifespan rodent carcinogenicity tests were not deterred. For example, in response to the FDA's report to the ICH EWG on carcinogenicity, Gerd Bode, a senior toxicologist at the pharmaceutical firm Roussel Uclaf, commented:

> We have to go on; we want to go to a situation in which not only the mouse but maybe in the next 20 years, we can also drop the rat. We have to stimulate the research on new models [of carcinogenicity testing]. (Bode 1996: 300)

Bode's comments reflect a recurrent theme in the discourse about carcinogenicity testing within ICH that the abolition of the regulatory requirement for some or all rodent lifespan studies would release new innovative drug testing. The fact that some novel and much less costly short-term tests (of less than six months duration) had been formulated, certainly led the ICH EWG to state:

> This project is concerned with making a harmonised change to take account of scientific developments ... The alternative methods which are being proposed take less than one tenth of the time currently assigned to a rodent carcinogenicity study. The resources freed up could be applied to refining some of the newer techniques being developed for cancer risk assessment. (ICH EWG on Safety 1996: 258, 260)

Alastair Monro, Director of Drug Safety Evaluation at Pfizer and a representative of the US drug industry at ICH, was even more explicit:

> Encouragement is given to manufacturers to be imaginative in designing protocols ... The EWG feels that a reduction in the dependency on rodent lifespan studies, plus the implementation of new emerging technologies represents progress. Beneficial impacts include an opportunity to divert resources into new methods that will result in better carcinogenic risk assessment. (Monro 1996: 266, 268)

Although DeGeorge was concerned that it would not be possible to identify trans-species carcinogens with a single-species carcinogenicity study, he conceded that this important regulatory information may not need to be derived from another *lifespan* rodent carcinogenicity study (DeGeorge 1996b). FDA scientists at ICH accepted for regulatory purposes that a single lifespan carcinogenicity study could be carried out in the most appropriate rodent species combined with a *new type of short-term in vivo* carcinogenicity study in the other rodent species. They were persuaded that this combination *could* be sufficient to identify trans-species carcinogens and capable of identifying compounds that produce mouse-only tumors of most regulatory concern (Contrera et al. 1997). However, this was little more than wishful thinking as the new tests had not, and have not, been shown to have such capability. Rather, DeGeorge justified the FDA's compromising stance by reference to an ostensible need not to hamper innovations in drug testing:

> We believe current long-term carcinogenicity testing requirements should not become an obstacle to the development of more effective and efficient alternatives. Innovative, flexible regulatory approaches need to be considered to encourage the development, validation and interpretation of new approaches to carcinogenicity assessment without compromising our current standards of safety for pharmaceuticals. (DeGeorge 1996b: 277)

The representatives of the European and Japanese industries and regulatory agencies agreed a new 'technical' standard for carcinogenic risk assessment that replaced a second rodent lifespan test with a new short-term test, which cost only about a fifth of the lifespan studies (DeGeorge 1998: 262). The ICH EWG said nothing of the immediate reduction in safety testing standards by this change, but rather emphasized hope for innovation in toxicological testing:

> Importantly, it [the new technical standard] does not fix in stone the methods available today for the pharmaceuticals of tomorrow, but rather allows for and even fosters the development of improved methods for the future. (DeGeorge 1998: 263)

Yet, according to ICH's own analysis, the new short-term tests with mice and rats available at that time, were either 'not satisfactory for detecting carcinogens', were 'problematic', and/or could detect only up to 80 per cent, and sometimes as few as 57 per cent, of compounds known to be carcinogens from lifespan studies (Mitsumori 1998).

Discussion

The ICH defined itself as a techno-scientific process, which involved solely expert scientists from industry and regulatory agencies. Formally, it is not politically accountable to anyone, although the regulatory agencies in the EU, Japan and US who have adopted the ICH standards are accountable to their governments. A convergence of social interests among the ICH experts is evident. Those from industry may reduce the time and costs of drug development, those from regulatory agencies may reduce their regulatory workloads. These interests have strongly shaped the construction of these standards. As with the triazolam case, producer interests in drug development have been predominant.

Moreover, this case study shows how social interests can create a multiplier effect on regulatory decision-making. The construction of these new standards was justified by permissive regulatory practices in the past. To put it another way, the ICH is converting permissive regulation into the new scientific standards of the future for carcinogenic risk assessment. These new scientific standards bear the imprint of social and political interests in increasing and accelerating access to markets for industry. These influences are neither neutral nor inconsequential because the new standards of regulatory science will determine the 'scientific knowledge base' regarding whether or not new drugs are carcinogens. Insofar as the new standards compromise safety testing of new drugs, then they are not consistent with the interests of public health.

As with the triazolam case, it is clear that a very different approach to new standards for carcinogenic risk assessment could have been adopted with equal, if not more, rationality in relation to wider interests of public health.

Conclusion

The sociological conclusion is that scientific expertise in regulatory settings should not be treated as if it operates in a social vacuum. Rather it needs to be related to social interests in a fairly thoroughgoing way—including the construction of regulatory standards and evidential interpretation by reference to standards. The political conclusion is that, at least in the pharmaceutical sector, the bipartite domination of industry and the regulatory state means that scientific expertise in drug regulation serves to shield the commercial interests of industry and the institutional interests of the state from critical scrutiny that might emphasize wider interests of public health, such as elevated standards of risk assessment and precautionary interpretations of safety and efficacy evidence.

Currently citizenship rights to private property dominate rights to security in health within pharmaceutical regulation. This only becomes clearly apparent when the interests of the pharmaceutical industry and those of public health diverge or conflict because it is only then that the state's use of the law via regulation involves having to prioritize one right over the other. If one wishes to develop more defensible science-based regulatory decision-making in the interests of public health, then expertise in regulatory settings needs to be drawn from wider constituencies and more robust systems of accountability need to be introduced into the regulatory process.

Note

1   Interview with Director of Regulatory Affairs at Schering-Plough, 12 December 1997.

Chapter 4

Protecting the Environment at the Margin: The Role of Economic Analysis in Regulatory Design and Decision-making

Marc A. Eisner

Introduction

In the past several decades, the politics of expertise and environmental protection have become tightly linked as debates have focused on what role, if any, economic theory and analysis should play in the policy process. Advocates of a more economically oriented environmental protection claim that a greater attention to economic analysis could make policy and administration more effective and efficient. When combined with a greater reliance on market-based instruments, it is argued, economics could provide a technical solution to many of the problems that have bedeviled regulation (e.g. excessive costs, rigidity, and a lack of incentives to go beyond regulatory requirements). Bureaucrats could employ economic analysis early in the regulatory process to consider the marginal costs and benefits of each additional increment of pollution reduction. They could establish enforcement priorities ex ante to maximize the impact of scarce budgetary resources. They could replace command-and-control instruments with market-based instruments to reduce compliance costs and alter the incentives facing businesses, thereby promoting innovations and higher levels of environmental quality (Freeman 2003).

Those who oppose a greater reliance on economics are not easily persuaded. They commonly view these claims as attempts to use the technical discourse of economics to justify and conceal a deeper desire to dismantle regulation and reify market outcomes. Economics, by necessity, would seek to determine optimal levels of pollution by finding the point where the marginal costs of mitigation were equal to the marginal benefits, with each element of the equation determined through reference to values that could be expressed in monetary terms. Environmental policy, they argue, should seek to promote environmental quality and preserve things that may be difficult or impossible to monetize (e.g. unique ecosystems, endangered species, biodiversity, and human life). Moreover, to the extent that costs are concrete and incurred immediately and benefits are probabilistic and realized in some distant future, discounting—a methodological pillar of economic analysis—would create insurmountable barriers for a host of policies.

This essay explores the demands for regulatory efficiency and a greater reliance on economic expertise as part of a larger dynamic of institution building in the United States. This exploration is prefaced with a discussion of how one might design a system of environmental protection if one wanted to follow the basic precepts of economics and make maximum use of markets. Next, the essay turns to consider the politics of regulatory design. Reform advocates commonly critique the US Environmental Protection Agency (EPA) as inefficient. Yet, there is precious little evidence that bureaucracies are designed with these values in mind (see Niskanen 1971; Moe 1989, 1997). Rather, bureaucracies, like the policies they implement, are designed, in part, to serve the interests of the political winners and insulate today's victories from an uncertain future. To illustrate the politics of regulatory design, the essay turns to examine the original design of the EPA. The essay then turns to explore the demands for economically oriented reforms through the lens of regulatory design, focusing on regulatory review, the growing use of market-based instruments, and recent efforts to reinvent regulation to leverage market forces and trends in corporate environmentalism.

Regulatory design as if economics mattered

Economics is the science of decision-making under scarcity. The market conveys information on the supply of and demand for specific resources. Actors adjust their behavior at the margin in such a way as to maximize utility. When a resource is scarce, prices signal consumers to adjust consumption patterns and producers to search for efficiency-promoting innovations or substitutes. In the end, markets promote efficient resource allocations. Markets are less successful in conserving scarce environmental resources, however, because private property rights are often poorly defined or nonexistent. Producers frequently externalize pollution rather than incorporating the costs of pollution control into their prices, forcing society to subsidize their products and creating a situation of overuse (a situation that is exacerbated by government subsidies). Although markets often fail to promote environmental quality, economics is well suited to identify market failure and suggest remedies (Cropper and Oates 1992: 675).

As a thought experiment, imagine that one could start anew and create a regulatory structure that reflected the core insights of economics. What would such a system look like? First, one would assign primary responsibility to markets on the assumption that market actors possess the information and the incentives necessary to make rational economic decisions and that these decisions, when aggregated, will preserve scarce resources. This would require the elimination of public policies that subsidize the use of scarce resources so that market prices could convey accurate information regarding costs. From a minimalist position, one could follow the insights of Ronald Coase (1960) and adopt a property rights-based system with strict liability for damages. For a property rights system to work, there must be 'private rights that can be *defined*, *defended*, and *divested* or transferred' (Yandle 1999: 15). When polluters infringe on property rights, injured parties could defend their rights through the courts and receive damages. The expectation that pollution beyond a certain threshold will give rise to a significant liability should create incentives to control pollution or purchase the property rights in question (Anderson and Leal 2001). The efficacy of this system would depend on the availability of information (e.g. information on whether rights were violated) and a lack of transaction costs. Indeed, Coase acknowledged that regulation could economize on transaction costs, although he was agnostic about whether it would yield net benefits.

Although a property rights-based system has inherent appeal, there are several problems, some of which Coase anticipated. First, one can imagine ways of assigning property rights to a scarce resource like water. In areas of scarcity, one could determine the sustainable flow from an aquifer and assign tradable water quotas to residents. Companies and agribusinesses, in turn, could purchase these quotas on markets. It is far more difficult, however, to assign rights to other resources like clean air. Second, it may be exceedingly costly for some parties to determine whether their rights have been infringed upon due to technological constraints, corporate secrecy, and difficulties of allocating responsibility among multiple sources. Third, transaction costs may make it prohibitively expensive for some parties to defend their rights. They may have to organize, creating collective action problems and imposing costs that are greater than the damages in question. Fourth, because some environmental issues involve transboundary pollution, the institutional infrastructure necessary for defending or transferring rights may not exist. Finally, some important environmental assets (e.g. unique ecosystems or endangered species) may be of no instrumental value to individuals and will be difficult to defend in a property rights-based system.

One can develop policy tools to compensate for some of these shortcomings. For example, Pigouvian taxes could force producers to incorporate the costs of pollution into their prices, although an effective tax rate would be difficult to set given informational constraints (see Cropper and Oates 1992). Alternatively, effluent charges might be employed for various substances, although, once again, one would need to negotiate large informational constraints and the ubiquitous pressures to set tax rates too low to affect behavior. To resolve these difficulties, it might be more useful to create a cap-and-trade system wherein optimal pollution levels are determined according to health standards, permits are issued, and either assigned to facilities or sold at auction with provisions for banking and sales. Market mechanisms would help insure that permit prices would reflect the incremental costs while creating incentives for cost reductions (Stavins 2000).

Under each system, regulators would need to determine the optimal level of pollution and administer a system of permits or taxes. Assuming that policy required the mandatory disclosure of performance data, the role of the state would be minimal. Producers would be forced to internalize the costs of pollution control and there would be incentives for firms to discover the most efficient means of doing so. Once markets get the prices right, actors can make rational decisions at the margin. With mandatory information disclosure, property holders would be better able to determine when their rights had been violated and use the courts to seek relief. Although one does not have the luxury of designing a regulatory structure de novo, it is a useful experiment insofar as it provides a sense of how far existing systems depart from what would be minimally necessary.

If a market-based system were deemed politically impossible, economics could still offer a number of tools to make environmental protection more effective and efficient. When setting environmental standards, for example, economic analysis could be used to identify optimal levels of environmental protection by weighing the marginal costs (under competing instruments) and marginal benefits of each additional increment of pollution control. Assuming that there is a fixed pool of resources to invest in environmental protection, a comprehensive application of cost–benefit or cost-effectiveness analysis could maximize impacts. Similarly, economics could offer a number of policy instruments that would allow for greater efficiencies in pollution control. Instruments like pollution taxes, effluent charges, pollution banking, and tradable permits can provide incentives for firms to find the most cost-effective means of controlling pollution, conserving on enforcement resources and allow the market to reinforce regulatory goals. This can occur, however, only to the extent that command-and-control regulations do not eliminate the flexibility necessary to respond to incentives and policymakers have the discretion to discover complementary mixes of instruments (see Gunningham and Sinclair 1999).

The politics of regulatory design

In the United States, the call for greater regulatory efficiency is nothing new nor is the effort to veil antiregulatory initiatives with the rhetoric of economics and reform. The attractiveness of this strategy (and its limited success) stem, in part, from a broad misconception of administration as being separate from politics—a conceptual legacy of the Progressive Era debates. In the words of Frank Goodnow (1900: 10–11) politics and administration are 'two distinct functions'. Politics refers to 'policies or expressions of the state will', while administration describes 'the execution of these policies'—a technical task that could be judged on the basis of its efficiency and effectiveness and improved through the application of new management tools (see Wilson 1887). Although most texts in public administration begin with a rejection of the politics-administration dichotomy, they invariably portray administration as a technical exercise (compare Abraham this volume). For the last several decades, critics of regulation have argued that a greater reliance on economics could open the door to greater administrative efficiency and effectiveness without compromising the political judgments that were foundational to the system of environmental protection.

Assuming, arguendo, that economic analysis could yield greater efficiencies in the use of scarce budgetary resources, one must ask why there has been such strong opposition? Environmental groups, environmental advocates in Congress, and regulators—presumably the actors with the greatest stake in promoting environmental quality through a more judicious use of resources—have provided vigorous resistance. Legislators have even created statutory prohibitions on the role of economic analysis, for example, barring the use of cost–benefit analysis in standard-setting. When economics has been integrated into administration, it has often been the result of protracted struggles or mandates imposed by the President. To understand this state of affairs, it is necessary to move from a discussion of technical merits to an exploration of the politics of regulatory design.

If there has been any consistent message from political science and cognate disciplines in the last two decades, it is this: institutions matter. Rules, roles, and formal structures are of critical important for understanding politics and policy (see March and Olsen 1989; Weaver and Rockman 1993). They shape elite and interest group access to sites of policy-making and determine the extent to which administrative agencies and executives are insulated from elective institutions. The way agencies are organized and staffed will determine whether policymakers have access to certain bodies of expertise (e.g. through professionalization) and the extent to which this expertise is integrated into decisions regarding resource flows, policy design, instrument choice, and evaluation. Similarly, institutional design will determine the ways in which other governmental and non-governmental actors are integrated into the policy-making and implementation structure. These factors will affect the focus, coherence, and performance of policy.

Although original decisions regarding institutional and policy design shape subsequent events, they are not strictly determinative. New designs are often superimposed upon the old as a product of subsequent contests over policy. Indeed, this is often a source of incoherence in agencies that must manage incompatible mandates and policy instruments. In addition, policy-learning continues to occur within agencies. Actors usually deal with uncertainty and ambiguity 'by trying to clarify the rules, make distinctions, determine what the situation is and what definition "fits"'(March and Olsen 1989: 161). Changes are usually incremental; officials seek to adapt existing institutional capacities to new circumstances. Yet new challenges often force them to work outside of existing routines and this experience expands the opportunity set available when addressing subsequent challenges.

In the study of politics, social scientists routinely assume that legislation reflects the interaction of self-interested parties involved in a political exchange. Interest groups and vote-maximizing politicians trade political support for policy. Institutional structures (e.g. the design of legislative committees, decision rules) will impact on the way in which coalitions are formed and group demands are translated into policy. Much of what constitutes public policy is simple rent- or transfer-seeking. That is, organized interests exchange political support for policies that produce benefits for group members, imposing the costs on the unorganized or insufficiently organized (see Buchanan, Tollison, and Tullock 1980; Rauch 1999).

Under the politics-administration dichotomy, one might assume the passage of legislation marks the end of politics and the beginning of the technical task of implementation. However, groups that win new mandates also need to manage uncertainty about their future through what Terry M Moe (1989) describes as 'the politics of structural choice'. They design structures that preserve their victories, but at a high cost.

> The driving force of political uncertainty ... causes the winning group to favor structural designs it would never favor on technical grounds alone: designs that place detailed formal restrictions on bureaucratic discretion, impose complex procedures for agency decision-making, minimize opportunities for oversight, and otherwise insulate the agency from politics. The group has to protect itself and its agency from the dangers of democracy, and it does so by imposing structures that appear strange and incongruous indeed when judged by almost any reasonable standards of what an effective organization ought to look like. (Moe 1989: 275)

Because much legislation requires compromise between opposing groups, those who were not in the majority may nonetheless 'have a say in structural design, and, to the degree they do, they will impose structures that subvert effective performance and politicize agency decisions' (Moe 1989: 277). The end result may be a structure that is overly complex, internally contradictory, and incapable of achieving its purposes.

One can characterize the politics of regulatory design in similar terms. Historically, economic regulatory policies provided classic examples of rent-seeking behavior. Industries relied on regulators to manage cartels (Stigler 1971); regional coalitions use regulations to shape the conditions of economic change (Bensel 1987; Sanders 1987). Rent-seeking behavior has also become common in social regulation. Policies that are promoted as being in the 'public interest' often reflect underlying 'Bootlegger–Baptist' coalitions, a term introduced by Bruce Yandle (1983) in reference to the coalitions that supported local laws banning the sale of liquor on Sundays in the United States. Thus, environmentalists (the Baptists) may promote more stringent air pollution regulations with the support of select economic actors (the Bootleggers) who shape the requirements to impose costs on the poorly organized and, ultimately, on consumers, as a means of claiming economic advantage. In the end, the compromises reached between the Bootleggers and the Baptists may guarantee passage while sacrificing effectiveness (see Yandle 2000).

When groups emerge victorious in the legislative mandates, they seek to insulate today's successes against future assaults or changes in the political landscape. This is accomplished through core decisions regarding regulatory design—decisions that structure future politics and the capacity of various groups (including the bureaucrats themselves) to shape policy outputs. Decisions must be made about an agency's vulnerability to external forces. Will it be formally independent and thus more subject to legislative pressures, or placed within an executive agency? What formal role will interest groups have in the development and implementation of policy? Will certain groups (i.e. the groups that proved victorious) be integrated directly into the agency through placement on advisory or oversight bodies? Decisions must be made about delegation and agency staffing. How much discretion will be delegated to bureaucrats? Will the legislature impose detailed and mandatory directives and statutory timetables? Alternatively, it could provide a broad delegation of authority, a strategy that may make the greatest sense in professionalized agencies when professional norms and bodies of expertise reinforce policy goals (see Eisner 1991). Will the agency have the flexibility to define precise policy goals and performance indicators? Will it have the latitude to select specific policy instruments or instruments mixes? These decisions will shape an agency's effectiveness and its relationship with regulated parties.

There is little reason to believe that these decisions will be driven by the quest for efficiency or effectiveness. Rather, they should reflect the goal of insulating today's victories from an uncertain future. Of course, nothing is permanent in politics. With each new political contest, winners will seek to preserve their victories by altering existing structures and processes or by imposing new structures and processes upon the old. The politics of regulatory design is never a one-stage game. Each stage may place new layers of rules, roles, and routines on top of those that already exist, resulting in far greater incoherence than anyone would accept under normal circumstances.

Environmentalism and regulatory design

One cannot understand key design decision in environmental protection in isolation from the political debates of the 1960s and early 1970s. Richard Nixon created the Environmental Protection Agency via executive order in 1970 to capitalize on the political saliency of the environment. Rather than creating the EPA from new cloth, he consolidated offices and programs from fifteen agencies, placing 5,743 bureaucrats in what was, in essence, a holding company for regulators drawn from agencies with vastly different missions and cultures (Eisner 2000: 140). The new agency was given a media-specific organization, a decision that was reinforced by the media-specific responsibilities of congressional subcommittees and, ultimately, the media-specific focus of the new legislation (e.g. the *Clean Air Act*, the *Clean Water Act*). Environmental groups had preferential access to sites of policy-making, creating a relatively well-insulated policy monopoly (see Baumgartner and Jones 1993).

Because the EPA's authority was not derived from an organic act, the authority it exercised was structured by the new regulatory legislation—in particular, the various amendments to the *Clean Air Act* and the *Federal Water Pollution Control Act* (or *Clean Water Act*). When drafting these statutes, as a result, extraordinary care was taken in creating provisions that would shape regulatory politics well into the future. The advocacy groups that mobilized around environmental protection were gravely concerned with the power of big business in American society and, more immediately, the problem of regulatory capture (see Harris and Milkis 1996: 230–32; Eisner 2000: 118–33). There was much evidence that business had been quite adept at capturing agencies in the past. Industry actors dictated core elements of regulatory design, or legislation was vague and delegation was great, creating the structural foundations for mutually beneficial exchanges between business groups and bureaucrats searching for political patrons (see Kolko 1963, 1965; Lowi 1969; Stewart 1975; Bernstein 1955; Stigler 1971). This history raised important questions for environmental advocates and their congressional supporters. How could regulatory design prevent capture—or, more to the point, capture by hostile interests? How could it prevent the erosion of governmental commitment over time, should the configuration of political forces change and environmentalism lose its political appeal?

The environmental initiatives of the 1970s were the product of a new policy subsystem that linked environmental interest groups, key congressional subcommittees and the EPA.[1] Environmental groups worked closely with their congressional allies to secure their victories through regulatory design. In contrast to the vague and skeletal regulatory mandates of the past, the new regulatory legislation like the *Clean Air Act* was exhaustively detailed to constrain the scope of delegation and bureaucratic discretion. Detailed and mandatory directives, statutory deadlines, and a strong reliance on command-and-control instruments and technological standards minimized the potential for industry influence and agency inaction. The mandates and instruments created an adversarial relationship between the regulated and the regulators, creating a further barrier to capture. Finally, the extended rulemaking process provided greater opportunities for environmental groups to participate in agency activities, and expanded standing allowed previously excluded groups to sue the EPA to force the execution of non-discretionary duties (Eisner 2000: 134–200; Landy and Cass 1997).

For present purposes, one of the most interesting features was the treatment of economic analysis in original regulatory design decisions. Consider the *Clean Air Act Amendments* of 1970, the statutory foundation of US air pollution policy. Congress directed the EPA to base primary National Ambient Air Quality Standards (NAAQS) upon air quality criteria, allowing a margin of safety to protect the public health. A consideration of compliance costs was statutorily prohibited. When setting secondary NAAQS, the EPA was allowed to consider a broader range of benefits—but costs were once again excluded from consideration. The National Emissions Standards for Hazardous Air Pollutants were also to be set on the basis of public health concerns without any consideration of costs of economic feasibility. The *Clean Air Act* was not an exceptional piece of legislation. The *Clean Water Act*, the *Safe Drinking Water Act*, the *Resource Conservation and Recovery Act*, and the *Comprehensive Environmental Response, Compensation and Liability Act* all placed limitations on the EPA's consideration of compliance costs, cost effectiveness, and economic impacts (Environmental Protection Agency 1987).

When taken together, these regulatory design decisions provided a level of certainty and dependability but at a significant cost. Detailed regulatory mandates, technology, rather than performance-based standards, and a heavy reliance on command-and-control instruments, dramatically constrained flexibility in compliance and undermined the potential for innovations. Regulated parties had to comply with multiple parallel policy processes and incur delays and the costs associated with vast amounts of regulatory duplication (e.g. separate paperwork requirements for media-specific permitting). Moreover, the design sacrificed performance for dependability. Resources were often devoted to media shifting rather than pollution prevention—something that would not have occurred under a system of integrated regulation that provided regulated parties with greater flexibility. There were no incentives for going beyond regulatory standards; policy created a regulatory ceiling rather than a floor. The high costs, long delays, and large penalties for noncompliance assured that protracted litigation would become a regular part of the policy process, exacerbating the culture of adversarial legalism and devouring scarce resources (see Kagan and Axelrad 1982; Vogel 1986). For many environmental groups that participated in regulatory design, the ability to insulate victories from future political assaults was worth these costs.

Economics and US environmental regulation

If one accepted the politics-administration dichotomy, one would find the case for economic analysis to be sufficiently strong to justify significant reform efforts. It would be relatively easy to identify the points at which the use of economic analysis and economic instruments could contribute to efficiency and effectiveness. When we understand that regulatory design is inherently political and driven, in large part, by the desire to structure future political contests, one becomes less sanguine when reviewing the prospects for overarching change. Let us examine the growing presence of economics at the EPA, focusing on (1) its role in regulatory review, (2) the use of market-based instruments in air pollution regulation, and (3) recent efforts to reinvent regulation to leverage market forces and corporate innovations.

Economic analysis and regulatory review

Environmental advocates and their congressional supporters clearly understood the challenge posed by economic analysis. Congress provided the EPA with little discretion in setting many goals and selecting among policy instruments. At the same time, Congress placed statutory constraints on the ability of the agency to employ cost–benefit analysis at critical points in the regulatory process. In part, this reflected an understanding that a comprehensive consideration of compliance costs could elevate the influence of business in the policy process, thereby reducing the agency's fidelity to goals established by Congress and supported by environmental groups.

When policy subsystems exclude actors, they frequently capitalize on salient events to recast the debates, expand the scope of conflict, or force policy deliberations into a friendlier venue. Even if the old policy subsystem remains in place, parallel subsystems may emerge that will represent different visions of policy, models of the underlying problems, bodies of expertise, and interests. The existence of multiple parallel policy subsystems is particularly common in nations like the United States with decentralized institutional structures (Baumgartner and Jones 1993). The environmental groups that structured the policy debates of the late 1960s and 1970s were motivated by a deep distrust of corporate America, both a product of the New Left critique of capitalism and the experience of the Vietnam War (Eisner 2000: 118–33). Although policy subsystem in Congress failed to recognize a role for business and economic analysis, the presidency provided another venue that was used quite effectively once regulation was linked rhetorically to the inflation and stagnation of the 1970s.

During the 1970s, poor macroeconomic performance combined with heavy business mobilization to force the consideration of regulatory impacts into a new venue (Vogel 1989: 146). Beginning in the Nixon administration, presidents began requiring regulatory agencies to conduct regulatory analyses of significant rules. In 1971, the Office of Management and Budget (OMB) instituted a Quality of Life Review process requiring agencies to accompany significant regulations with a summary description comparing the costs and benefits of the alternatives and a justification for the decision. During the Ford presidency, Executive Order 11821 (1974) created the Inflation Impact Statement, which was replaced in 1976 by the Economic Impact Statement (Executive Order 11949). In each case, significant regulations were to be accompanied by an analysis of costs, benefits, and economic impacts. These efforts were continued during the Carter presidency, with Executive Order 12044 (1978) which mandated a Regulatory Analysis, considering costs and economic impacts, and required agencies to select the 'least burdensome' alternative (Environmental Protection Agency 1987). The impacts of these review processes on the EPA were mixed. Some of the EPA's rules were statutorily exempt and it is unclear across regulatory agencies whether decisions were based on analyses or simply justified ex post (Miller 1977). Yet, these initiatives unquestionably elevated the status of economists and economic analysis within the EPA. Economic professionalization occurred in other agencies as well, creating powerful internal constituencies for economically informed reform (see Eisner 1991; Tunstall 1986; and Derthick and Quirk 1985).

Regulatory analysis was a centrepiece of the Reagan administration's regulatory agenda. It provides the single best example of how economic analysis can enter into the politics of regulatory design. Reagan's reform strategy had several components. Loyalists were placed in key management positions and, where possible, functions were delegated to state-level regulators. Draconian budget cuts forced a reduction of regulatory staff. In the case of the EPA, the agency lost one-third of its operating budget and one-fifth of its staff, including a cadre of scientists who generated the scientific foundations of new rules and initiatives. A new Task Force on Regulatory Relief, under the direction of then Vice President George HW Bush, was touted as a place where businesses could appeal agency decisions if they felt that they had not been given a fair hearing within the agency. In essence, new access points were created for interests that had been systematically excluded under the original regulatory design (Vig 2003; Eisner 2000: 170–200).

Most important, the administration built on earlier initiatives to introduce a system of centralized regulatory clearance. Under Executive Order 12291 (1981), all major proposed rules had to be accompanied by Regulatory Impact Assessments (RIAs) that subjected the rule to cost–benefit analysis, applying discount rates that set a high threshold for most initiatives. The RIAs were reviewed by the Office of Management and Budget's Office of Information and Regulatory Affairs (OMB–OIRA), a body that was controlled by the President and explicitly charged with regulatory clearance. Noncompliance would result in the suspension of the rulemaking process. Reflecting the administration's strategy of regulatory design, the importance of economic analysis was elevated in each major regulatory agency. Thus, although the EPA suffered unprecedented budget cuts that threatened its capacity to execute its core functions, its economics unit (the Office of Policy, Planning, and Evaluation) expanded, receiving larger budgets and a growing staff. Its influence in the agency grew, creating internal pressures for economic analysis and market-based instruments (McGarity 1991: 271–91; Harris and Milkis 1996: 251–65).

Subsequent presidential administrations did not share Reagan's aversion to regulation. Yet, they reinforced the importance of cost–benefit analysis and regulatory review through executive orders. Moreover, the Republican-led 104th Congress made the reduction of regulatory burdens central to its regulatory agenda and the Contract with America. It imposed additional cost–benefit analysis requirements through important statutes, including the *Unfunded Mandates Reform Act* of 1995 and the *Small Business Regulatory Enforcement Fairness Act* of 1996, both explicitly designed to force the analysis of regulatory impacts on entities that received little attention under the EPA's original design (Eisner, Worsham, and Ringquist 2000: 35–7). While original regulatory design decisions continued to structure environmental protection, economic analysis had gained an important foothold.

Economic instruments and the regulation of air pollution

Largely as a result of economic professionalization and the imposition of regulatory review, there was a growing willingness within the EPA (and ultimately, in Congress) to experiment with market-based instruments. Market-based instruments, it was argued, could reduce compliance costs and stimulate innovations. Instead of requiring that all firms (or facilities) achieve a uniform level of pollution control, market-based instruments could create incentives for firms (or facilities) that can control pollution at the lowest cost to achieve even greater reductions and sell them to other firms or use them internally. If provided with sufficient flexibility, companies could have greater incentives to innovate and discover new technologies or changes in product and process design that could achieve reductions at the lowest possible cost (Stavins 2000). Let us turn briefly to examine the use of economic instruments in air pollution regulation.

Creating markets for pollution. A greater role for economic instruments was stimulated, ironically, by the constraints created by the *Clear Air Act* and its judicial interpretations. The 1970 Act established some 247 Air Quality Control Regions, each of which was classified as being an attainment or nonattainment region based on the NAAQS. The policy design was relatively straightforward: Factories in nonattainment regions would be required to install pollution control equipment that represented 'reasonably available control technology'. New Source Pollution Standards (NSPS) required that new facilities meet a higher standard of best available control technology. The goal of policy was to bring nonattainment areas into compliance with NAAQS. An obvious means of doing this would be to shift industry to attainment areas, thereby decentralizing pollution sources. The Sierra Club sought to prevent this outcome through the courts (Melnick 1983: 71–

112). In *Sierra Club v. Ruckelshaus* (1972), the district court for the District of Columbia required that the states prevent the deterioration of airsheds in attainment areas through provisions in their state implementation plans. This created a clear regulatory problem. Pollution in populated areas could not be mitigated by moving facilities to pristine areas with sparse populations. At the same time, additional investments in nonattainment areas could worsen environmental conditions, exacerbating rather than relieving pollution.

The EPA began to develop means of negotiating the statutory obstacles. The first major innovation is this area was 'netting'. In 1974, the agency allowed companies in nonattainment areas to create new sources of emissions only if they achieved equal reductions in emissions elsewhere in the plant and installed control equipment that met Lowest Achievable Emission Rate standards. The net impact of the new emission source would be zero. Two years later, the EPA began to experiment with limited emissions trading. New facilities could now be built in nonattainment areas if they could purchase offsetting pollution reductions from other firms in the area. The EPA's Offset Policy was authorized by the *Clean Air Act Amendments* of 1977. With new statutory foundations in place, the agency continued to experiment. In 1980, it introduced 'the bubble'. Firms could place an imaginary bubble over their facilities, treating them as a single emission source and pursuing reductions where they could be achieved cost effectively. They could bank emission reduction credits to offset future emissions or to sell to other firms (Rosenbaum 1998: 172–3).

Although the trading policy was formalized in 1986, participation rates were lower than anticipated. The innovations were hard to reconcile with the original regulatory design. For example, bubbles had to be approved through a revision of State Implementation Plans, 'a factor that has discouraged their use' (Environmental Protection Agency 2001b: 73). As the EPA (2001b: 75) notes, in a review of the use of economic incentives in regulating the environment:

> Emission trading has not lived up to expectations; trades have been fewer and offset prices lower than many had expected. Several factors seem to have limited the appeal of the emissions trading policy. In order to assure that air quality did not deteriorate, state environmental administrators often required expensive air quality modeling prior to accepting proposed trades between geographically separated parties. Deposits to emission banks typically were "taxed" by the air quality management authority to meet SIP [state implementation plan] requirements or to generate a surplus that the area could offer to attract new firms. Offset ratios greater than unity further depressed the value of ERCs [emission reduction credits]. In many areas, it appears that ERCs had an economic value less than the transaction costs of completing a sale to another party.

The effort to create pollution markets as a means of reconciling economic growth and environmental protection was an important experiment, albeit one which was difficult to harmonize with the existing regulatory design that permitted ongoing efforts to control the terms of trade. Markets cannot function effectively when property rights are poorly defined and parties are subjected to high transaction costs.

Emissions trading and acid rain. Early experiments in emissions trading provided experiences that would prove invaluable in other areas (e.g. chlorofluorocarbon reductions under the Montreal Protocol). However, the largest application of trading came with acid rain regulation under Title IV of the *Clean Air Act Amendments* of 1990. This emerged as the result of a complex set of debates involving the Bush administration, Congress, industry, and environmental groups. Earlier regulatory decisions permitted coal-fired power plants to disperse pollutants through the construction of tall smokestacks. The resulting atmospheric concentrations of sulfur dioxide (SO_2) and nitrogen oxides (NO_x) produced acid rain. The costs and benefits of regulation would fall on different regions of the country, thereby creating regional coalitions that were not easily captured by standard partisan politics. High sulfur coal producers, the United Mine Workers, and Midwestern utilities had the most to lose from regulations. Low sulfur coal producers (largely in the West), Western utilities, and Northeastern states that had been most severely impacted by acid deposition would claim the greatest benefits (Layzer 2002: 274–5). These regional disputes, combined with Reagan administration opposition to *Clean Air Act* reauthorization, prevented the US from developing viable regulations.

George HW Bush's decision to embrace the environment in the 1988 campaign combined with changes in Senate leadership to create a window of opportunity. The administration, strongly committed to market-based instruments, promoted a cap-and-trade approach that had been developed, in part, by the Environmental Defense Fund and was supported by EPA economists. After lengthy negotiations, Congress passed the *Clean Air Act Amendments* of 1990, creating (among other things) a cap-and-trade regime for SO_2. Under the Act, reductions in SO_2 were to be realized by setting a cap on emissions that would reach approximately one-half of the 1980 level. Utilities were given allowances (2.5 pounds of SO_2 per million Btu, multiplied by average Btu consumption for 1985–7) with additional allowances to help offset compliance costs and secure congressional coalitions. This allowance rate would be reduced in Phase II. Allowances that were not used could be banked or sold through bilateral transactions or auctions. New sources were required to purchase allowances and meet NSPS (Environmental Protection Agency 2001b: 75–85).

The EPA plays a relatively minor role in implementation. Due to the reliance on markets and the requirement that all facilities install continuous emissions monitoring systems (a demand of environmental groups) and submit hourly emissions readings on a quarterly basis, emissions and allowances are reconciled on an annual basis. If utilities exceed their allowances, they are penalized at a rate originally set at $2000 per ton (and indexed for inflation). Penalties have been rare. The cap-and-trade system created strong incentives for innovations in pollution control, as reflected in the fact that reductions have occurred well ahead of schedule and created a surplus of allowances (see Burtraw 2000). Indeed, the clearing price in the most recent (2003) EPA auction was $171.80 per ton, about one-tenth of original estimates (see Burtraw and Mansur 1999). Only one of the twenty successful bidders was a company (American Electric Power); the others included environmental groups, environmental economics classes, and elementary schools hoping to prevent pollution by purchasing credits.[2]

Although some question the adequacy of the targets set under the 1990 Act, there is a strong consensus that the cap-and-trade system has provided the means of achieving rapid implementation at a fraction of the anticipated costs (see Environmental Defense 2000). Despite heated controversies about the legitimacy of any system that allowed corporations to purchase the right to pollute, much of the environmental community has acknowledged the value of market-based instruments. There has been policy learning in Congress and the EPA as well. The regulatory constraints imposed in earlier trading regimes are notably absent.

Corporate environmentalism and regulatory reinvention

The success of the cap-and-trade system was partially attributable to corporate efforts to search for more innovative ways to manage their pollution. These innovations were part of a much larger trend in the corporate economy. There is much evidence that corporations are being driven by market forces to pursue higher levels of environmental quality. Companies have employed a number of tools in pursuit of green production, including life cycle analysis, design-for-environment, industrial ecology, environmental management systems (EMS), and environmental auditing (see Porter and van der Linde 1995a, 1995b; Elkington 1998; Fussler 1996; DeSimone and Popoff 1997; and Prakash 2000. For a critique, see Walley and Whitehead 1994; Tokar 1997). Why would profit-seeking firms voluntarily go beyond regulatory requirements? Rather than celebrating the emergence of norms of social responsibility, it is more realistic to accept an instrumentalist position and conclude that voluntary pollution reduction reinforces the fiduciary responsibility to maximize shareholder wealth. Indeed, there is some empirical evidence that companies that proactively manage their environmental impacts are realizing higher levels of profitability (see Russon and Fouts 1997; Klassen and Whybark 1999).

Although corporate environmental policy may reduce costs through waste reduction and lessened legal liability, it is more important in supporting differentiation-based strategies. There are strong market pressures for green production. Beyond consumer markets that are of limited impact (Speer 1997; Frankel 1998: 138–40), there are powerful forces in the business-to-business, government procurement, and financial markets that are rewarding firms with a positive environmental record (see Moltke and Kuik 1997; Organisation for Economic Co-operation and Development 1999; Blumberg, Korsvold, and Blum 1996; Schmid-Schönbein and Braunschweig 2000). Indeed, some 49, 462 firms in 118 nations have been certified as compliant with the International Organization for Standardization's ISO 14000 series, the international standard for environmental management systems (International Organization for Standardization 2003: 18). Many of these firms have made ISO 14001 certification a key criterion in establishing supplier and distributor relationships (Rodgers 1996). Thus, even if a company is otherwise not persuaded of the merits of environmental policy, the forces of coercive isomorphism or resource dependency may force change (DiMaggio and Powell 1983; Nohria and Gulati 1994; Pfiffer and Salancik 1978).

As a green revolution was occurring within the corporate economy, the EPA began to pursue regulatory reinvention, an exercise informed by agency critiques, examples of corporate innovations, and the lessons of economics. A central goal was to delegate greater authority to regulated parties, provide greater flexibility, and develop collaborative relationships with businesses to leverage corporate innovations as a means of realizing regulatory goals. In presenting its reinvention efforts, the Clinton administration noted:

> We have learned that pollution is often a sign of economic inefficiency and business can improve profits by preventing it. We have learned that better decisions result from a collaborative process with people working together, rather than from an adversarial one that pits them against each other. And we have learned that regulations that provide flexibility—but require accountability—can provide greater protection at a lower cost. (Clinton and Gore 1995: 2)

Rather than designing policies to regulate by pollutant or medium, 'attention must shift to integrated strategies for whole facilities, whole economic sectors, and whole communities'. The goal would be to 'efficiently tailor solutions to problems'. Moreover, it was argued, policy must adopt performance standards so that success 'will be measured by achieving real results in the real world, not simply by adhering to procedures'. It would 'encourage innovation by providing flexibility with an industry-by-industry, place-by-place approach to achieving standards'. This promised to have major implications for green production. According to the administration, businesses would be encouraged to 'accept their responsibility for environmental stewardship'. Through the provision of better information, they would be able to 'identify and eliminate inefficiencies that create pollution and reduce profits' and 'make environmental protection a strategic consideration that will be designed into their products and services, not considered after the fact (Clinton and Gore 1995: 4–5).

The administration's goals were broad and ambitious. Twenty-five high priority projects were introduced in 1995, with new programs being introduced every year thereafter (Rosenbaum 2000). By February 1997, the EPA created the Office of Reinvention to coordinate myriad agency initiatives. Some projects— such as Project XL—had broad economy-wide significance. Others—such as the Great Printing Project which strives to make 'pollution prevention a standard business practice of the Great Lakes states lithographic printing industry'—were narrowly focused.

The results were less than one might have hoped, doubtless reflecting the power of the EPA's bureaucratic culture and the original tenets of regulatory design. The media-specific organization of the EPA has survived and there have been no significant efforts to redesign core environmental statutes. Even the reinvention projects have had limited results. Consider the case of Project XL, presented by the EPA as the centrepiece of reform. Project XL was designed to provide top companies with strong environmental records with the flexibility to pursue innovative means of managing environmental impacts. The requirements were sufficiently stringent to limit participation to the firms that were already well beyond compliance. The delays in approval, ongoing demands for information, and the resistance of the EPA led many applicants to withdraw their applications (see Blackman, Boyd, Krupnick and Mazurek 2001). Although there were some success stories, most of the applicants were either rebuffed or refused to continue participation when they discovered that the costs of EPA's demands for information, analysis, and stakeholder engagement would vitiate potential savings. In the end, one would have to declare reinvention to be a failure—an experiment that could not break free of the original regulatory design. In the words of EPA's Daniel J. Fiorino (1996: 442): 'nearly all recent efforts to reinvent environmental regulation in the United States have come to little more than a tinkering with specific elements of a highly complex system'. They 'graft flexibility onto parts of an inflexible whole ... However laudable these improvements may be, they rarely, except rhetorically, deliver the systemic change that the term "reinvention" implies'. Thus, as with the early experiments in emissions trading, original regulatory design has continued to limit the scope for economically informed innovations.

In addition to these projects, the EPA introduced a new regulatory green track, the National Environmental Performance Track (NEPT), in 2000.[3] Businesses need to employ a high quality EMS, demonstrate a commitment to continuous improvement, commit to public outreach and reporting, and demonstrate a sustained record of regulatory compliance. They must demonstrate performance by documenting measurable improvements (and expected future improvements) in several categories, including energy use, water use, emissions of key air pollutants, chemical releases, wastes generated, discharges to water, product performance, and restoration/preservation. The EPA has promised a host of benefits, including public recognition, enhanced access to regulators, technical assistance, and lower inspection priority. More importantly, it is considering streamlined reporting and paperwork (Environmental Protection Agency 2001).

Within 18 months of its creation, the EPA had accepted 280 'members' into the program, including one or more facilities from Dupont, International Paper, IBM, 3M, and Marathon Ashland (Environmental Protection Agency, *Environmental News*, February 11, 2002). It is far too early to assess NEPT. Yet, two concerns automatically come to mind. First, will participation be short-lived, as was the case in many of the other EPA initiatives? Some of NEPT participants also attempted to participate in Project XL, but withdrew their applications, as it became clear that promises of greater delegation and flexibility were largely hollow and regulatory transaction costs were greater than any projected savings. If the same kind of restrictions hampers the performance track, the same result may be forthcoming. More important, because NEPT, like green tracks more generally, court large firms with exemplary records, even success may have limited environmental implications. Firms that should be of the greatest concern to regulators (e.g. small and medium enterprises and firms that are not yet in compliance and thus could realize greater gains at lower marginal costs) are formally excluded from agency innovations.

Lessons from the Environmental Protection Agency

Economic analysis has much to offer environmental regulation and there is much evidence that its role in policy-making and implementation has increased significantly over the past several decades. The history presented above offers a few insights into the process. First and foremost, regulatory design is inherently political. The interests that prevailed in securing early regulatory legislation used regulatory design to achieve pollution reductions *and* to insulate their victories from an uncertain future. As a result, many of the features of environmental regulations that critics would identify as design flaws were fully intended to serve an important political purpose. Second, policy effectiveness and efficiency, while not unimportant, were not the key evaluative criteria for those engaged in the politics of regulatory design. Even if there were unquestionable evidence that a greater reliance on economics would produce better results, this would be relevant only to the extent that it did not come at the cost of enhanced vulnerability to change.

Third, although economics has assumed an increasingly important role, this has occurred within the larger dynamic of the politics of regulatory design. It would be a mistake to characterize regulatory review as being the imposition of rational decision processes on a flawed system or a triumph of expertise over politics. Presidents have responded to the demands of interests excluded from the policy subsystem by forcing regulatory agencies to formally analyze costs and benefits. One cannot understand the imposition of economic analysis separate from the demands that greater emphasis be accorded to the costs incurred by business. Fourth, the imposition of new review procedures reinforced by budgetary flows created pressure for organizational change. Professionalization, the creation and expansion of economic staffs in the EPA and other regulatory agencies, created an internal constituency for economic analysis and market-based instruments.

Fifth, despite the growing support for economic analysis and market-based instruments, original regulatory design decisions and the EPA's bureaucratic culture continued to place constraints on the extent and rapidity of change. Although command-and-control instruments and market-based instruments may be used in conjunction as part of a larger regulatory strategy, it requires careful consideration of the potential conflicts (see Gunningham and Sinclair 1997). In the case of emissions trading, for example, demands for data, requirements that bubbles be approved through changes in state implementation plans, taxes on deposited credits, and the manipulation of offset ratios increased transaction costs and created instability in property rights, essentially vitiating many of the benefits of this innovation. Similar constraints bedeviled some of the EPA's reinvention initiatives, including Project XL.

Sixth, despite these constraints, there is evidence of considerable institutional and political learning. The growing role of economics is not simply the product of external coercion, as exhibited by the fact that economic impacts are now routinely given some consideration even when not required by statute or executive order. Moreover, even if the EPA's original regulatory design has survived for decades, there is a growing willingness to allow market-based instruments to function free from excessive interference. Environmental groups are increasingly acknowledging a role for market-based instruments. Title IV of the *Clean Air Act* provides the single best example of a successful cap-and-trade program that was instituted with minimal constraints. The basic design was generated by the Environmental Defense Fund and concerns over implementation were resolved with technology (continuous emissions monitoring systems) rather than new layers of regulatory restrictions. The positive results of the acid rain program suggest that the future of market-based instruments is far brighter than one would have predicted a few decades ago.

The final point is perhaps the most important. Bureaucracies and the policies they implement evolve over time, both as a response to new contests over the shape of the regulatory state and practical experiences with the design and implementation of public policy. In the end, the greatest testament to the importance of the contribution of economic analysis and instruments is that they have gained influence in spite of the considerable barriers. Is it better to regulate with marginal gains or to regulate at the margin? As policymakers, regulators, and members of the environmental movement have been confronted with this question, they have conceded, albeit grudgingly, that economics has an important contribution to make.

Notes

1   William Ruckelshaus, the first administrator of the EPA, recalls: 'In the early days of EPA, we accepted much of the initial agenda of the environmental movement. In fact, the new agency worked with environmentalists, whose demands helped create EPA in the first place. They were allies, at least in part; not locked in the confrontation that exists today between the agency and the environmental community. There still is a so-called "iron triangle" relationship between the environmental movement, the EPA staff, and the Congressional committee staffs. Some of it has to do with job security; some of it has to do with a certain amount of zealotry inside EPA ... Basically, the three parties have used each other. There has existed among them a symbiosis, in which the environmental movement used the agency as an antagonist to raise money and get more members; and the agency used the environmental groups to sue for objectives they were trying to accomplish, but could not otherwise gain. The same is true of the Congressional committees',
     <http://www.epa.gov/history/publications/ruck/index.htm>.
2   <http://www.epa.gov/airmarkt/auctions/index.html>.
3   The National Environmental Performance Track was based on the experimental Star Track in EPA Region 1. This was not the only EMS-based regulatory experiment. A number of states (including Connecticut, Illinois, New Jersey, Oregon, and Wisconsin) implemented new regulatory programs with similar features. The Multi-State Working Group on Environmental Management Systems—a consortium of fifteen state agencies, the EPA, non-governmental organizations, industry representatives and academics—has provided an important network for conducting research on the regulatory implications of corporate environmentalism and sharing results.

Chapter 5

Hyper-experts and the Vertical Integration of Expertise in EMF/RF Litigation

David Mercer

Introduction

In the following discussion I will provide a preliminary theoretical sketch of how the concept of *vertically integrated expertise* may be used as a way to help describe a form of expertise that has emerged in recent years in the debate surrounding the possible health risks of EMF/RF (electric and magnetic fields/radiofrequency radiation). Because the EMF debate has also been frequently linked to debates about 'junk science' and tort reform, characterizing the nature of expert knowledge in the EMF/RF debate has broader theoretical and political relevance.

The debate surrounding whether or not electric and magnetic fields and low level radiofrequency radiation (EMF/RF) constitute a health risk is more than twenty years old. While there has been some evidence of regulatory fatigue the debate continues. This longevity has been assisted by the tendency for the debate to have become scientifically polarized (Miller 2004) between so-called thermalist (energy) perspectives and non-thermalist (information) perspectives. Thermalist perspectives are relatively easy to explain within existing mainstream physical sciences. They suggest that the only possible risks of EMF/RF are levels of exposure high enough to cause heating or electrocution. From a thermalist perspective the risks of exposure to low levels of EMF/RF are likely to be trivial or nonexistent (Park 2000). Non-thermalist perspectives draw upon a patchwork of scientific studies from a variety of scientific fields. Low levels of exposure are linked to subtle interruptions to the endocrine system, brain chemistry and intercellular communication; these interruptions are interpreted as potential cancer promoters. Among non-thermalist approaches there is a lack of agreement about a simple unifying causal mechanism to explain how EMF/RFs may be linked to harmful biological effects. The debate between thermalist and non-thermalists has been played out against the backdrop of a number of epidemiological studies which have been indecisive but unable to dismiss EMF as a health risk, especially the case of EMF exposure and the raised likelihood of childhood leukemia (Neutra et al. 2002). Within the epidemiological literature it has been deceptively difficult to reach agreement on exposure models and in cases of new RF emitting technologies, such as mobile telephones, the relevance of current studies are often challenged on the basis that there has been insufficient time to map possible long term effects (Stewart 2000; Graham-Rowe 2003). The EMF/RF debate has enormous economic implications for industry and government. The ubiquitous nature of power distribution and electrical and telecommunication devices, especially mobile telephones, means that establishing risk could lead to a massive number of personal injury suits and exert pressure for major changes to the way electrical and telecommunication infrastructures are organized (Walsh et al. 1997).

The EMF/RF health and safety issue has appeared in litigation in three different forms: *contested environmental impact assessments*—such as whether or not such assessments have adequately taken into account the health risks of proposed telecommunication and electricity transmission infrastructure; *compensation for the reduction of home values*—that RF or EMF infrastructure has produced health risks, or fear of health risks, which have diminished home values; and, *personal injury claims*—that living or working with EMFs and RFs has caused illnesses such as cancers, brain tumors and leukemia. The results of litigation have generally not been supportive of plaintiffs' claims (Depew 1994; Gerjuoy 1994; Grasso 1998). Over the last twenty years most, but not all, government panels and public inquiries which have reviewed similar questions have generally been indecisive, following a pattern of downplaying the scientific basis for compensation and public fears while emphasizing the need for more research (Mercer 2002).

In anticipation of possible social, economic and legal impacts, the EMF debate has had a rich legal–regulatory history. It has been the subject of numerous public and government inquiries (Mercer 2002), an important site for experiments with science court proposals (Mazur 1981), and has been used as a popular example of a 'phantom risk' and 'junk science' by proponents of tort reform such as Peter Huber (1991), Robert Park (2000) and various politically conservative US think-tanks such as the Atlantic Legal Foundation (ALF) and Manhattan Institute (ALF 2002; Mone 2004).

Vertically integrated expertise

Many studies of expertise have emphasized the importance of understanding the processes of the increasing professionalization, specialization and differentiation of knowledge in modern societies (Barnes and Edge 1982). Most traditional epistemologically realist studies of these processes have been prefigured by an implicit spatial metaphor, that expertise has its origins in specific expert locations. Following the logic of this metaphor one of the main challenges to policymakers has been to make sure that the knowledge generated in such privileged sites is true and objective to start with, and that when it is 'transported' to other sites it is done so without distortion. Expert identity is similarly viewed as static and mono-centric. Ideally, experts should be careful to only speak about matters that fall within their own field of specialization. Given these kinds of assumptions, when expertise is drawn upon for the purposes of regulation and litigation, questions have often been raised such as whether in the processes of simplification and translation, social values have distorted original knowledge; whether the legal/regulatory question actually matches, or is beyond, available expertise and knowledge (trans-science); and, whether social and psychological pressures have encouraged experts to adopt polarized positions, become partisan and fail to acknowledge uncertainties (Mazur 1981). Social constructivist approaches in science studies have framed similar questions quite differently suggesting that the process of setting boundaries between specializations (Geiryn 1998), evaluating the veracity of simplifications (Hilgartner 1990), determining the lay–expert divide (Irwin and Wynne 1996), are all subject to social and political negotiation. While many of these studies have tended to focus on the politics of creating expert knowledge in specialist settings, for example defining and studying narrow core sets of relevant knowledge producers working in settings such as laboratories (Collins 1985), there has also been a growing body of studies which have attempted to model the ways expert knowledge is produced at multiple sites in society. These studies have included concern with the politics of scientific exposition and popularization (Shinn and Whitley 1985); the industrialization of science (Ravetz 1971; Nowotny et al. 2001), and the role of social activism and situated knowledge (Epstein 1996). Without drawing upon their arcane vocabularies and theoretical formalisms, 'actor network' studies have also made valuable contributions by emphasizing that experts may take on the role of the multi-skilled builder of socio-technical networks (Law 1987). Bruno Latour's (1983a) well-known analysis of Pasteur, for instance, attributes Pasteur's success to a network of strategic alliances which allowed him to create a favorable environment for the reception of his work. His efforts did not stop at the laboratory door but rather, to paraphrase Latour, Pasteur turned France into *his* laboratory. The metaphor of vertical integration is consistent with these later approaches and constitutes an addition to this literature by offering a useful model for helping illustrate some of the ways that the environments in which socio-technical expertise operates are linked to the forms that expertise adopts.

I have borrowed the metaphor of 'vertical integration' loosely from studies of the economics of innovation. The use of economic metaphors to help understand the social aspects of science is not new (Mirowski and Sent 2002). Rather than take direct inspiration from these studies my notion of the vertical integration of expertise draws in a theoretically more informal way upon a number of classic studies of the emergence of the 'modern' (i.e. 20th century) corporation. Theorists such as JK Galbraith (1967) highlighted the way that the various imperatives of long term planning and investments in knowledge and production processes encouraged large firms and their entrepreneurs to attempt to 'internalize the marketplace', to control product, process and even demand. This helped overcome the fact that markets for the new mass-produced manufactured products were initially too unpredictable to sustain demand. Without drawing too literally on the intricacies of the economic meanings of vertical integration let me suggest that similar processes of 'vertical integration' can be observed over the last decade, in particular, in the EMF and, most likely, other similar controversial scientific, legal and regulatory debates. I will show how various key experts, institutions and political actors have encouraged the vertical integration of expertise to help counter the difficulties of managing knowledge and expertise in longer standing civil litigation and regulation involving scientific controversy. Like the economic vertical integration strategies outlined above, these processes have involved the efforts of conspicuous multi-skilled experts and their institutional supporters to privilege certain types of knowledge/product and have involved attempts to manipulate demand for this knowledge by reshaping the 'marketplace' (courts and jurisprudence) to be more amenable to a particular style 'product' (blended/hybrid law–science knowledge).

In keeping with the economic metaphor of vertical integration I will divide my discussion of examples into three quasi-economic categories: *producers*—experts with 'multiple expert identities' (hyper-experts) who can function at a variety of points in the knowledge 'production process'; *products*—packages of blended law–science knowledges; and, *marketplaces*—audiences that are receptive to and help reproduce vertically integrated expertise. I will follow this conceptual mapping exercise by sketching some hypotheses to account for the emergence of vertically integrated expertise.

Producers

There are a number of scientists who have participated in the EMF/RF debate who qualify as hyper-experts. Two examples are Kenneth R Foster and Michael H Repacholi. The brief sketch below serves to illustrate the variety of socio-technical arenas that hyper-experts from long standing scientific controversies may participate in.

Kenneth Foster has published a number of scientific studies and policy reviews on the EMF/RF question. This has included articles in influential scientific generalist journals such as *IEEE Technology and Society* (Foster and Veccia 2002/2003) and *Science* (Foster et al. 2000). His interests in policy have extended to legal matters where he co-authored the book *Judging Science* (1998) with Peter Huber of the Manhattan Institute. *Judging science* provided a detailed analysis and commentary on the implications of the *Daubert v Merrell Dow Pharmaceutical, Inc.* (1993) case on US Federal jurisprudence and has been cited in a number of US Federal Court judgments (see Edmond and Mercer later in this volume). Foster has also been a signatory to an *amicus* brief submitted in EMF litigation submitted by the tort reform lobby group, the Atlantic Legal Foundation (ALF). The ALF has submitted *amicus* briefs to most of the leading US appeals cases over the last decade which have been concerned with interpreting the rules for the admissibility of expert evidence (ALF 1999, 2002). Foster is also Professor of Bio-engineering at the University of Pennsylvania, immediate past president of the Institute of Electrical and Electronics Engineers Inc. (IEEE) Society for the Social Implications of Technology, and immediate past president of IEEE Engineering in Medicine and Biology Committee on Man and Radiation (COMAR) (Foster 2004).

Michael Repacholi has made numerous appearances as an expert witness in litigation and public and government inquiries. For more than a decade he has been one of the central figures in attempts to establish uniform international health and safety guidelines in relation to RF and EMF. Repacholi has authored and co-authored dozens of reports, scientific overviews and position papers on the EMF debate; most of them under the auspices of the International Committee for Non-Ionizing Radiation Protection (ICNIRP) of the World Health Organization. He has also coordinated laboratory experiments, acted as a consultant for electricity authorities and advised committees of the Australian National Health and Medical Research Council (NHMRC) (Fist 2004).

It is difficult to imagine many possible contexts involving the EMF/RF debate in which Foster and Repacholi have not been active participants. Both have produced scientific research papers, written reports designed for use in legal and regulatory settings, acted as expert witnesses or provided support to parties involved in litigation, and published popular overviews of the debate and commentaries hoping to influence the way courts and regulators interpret, not only the science of EMF/RF, but science more generally. Both have also had their work received favorably by regulators and courts, although Repacholi's multiple roles have meant that he has occasionally been subject to criticism from activists and other scientists (Mercer 2001: 94).[1]

Products

As noted above, hyper-experts not only participate in producing scientific papers but are active in the production of things such as *amicus* briefs, submissions to public inquiries, scientific literature reviews, reports to government inquiries, and editorial commentaries. These types of products will often reflect the hybrid roles of the hyper-expert, blending together different forms of legal and scientific authority. Unlike the traditional specialist scientific paper, these products are much more likely to indicate how scientific conclusions should be put to work and are more likely to engage in explicit discussion of the nature of science-in-general and the way models of science may be applied to the question at hand (Mercer 2002). While the regular injunction in many policy-making models is for there to be a separation of factual from advisory or value questions (Mazur 1981) these 'products' appear to seamlessly blend these questions. Bolstered by multi-dimensional models of scientific and legal authority the decision-maker is 'told' what decision the science demands. A typical example of a vertically integrated knowledge product in the EMF/RF debate is an *amicus* brief submitted by the Atlantic Legal Foundation to the EMF case of *Covalt v San Diego Gas and Electric*.[2]

Covalt v San Diego Gas and Electric. In 1993 the Covalts filed a suit against San Diego Gas and Electric for loss of property value and fear of health risks from EMFs which had been produced by a 1990 upgrade of power lines close to their house. At this time a number of other EMF cases involving property devaluation and personal injury claims were pending so *Covalt* became something of a test case for the EMF issue (Park 2000).

The case attracted a number of *amicus* briefs. These briefs can be submitted to the court by interested parties. Judges are free to disregard them. The brief which arguably had the greatest impact on the *Covalt* case was that filed by the Atlantic

Legal Foundation. The brief was signed by fourteen eminent scientists, six of whom were Nobel laureates. Many of these signatories were regular 'clients' of the ALF. Kenneth Foster, discussed above, is a 'client' of the ALF and became a signatory to a later Atlantic Legal Foundation EMF brief, basically a copy of the *Covalt* brief, filed in the later case of *Ford v Pacific Gas and Electric Company*.[3] The ALF had filed *amicus* briefs in *Daubert v Merrell Dow Pharmaceuticals, Inc.* (brief of Bloembergen et al. 1993) and many other important US appeal cases involving the admissibility of expert evidence (Atlantic Legal Foundation 1994). This included landmark cases such as *General Electric Co v Joiner* (brief of Ames et al. 1997) and *Kumho Tire Co Ltd v Carmichael* (brief of Bobo et al. 1999). These briefs were quite often similar in form, involving a summary of the key scientific issues before the court, a short summary of relevant evidence jurisprudence and models for how these things should be linked together. In this later context, the briefs play the role, to borrow a term from TS Kuhn (1962), of providing 'exemplars' or 'ideal problem solutions' to law–science problems.

The ALF's *Covalt* brief opens by stating the interest of the amici and blends general statements of science with an endorsement of existing California EMF policy:

> *Amici* are scientists who have studied the issue of the health effects of electromagnetic fields [EMF] and believe that the current concern that EMF causes disease, particularly cancer, is not supported by the weight of credible scientific evidence. *Amici* further believe that the 1993 policy statement by the California Public Utilities Commission [PUC] correctly evaluates and assimilates the current state of scientific knowledge regarding the health effects of EMF. *Amici* are concerned that any decision which even implicitly can be seen as support for the concerns about EMF would lend credibility to beliefs which are essentially without scientific foundation and based on irrational and speculative fear of injury. (Brief of Adair et al 1996: 1-2)

The brief offers a compressed review of EMF 'science'. Its main focus is on diminishing the scientific value of epidemiological studies of EMF and the failure for EMF studies to be able to be explained by physical causal mechanisms. The brief 'anchors' this discussion to the nine so-called *Bradford Hill Criteria* for assessing epidemiology. These criteria help to give the brief structure and generic authority. The ALF strengthen their interpretation—that EMF science fails to meet the Hill criteria—by stressing that it also fails to meet ordinary scientific standards such as repeatability and that this concept is supported by the relevant jurispurudence of *Daubert*.

> Hill also mentions, under this heading [attribute 7] coherence with laboratory experiments on animals and *in vitro*. Many experiments on the effect of electromagnetic fields have been quoted as evidence that low intensity magnetic fields cause effects in biological systems. It has been suggested that the experiments on calcium efflux on chicken brains substantiate the epidemiological results. There are two problems with such a statement. Firstly the results of these efflux experiments have not been closely similar when repeated, so that the ordinary scientific concept of *repeatability*, which can and should be applied to laboratory

experiments and which is closely connected with factor (3) on the United States Supreme Court's list of criteria in *Daubert v. Merrell Dow Pharmaceuticals, Inc.* ... is not satisfied. (Brief of Adair et al. 6, emphasis in original)

The brief also reminds the reader that the failure of EMF science to satisfy 'Hill's principles' can be confirmed by recourse to the opinion of 'responsible public bodies and professional associations' such as the WHO. This type of association is the 'home' of hyper-experts such as Foster and Repacholi.

It would be inappropriate for a court to allow the introduction of "scientific" evidence that satisfies few of Hill's principles, without extensive evidence also being proffered on the principles themselves and the logic behind them. Of course opinions can differ on whether these principles are met, since there is a difference of opinion, one might refer to reviews by committees composed of distinguished and competent persons and set up by responsible public bodies and professional associations. We list some reviews below. [The reviews included those of the WHO, chaired by Repacholi, and the American Physical Society] (Brief of Adair et al. 6)

The brief offers an excellent example of a hybrid blend of integrated law–science knowledge. It seamlessly links disparate scientific standards, the authority of mainstream scientific institutions, appeals to common sense, legal precedent and specific scientific studies. This streamlined package would appear to have been well received by its legal audience.

Justice Stanley Mosk rejected the Covalts' claim and cited with approval the ALF brief (amongst other mainstream science views) as an important authority for his decision (Slesin 1996):

[The] AMA likewise adopted a policy statement declaring that the association 'will continue to monitor developments and issues relating to the effects of electric and magnetic fields, even though no scientifically documented health risk has been associated with the usually occurring levels of electromagnetic fields.' ... The same conclusion is expressed in an *amicus curiae* brief filed in this court by 17 prominent physicists, epidemiologists, biochemists and physicians including among their number six Nobel laureates. (cited in Slesin 1996: 4)

Markets

To continue structuring my discussion according to the economic metaphor of the vertical integration of expertise, it is useful to think of judges and regulators and the public as the market for such packages of EMF/RF knowledge. While the *Covalt* judgment above suggests that some courts have been favorably disposed to such packages and the ALF has claimed that their lobbying strategies can be linked to a general decline in EMF/RF litigation, such evidence, nevertheless, still only offers a circumstantial way of assessing the 'positive' impact of vertically integrated EMF expertise. While it is beyond the scope of this preliminary theoretical sketch to provide a lengthy detailed investigation of EMF/RF judgments we can gain some sense of the impact of such expertise, albeit rather impressionistically, by evaluating an important EMF/RF judgment in a case heard in the New Zealand Environment Court, *Shirley Primary School v Telecom Mobile Communications Limited* (1998).[4] As I will show in more depth below, the judge not only responded favorably to EMF/RF claims packaged in an integrated form, but also blended and hybridized various forms of legal and scientific authority in a similar manner himself.

Shirley Primary School v Telecom Mobile Communications Limited. This case involved an appeal by Shirley Primary School Trustees (SPS) against the resource consent granted by Christchurch City Council to an application by Telecom New Zealand Ltd (hereafter Telecom) to build a cellular radio base station 14 metres from the school's boundary. Telecom also appealed against one of the conditions of Christchurch City Council's resource consent which had imposed a limitation on the power to be emitted by the cell site. One of the major grounds for the school's objections was potential health risks. A number of commentators have suggested that the case became especially prominent as it took place during the process of Standards Australia and New Zealand negotiating a revised safety standard for RF radiation. This process had become drawn-out and controversial so the Court's assessment of the relevant scientific claims fed back into the regulatory process and the EMF/RF scientific debate more generally (Mercer 2001). The judgment handed down in December 1998, rejected SPS's claims and supported Telecom's appeal against the conditions imposed on it by Christchurch City Council. Further, it suggested that 'the members of the school community greatly exaggerated the risks of exposure to RFR' (*Shirley* 1998: 123). The judgment also provided a lengthy discussion supporting the existing RF safety standard-setting rationales supplied by institutions such as the ICNIRP of the WHO.

As with *Covalt*, the authoritative image of mainstream science and consensus reviews played a major role:

> We respectfully agree with ICNIRP that, *overall the literature on athermal effects ... electromagnetic fields is so complex, the validity of the reported effects so poorly established, and the relevance of the effects to human health so uncertain, that it is impossible to use this body of information as a basis for setting limits on human exposure to these fields.* (*Shirley* 1998: 89)

The judgment also explicitly defers to the authority of ICNIRP and hyper-expert Michael Repacholi:

> [T]urning to the ICNIRP Standard, the individuals who comprise ICNIRP including Dr Repacholi as Chairman Emeritus explain that ... [t]he ICNIRP standard was the last word in scientific consensus on the issue of athermal effects from chronic exposure to RFR at the time we heard the case. We are reassured to find that it confirms our findings on the other evidence before us that risk of adverse health effects on humans of chronic low-level exposure to RFR is very low. (*Shirley* 1998: 109)

The judgment also draws on the authority of US jurisprudence. Whether this authority is legal or scientific is not altogether clear. For instance, the judgment noted the limits of applicability of these 'admissibility' decisions to the NZ

Environment Court, as the Court did not rely on a jury and the matter was not one of admissibility, but nevertheless affirmed their value in assessing expert evidence more generally. In a five-point checklist for assessing expert evidence *Daubert* becomes a 'legal-scientific authority' for judging the veracity of the 'hard sciences':

> In assessing the expert evidence (including rebuttal and cross-examination) on any issue we have to take into account and evaluate (inter alia) the following factors: ...
> (5) Especially for 'hard' science - the research or papers referred to by the witness in reaching their opinions with respect to whether:
> (a) the techniques used are reliable
> (b) the error rates are known and published (and the research is shown to be statistically significant)
> (c) the research or papers have been published
> (d) the research or papers have been subject to peer review
> (e) the research is repeatable (and has been replicated). (*Shirley* 1998: 67)

A footnote to this checklist suggests that 'Loosely these are the *Daubert* criteria' (*Shirley* 1998: 67). At a later point the US case of *Joiner* is put to similar use, as a 'legal-scientific authority', this time to dismiss animal studies unless they are accompanied by epidemiological evidence:

> As for the existence of animal studies these suffered from a number of defects also. There were no attempts to explain why there was no or little epidemiological evidence of actual adverse health effects. In the absence of such explanations the usefulness of animal studies is very doubtful. (*Shirley* 1998: 88)

The footnote for this point reads: 'There is significant jurisprudence on this in the USA - see for example: *General Electric Ltd v Joiner* 118 S.Ct. 512' (*Shirley* 1998: 88 n109).

Immediately below this discussion of epidemiology and animal studies, the judgment yet again melds legal and scientific authority. The jurisprudence of *Joiner* is linked to the authority of Repacholi (quoting from a 1998 'survey review' by Repacholi from the journal *Bioelectromagnetics*):

> In addition, as we have already pointed out, the existence of an effect does not necessarily mean they are harmful. As Dr Repacholi himself has recently written of animal studies: ... "*It is questionable whether reported 'effects', even if substantiated, can be considered to represent evidence of a hazard simply because the significance of the effect on the organism is not understood. ... Not all biological effects of exposure are necessarily hazardous; some may be helpful under certain conditions.*" (*Shirley* 1998: 88)

The extracts above show a pervasive acceptance of vertically integrated expertise. The judgment presents some of its strongest arguments to reject and understand the nature of EMF/RF claims by melding together the opinions and authority of a hyper-expert Michael Repacholi with the US jurisprudence of *Daubert* and *Joiner*.

Discussion

There are a number of possible hypotheses which can be proposed to help explain why vertically integrated expertise has assumed an important role in the EMF/RF debate. The explanations I will sketch below are largely impressionistic, and indicative of areas which warrant further research, rather than a definitive analysis.

Scientific controversies like EMF/RF, which develop over time, tend to become increasingly complex and offer opportunities for experts to participate in numerous points of knowledge construction

In debates such as EMF and RF various experts are provided with the opportunity to learn and shape their knowledge claims in anticipation of legal and regulatory needs. During the 1980s and 1990s in response to ongoing demands of litigation and regulation many power authorities and electrical utilities retained legal and public relations firms to help them manage the EMF/RF 'problem'. In the context of litigation for instance, the Washington DC-based firm Crowell and Moring managed the legal campaigns of many of the world's electrical utilities. This meant that a 'stable' of experts could be repeatedly drawn upon and legal and scientific strategies refined. By the early 1990s some experts could boast more than twenty court appearances in EMF campaigns (Brodeur 1989). Affidavits of evidence, submissions to inquiries and government reports bootstrapped their authority to each other and versions of scientific method and standards for the adequacy of evidence were developed in a manner more or less sensitive to emerging legal and regulatory needs. Activists and industry opponents engaged in similar exercises with less refinement and funding (Mercer 2002). It is possible to observe, over time, the development of 'scientific method discourses' which were relatively portable, which could be carried over and adapted from one EMF engagement to the next. Submissions in litigation over potential risks of high voltage power lines in New York could be transported and adapted to litigation in Sydney and be reworked yet again in submissions to a New South Wales Government Inquiry. The outcomes of this inquiry could then be recycled yet again and quoted in contexts shaping EMF policy in Europe and the UK (Mercer 2002). The tendency for refined positions to develop has been observed in other scientific controversies, such as nuclear power (Mazur 1981). The way the needs of litigation may also permeate a scientific debate has also been noted in the Bendectin litigation (the debate which spawned the *Daubert* decision). Over time the scientific/legal standards for evaluating evidence for the risks of Bendectin shifted in response to various pressures of litigation. Particular forms of epidemiological evidence came to take priority over toxicology and animal studies. This occurred without any single decisive specialized scientific work taking place separate from litigation. It was instead the by-product of key legal decisions, the possible influence of editorials in generalist scientific journals, and political pressures to resolve a matter that policymakers believed had gone on for too long (Green 1996; Sanders 1998, Edmond and Mercer 2000).

The vertical integration of expertise protects against risks of the deconstruction or legal criticism of expert claims

Many SSK studies have noted the way the slippage between ideal images of science and the messy realities of scientific practice provide a particularly fertile source for the legal 'deconstruction' of science—especially in adversarial settings (Smith and Wynne 1989; Lynch 1998). In such contexts, courts and regulatory institutions often have the opportunity to contrast the practices and knowledge of scientists against standards of conduct and proof provided by ideal images of scientific norms and method. By comparing artificial and ideal images of science and expertise to the messier realities of scientific work, an interpretative space is created for the deconstruction of scientific authority. Experts who are adept at understanding/manipulating legal and regulatory needs, as well as scientific and technical principles and policies, may find themselves in a strategic position to anticipate and absorb potential pressures of deconstruction. A good example is the controversy over DNA typing in the OJ Simpson trial (Jasanoff 1995). Because of an absence of formal standards and protocols, DNA typing as a relatively novel technology initially appeared vulnerable to potential legal deconstruction. But in a manner reminiscent of the ALF's EMF *amicus* brief, anticipated deconstruction was averted through efforts by scientific authorities, external to courts, developing a legal and scientific standard for the technique. In an era of enhanced judicial sensitivity to the form in which scientific and expert claims are presented to courts, vertical integration of expertise enhances the translation of concepts from specialized to more generalist contexts in ways that might help counter problems of deconstruction.

Pressures of judicial gatekeeping are predisposing judges and regulators to encourage the development of vertically integrated expertise

In the wake of the spread of perceptions of legal and regulatory crisis because of the increased entry of 'junk science' into courts as well as the problems of managing the scale and persistence of mass tort actions there have been increasing pressures on judges and regulators to develop new ways to manage scientific disagreements. To satisfy this task they are increasingly drawn into making 'scientific judgments' which prioritize 'mainstream' scientific and technical claims and administrative solutions (Jasanoff 2002). Vertically integrated expertise which has been packaged in a legally tractable form and carries the imprimatur of scientific associations, eminent scientists and other 'public' signifiers of authority fits in with these legal and regulatory needs much more effectively than the knowledge of the more traditional specialist, which is far less likely to be packaged/simplified and blended to suit legal and administrative needs.

Politically conservative lobby groups have promoted vertically integrated expertise as a by-product of their direct engagement in various scientific/legal controversies

By helping to promote wider perceptions of a 'junk science' crisis and by demanding greater judicial attentiveness to scientific gatekeeping (Edmond and Mercer 1998a, 2004) groups such as the ALF have indirectly assisted in encouraging legal environment(s) which are more amenable to vertically integrated expertise. The ALF has also played a more direct role by producing and promoting vertically integrated expertise packages in specific controversies. As my earlier discussion of the ALF's involvement in the *Covalt* case shows, their activities have extended from promoting particular models of judicial gatekeeping to providing examples, supported by the authority of eminent scientists, of how judicial gatekeeping should be applied to specific scientific debates. In having the energy and financial resources to facilitate the links between scientific, legal and policy dimensions of controversial areas of science and law, groups like the ALF have directly encouraged the development of vertically integrated expertise.

While the ALF would not perhaps describe their activities in terms of the vertical integration of expertise, they have no doubts that their efforts have exerted influence.

> In 1990 it was estimated that these claims [that EMF causes leukemia or brain cancer] had already cost the United States a billion dollars as utility companies buried and rerouted power lines, and fended off law suits. Many law suits were instituted. The Atlantic Legal Foundation, representing a number of distinguished amici in each case, filed briefs of amicus curiae in several key cases. The most crucial was before the supreme court of California where a Mr Covalt had sued San Diego Power and Light Company. The case was dismissed in this court. Mr Ford's case in a lower California Court was rejected on appeal. No legal case claiming an effect has ever survived appeal. *ALF believes that was largely due to its activities.* (Wilson 2004: 3, italics added)

Conclusion

While the sketch of vertically integrated expertise provided above is rather preliminary, it offers a useful metaphor to guide further research beyond static models of expertise. In particular, moving beyond monocentric models encourages greater sensitivity to social contexts and the processes involved when hybridization and blending of different forms of knowledge take place (Rip 2003). Most sociologically informed approaches to professionalization and expertise encourage examination of the ways experts endeavor to set the boundaries between themselves and competing experts and non-experts (Gieryn 1998) and have often emphasized that there have been trends for the increased specialization of expertise and appeals to mechanical rule-based forms of objectivity (Porter 1995). The vertical integration of expertise highlights the need to keep in mind the flexibility of boundary maintenance and the ways in which ideals of objectivity may be interpreted (Timmermans and Berg 2003). For instance, drawing from traditional models of expertise, hyper-experts such as Repacholi and Foster could appear vulnerable to criticisms that they are speaking beyond their appropriate specialist domain, or that they have conflicts of interest and therefore lack objectivity. But while these criticisms are possible they overlook that hyper-experts may claim legitimacy for their expertise by claiming that the breadth of their knowledge places them in a unique position to set the standards for, and judge what counts as, relevant and objective knowledge. The political implications of legitimating expertise in this way, and the processes required to create and sustain such forms of expertise, warrant further study.

Notes

1   It is important at this juncture, nevertheless, to indicate that it is not my intention in the current discussion to criticize Foster or Repacholi or other experts who have taken on multiple roles in the EMF/RF debate.
2   *Covalt v San Diego Gas & Electric Co.*, 55 Cal.Rptr.2d 724, 920 P.2d 669 (1996).
3   *Ford v Pacific Gas & Electricity Co.* 70 Cal.Rptr.2d 359 (1997).
4   In the matter of the resource management act 1991 and in the matter of appeal under section 120 of the act between Shirley Primary School (rma 343/96) and Telecom Mobile Communications Limited (rma 429/97), Decision No: C136/98, Environment Court of New Zealand, Judge JR Jackson (presiding), Mrs R Grigg, Ms N Burley.

Amicus curiae briefs

Brief amici curiae of Robert K. Adair et al. in support of Petitioner (*Covalt* 1996).
Brief amici curiae of Eleanor R. Adair et al. in support of the Defendant-Respondent (*Ford* 1997).
Brief amici curiae of Bruce N. Ames et al. for the petitioner (*Joiner* 1997).
Brief amici curiae of Nicolaas Bloembergen et al. in support of Respondents (*Daubert* 1993).
Brief amicus curiae of Stephen N. Bobo et al. in support of Petitioner (*Kumho* 1999).

Chapter 6

Jackson Pollock, Judge Pollak, and the Dilemma of Fingerprint Expertise

Simon A. Cole

Introduction

One day in 1992—or it may have been 1993—a long haul truck driver named Teri Horton walked into Dot's Thrift Shop in San Bernardino, California. Inside, she found a large, stretched canvas painting that was 'so ugly' that she decided to buy it as a gag for a depressed friend. Horton paid US$5 for the painting. At first glance, the painting looked like the result of a child hurling paint at the canvas. But, of course, when they first appeared, in the 1940s, that was an invective often flung at the now world famous drip paintings of Jackson Pollock (Reed 2003; Sauerwein 2003).

In 1989, an authenticated Pollock drip painting of similar size sold for US$11.5 million (Sauerwein 2003). After art connoisseurs pointed out the resemblance of her painting to authenticated Pollocks, Horton set about trying to authenticate her painting. This was not due to an artistic awakening analogous to that of the art world at large, which at first despised Pollock and then embraced him. Says Horton: 'I still think it's ugly, but now I see it with dollar signs' (Reed 2003).

Several art experts noted the similarity of the Horton painting to authenticated Pollocks. The artist's brother Charles lived in the area of Southern California near where the painting was purchased. Charles Pollock died in 1991. According to Horton's son Bill, the owner of Dot's Thrift Shop claims to have purchased the painting at an estate sale in Victorville, California (Biró 2003).

Sometime before April 2001, Horton had the painting examined by Peter Paul Biró, a forensic art expert. In addition to taking paint samples and so on, Biró located hairs and two fingerprints on the painting. One fingerprint, on the painted side of the canvas, Biró deemed insufficient for identification. The second fingerprint, on the back of the canvas, contained 16 'identifiable characteristics,' which Biró found sufficient for identification.

Biró first sought to match the Horton fingerprint to fingerprints he identified in art book reproductions of Pollock's work. Due to the intimate nature of Pollock's painting style, Biró was able to discern Pollock's (presumably) fingerprints in Pollock's own paintings. Using digital enhancement technology to remove the effects of the weave of the canvas and the offset dots from reproduction and to image the prints in 3-D, Biró found 12 corresponding characteristics between the Horton print and a print found in a reproduction in Varnedoe (1998) of 304 [Red Painting 4], 'an undisputed Pollock'.

Interestingly, because Biró was working from a reproduction, his 'known' print was not to scale. Upon scaling the known print, he found that it was 'larger than expected'. Biró was forced to posit an ad hoc hypothesis: that Pollock's finger was swollen through trauma such as an insect sting or bite or injury when he left the print in Red Painting 4. Still somewhat 'uncomfortable' with this fingerprint match, Biró sought corroborative evidence. He obtained permission to canvas Pollock's East Hampton, New York studio, which has been preserved as a historic site, for fingerprints.

Biró located 33 fingerprints, preserved in paint, in Pollock's studio. Among these he was able to find one—discovered on a paint can in the studio—showing ridge detail matching the Horton print. Biró does not say how many corresponding ridge characteristics he found between the Horton print and the print on the paint can, but he does report that it was 'a match'. This conclusion was later confirmed by André Turcotte, a fingerprint examiner for the Royal Canadian Mounted Police.

In the meantime, Horton submitted the painting for authentication to the International Foundation for Art Research (IFAR), a New York non-profit organization that authenticates art. In June 2003, IFAR issued a report denying authenticity. While the report has not been made public, media accounts report that IFAR objected to the painting's lack of 'provenance'—that is, a documented history of ownership (Davis 2003; Sauerwein 2003). According to Biró, IFAR also noted the use of acrylic paint, a commercially primed canvas, and lack of a 'bare' border (that is, a less densely painted border which would suggest that the canvas was cut *before* painting), each of which it deemed inconsistent with Pollock's work habits during the drip period. In rebuttal to the latter points, Biró musters historical evidence indicating that Pollock was indiscriminate in his choice of surfaces and paints and that, while his larger canvases were painted 'from the inside out' and showed bare borders, on the smaller canvases, 'the trajectories of flying paint extend beyond the bounds of the canvas'. He also performed chemical analyses which revealed both acrylic paint in Pollock's East Hampton studio and non-acrylic paint (though acrylic is also present) in the Horton painting (Biró 2003).

Fingerprints v provenance

The attraction of this story for a book on expertise, of course, lies in its fascinating juxtaposition of expert knowledges: the fingerprint versus provenance. In this story, one form of expertise, forensic science, appears to be 'hard,' 'scientific,' based on sample scrapings, microscopy, digital imaging tools, chemical assays. The other, art connoisseurship, seems 'soft,' humanistic, based on texts and documents, visual inspections, educated interpretations of an artist's seemingly ineffable 'style.' One can sympathize with Biró's scientist frustration with IFAR and his 'sincere hope that the forensic evidence described here will be weighed, examined and accorded the same consideration as scientific evidence normally is in the many venues of daily life' (Biró 2003). One can similarly sympathize with Horton, who somewhat more bluntly describes IFAR as 'a monopoly that has never authenticated one Pollock painting, and that of course raises prices. They can take a hike. I'm going the scientific route' (Reed 2003). IFAR has not helped its case with its obscurity—its refusal to publish its report or even identify its authors, the lack of evidence the authors offer other than the simple conclusion, 'I don't feel that this is a painting by Pollock's hand' (quoted in Biró 2003). But, interestingly, thus far the soft science has won. In the art world, IFAR has 'the last word on genuine works' (Reed 2003), and Horton has been unable to convert her painting into the dollars she covets. Art, apparently, is one of the few remaining fields in which humanists outweigh scientists.

And yet, the distinction between hard and soft science turns out to be not quite as clear as it might at first seem. The juxtaposition of fingerprint identification and art connoisseurship in the case of the disputed Pollock caught my eye for another reason: its uncanny echoing of events surrounding a different Pollak. This Pollak is not as well known as Jackson, perhaps, but quite eminent in his own right: Louis Pollak, federal Judge in the Eastern District of Pennsylvania, former Dean of Yale and University of Pennsylvania Law Schools. Around a year earlier, in March 2002, in what has by now become an influential ruling on the admissibility of forensic fingerprint identification, *United States v Llera Plaza,* Judge Pollak, in words that were quickly picked up by the legal press (Duffy 2002), wrote:

> I conclude that the fingerprint community's "general acceptance" of ACE-V [Analyze, Compare, Evaluate—Verify, fingerprint examiners' term for their source attribution methodology] should not be discounted because fingerprint specialists like accountants, vocational experts, accident reconstruction experts, appraisers of land or of art, experts in tire failure analysis, or others have "technical, or other specialized knowledge", rather than "scientific ... knowledge", and hence are not members of what *Daubert* termed a "scientific community".[1]

Legally, this passage is of minor importance and also wrong.[2] But the words themselves are startling. How could fingerprint examiners not be a scientific community and be analogized to art and land appraisers?

The *Llera Plaza* opinion quoted above was in fact the second *Llera Plaza* opinion that Judge Pollak had written within the space of three months. The first opinion, issued on 7 January, was the true 'landmark' decision in that it was the first legal decision anywhere to limit the admissibility of expert testimony by forensic fingerprint examiners. Judge Pollak found that forensic fingerprint identification failed to meet the *Daubert/Kumho* standard set down by the United States Supreme Court for admissibility of expert scientific, technical, or specialized evidence.[3] In light of fingerprint evidence's long history of courtroom use and broad presumption of reliability, Judge Pollak, instead of excluding the evidence altogether, limited the scope of fingerprint examiners' final conclusions—their attributions of source. In the 13 March opinion, Judge Pollak withdrew those limitations, though he reiterated, and even explicated, his opinion that fingerprint evidence was not science, as well as his finding that forensic fingerprint evidence failed to meet some of the *Daubert/Kumho* prongs including, notably, the 'testing' prong.

Though the fingerprint community celebrated the reversal by the eminent jurist as a great victory in the ongoing war over the validity of fingerprint identification, it may more interestingly be read as a watershed in the ongoing *diminution* of fingerprint examiners' claims to expert knowledge. Though fingerprint examiners retained their legal warrant to testify as expert witnesses in *Llera Plaza II*, as the second decision has come to be called, they did so as nonscientists and with a degree of expert knowledge that was analogized not to, say, forensic DNA analysts or mathematicians as they might have preferred, but to land and art appraisers. This marked a rather stunning demotion for a brand of expertise that scarcely a year and a half earlier had been described by a sister federal district court as providing 'the very archetype of reliable expert testimony'.[4]

Until *Llera Plaza II,* we might have thought that history would read *Llera Plaza I* as a significant milestone in the eventual exclusion, or abandonment, of fingerprint evidence. That no longer appears to be the case. But history may well read *Llera Plaza II* as a significant milestone in the reconfiguration of fingerprint examiners' knowledge claims, from something commonly understood as 'science' to something closer to what is commonly called 'appraisal.' In order to understand this reconfiguration, it is necessary to briefly explore the history of how the testimony of fingerprint examiners has been conceptualized as expert knowledge by courts.

Background

In the beginning, there was a brief period in which it was thought that the interpretation of forensic fingerprint identification might not require expert interpretation at all. Sir Francis Galton (1893), a pioneer of the technique, predicted that expert testimony regarding fingerprint evidence would only be required for a short period of time. Once the novelty of the technique had worn off and laypersons were familiar with the idea of fingerprints, the evidence might simply be submitted to the jury for analysis and comparison. The evidence, in short, would speak for itself, rather than having expert testimony speak in its place. In *Emperor v Abdul Hamid* (1905), an impersonation case in India, for example, although expert testimony was offered by the prosecution, the judges and assessors examined the fingerprints themselves and considered themselves fully qualified to render opinions agreeing or disagreeing with the expert (Cole 1998).

The period after the turn of the century was characterized by the efforts of a group of individuals calling themselves 'fingerprint experts'—consisting mostly of clerks in police identification bureaus who, in the process of maintaining criminal records indexed according to inked fingerprint patterns, had acquired familiarity with fingerprint patterns—to preclude this type of lay interpretation of fingerprint evidence. Fingerprint examiners were seeking to win exclusive 'jurisdiction' over the field of forensic fingerprint identification (Abbott 1988). But the goal was not only to fend off rival experts but also to ensure that the area was considered a proper subject of expert, as opposed to common, knowledge. This move proved remarkably successful. Anglo–American courts (and, so far as I know, those elsewhere) affirmed not only the admissibility of forensic fingerprint evidence but also self-professed fingerprint experts' authority to interpret fingerprint evidence. At the same time, fingerprint evidence was distinguished—forever, not for the limited period Galton suggested—from types of evidence that *were* subject to lay expertise, such as footprints. As the Court wrote in *People v Jennings* (1911), the earliest US appellate decision upholding the admissibility of expert evidence concerning fingerprints:

> In view of the knowledge and experience of men in identifying by footprints as compared with their knowledge and experience in identifying finger prints, it is manifest that opinions by experts might be entirely proper as to the latter class of testimony when they would not be with reference to footprints. The jury, if the facts were all stated, would be able to draw conclusions as to footprints as well as could expert witnesses.[5]

The *Jennings* Court was also clear that the claimed expertise of fingerprint examiners was to be treated as a claim of *scientific* knowledge:

> [S]tandard authorities on scientific subjects discuss the use of finger prints as a system of identification, concluding that experience has shown it to be reliable. (*Jennings* 1911: 1081)

And,

> From the evidence in this record we are disposed to hold that the classification of finger print impressions and their method of identification is a science requiring study. (*Jennings* 1911: 1083)

Other early cases were equally clear that fingerprint evidence was to be evaluated as 'science'.[6]

At the same time, there was a small amount of contestation by rival experts. One of the few challenges to these new 'fingerprint experts' illuminates the nature of the expertise that was being constructed. Two experts sought to supersede the expertise of fingerprint examiners on the grounds of having greater scientific training. One was Henry Faulds, a physician who had played an important pioneering role in the development of the British system of fingerprint identification and in articulating both the idea and practice of forensic fingerprint identification (Beavan 2001). The second was John Garson, also scientifically credentialed, who ran the Home Office's Identification Bureau. In government hearings on identification (Belper et al. 1901) and, most notably, at the 1905 Deptford Murder Trial, Faulds and Garson challenged the notion that fingerprint identification should be left in the hands of police personnel without scientific training (Joseph 2001). Garson insisted on calling the identification office a 'laboratory,' and argued that it should be headed by a scientist; his vision was challenged by a rival who successfully argued that biometric identification was more a bureaucratic function than a scientific one (Cole 2001: 92–3). Both Garson and Faulds criticized the Crown's evidence in the Deptford Murder Trial, arguing that forensic fingerprint identification should be performed by scientific men like themselves rather than by, as Faulds put it, 'subordinate officials untrained in scientific observation' (Faulds 1905: v).

Garson and Faulds's scientistic vision did not succeed. Overwhelmingly, 'fingerprint experts' were police and prison officials without scientific training, whose expertise was experience-based. The claim to expertise voiced by the rank-and-file fingerprint examiner was not as a scientist, as such, but as one who applied a science that had been established by other persons. Knowledge, about say the anatomy of friction ridges or the statistical basis for making an identification, was irrelevant. The visual skill of fingerprint identification, the acuity at recognizing and matching friction ridge features, was supposedly acquired through experience and only through experience. One could not identify fingerprints without experience no matter how much scientific knowledge one had.

As fingerprint identification became increasingly familiar and increasingly taken for granted in the courts, a curious ambiguity arose about whether fingerprint evidence was 'opinion' evidence. In both their own literature and courtroom testimony, fingerprint examiners sought to distinguish their conclusions from 'opinions' and to suggest that they were more akin to 'facts.' The rationale for this seemingly curious move was twofold. First, the conclusions of fingerprint examiners were expressed in positive terms without allowing any room for error or doubt. Therefore, they were distinguished from what we would today consider the 'proper' expression of other types of expert testimony through the use of disclaimers like 'to a medical certainty' or 'in my expert opinion.' At the *Jennings* trial, for example, one witness, Edward Foster, made this point quite forcefully:

> Q: In comparing these fingers it is your opinion that the lines in those photographs were made by the same person?
> A: I am positive. It is not my opinion. (1910: 139)

Second, the conclusions of fingerprint examiners were presented as indisputable. In other words, fingerprint examiners were supposed to restrict themselves to conclusions that were so unambiguous that no qualified examiner would testify against them: 'The testimony of a finger print expert is not subject to contradiction by another finger print expert, for the reason ... that the print is from the person' (Kuhne 1917: iv). And, 'The finger print expert has only facts to consider; he reports simply what he finds' (Gribben 1919).

Mnookin (2001) has convincingly argued that the reason for this strengthening of fingerprint examiners' conclusions lies in the judicial world's disappointed expectations for scientific evidence around the time that fingerprint evidence was introduced. Legal scholars were shocked and disappointed to discover that scientific evidence, far from bringing a burst of clarity to questions of fact, tended to confuse matters even more. Fingerprint identification was the first, and perhaps the only, form of evidence to present itself as an escape to this problem: an unambiguous form of evidence, offering clear truths, unmarred by the 'dueling experts' syndrome. And, judges, therefore, anointed it as a virtually infallible form of evidence (Cole 2004).

This engendered a potential legal paradox in that expert witnesses are supposed to testify only to opinions and never to facts. This paradox was not seized upon by anyone, however, until an Iowa burglary case, *State v Steffen* (1930) in which an overzealous prosecutor forced it upon the Court with direct examination like the following:

> Q: Now, you may examine Exhibit 4, the glass, your comparison of that print found that particular glass with the finger print taken from the left index finger of Steffen. I will ask you to state whether or not you are able to say whether or not those two prints, the one on the glass, and the one you took from the finger of Clem Steffen, were both made by the same finger? (Objected to as incompetent, immaterial, and irrelevant, calling for an ultimate fact to be determined by the jury. Overruled. Defendant excepts.)
>
> A: They were.
>
> Q: What is the fact? (Objected to as incompetent, immaterial and irrelevant, calling for an ultimate fact to be determined by the jury. Overruled. Defendant excepts.)
>
> A: They are the same.[7]

Given this testimony and several exchanges like it, the Supreme Court of Iowa had little choice but to take up the vexing question of whether fingerprint evidence really was opinion evidence and, if not, whether it was proper expert testimony. It was also forced to address the somewhat less vexing question of whether a fingerprint examiner might testify to the ultimate fact.

Five judges voted to reverse Steffen's conviction, in part because the fingerprint expert had strayed into the province of the jury by testifying to the ultimate fact. Three judges dissented, principally because 'whether the finger prints were the same is not the ultimate fact in this case. The ultimate fact is whether or not the defendant was guilty of the crime charged, and the evidence relative to finger prints was a mere item of evidence' (539). Since this is a valid argument, we can only assume that the majority was taking the position that identification evidence, under such circumstances where there is no 'legitimate access' defense available (that is, no innocent explanation for the presence of the identifying material), is tantamount to the ultimate fact. In addition, the majority referred to *Jennings*, writing 'It is to be noticed that in the *Jennings* case the expert witnesses, with the possible exception of one, testified to their judgment, belief, or opinion ...' (538). The exception appears to be Foster, who I quoted above. Thus, the *Steffen* majority opinion may be interpreted as a reminder that fingerprint expert evidence remains opinion evidence.

Scientific v technical rhetoric

What, however, is the basis for this opinion evidence? Elsewhere I have argued that two general streams of thought have coexisted within the fingerprint community (Cole 1999). The first, which I have labeled a 'technical rhetoric,' holds that the fingerprint examiner is a technician, not a scientist, and the process of fingerprint identification is a routine, technical process. Fingerprint identification, in this mode, is something like an 'applied science.' Crucial to this rhetoric was something called a 'point standard,' a set number of corresponding friction ridge characteristics which enabled the examiner to conclude that the known and unknown samples derived from a common source. The technician was therefore able to refer to this point standard to vouch for her.

We have already heard the glimmerings of the critique of this position in the words of Garson and Faulds: fingerprint examiners should not be technicians; they should be scientists whose opinions about the common source of fingerprints is based on their own knowledge of the formation of friction ridge characteristics, their frequency in human fingertips and so on. If the fingerprint examiner is a scientist, point standards are improper and unnecessary; the question of when to reach the conclusion that two samples derive from a common source can be made simply on the basis of the individual examiner's knowledge and experience (Ashbaugh 1999).

The competition between these two positions became more heated beginning around the 1970s when some North American examiners became more vociferous in their opposition to the use of point standards. The movement gained significant ground in North America during the 1970s and 1980s, less so elsewhere. Despite the inroads made by scientific rhetoric, 'point counting' remained the way the vast majority of judges, attorneys, and the public *imagined* fingerprint opinions were formed.

The technical rhetoric implied that the point standard had been validated by some scientist somewhere; the technician was merely applying a validated standard. Fingerprinting's 'dirty little secret' was that this validation had never occurred. Unbeknownst to almost anyone other than fingerprint examiners themselves, the standards for declaring a match were:

1. Not empirically generated, but simply postulated by fiat; never subsequently tested against reality.
2. Not uniform; they varied from nation to nation, jurisdiction to jurisdiction, agency to agency.
3. Misleading, in that the number of similarities present is not really an accurate measure of the similarity of two prints.

An unheralded federal case, *United States v Parks* (1991), plainly illustrates the moment of one judge's awakening to the fact that fingerprint examiners' expertise was not the kind of expertise he had assumed it was.[8] In this case, the examiner opined that there were ten matching points between the latent and the known in the case at hand and that her personal minimum point standard was eight matching points. The judge remarked that, in his experience as a trial judge, the examiner's minimum had a curious way of always seeming to be *two less* than the number of matching points in the case at hand:

> THE COURT: I've never heard that eight number before yesterday, never; and I have heard 10 when it is 12. And I did predict that your testimony would come out, when asked, that you had 10, and that bothered me. I didn't like to have that prediction come true. It bothered me a lot. (*Parks* 1991: 554)

'The Court', therefore, demanded to know what the scientific literature stated the minimum point standard should be, but the examiner was unable to refer to any such literature.

> THE COURT: I want to know what the accepted level is generally. If all of the treatises of all the work done in this area says 10 is fine, that's fine; then 8 isn't fine. If it says 8 is fine, that's different. I don't know why I never heard 8 before if that's true ...
> There are books written by people who do this, I hope. If there aren't, it's a bad expertise and I'm just not going to have any more fingerprinting testimony. I don't think that's the fact.
> I think there are—there must be—some scholarly works. There must be, notwithstanding her testimony. There have to be some compilations of this. It cannot be that it was just an *ipse dixit*, that no two people have the same; it's simply not so. (*Parks* 1991: 555–6)

'The Court's' confusion and desperation are palpable:

> There are some studies; there have to be. If there aren't, then this is not a science and there are no experts in it. (*Parks* 1991: 555)

Sensing trouble, the government brought in a second examiner to explain the philosophy of having no minimum point standard to the judge:

> THE COURT: But what I want to know, outside the department—
> THE WITNESS: Okay.
> THE COURT:—what is the literature and what does it say?
> THE WITNESS: Okay. The thing you have there is that each department has their own goals of their own rules as far as the number of points being a make.
> I think the Sheriff—if I'm not mistaken, there's [sic] is a lot more than 10. I think there's [sic] is 12 or 15, if I'm not mistaken.
> Scotland Yard uses 18 [sic, actually 16] in order to have a comparison make, so that number really just varies from department to department.
> THE COURT: I don't think I'm ever going to use fingerprint testimony again; that simply won't do ...
> THE WITNESS: That just may be one of the problems of the field, but I think if there was a survey taken, you would probably get a different number from every department that has a fingerprint section as to their lowest number of points for a comparison and make.

THE COURT: That's the most incredible thing I've ever heard of. Is there no literature about it? (*Parks* 1991: 560–61)

The next day the government introduced a third fingerprint examiner to, in the judge's words, 'resuscitate these fingerprints' (*Parks* 1991: 567).

THE COURT: What is the largest number of points thought to be identical and thereby proven which indeed were erroneous?
THE WITNESS: Well, in my own experience—
THE COURT: There is no literature to this; nobody had ever studied this; we just don't know?
THE WITNESS: Okay. I can only relate to—
THE COURT: That's a question; it's not an answer. So far as you know, no study has ever been made to find out the largest number of points thought to be matching that were still erroneous?
THE WITNESS: I think there has [sic] been some studies by individuals that I don't think have ever been published, but I do remember when my employment with the Federal Bureau of Investigation, there were several 7-point identifications that—
First of all, the number of points doesn't mean too much, it's the location of the points and as they relate to each other. That means an awful lot more than the number itself. (*Parks* 1991: 569–70)

This last exchange perfectly illustrates the fingerprint community's dilemma. Those examiners who believed that the 'point system' was corrupt nonetheless continued to allow themselves and their colleagues to use it in court because it was so rhetorically useful. The point system provided an air of quantification, of precision, and of rigor that sat well with both judges and juries. In *Daubert* hearings, scientifically minded fingerprint examiners have claimed that 'points' are merely an explanatory device for the courtroom, 'a simplistic way of explaining the identification process to the jury', positing a disconnect between what goes on in the laboratory and in the courtroom.[9] In the *Parks* case, however, fingerprint examiners paid the price for this mild deception. Having allowed judges to persist in the delusion that identifications are vouched for by a certain number of corresponding points, fingerprint examiners are forced to defend this imaginary system. At times, the fingerprint examiners themselves get caught up in the illusion, as in the last exchange, where the examiner begins answering the question in terms of points, realizes that he is heading in a dangerous direction (will the interrupted paragraph end with testimony that 7-point matches have turned out to be erroneous?), and then returns to 'reality' by insisting that counting points is not the proper method.

Since the above colloquy dates from 1991, it offers a convenient snapshot of the situation on the eve of the seminal *Daubert v Merrell Dow* (1993) opinion. In 1993, the United States Supreme Court ruled that Federal Rule of Evidence 702 concerning scientific evidence had superseded the case law established by *Frye v United States* (1923).[10] Whereas *Frye* (1923: 1014) required 'general acceptance in the particular field' to which the expertise belongs, *Daubert* (1993: 589) required that evidence be 'not only relevant, but reliable'. *Daubert* imposed a 'gatekeeping' requirement on federal trial judges to ensure that scientific evidence put before fact-finders was 'reliable'. In order to demarcate reliable from unreliable science, the *Daubert* Court specified four (or five, or three, see Denbeaux and Risinger 2003: 31), non-binding guidelines:

1. Whether the theory or technique has been tested.
2. Whether the theory or technique has been subjected to peer review and publication.
3. Whether standards have been promulgated and error rates measured for the theory or technique.
4. Whether the theory or technique is generally accepted by the relevant scientific community. (*Daubert* 1993)

Kumho Tire v Carmichael (1999) extended *Daubert's* reliability requirement to non-scientific expert evidence.

Fingerprinting after *Daubert/Kumho*

Fingerprint examiners were no doubt somewhat befuddled at first as to how to go about vouching for their expertise. What did the famously vague *Daubert* guidelines mean, and how did they map onto fingerprint identification? The problem was exacerbated by the fact that neither fingerprint examiners themselves nor anyone else had ever sought to test fingerprint examiners' ability to accurately make source attributions. Fingerprint examiners could not therefore simply point to a peer reviewed and published validation study that established an error rate and a standard enjoying general acceptance in the scientific community. Three general lines of thought have emerged as to how fingerprint identification might pass *Daubert* muster:

1. Fingerprint examiners are scientists in that each fingerprint identification is akin to a scientific experiment.
2. Fingerprint examiners are applied scientists or technicians in that the requisite scientific knowledge has been developed by research/experimental scientists and fingerprint examiners operate within the strictures set down by these scientists.
3. Fingerprint examiners are skilled technicians, whose skills are rooted in experience, not in scientific knowledge. Their knowledge is no less reliable, though.

Fingerprint identifications (and criminal trials) as experiments

Characteristic of the first approach are somewhat tortured efforts to fit forensic fingerprint identification to some idealized version of 'the scientific method.' Thus, for example, David Ashbaugh (2002) describes forensic fingerprint identification as a seven-step process that, he claims, is indistinguishable from 'the scientific method' used by Newton himself. The steps are:

1.   Statement of Problem
2.   Hypothesis
3.   Observation
4.   Experimentation
5.   Conclusion
6.   Repetition
7.   Report

These steps, in Ashbaugh's view, are repeated with every latent fingerprint analysis. Fingerprint examiners are thus able to construe their process as scientific by restating the hypothesis from the general to the specific. Whereas defendants contend that the relevant falsifiable hypothesis is: 'Fingerprint examiners can accurately match latent fingerprint impressions to their correct source finger', fingerprint examiners restate the hypothesis as: 'This latent print belongs to this source finger'. This hypothesis is then 'tested' through 'experiment' (comparison). Replication is achieved by having a colleague 'verify' the conclusion. Falsificationist forensic scientists like Stoney (2001), however, point out that general claims can be tested through controlled experimentation, whereas specific claims cannot.

Indeed, were one to attempt to validate the methodology of forensic fingerprint identification in general—producing, presumably, a statement along the lines of 'When performed under such-and-such conditions, forensic fingerprint identification is accurate XX% of the time'—one would only be able to extrapolate that generalized error rate to the specific case at hand. Ashbaugh, in yet another of his many brilliant rhetorical moves, argues that such statistical generalizations (which are routine for DNA evidence) are prejudicial to the defendant. Ashbaugh (2002) paraphrases one of his own cross-examinations:

Q: Why can't you attach a probability to your conclusion in the way that a DNA expert would?
A: Because it wouldn't be fair to your client.

Ashbaugh suggests that the defendant is rendered safer by having the fingerprint examiner evaluate the specific case on its own merits. In other words, the fingerprint examiner must decide whether the specific evidence before him crosses his personal threshold of certainty, rather than take refuge in a generalized statistical statement that he is right XX per cent of the time, so he is probably right this time. Defendants are safer, he argues, if the examiner treats each comparison as a scientific experiment, than if the examiner treats the comparison as a routine process whose accuracy has been measured and attested to by someone else. And he may well be right.

Legal rulings

The legal parallel to the argument that each fingerprint analysis was a scientific experiment was the claim that each criminal trial was a scientific experiment testing the accuracy of the fingerprint examiner's source attribution. In *United States v Havvard* (2000: 854), the Court wrote, 'The methods of latent print identification have been tested. They have been tested for roughly 100 years. They have been tested in adversarial proceedings with the highest possible stakes—liberty and sometimes life'.

The *Havvard* interpretation stood for around a year until it was effectively refuted by the first *Llera Plaza* (2002) decision. The *Llera Plaza* Court ridiculed the notion of 'adversarial testing' noting that that could not possibly be what the Supreme Court meant by 'testing.' Forensic fingerprint identification failed to satisfy testing, peer review and publication, or standards and error rate. Fingerprint identification met only the last guideline, 'general acceptance,' but the Court noted that *Daubert* called for especially strict vigilance for a technique that met only this criterion. Using a strict reading of the *Daubert* guidelines, *Llera Plaza I* became the first US (or, for that matter anywhere) decision to flunk fingerprint identification.

The Government's Memorandum for reconsideration

The Government immediately filed a motion for reconsideration. The Government's Memorandum ('the Brief') was an extraordinary document in the degree to which it *diminishes* the expert knowledge claims of forensic fingerprint identification. Rather than arguing that fingerprint identification is 'the archetype of reliable expert testimony' under *Daubert/Kumho,* as did the *Havvard* Court, the Brief's principal argument is that *Daubert* actually set the bar lower than Judge Pollak set it. The Brief noted that the Advisory Committee Notes to Rule 702 state 'an expert opinion "not rely[ing] on anything like a scientific method" may be admissible, if "it is properly grounded, well-reasoned, and not speculative"' (Memorandum 2002: 3). 'FBI examiners express opinions based on a careful, scientific analysis, and that those opinions are relied upon throughout American law enforcement and civil communities', the Brief insisted. '*Daubert* demands no more' (Memorandum 2002: 26–7).

In *Daubert*, the Brief argued, the Supreme Court 'drew the line at what is colloquially referred to as "junk science", the attestations of purported experts without any reliable basis in fact or study. Apart from such extreme circumstances', the Brief argued citing the Third Circuit, 'the reliability "standard is not that high"' (Memorandum 2002: 16–17). The Brief's juxtaposition of types of expertise here is fascinating. The 'junk science' cited includes epidemiology, mechanical engineering, and meta-analysis. The Brief's use of epidemiology (*Joiner* 1997), meta-analysis (*Daubert* 1993), and mechanical engineering (*Kumho* 1999) as 'junk science' foils is especially interesting in light of Edmond and Mercer's demonstration that the construction of these specific forms of expertise as 'bad science' or 'inadmissible evidence' was far more contingent than either the legal opinions themselves or the mainstream scholarly accounts of them would have us believe (Edmond 2002c; Edmond and Mercer 2000). But certainly, all of these fields enjoy greater superficial trappings of 'science' than does fingerprint identification, which is generally practiced by high-school graduates, lacks degree programs in universities, and whose journals do not look as 'scientific' as do, say, epidemiology journals.

Similarly, the Brief cited the admissibility of psychological testimony: 'it cannot be said that a judicial system which accepts expert opinions based on, say, a psychologist's view regarding a patient's mental disease, will not accept an opinion based on a test with such a proven success rate' (Memorandum 2002: 46). Here the Brief referred to the longstanding admissibility of many forms of psychological testimony, despite a lack of evidence of its accuracy or even substantial evidence of its inaccuracy. Most notorious in this regard is the *Barefoot v Estelle* (1983: 920–21) case in which the Supreme Court upheld the admissibility of psychiatric testimony predicting future dangerousness, despite an *amicus curiae* brief by the American Psychiatric Association stating that their 'best estimate' was that predictions of future dangerousness were incorrect two out of three times, or more often than not.[11] The Brief's implicit appeal to the *Barefoot* standard—that even reliability is not necessary for expert testimony—for *fingerprint identification*, of all things, is nothing short of extraordinary.

Invoking the supposed liberality of *Daubert*, the Brief seeks to establish an irony in holding inadmissible under *Daubert* a technique which was (presumably, though not explicitly) admissible under *Frye* because 'fingerprint identification is the paradigm [by which it presumably means 'paragon'] of a "generally accepted" test' (Memorandum 2002: 15). Since '*Daubert* was aimed at expanding, not restricting, the admissibility of expert opinion' (Memorandum 2002: 14), the Brief claimed

> [i]t would thus be incongruous, to say the least, if a method of evaluation which has received such overwhelming acceptance and consistent use as the FBI's identification method would fail under a rule of evidence meant to be *less* stringent than the general acceptance test of *Frye*. (Memorandum 2002: 16)

While it is true that evidence scholars initially perceived *Daubert* as more liberal than *Frye* (because it might take time for reliable evidence to gain general acceptance), they now generally recognize that 'reliability,' in many if not most cases, is a more stringent requirement than 'general acceptance' (Cranor and Eastmond 2001; Graham 2000; Saks 1998). Moreover, the Brief's incongruity is somewhat disingenuous, in that fingerprinting is not, as the Brief implicitly suggests, a technique that was *inadmissible* under *Frye* that should be admitted under the 'more liberal' *Daubert* standard. Rather, fingerprinting is a technique that was *admissible* under *Frye* because it passed the general acceptance test without having had to demonstrate its efficacy.

In general, the Brief, despite the aggressive tone that is customary for a legal argument, may be viewed as a significant retreat. Fingerprint identification is no longer held out as the epitome of science. While fingerprint examiners on the sideline boldly denounced the so-called *Kumho* exemption—asking to be held to a lower standard in exchange for giving up the claim to the mantle of 'science' and accepting a designation as 'technical' or 'specialized' knowledge—as 'the chicken's way out' (Pat Wetheim quoted in Cho 2002), the Brief barely even argued this point and in fact conceded it, calling fingerprint examiners' expertise 'an amalgam' of 'scientific, technical, or other specialized knowledge' (Memorandum 2002: 50, n. 13). Rather than suggesting, as the Government did in *Mitchell* and *Havvard,* that fingerprinting passes all the *Daubert/Kumho* factors with flying colors, the Brief sought exemption from the factors. It asked the Court for a weak reading of *Daubert* in which there is but one factor: reliability. Even this factor fingerprint examiners cannot meet, so 'reliability' was watered down to 'good grounds.' That fingerprint examiners, for nearly a century the so-called '"gold standard" of forensic scientific evidence', should profess little more than 'good grounds' for their opinions itself signals a dramatic reversal of fortune (Lynch in this volume) and demonstrates how much anxiety the first *Llera Plaza* decision generated.[12]

Llera Plaza II

The *Llera Plaza* Court reversed its decision less than two months later, issuing a second, equally lengthy, decision known as *Llera Plaza II*. Nonetheless, *Llera Plaza II* let quite a few things stand from *Llera Plaza I*. Forensic fingerprint identification was still not a 'science' though it was 'rooted in science'; its admissibility, therefore, fell under *Kumho*, not *Daubert*. Forensic fingerprint identification continued to fail the testing criterion. Fingerprint examiners' ability to express conclusions was restored, not because fingerprint identification met the *Daubert/Kumho* guidelines, but because the Court acceded to the government's request that it exercise its discretion to ignore them and engage instead in a 'flexible' analysis of the technique's reliability. In so doing, *Llera Plaza II* marks a significant development in the discourse surrounding fingerprint examiners' expertise.

Interestingly, what little evidence there is from the brief period during which *Llera Plaza I* stood suggests that it would not have had a very big impact within the legal community. At least one court saw fit to completely dismiss the 60-page *Llera Plaza I* opinion in a few short paragraphs.[13] It even defended the *Havvard* Court's notion of 'adversarial testing,' seemingly so effectively demolished by *Llera Plaza I*. Had the *Llera Plaza* Court not reversed itself, it may well have been dismissed as an outlier among the tide of less exhaustive opinions upholding the admissibility of fingerprint evidence. In reversing, in yet another 60-page opinion, however, *Llera Plaza II* has usurped *Havvard* as the most definitive post-*Daubert* decision. Paradoxically, in so doing, the *Llera Plaza* Court may have done more damage to forensic fingerprint identification than if it had let *Llera Plaza I* stand. This is because under *Llera Plaza II* fingerprint expertise, though admissible, is no longer 'the archetype of reliable evidence'. Nor is it some sort of Popperian, tested-through-experiment type of expertise. Instead, fingerprint examiners' opinions are admissible, not because they have survived falsification nor because they are derived from scientific experiments, but merely because the Court, based on a potpourri of non-dispositive pieces of evidence, has concluded that fingerprint examiners probably do have some sort of expert knowledge.

Fingerprint examiners, then, were to be admitted as experts, but not as the sort of archetypal, faux-Newtonian/Popperian experts constructed by the *Havvard* Court. *Llera Plaza II* abandoned the strict reading of *Daubert* adopted in *Llera Plaza I* and emphasized the flexibility called for in *Daubert* and even more so in *Kumho*. Without going into the—rather bizarre and perplexing—specifics that led the Court to 'change its mind' (see Cole 2004), it appears that—far more than the government's 'new evidence' of previously unknown proficiency testing conducted by and at the FBI, evidence which was effectively demolished by defence witnesses—it may have been the government's reduction of the threshold to 'good grounds' that persuaded the Court. Hence the Court's remarkable comparison of fingerprint examiners to land and art appraisers.

Fingerprint identification and art appraisal

By now, the resonance of Judge Pollak's analogy between fingerprint identification and art appraisal should be clear. Fingerprint identification, like connoisseurship (as opposed to appraisal, which seeks to calculate the value of an artwork), is a process of *source attribution*. A fingerprint impression was made by Carlos Llera Plaza's finger. A painting was made by Jackson Pollock's hand. It has long been held that connoisseurship relies on a *gestalt* judgment, rather than on the application of specific measurements or standards. Of course, connoisseurs can identify reasons for their conclusions and communicate these reasons to one another, their clients, and the general public, e.g. 'the style, colours or material are consistent with Pollock.' But connoisseurs would never allow the existence of any algorithmic method for making source attributions, e.g. 'any painting bearing seven of the following nine characteristics may be attributed to Pollock.' Thus, while connoisseurs might identify rules of method of making source attributions—e.g. 'brushstrokes, colour palette, materials, and subject matter are important'—they would always reserve the right to make final judgments for themselves, on the basis of an overall evaluation of all the available evidence, rather than grant it to the rules. At some point in a competent cross examination, a connoisseur would be forced to fall back on a modification of Justice Stewart's famous line about pornography: '[I am an expert, and] I know a Pollock when I see it'.[14]

Fingerprint examiners—reasonably, one might argue—do much the same thing. As described above, rules governing source attributions have proven just as problematic for fingerprint examiners as they have for connoisseurs. Erroneous source attributions have purportedly occurred even under the 16-point standard (Jofre 2001). And, many potentially correct source attributions are probably lost due to strict adherence to a point standard (Champod 1995). In short, a fingerprint match is more like a medical diagnosis than like the output of scientific instrument. That fingerprint expertise, like connoisseurship, relies on subjective, expert judgment does not, of course, invalidate its knowledge claims. Indeed, etymologists would be surprised by any claim that connoisseurship is not knowledge. The problem, however, is that somehow the courts, the general public, and many fingerprint examiners themselves have acquired the mistaken impression that fingerprint examiners do something qualitatively different from exercise experience-based judgment. The quantitative point system conveyed an air of precision that turned out to be misleading, to the great surprise of at least one judge. The *gestalt* system is less explicitly misleading, but, even under that system, fingerprint examiners' inflated claims to accuracy (through signifiers like the term 'positive identification' and 'zero error rate') imply that fingerprint matches are something more than expert judgments.

Testing, the first and perhaps most important of the *Daubert/Kumho* prongs, poses difficulties for both connoisseurs and fingerprint examiners. Since both are fields of expertise that claim proficiency at source attribution, tests of their claimed skills are easy to envision: the expert is provided with exemplars whose true sources are known to the test-giver, and asked to attribute them to the correct source among a set of possible sources, whose true source is also known. But, of course, it would not be feasible to devise such a test for the claimed expertise of connoisseurship simply because the universe of authenticated Pollocks is not large enough.[15] Testing of fingerprint examiners' claimed expertise poses no such insurmountable difficulties, although a well-designed testing regime would certainly be a sizable undertaking (Faigman 2002). To be sure, sociologists of science have demonstrated that determined advocates could contest the interpretation of the results of any such tests (Collins 1985). But during the century over which fingerprint identification has been used for forensic identification, no such testing has ever been attempted. There are various reasons for this, too complicated to explore here, though primary among them is that courts have not *demanded* such tests (Cole 2001).

Thus, neither connoisseurs nor fingerprint examiners can point to rules that govern their source attributions. Further, neither connoisseurs nor fingerprint examiners can point to validation studies that establish a confidence level to attach to their source attributions. On what basis, then, and with what degree of confidence, ought we to believe these experts' source attributions? In the end, it comes down to trusting the experts. Connoisseurs respond to this dilemma through certificates. Confidence in connoisseurs is generally based on the certificates they possess, e.g. degrees in art history, perceived expertise in the subject area as attested by respected peers, experience studying and working in the subject area, and, crucially, the lack of known misattributions. Of course, it is well understood that it would be difficult to expose a misattribution since in most cases the 'ground truth' is usually established by the various experts who make the attribution; as noted above, connoisseurs usually have 'the last word' on source attributions (Reed 2003).

No one is surprised to learn that our confidence in connoisseurs derives from nothing better than certificates; but it has come as a great surprise to many to find that the same is true of fingerprint examiners. Lacking standards or validation studies, in the final analysis our confidence in fingerprint examiners' source attributions is based on certificates: voluntary certification programs, individual proficiency testing, years of experience, laboratory quality control procedures and the number of known misattributions.[16]

That an expert's knowledge claims can be supported by nothing more than certificates does not, of course, necessarily imply a lack of expertise, nor that the expert should be prevented from testifying in court. One could presumably generate general agreement that a professor of art history with expertise in the work of Pollock should be permitted to testify in a putative civil case involving the Horton painting. But knowledge vouched for by certificates does imply limits on the sorts of knowledge claims the expert could reasonably make. One could presumably also generate general agreement that the art history professor should not be permitted to testify that she has scientifically determined that Pollock painted the Horton painting or that the Horton painting *is* a Pollock.

But while we easily accept this sort of expert knowledge from art historians, we seem to have difficulty accepting it from fingerprint examiners. Historically, courts have overvalued fingerprint evidence (Cole 2004). Today, the idea that 'the matching of prints is an art rather than an exact science' is regarded as a scandal (Osborne 2002).

We can see, then, that the seeming opposition of 'scientific' knowledge as embodied by fingerprint analysis and 'softer' knowledge as embodied by connoisseurship is not as clear-cut as it first appeared. Indeed, even Biró's account of his investigation strangely mixes 'hard' and 'soft' knowledge claims. Biró uses connoisseurship himself and claims a sort of 'hybrid knowledge' (Valverde 2003) that makes it sound a lot like the *gestalt* method usually attributed to connoisseurs: 'In addition to traditional connoisseurship, my specializations embrace a forensic approach coupled with modern scientific methods of detection that are not specific to any individual artist but rather encompass elements universal to them—the artistic process' (Biró 2003). As evidence of Pollock's authorship, Biró created a collage composed from the Horton painting and Number 5, claiming, 'Selection of colours and their relationship to each other are highly comparable' (Biró 2003). Biró's collage recalls the notorious fingerprint collage created by Bertillon in 1912 to question fingerprint identification's claims to reliability, fabricated prints from different sources that purportedly showed 16 points in common (Champod et al. 1993; Evett and Williams 1996). On another occasion, Biró juxtaposes two details from the Horton print and one from an authenticated Pollock, claiming 'The behaviour and form of the paints in both images appear identical' (Biró 2003). The claim is reminiscent of fingerprint examiners' claim that two prints, which—due to pressure distortion and the fact that one is latent and one is inked—are, in any lay understanding of the term, clearly not 'identical' at all, are 'identical' because they have been attributed to a common source.

Biró's deployment of fingerprint analysis, meanwhile, as is normal for fingerprint analysis, hardly adopts the canonical method of scientific investigation. On the first fingerprint match, Biró does not specify the point threshold at which he would reach a conclusion of a match noting only that 'The number of points that have to match is not universally agreed on; however, 6 to 8 points are often sufficient' (Biró 2003), a rather understated account of the vexing nature of this problem. The statement is typical of the fingerprint community's pronouncements in this area: a statement that sounds definitive when read as a whole, but, on closer inspections, turns out to be laden with imprecision (does '6 to 8' mean 6,7, or 8?) and caveats ('often'). On the second match, Biró admits that he had 'memorized' the Horton print to which he was trying to match the prints from Pollock's studio. To any canonical scientist this would raise immediate bias problems, but fingerprint examiners—and, indeed, forensic scientists in general (Risinger et al. 2002)—dismiss such concerns. Similarly, Biró has the match confirmed by a professional fingerprint examiner, again evincing no apparent concerns about bias or efforts to blind the confirming examiner. Finally, Biró's report is curiously open about his own potential biases. 'It has been my privilege to work on this project', he notes, and he characterizes Horton as having 'persevered in her brilliant and single-minded pursuit of what she perceived as being right', when Horton herself admits, understandably, to being solely interested in money, rather than truth (Biró 2003; Reed 2003).

Connoisseurship and fingerprinting

That a connection might be drawn between connoisseurship and fingerprint identification would come as no surprise to the historian Carlo Ginzburg, who makes precisely that connection in his famous essay linking the 19th century art connoisseur Giovanni Morelli with Freud, Sherlock Holmes, and fingerprint identification. Morelli felt that attributions could be made more accurately by looking at seemingly minor details, such as earlobes and fingernails, rather than the signature attributes of an artist's style, such as the smiles of Leonardo's women (Ginzburg 1983: 81–2). The discussion is especially interesting when it concerns Pollock's drip paintings, which, to some, epitomize the familiar criticism of modern art—that 'anyone could do it.' Others argue that Pollock's drip paintings are not nearly so haphazard as they appear. Indeed, the art critic Robert Hughes once claimed 'It is impossible to make a forgery of Jackson Pollock's work' (quoted in Biró 2003). Biró himself echoes Morelli, writing,

> A forger could not create the innate flow and rhythm of patterns and combination of colors that came naturally only for Pollock. His painting 'ritual' arose from his unique personal temperament, intellect and psyche—each determining factors that cannot be designed at will without the design effort showing through in an actual attempt to imitate. (Biró 2003)

These sentiments echo those with which fingerprint examiner G. Tyler Mairs (1945) supported the uniqueness of fingerprint patterns:

> Duplication is impossible because of the inherent variability of controlling growth factors during fetal development. Even Nature cannot duplicate them as she has no "master mold" into which all human life can be poured. Each creation represents the master "blue print," but exhibits all the variables inherent in individual workmanship.

For Ginzburg, connoisseurship and fingerprint analysis share an epistemological approach that is rooted in medical diagnosis. Both claim to be able to determine authorship—of a painting or a fingerprint—through minute, involuntary traces. Connoisseurship and fingerprinting, Ginzburg argues, fall into the epistemological category characterized by the human sciences, which split off from what he calls a Galilean method (though Ginzburg is careful to note that this method was an ideal that may not even have been fulfilled by Galileo himself) that ignores individual differences in favor of experimental control, abstraction, quantification, and generalization. The human sciences, Ginzburg shows, are constantly dissuaded from making the leap into the Galilean model by the individual case. The minute differences between each individual case militate against the Galilean leap into generalization and abstraction. The paradigmatic human science, in this respect, is of course medicine, and medicine also provides the link between connoisseurship and fingerprinting (through the Czech physician Jan Purkynê, who was the first to sort friction ridge patterns into types) (1823).

This emphasis on the individual case is, of course, the reason clinicians' deployments of expert knowledge are always so maddeningly laced with caveats and uncertainties. And, of course, clinicians are the expert community that most prominently defies the *Daubert/Kumho* framework's narrowly Galilean conception of expert knowledge with its emphasis on testing, standards, and error rates. The implication of the government's *Llera Plaza* brief and *Llera Plaza II* that fingerprint examiners are in fact better understood as clinicians than as experimental scientists is consistent with Ginzburg's reading of the origins of the discipline. What Ginzburg's history suggests, but does not fully spell out, is why a confusion arose over which epistemological camp fingerprint identification fell into. This, in turn, might explain why people like myself think there is something the matter with forensic science (Cole 2004; Risinger et al. 2002). The distinctive attribute of *forensic*, as opposed to 'academic' science, is widely believed to be its emphasis on the specific rather than the general; forensic scientists deal in specific cases; academic scientists try to produce generalizable truths (Inman and Rudin 2001). This places forensic science squarely with the realm of the human sciences, in Ginzburg's typology, with their emphasis on the individual case. And, of course, this can readily be seen in fingerprint examiners' answer to critics' demands for standard: 'Show me the print'—universal standards cannot do justice to the individual case (Wertheim 1990: 66).

This is a perfectly reasonable response for a clinician to make; we would accept it from a physician. The trouble with forensic science, perhaps, is that, though it is a clinical form of expertise, it sometimes uses the same methods as Galilean experts like chemists. Forensic science has, therefore, become confused about its own epistemological origins and presented itself as Galilean science, when in fact it is clinical expertise. Thus, Ashbaugh's insistence that the individual case defies generalization is reasonable for a clinician; it is his attempt to map fingerprinting onto a Newtonian (which could just as well be Galilean) model of science that is misguided.

Conclusion

This confusion, of course, has real manifestations. One is seen in the way that fingerprint examiners express their conclusions. The conclusion of 'positive identification' is a Newtonian conclusion, not a clinical one. The mismatch is made even more apparent by the fact that fingerprint examiners deny the existence of measurement error, which would be fundamental for a Newtonian. Another manifestation is in the fingerprint community's casual approach toward certificates. Physicians, for example, have a strong enforcement of certificates— medical school is rigorous, boards are difficult, and so on—perhaps because they recognize that it is the foundation upon which their knowledge stands. Fingerprint examiners have neglected to build strong certification, which they are now hastily trying to erect, perhaps because they did not realize that it really was the foundation upon which their knowledge stands. Fingerprinting now stands at a crossroads. Statistically minded thinkers want to take it in a Galilean direction in which the confidence level attached to conclusions of identity could be quantified (Champod 1999; Champod and Evett 2001; Stoney 1985; Stoney 2001). The fingerprint community appears to prefer the clinician's route in which confidence is attested by the strength of quality control/quality assurance (QC/QA) measures. There is nothing necessarily wrong with the latter—indeed, it may be the better choice—but the confidence level with which fingerprint examiners should be permitted to express themselves would not be as high under such a regime, and it would be highly dependent on the rigor and independence of the QC/QA regime.

This comparative analysis of Pollock and Pollak's dilemmas suggests that some of the courts' most vexing problems concerning expert knowledge stem not, as is commonly stated in the legal discourse on *Daubert* and *Kumho*, from the inability to distinguish 'good' and 'bad' expertise (Faigman et al. 2000; Imwinkelried 1999), but rather from mismatches between experts' epistemological foundations and their knowledge claims. In the specific case of source attributions, it is clear that certain epistemological foundations would support greater confidence in source attributions than others. Trusting experts because they have created a self-credentialing body is different from trusting them because someone—even better, a relatively disinterested party—has sought to validate their knowledge claims.[17] Although the latter certainly does not provide for completely unproblematic knowledge claims, it may allow for greater confidence in the expert. A way forward might be to evaluate—or *appraise*—expert knowledge claims' epistemological foundations (see Table 6.1).

It remains only to note that what I am proposing to do as analyst is also, of course, an appraisal. As described elsewhere (Lynch and Cole 2004), the question of what sort of an expertise the science studies scholar possesses can be quite vexing. While science studies can be empirical, it cannot claim to adhere to a Galilean or Popperian model of science either. But perhaps, as Collins and Evans (2002) suggest, however provisionally, what it may be able do is provide an informed, empirically generated, appraisal of expert knowledge claims.

Table 6.1 Proposed instrument for appraisal of expert knowledge claims in source attribution

Knowledge claim			Epistemological basis
I know that X can be attributed to Y because ...	... I am an expert, and I know the products of Y when I see them.	You can trust my source attributions because ...	... my ability to make source attributions has been tested under conditions of Z stringency, and have yielded correct results N% of the time.
			... I possess M certificates in the attribution of Xs to Ys.

Acknowledgement

Thanks to Peter Paul Bíró and Teri Horton.

Notes

1   *US v Llera Plaza* 188 F.Supp.2d 549, 563–4 (E.D.Pa. 2002) (hereafter *Llera Plaza II*); *US v Llera Plaza* 179 F.Supp.2d 492 (E.D.Pa. 2002) (hereafter *Llera Plaza I*).
2   Contrary to what the passage implies, in *Llera Plaza I* the Court had not discounted the general acceptance of fingerprint identification among fingerprint examiners because fingerprint examiners possess 'technical' rather than 'scientific' knowledge. Rather, the Court discounted general acceptance because the Supreme Court in *Kumho Tire* cautioned that general acceptance does not 'help show that an expert's testimony is reliable where the discipline itself lacks reliability' (515). Since nowhere in *Llera Plaza II* does the Court recognize any evidence of reliability, it is difficult to see why designating fingerprinting an area of 'technical or specialized knowledge' should impact its analysis at all.
3   *Daubert v Merrell Dow Pharmaceuticals, Inc.* 509 U.S. 579, 125 L.Ed.2d 469, 113 S.Ct. 2786 (1993). *Kumho Tyre Co. v Carmichael* 526 U.S. 137, 143 L.Ed.2d 238, 119 S.Ct. 137 (1999).
4   *US v Havvard* 117 F.Supp.2d 848, 855 (S.D.Ind. 2000).
5   *People v Jennings* 96 N.E. 1077, 1082–3 (Ill. 1911).
6   *State v Cerciello* 90 A. 1112, 1114 (N.J. 1914); *State v Kuhl* 175, 191 P. 190 (Nev. 1918); *Lamble v State* 114 A. 346, 348 (N.J. 1921).

7   *State v Steffen* 230 N.W. 536, 537 (Iowa 1930).
8   *United States v Parks* CR-91-358- JSL Tr. trans. Vol. 5 (Cent.D.Cal. 10 December 1991).
9   *US v Mitchell* Cr. No. 96–407 Tr. trans. (E.D.Pa. 1999).
10   *US v Frye* 293 F 1013 (D.C.Cir. 1923).
11   *Barefoot v Estelle* 463 U.S. 880 (U.S. 1983). Of interest here is the fact that the Court dismissed the APA's argument on legal grounds without even resorting to the obvious move of deconstructing its positivist claim that it could produce a reliable estimate of the accuracy of future dangerousness predictions. Perhaps the Court saw the deconstruction of positivist claims, in general, as too great a threat to the legitimacy of the expertise whose admissibility it wished to preserve.
12   The Brief was a retreat in another way as well. It marked the first time that either the government or the fingerprint community had limited its defence to a single laboratory rather than defending the profession or methodology as a whole.
13   *US v Cline* 188 F.Supp.2d 1287, 1294–5 (D.Kan. 2002).
14   *Jacobellis v Ohio* 378 U.S. 184 (1964).
15   There is also perhaps a regress problem, in that it is not clear how one could ever actually know that any painting was in fact painted by Pollock. Testing appraisal poses difficulties as well since the 'ground truth' is established by a market, which is usually itself impacted by the appraisal.
16   Of course, the same problem applies here as in the case of connoisseurship: exposed misattributions are likely far rarer than actual misattribution because in most real world criminal cases, fingerprint examiners, for all practical purposes, have 'the last word' on the guilt or innocence of the suspect.
17   Legally, this might be likened to the difference between meeting *Frye* and meeting *Daubert*—or at least a reasonably strict interpretation of *Daubert*.

Chapter 7

'Science above all else': The Inversion of Credibility between Forensic DNA Profiling and Fingerprint Evidence

Michael Lynch

Introduction

This chapter is based on an ongoing study of the historical and epistemic relationships between DNA profiling and fingerprinting.[1] It is a study of key court cases, numerous documentary sources, and interviews with contemporary lawyers, forensic scientists, police, and other active participants in controversies about forensic DNA profiling ('DNA fingerprinting') and friction ridge identification ('fingerprinting').[2] The study's narrative is framed chronologically, starting in the mid-1980s, with the development of DNA profile methods, and continuing through phases of controversy, closure, and post-closure. In some respects it is a 'controversy study': a social–historical case study of a controversial innovation.[3] Like other historical and ethnographic case studies of technical controversies, it focuses on disputes among key participants about novel innovations. It differs in some important respects from a study of a scientific controversy because it is framed by legal questions and legal decisions. In this case, disputes in criminal cases about the admissibility of forensic evidence made up some of the key episodes in the controversy. Scientists and technical specialists participated in these disputes, but nonscientists involved in court decisions and serving on advisory panels helped set the agenda and were key players in opening and closing the controversy. In addition to discussing a techno-legal controversy embedded in a hybrid field, this chapter examines the interplay between two contemporaneous controversies.

The main theme of the chapter is an *inversion of credibility* that began in the late 1990s and is continuing today. This inversion had to do with the relation between recently developed techniques of DNA profiling and established methods of fingerprinting. I argue that this inversion is part of a more general shift away from 'experiential' grounds of expertise toward institutionalized 'objective' expertise. What follows is a brief sketch of the phases of a much more elaborate story.

Two forms of 'fingerprinting'

In the mid-1980s, when DNA profiling was introduced to the world of criminal forensics, it was given the name 'genetic fingerprinting' (Jeffreys et al. 1985). The expression 'DNA fingerprinting' was frequently used by the media and also, with greater qualification, by forensic specialists. The analogy with fingerprinting (dactyloscopy; friction ridge identification) drew attention to similarities between the two forensic technologies. Both were used to analyze crime scene evidence (bodily marks and material traces, and 'crime stains' such as semen recovered from rape victims) and compare such evidence with prints, test results, and material samples taken from suspects in custody. (In some cases, such as the OJ Simpson case (*CA v Simpson* 1994), bodily samples of blood or other material recovered from victims also are compared with bodily samples or trace evidence recovered from searches of a suspect's clothing, vehicle, or residence.) The fact that fingerprinting was well established and broadly accepted in criminal justice systems throughout the world lent credibility to the analogy. Police detectives and criminalists trusted fingerprinting, and were accustomed to the routines of collecting latent fingerprints at crime scenes, taking prints from suspects at police stations, and maintaining fingerprint files. Fingerprint examiners were rarely challenged when they testified in criminal trials, and they were allowed to declare, categorically, whether or not a particular latent print collected from a crime scene derived from a rolled print taken from an individual suspect. They were not required to qualify their reports with quantitative estimates of the likelihood of error. Some national systems used a given number of 'points', (such as the 16 points system used, until very recently, in the UK), to act as a threshold for declaring matches. Such declarations were either-or judgments, rather than probabilistic estimates of evidential weight.[4] Other techniques like blood protein analysis could be used to exclude a suspect by demonstrating that the suspect's blood group differed from that of a presumed perpetrator, but unlike fingerprinting, such techniques did not furnish evidence of individual identity.

DNA profiling was adopted for criminal investigations with remarkable speed,[5] and by 1987 it had begun to appear in US trials (it had been used even earlier in the UK, where it was first developed).[6] The earliest method used was the Multi-Locus Probe (MLP) method, a procedure for identifying Variable Number Tandem Repeat (VNTR) regions that recur at thousands of loci in the double-helical strands of human and non-human DNA. The MLP method used radioactive 'probes' that bind to an indefinite number of VNTR sites in a given genome and, when developed through gel electrophoresis and autoradiography (x-ray photography of the pattern of bands on a gel), the resulting patterns were sometimes likened to a supermarket bar code (Marx 1988: 1616). When Alec Jeffreys (now Sir Alec Jeffreys) first introduced 'genetic fingerprinting' he made strong claims about the individuating power of the technique: '... the pattern is so varied (hypervariable) that any particular combination of the segments is as unique as a fingerprint' (Jeffreys, quoted in *The Times*, 12 March 1985). Police spokespersons also emphasized unique identity. A Home Office spokesman was quoted in the *The Times* (27 November 1985), claiming '[t]he procedure is very complicated but it provides the scientists with a DNA fingerprint which has been shown to be specific to a particular individual'.[7] In popular accounts, DNA profiling was heralded as '... the perfect fingerprint: unfakeable, unique, and running in families' (*The Economist* 1986).

In retrospect, such unqualified acceptance seemed strikingly naïve, as Neil McLeod pointed out in a law review article on problematic cases in the US, UK, and Australia:

> In the popular mind the test became confused with the mapping of human genes, whereas in fact it probes only a handful of points on the chromosomes and ones which have no known function in determining physical makeup. The often faint, fuzzy, and distorted bands produced on autoradiographs were likened to the precise and unambiguous patterns of supermarket bar-codes. The chances of an innocent, coincidental match were touted at figures as low as 738,000,000,000,000,000 to one. The process was stated to be incapable of yielding a false match. (McLeod 1991: 583)

McLeod adds that defendants confronted with the evidence 'rolled over' and pleaded guilty, and prosecution expert witness testimony was accepted unchallenged.

A technical basis of such claims to extraordinary probative value—and of the analogies with fingerprints and bar codes—is that the 'probes' used in the MLP technique were not specific to one or even a few polymorphic DNA loci. The 'bar code' pattern produced by separating fragments of DNA marked by the probe produced a document of the size, or molecular weight, of the various VNTRs 'lit up' by the probe. Within a specified region of a gel, an analyst was likely to find ten or more 'bands'. Like matching points in fingerprint examination, matching MLP bands documented specific details in a complex pattern. So, for example, when a latent fingerprint lifted from the windowsill of a burglary matches a rolled print taken from a suspect at a police station, the examiner should be able to identify a complex pattern of corresponding details (branching ridges, whorls, and even skin pores). Similarly, when an MLP profile developed from a semen stain recovered from a rape victim's body or clothing matches one developed from a suspect's blood sample, numerous matching bands, and no mismatching bands, should be detected.[8] Because of the complexity of detail, forensic scientists deemed it extraordinarily unlikely that matching MLP probes would come from two different individuals (identical twins excepted).

However, the complexity of MLP patterns was a mixed blessing. Because of the large and indefinite number of VNTR sites potentially marked by a probe, this technique was not easily quantified. The large, and indefinite, number of bands developed in an MLP profile also enhanced the likelihood that artifactual bands (or the artifactual suppression of bands) would appear, and unless they were discounted such apparent mismatches could lead to the exclusion of evidence.[9] By the end of the 1980s, because of these and other practical and interpretative difficulties, forensic organizations had largely replaced that technique with the single-locus probe (SLP) technique. The SLP technique employed separate 'probes' to identify highly variable regions of the human genome. Probability estimates assigned to matching profiles depended upon the number of SLP markers used, the specific constellation of alleles identified in a given analysis, and the frequency of each allele in the human population and specific 'racial' subgroups. In some cases extremely low probability estimates were given, to the order of one chance in many billions of finding a given profile in a comparison population. By the end of the 1980s DNA profiling had been used in hundreds of cases, and in the vast majority of these cases it was accepted by judges and juries as a powerful, highly reliable, forensic tool. A few challenges occurred, but not many defence attorneys had the training, expert assistance, or equipment necessary to mount convincing arguments against such powerful evidence. Defence attorneys sometimes commissioned the technique as a basis for exonerating defendants, but more often the police and prosecution employed it to investigate crimes and develop trial evidence. The expense of the technique, access to the equipment, and the restricted availability of public funds for indigent defendants to pay for expert evidence were significant and chronic parts of the story, especially in the US system of 'justice'.

Criticism of the method began to mount in the late 1980s. A few molecular biologists, population geneticists, and legal scholars expressed doubts about the extraordinarily tiny numbers given in forensic experts' testimony—running to one chance in hundreds of billions that a given profile would be found at random in a population—and these critics argued that such estimates were based on dubious genetic and statistical assumptions. Doubts were raised about the methods and quality control standards practised by the private and public forensic labs that conducted DNA profile analysis. These criticisms were publicly aired during the admissibility hearing in the 1989–90 double-murder case *NY v Castro*.[10] In the early 1990s, the pages of *Science* and *Nature* covered a heated dispute that was dubbed the 'DNA wars'—a dispute that concerned, among other things, the way *Science* and *Nature* covered the contending positions—and countless studies and argumentative essays were published in law journals, police and forensic journals, and newspapers.[11]

Dissociation between 'DNA' and 'fingerprinting'

During the 'DNA wars' of the early 1990s, critics and proponents alike questioned the analogy between DNA profiling and fingerprinting. It became common to qualify the analogy by placing quotation marks around 'fingerprinting', or to avoid the term altogether in references to DNA *typing* and DNA *profiling*.[12] According to the first NRC report:

> In the publications in 1985 by Jeffreys and colleagues, the term 'DNA fingerprint' carried the connotation of absolute identification. The mass-media coverage that accompanied the publications fixed in the general public's minds the idea that DNA typing could be used for absolute identification.[13] Thus, the traditional forensic paradigm of genetic testing as a tool for exclusion was in a linguistic stroke changed to a paradigm of identification. (National Research Council 1992: 27)

Several reasons can be given for downplaying the analogy with fingerprinting:

- Unlike fingerprints, which are assumed to be unique to individuals, DNA profile patterns are shared by identical twins, and, because an SLP pattern involves a rough size comparison of a small sample of DNA segments from the entire genome, in a large population it is possible (even likely) to find multiple unrelated individuals with the same profile.

- Unlike fingerprints, which are declared categorically to be matching, not matching, or inconclusive, reports of DNA profile evidence include quantitative estimates of the frequency of the particular combination of alleles in a relevant population group. Such estimates are based on studies of blood samples taken from national and regional populations and 'racial' subpopulations (for most purposes of subpopulation analysis, US forensic organizations use the evidently crude categories 'Hispanic', 'Caucasian', and 'African–American').

- Unlike fingerprints, DNA profiles involve genetic patterns that are inherited. Persons who are closely related are more likely to share alleles than unrelated persons. Consequently, estimates of the frequency of a given pattern of alleles in a 'relevant' population—a group or subgroup made up of all persons who could possibly have 'donated' to the crime scene the bodily traces under analysis—will depend upon the genetic relationships among the members of that population. If the pool of suspects for a given crime includes members of an extended family, inbred village population, or ethnic enclave, then calculations of allele frequency should be adjusted accordingly.

- The ability to identify matches between crime scene marks and suspect fingerprints is assumed—perhaps erroneously—to be unproblematic.[14] The large literature on DNA profiling and testimony at many court cases provide abundant documentation of sources of error, mistake, and deliberate fraud in the handling, processing, and analysis of DNA samples. Innumerable sources of pre-analytical, analytical, and post-analytical error have been documented. Possible sources of error (or deception) arise from the point of evidence collection, all the way through to the reporting of probability estimates in the trial court. In principle, and in some cases in practice, fingerprinting can be subject to similar sources of error, fraudulent 'planting' of evidence, and misleading reporting in court, but it was widely *assumed*, until recently, that fingerprint identification was, for all intents and purposes, infallible.

- Unlike fingerprinting, which was a well-established routine in police stations and a familiar form of expertise in the courts, forensic DNA profiling included an evolving set of techniques which, in the late 1980s and early 1990s, were not closely supervised or regulated by administrative bodies. Police officers and civilian employees who were charged with collecting samples often had limited, if any, training in techniques of DNA evidence-handling, and private and public forensic labs were criticized for being sloppy and haphazard in the way they analyzed and kept track of samples.

Controversy and closure

In part, as a direct result of the bad publicity about forensic DNA 'fingerprinting' that came out of the fractious admissibility hearing in *NY v Castro*, the FBI, the National Research Council (NRC), and other regulatory and advisory groups took up the task of evaluating the state of the art of forensic DNA profiling (National Research Council 1992; 1996).[15] Typical of the NRC, the two committees that reported on the state of the art of forensic DNA profiling assumed a high-church vantage point, considering whether *forensic* work met standards of *science*. The auspices of 'science' seemed appropriate for the evaluation of forensic DNA testing, insofar as the 'same' techniques, such as Southern Blotting and the Polymerase Chain Reaction (PCR), and much of the same equipment, were used in forensics, diagnostics, and numerous academic research fields. The question was whether forensic scientists used these techniques in the manner prescribed in bona fide areas of science. (What was not pursued with equal vigor was whether scientists, medical researchers, and corporate R&D outfits in various fields of biology, biomedical engineering, and diagnostics used the techniques in the manner prescribed.) The NRC noted that forensic crime scene samples are found under uncontrolled conditions: the amount may be limited, the condition degraded, and the purity doubtful. Diagnostic samples, in contrast, are drawn under clinical conditions: amounts are sufficient for analysis, and samples are preserved from spoilage and maintained in sterile conditions. Less evident in explicit evaluations of forensic DNA profiling, but abundantly evident in cross-examinations of forensic scientists, is the association of forensics with low academic and epistemic status. Invidious comparison with 'real' science ignores the fact that researchers in some academic fields (archeology, for example) also collect samples where they find them, and 'basic' research can involve small batches and customized techniques which can produce highly variable results. In contrast, large forensic labs that handle thousands of samples, have the capacity and incentive to develop standardized routines that are, at least in principle, less capricious than those used in 'basic' research (Jordan and Lynch 1992, 1993).

Even before the OJ Simpson case treated a vast media audience to an exhaustive, if tendentious, tutorial on the contingencies of forensic analysis, proponents (and even former critics) of DNA profiling began to declare that the controversy was closed (Lander and Budowle 1994). The actual and anticipated endorsement of forensic DNA profiling by authoritative spokespersons for science (especially the NRC) was a primary basis for such declarations of closure. Such declarations were contested, and critics like Richard Lewontin and William Thompson continued to contest them, but closure was announced with increased regularity and assurance in the late 1990s (cf. Dawkins 1998). More importantly for legal purposes—and we must keep in mind that the controversy about forensic DNA profiling was a 'scientific' controversy framed by legal considerations, and especially considerations having to do with the admissibility of expert evidence in the US courts—was the fact that by the late 1990s, DNA profiling evidence and DNA databases had become institutionalized in the UK, many US states, and many European and non-European nations. Together with this institutional acceptance were technical developments, the adoption of standard procedures, and the promulgation of quality assurance/quality control recommendations (and, perhaps, occasional adherence to them).

By mid-1990s, the British Forensic Science Service, and soon after that many other forensic organizations, began to adopt the Short-Tandem Repeat (STR) system. Both national and international efforts were made to adopt the same markers, manufactured reagent kits, and laboratory equipment. A degree of flexibility was allowed within these developing standards, in part to enable more or less precise (and thus more or less costly) versions to be deployed for different purposes, and to accommodate variations among the techniques (some of which were proprietary) used by different government and private forensic labs.

Inversion of credibility

By the end of the 1990s DNA profiling had become so well accepted that it began to be used as a basis for calling all other forms of evidence into question. Barry Scheck and Peter Neufeld, who became prominent years earlier as 'DNA lawyers' who criticized forensic DNA 'fingerprinting' in the *Castro* and *Simpson* cases, were prominent in the Innocence Project (Dwyer, Neufeld and Scheck 2000). This project advocates (and sometimes commissions) DNA analysis of available physical evidence from cases that had resulted in convictions years, and sometimes decades, earlier. Prior convictions have been overturned in more than a hundred cases, including the murder convictions of several death-row inmates. In addition to resulting in dramatic stories of inmates released after years of confinement, and renewing criticisms of capital punishment, the innocence project encouraged broader questioning of the forms of evidence that had led to the convictions. 'DNA' became synonymous with a bedrock of scientific certainty that cast into relief the abysmal state of criminal justice: the fallibility of eyewitness testimony (a long-standing issue for Elizabeth Loftus (1979) and other psychologists[16]); the ineffectual defences mounted for indigent defendants; the false confessions extracted under duress; and the reliance on the testimony of jailhouse snitches and corrupt forensic 'experts'. 'DNA' was the new gold standard for revealing the fallibility of all other forms of evidence. Even *fingerprinting*—the previous gold standard—came into question, as parasite and host changed places (cf. Hacking 1992). Where forensic DNA had once borrowed the name 'fingerprinting' from the older technique, with its associations of credibility, certainty, and singularity of identification, the former 'host' (the established precedent and source of borrowed credibility) began to be reviewed, critically, in light of its successful parasite. To mix metaphors: parasite became parricide.

In the 1990s, there were a few cases in the US and UK in which embarrassing fingerprint misidentifications occurred (Specter 2002). These misidentifications did not lead the courts to entertain doubts about the dogma that all fingerprints are unique, but they did motivate questions about the adequacy of the existing methods for comparing latent and rolled prints. The 'points system' in the UK was held to be inadequate—to have no firm scientific basis—and it was abandoned in 2001. In the US, starting in 1999 with the case *US v Mitchell*, fingerprinting was challenged in a series of admissibility hearings, and while the courts have rejected each of the growing number of challenges that have been conducted thus far, the very occurrence and persistence of such challenges demonstrates a degree of questioning that had not occurred earlier.

A flurry of publicity accompanied the decision in January 2002 by Federal District Court Justice Louis H. Pollak in *US v Plaza*. Pollak, former Dean of Yale Law School, reviewed the evidence in *Mitchell*, and created a stir by ruling that fingerprint examiners should be prohibited from using the word 'match' in trial court. After the forensics community, led by the FBI, requested a re-hearing on the matter, Pollak reversed his earlier judgment in March 2002. Perhaps most interesting is an analytical challenge to the non-probabilistic way in which fingerprint evidence is reported; a challenge that, thus far, has not had discernible impact on the practice of fingerprint analysis or the testimony of fingerprint examiners. A decade ago, the word 'fingerprinting' was dissociated from 'DNA', because DNA profiling was *merely* probabilistic, and not uniquely identifying. Today, at least in the view of two prominent spokesmen for a particular (Bayesian and quantitative) view of science, the lack of probabilistic foundation marks fingerprinting as *un*scientific:

> With the extensive use of DNA—probability based—evidence and the evolving requirements for the admissibility of scientific evidence, older identification fields like fingerprints are becoming subject to more rigorous scrutiny and under the pressure of a growing demand of scientific data to underpin the identification of fingerprints. (Champod and Evett 2001b: 100)

The US Supreme Court has lent its weight to a 'more rigorous scrutiny' of older forensic expertise. Two key decisions in the 1990s—*Daubert v Merrell Dow Pharmaceuticals, Inc.* (1993) and *Kumho Tire v Carmichael* (1999)—allow considerable judicial discretion in admissibility decisions, but the Court majorities express a view of expertise that stresses 'science' and various (alleged) indicators of scientific reliability (peer-reviewed publications, general acceptance in a relevant field, testability, etc.) rather than personal experience and first-hand knowledge.[17] The fingerprint examiner's expertise has become vulnerable to being reduced to 'intuition' lacking 'transparency':

> The traditional role of expertise in forensic science is well recognised and it is something of a stereotype to visualise the distinguished, greying individual on the

stand saying, 'my opinion is based on my many years of experience in this field'. Whereas we do not for one moment deny the value of experience, we claim, as a matter of principle, that the scientist should, as far as possible, support his/her opinion by reference to logical reasoning and an established corpus of scientific knowledge. This is what we mean by 'transparency': the former 'in my experience' justification we refer to as 'obscurity'. (Champod and Evett 2001b: 98)

In addition to warranting an inversion of credibility between DNA typing and fingerprinting, this conception of transparency itself marks a conceptual inversion. During the 'DNA wars' concern was raised about the extent to which judges and jurors could understand the molecular biology, population genetics, and statistics employed in testimony about DNA evidence. Critics argued that the impressive probability figures would mislead jurors into assuming that a match meant certain guilt and confuse them with a complicated nest of assumptions about the makeup of suspect populations, population genetic relationships between persons and alleles, and methods of statistical sampling. Richard Lewontin recommends that probability figures should be kept out of the courtroom, because they demand a degree of competence from average jurors that many Harvard undergraduates fail to attain after a semester of study in Lewontin's courses on population genetics.[18] The comparative concreteness, and apparent simplicity, of fingerprint recognition might seem less 'obscure' and more 'transparent' to laypersons when demonstrated in court.[19]

The 'transparency' of DNA profiling—and of a suitably reformed fingerprint practice—is qualitatively distinct from the 'transparency' of the older forms of witnessing that are now in question (confession, eyewitness identification, surface matches in the conformation of threads, hairs, and fingerprint ridges). Whereas the old transparency is a matter of 'intuitive' or 'obvious' relation to lay sensibilities, the new transparency is organizational and authoritative: it consists in what we might call 'administrative science'—credibility achieved through the presentation of records of administrative certification, reports of tests, and quantitative figures, all of which may go over the head of the hapless juror.[20]

A key feature of administrative science, in practice, is that the 'transparency' of evidence in Champod and Evett's sense of the word, is supported (and, in some cases, undermined) by trails and archives of records, forms, signatures, bar codes, and electronic recordings. As in the case of 'fingerprinting', we can find various alignments and re-alignments of metaphoric entities with their 'real' counterparts. Where a DNA profile is likened to a fingerprint, which, in turn, is often likened to an individual signature, real signatures on evidence forms testify to the identity of evidence at one time and place to evidence at another time and place (Lynch and McNally 1999b). Where DNA 'fingerprinting' is likened to a bar code, real bar codes imprinted on stickers accompany the movement of evidence samples from crime scene to lab, and from one lab space to another. If, in Champod and Evett's formulation, we should no longer trust the word of the 'graying individual' who pronounces, 'my opinion is based on my many years of experience in this field', we now are faced with trusting (or, in the case of a savvy defence lawyer, distrusting) the paper trails—with their human signatures, automatic codes, and electronic traces—that testify to the chains of custody, which, in turn, secure the identity of a sample with itself, nurture that identity through a series of material transformations and support the 'scientific' declaration of correspondence between DNA samples.

Conclusion

DNA 'fingerprinting' has displaced its nominal predecessor as the 'gold standard' of criminal forensics. There may be reason to celebrate the ascendance of 'DNA' to unrivalled status as evidence with which to trump all other forms of criminal evidence. The reanalysis with the new techniques of material evidence from old cases has resulted in freeing convicted criminals, some of whom had spent decades on death row in Texas and Oklahoma. It has provided strong leverage for demonstrating that death penalty convictions have been based on flawed evidence; in some cases, evidence that seemed unassailable at the time, and in other cases evidence that was dubious at the time but not challenged by poorly prepared, sometimes sleeping, lawyers. Inspired by 'DNA', there has been much talk, and some action, in favor of upgrading standards for certifying forensic examiners, and conducting reliability and proficiency tests for the broad range of forensic practices.

There is also a downside: as was the case earlier in its history, 'DNA' has become synonymous with certainty. But where earlier it had been held certain because of a naïve analogy with fingerprinting, now it is held certain because it has passed through a series of stringent trials. Newspaper stories report the results of DNA testing without qualification, and some proponents in the technical community now argue that with current technology the probability of a coincidence match in the human population has vanished to zero (Budowle et al. 2000). Much like the fingerprint examiner's unqualified declarations, but with a new science to back it, the 'DNA' expert can declare that a match points uniquely to a suspect. Ironically, at a time when the declarative force of the 'traditional' fingerprint expert's pronouncements has been called into question, we are being advised to relieve the 'DNA' proponent of the burden of probabilistic qualification. Worse, just as 'DNA' is cited as a basis for innocence, so it is cited as a basis for 'guilt'.

All too predictably, in the wake of the innocence project comes a proposal to initiate what might be called the 'guilty project'. Governor Mitt Romney of Massachusetts on 23 September 2003 stated that he favored reinstating the death penalty in Massachusetts, now that there is a certain means for ascertaining that no innocent person would be executed. According to the *Boston Globe*:

> 'We want a standard of proof that is incontrovertible', Romney said as he stood at a State House press conference with members of his newly formed Governor's Council on Capital Punishment. He said he wants to put 'science above all else' in capital murder cases. The governor said he is directing the panel, which is made up of well-known forensic and legal specialists, to craft a narrowly defined capital punishment

law that will deal with those who have committed multiple murders through acts of terrorism; killers of those in the criminal justice system, such as judges, prosecutors, and police officers; and those who commit the 'most heinous violent crimes' … 'Just as science can be used to free the innocent, it can also be used to identify the guilty', Romney said. (Phillips 2003)

Romney's proposal received heavy criticism, and was likely to encounter resistance in the state legislature, but the way his statements conflate 'science' and the determination of guilt and innocence holds broader, and possibly more persistent, implications. As a recent scandal in the Houston Police Department crime laboratory has shown, DNA evidence has fragile properties which are obscured by the use of 'DNA' as the emblem for a certain and unique method of identification.[21] Its credibility in any particular case had to do with its marvelous technical properties, but this did not relieve juries and judges from judgments about the competence of forensic researchers and the motives of police, the very uncertain and conceptually murky judgments that Governor Romney would transcend with 'science'. The lesson to be taken from the 'DNA wars' is not that DNA profile evidence successfully met the challenges raised by courtroom lawyers and sceptical population geneticists, so that it can now be taken as certain. Instead, it is that closure was administrative—performed by court decisions and official review panels—and that the credibility of DNA evidence is as much a product of administrative regimes—with their audits, tests, tracking devices, and paper trails—as it is of 'science above all else'.

Acknowledgements

This chapter is based on a long-term study. At different phases of the study I have collaborated with Ruth McNally, Kathleen Jordan, and Simon Cole, and their input has been essential to what I discuss in this chapter. An earlier version of this chapter was presented at the conference, 'Law's Experts', held at The Australian National University, Canberra (23–4 August 2002), sponsored by Law Program, Research School of Social Sciences (ANU), RegNet and the National Institute for Government and Law (NIGL). I would like to thank Gary Edmond for organizing the conference, and for providing helpful comments on this chapter. The research has been supported by grants from the National Science Foundation (US) and the Economic and Social Research Council (UK).

Notes

1   Ruth McNally, Kathleen Jordan, and Simon Cole have collaborated with me on different phases of the research. For publications based on the research, see Jordan and Lynch (1992; 1993; 1998); Lynch and McNally (1999a, 1999b; 2003); Lynch (1998); and Cole (1998).

2   The study also benefits from Simon Cole's involvement as a consultant and witness for the defence in a number of legal challenges to fingerprint evidence. For a discussion of a case in which Cole underwent an admissibility hearing as an expert witness for the defence, see Lynch and Cole (forthcoming).

3   Although their approaches to the analysis of controversies differ, both Collins (1985) and Latour (1987) accord special significance to episodes of technical controversy. Both draw upon the philosophical idea that discord about and troubles with statements of fact and/or with claims of inherent efficacy disrupt the transparency of the facts and technologies in question and draw attention to, otherwise non-obvious, contingencies that set up and maintain unqualified accounts about natural reality and technical efficiency. Philosophical sources include Heidegger's (1967) example of the broken hammer as a way to disclose the existential horizons of use, or, in his language the ontological property of 'ready-to-hand'; and Merleau-Ponty's (1962) orientation to bodily injuries and dysfunctions as sources of the ontologically fatal insight that sees the 'world itself' to be framed by and infused with an embodied 'grasp' of it. Literary critic Kenneth Burke (1969) and sociologist Harold Garfinkel (1967) also treat trouble, disruption, and discord as affording 'perspective by incongruity': a turning of attention to previously taken-for-granted conditions for the appearance and stability of 'things themselves'. Discord and disruption tend to shift focus from things and facts to *accounts* of things, *reports* of fact, and the local–historical circumstances that frame the intelligibility and motivate the acceptance of such accounts and reports. This does not necessarily encourage a regressive interest in 'subjectivity'; instead, it alerts us to the importance of language use, and the organized conditions of that use. Language use is always at hand (or at the tip of our tongues) when 'the world' is in question, and, by implication, when it is *not* in question. Legal wrangling about science and technology also has attracted the attention of STS scholars because of the way adversary disputes that enlist experts produce public spectacles of 'deconstruction', so that the public is treated to, and learns to expect, that unqualified 'facts' are likely to be attacked by the adversary as being infused with partisan interest, subject to systematic doubt, and dependent on the nuances of *just how* the evidence is reported (Jasanoff 1995; Fuchs and Ward 1994). Lynch (1998) speaks ironically of a 'sociology of knowledge machine' that is produced through adversary attacks on expert evidence. A sceptical view of the lawyerly arts of 'deconstruction' can be encouraged by reading a brief primer for lawyers who would attack state forensic witnesses in drug cases (Oteri et al. 1982).

4   It is not strictly an either-or judgment. An examiner can declare insufficient evidence when a latent print is deemed to be too faint or smudged either for positively declaring a match or definitely excluding the possibility of a match.

5   The first trial in the US in which DNA profiling evidence was deemed admissible is often said to be *Florida v Tommie Lee Andrews* (1987). Peter Neufeld and Barry Scheck (interview, May 2002) indicated that there may have been earlier cases, but I have not found specific references to such cases.

6   Crime novelist and former LAPD officer Joseph Wambaugh (1989) wrote a popular true-life mystery of the first case in which DNA profiling was used in a criminal investigation. Police investigating two rape-murders in villages near Leicester, England, where Alec Jeffreys (the inventor of the MLP technique) worked, enlisted Jeffreys to assist with a mass screening of men living in and around the two villages in which the murders occurred. The story became interesting for a number of reasons. First, a suspect whom the police were convinced was the murderer was excluded by the DNA evidence, and, second, the aptly named Colin Pitchfork, who eventually was convicted of the murders, initially evaded suspicion by using the familiar ploy of using another man's blood sample when he appeared for the test. When the donor of the sample mentioned this ploy in a conversation months later, it was reported to the police, and they retested (and positively identified) Pitchfork.

7   Even after DNA profiling started to run into difficulty in the courts, the claim of uniqueness persisted in press accounts. One of the more spectacular claims was expressed with the following analogy: 'Suppose we could test a million people every second. How long would it take to find one exactly the same? The answer is, the universe itself would die before we found one the same. It is simply an incomprehensible number' (Grove 1989).

8   Challenges to MLP results in the UK case *R v Deen* (1993) and the US case *NY v Castro* (1989) revealed that forensic scientists sometimes discounted apparent mismatches (the presence of a band in one autoradiograph and not in the one with which it was compared) by invoking technical contingencies such as insufficient quantity of material in the crime stain, band shifting due to inconsistencies in the gel apparatus, and more arcane possibilities that could suppress the appearance of a band. According to William Thompson, even when using more recently developed techniques, forensic scientists have been found to preserve their declaration of matches in the face of apparent counter-evidence. Recent challenges to fingerprint evidence also make an issue of the examiner's practice of discounting anomalous traces (especially on a latent print) by invoking properties of the substrate, and the incomplete or inconsistent registration of dermal ridges and skin pores.

9   Forensic examiners sometimes attempted to discount apparent mismatching bands in MLP profiles, by declaring them artifacts, but as any Popperian philosopher (or criminal defence attorney) should know, such discounting practices recall the spectre of ad hoc reasoning designed to 'save' the evidence (this issue arose in the 1993 English appeal case *R. v Deen*).

10   According to Barry Scheck and Peter Neufeld (interviewed by Michael Lynch and Simon Cole, May 2002), the run-up to *Castro* involved an interesting combination of happenstance and directed effort. According to their account, Scheck and Neufeld, who had no specialized training in molecular biology, were contacted by the public defender in *Castro*, who they had met at a seminar on DNA profile evidence. However, Scheck and Neufeld added, they already had been concerned about the various low-grade forms of comparison evidence that pass for forensic science in the courts. In part, DNA evidence represented a strong point of leverage to expose the dubious practices and standards associated with other forensic (and non-forensic) methods, but consistent with their ideal of strengthening the standards of so-called 'scientific' evidence, Scheck and Neufeld also took a strong interest in the way prosecutions overplayed the power of DNA evidence. They represented a libertarian side of the 'junk science' debate that led to the 1993 Supreme Court judgment, *Daubert v Merrell Dow Pharmaceuticals, Inc.*

11   There is a large literature on the 'DNA wars'. A few of the more notable contributions to, and discussions of, the conflict surrounding *NY v Castro* are a series of articles by science journalist Leslie Roberts (1991; 1992), and contributions by participants, such as Lander (1989; 1992); Neufeld and Colman (1990); Lewontin and Hartl (1991); and Chakraborty and Kidd (1991).

12   Quotation marks or 'scare quotes' are often associated with a sceptical or cynical effort to, as philosopher DC Stove (1984: 23) once put it, 'neutralize success words' like 'truth', 'fact', or 'reality'. In a triumphant announcement of the closure of debate about DNA profiling, an editorial introduction to an essay by Richard Dawkins (1998) in the magazine *The Sciences* made an issue of the quotation marks: 'How times have changed! Almost nine years ago *The Sciences* published "A Question of Identity", by Simon Ford and William Thompson [1990], an article that took a dim view of the claims then being made about the value of DNA evidence for identifying crime victims and perpetrators. The subtitle set the tone, archly placing the word *fingerprints* in

ironic quotation marks. Ford and Thompson cited the potential for contaminated or deteriorated samples; for sloppy laboratory work; for inconsistencies in the expert interpretation of results; and for overestimates on the statistical chances against a random event posing as a significant finding. Now, as this issue goes to press, the FBI has announced it has assembled a national database of DNA fingerprints (no ironic quotes), which will enable law enforcement officers to scan criminal records throughout the country for a match with biological evidence recovered from a suspect, from a victim or from the scene of a crime' (Brown 1998: 2). What the writer of the essay overlooks is that the quotation marks, qualifying the analogy with fingerprinting, were favored by proponents as well as critics of DNA profiling. When it became apparent that forensic experts would be challenged when they presented DNA matches as certain indication of individual identity, proponents dropped the troublesome analogy and sought other means of supporting the weight and scientific status of DNA evidence. They succeeded so well in this effort that the success of DNA 'fingerprinting' has rebounded against its namesake (the original and 'real' kind of fingerprinting).

13   As indicated by some of the quotations above 'the mass media' were not alone in promoting the idea that DNA profile patterns were unique to individuals.

14   Before it became controversial, DNA 'fingerprinting' proponents portrayed the work of recognizing matches as unproblematic. Eric Lander (1989: 505) quotes from a Lifecodes scientist, Kevin McElfresh, who testified in *Georgia v Caldwell* (1990), a death penalty rape-murder trial, that declaring a match is a 'very simple straightforward operation ... there are no objective standards about making a visual match. Either it matches or it doesn't. It's like you walk into a parking lot and see two blue Fords parked next to each other'.

15   *Castro* was the first case in the US in which the admissibility of DNA evidence was successfully challenged by the defence. However, problems with DNA evidence had surfaced in earlier cases in the US, UK, and Australia. The *Neysmith* case (1987) involved some hilarious problems (see Lander 1992). *Neysmith* involved evidence commissioned by the defence, however, and there may be an asymmetry in the courts' handling of defence-commissioned and prosecution-commissioned evidence. In *Castro* the thing that was unusual was that the 'expert lawyers' called in some heavyweight scientists (most obviously Eric Lander) to counter the testimony of prosecution expert witnesses. The 'consensus about lack of consensus' that came out of the scientists' ad hoc meeting during the *Frye* hearing was pointedly directed at several problems with the way the prosecution and its contracting company (Lifecodes) handled the evidence and presented the results.

16   An interesting spin-off of the establishment of DNA evidence is that successful efforts to use DNA 'exclusions' to overturn guilty verdicts based on eyewitness testimony have worked to the benefit of psychologists. For years, the US courts have made inconsistent and ambivalent decisions about the admissibility as expert witnesses of psychologists who offer to testify about the fallibility of eyewitness testimony. Courts that ruled against the admissibility of psychologists in such cases objected that psychologists are divided among themselves, and that what they have to offer is, in any case, 'common sense'. Since jurors are properly assigned the 'common sense' job of deciding if an eyewitness had a good look at the perpetrator, is honest, had a good memory of the event, and so forth, an 'expert' reporting on experiments might muddy the waters and usurp the jurors' collective responsibility to decide what happened, commonsensically. In light of the way DNA reanalysis of evidence 'exposed' errors by eyewitnesses who professed absolute certainty (some of whom continue to object strenuously to the overturned convictions), the New York Supreme Court recently

ruled in favor of the admissibility of psychologists as expert witnesses on matters pertaining to eyewitness testimony.

17 See Solomon and Hackett (1996), and Jasanoff (1995) on *Daubert*, and Edmond (2002c) on *Kumho*. See Mnookin (2001) for discussion of how *Daubert* and *Kumho* apply to the DNA profiling/fingerprinting controversies.

18 Richard Lewontin, interviewed by Kathleen Jordan, using a schedule of questions prepared by Ruth McNally and Michael Lynch (Harvard University, 7 April 1998).

19 Cole's (2001) history of fingerprinting notes that courtroom demonstrations, though part of the popular legacy of fingerprinting, occur rarely.

20 See Shapin (1995) on credibility, Porter (1995) on trust in numbers, Latour (1995) on paper trails, and Dear (1995) on the transition from experience to experiment in 16th and 17th century natural philosophy.

21 The Houston Police Department crime lab was shut down in the wake of scandals arising from the case of Josiah Sutton, who was released from prison after having served four and a half years of a 20-year term following a 1999 rape conviction. The *Houston Chronicle* headlined that this case was another DNA exoneration: 'New DNA Test Casts Doubt on Man's 1999 Rape Conviction' (Khana and McVicker 2003). The headline uses a commonplace grammar that positions 'new DNA test' as the subject and agent that 'casts doubt' on the conviction. Reading further, however, one learns that DNA tests were also a crucial part of the evidence that led to Sutton's conviction in 1999. The doubts that were cast were not simply a matter of new tests replacing old. The problems with the original tests and the conditions under which they were implemented were legion. Many news articles mentioned the leaky roof in the crime lab, perhaps as emblematic of the less-than-watertight quality of the evidence produced under that roof. It is also significant that the lab in question produced evidence for a district that has held the dubious record of producing more death penalty cases than any other. Incompetence interacted with political pressures to produce convictions. No doubt, a 'new DNA test' proved to be powerful leverage for the civil libertarians who contested all-too-familiar patterns of injustice in the case, but nothing guaranteed that DNA's mystique would stay in their hands rather than in those of the police and forensic scientists who were now branded as incompetent and corrupt.

Chapter 8

Judging Facts: Managing Expert Knowledges in Legal Decision-making

Gary Edmond

Introduction

How is it that judgments, written by legal specialists, can withstand criticism from technical experts, such as scientists, accountants, medical practitioners and epidemiologists, with respect to the incorporation of expert evidence? Expressed more abstractly: why don't concerns about accuracy and truth—what we might call the *rule of fact*—displace the range of rights, procedures and values conventionally associated with the *rule of law*? This chapter offers some tentative explanations. My general contention is that by maintaining responsibility for the interpretation of laws and procedures, and the ultimate resolution of disputes, judges are able to qualify, insulate, influence and control the ways in which expertise is received and understood throughout the legal system, its shadowlands and occasionally beyond. This chapter endeavors to examine some of the techniques, strategies and institutional arrangements which enable judges to mediate the influence of law *and* fact as well as protect their decision-making from exogenous critique.

In undertaking this analysis, it is my intention to incorporate perspectives on the simplification of scientific knowledge (e.g. Shinn and Whitley 1985). Examining the rhetorical functions of popularization, sociologist Stephen Hilgartner sought to explain why scientists often encountered difficulty extending, and sometimes even maintaining, authority as their expert knowledge moved from professional arenas into policy contexts and public debates. For Hilgartner, these tendencies were inconsistent with the 'dominant view':

> The dominant view establishes genuine scientific knowledge, the epistemic 'gold standard', as the exclusive preserve of scientists; policy makers and the public can only grasp simplified representations ... this view of popularization grants scientists broad authority to determine which simplifications are 'appropriate' (and therefore usable) and which are 'distortions' (and therefore useless — or worse!). (Hilgartner 1990: 520, 2000)

In response, Hilgartner suggested that notwithstanding the 'depth and sweep of the epistemic authority that the dominant view of popularization grants scientists' there were practical limits to the influence scientists could bring to public discourse relating to expertise (Hilgartner 1990; Michael 1998). The following discussion explores these 'practical limits' in relation to judicial responses to expert evidence. It examines the institutional mechanisms and techniques which enable judges to invoke the epistemic authority of science without becoming beholden to scientists, or having to accept the implications of every expert pronouncement.[1]

Consequently, this chapter is not concerned, *per se*, with simplistic comparisons between formal judicial articulations of expert evidence and some putative, extra-legal 'golden standard' of science (or expertise). Recognizing, along with Ravetz (1971), that knowledge does not always remain stable across contexts of use, it aims to transcend simplistic attributions of legal distortion. By focusing on the special circumstances associated with litigation and judicial decision-making—such as legal causes of action, established rules and procedures, conflicting evidence, temporal and financial constraints, policy implications, and sensitivity to the social legitimacy of legal institutions and decisions—I am proposing to examine how judges as non-technical experts manage the role and scope of expertise; in particular, how judges operating in a public idiom and appealing to pervasive ideals of transparency, accountability and rationality, in accordance with liberal democratic 'rule of law' ideology, produce persuasive and socially compelling decisions.

As a preliminary methodological concern, those resistant to degrees of epistemological indeterminacy may wish to argue that judges avoid criticism because their assessments of the evidence are generally correct. An alternative, but theoretically similar, formulation suggests that we can assess judicial performances against some putatively proper value of the evidence. It is my intention to discount such approaches at the outset. If accepted, they would eliminate the need to study the judicial treatment of expert evidence. Those occasions where the legal system makes (what come to be understood as) mistakes, such as in notorious miscarriage of justice cases, might be among the few exceptions (Edmond 2002c). Commitment to a *proper* means of evaluating evidence naturalizes legal methods and (the vast majority of) judicial narratives. It often leads to proposals for highly artificial procedural reforms (Edmond 2003). Assuming that judges typically apply procedures and evaluate evidence correctly precludes serious study of how they practically manage evidence during the trial and in the judgment: that is, how legal *truth effects* are generated (Collins and Pinch 1993: 142). It also converts decision-making into a search for the right answer rather than examining how judges are implicated in these answers—through the production of methodological propriety and forms of evidentiary reliability. Further, to focus exclusively on evidence, or to think that only evidence, and not substantive law, procedure and strategy, have epistemological effects is naïve.[2] Such assumptions prevent us from examining the (institutional, professional and other forms of) politics associated with the attribution of *proper* values and *correct* evaluations as well as the manner in which judicial closure is often a peculiar situational accomplishment.

Rather than approach judgments on the basis that they are simply right or wrong, this chapter will adopt a more agnostic stance (Bloor 1976; Barnes and Bloor 1982). Such an approach enables the analyst to go beyond a narrow 'technical' focus and to incorporate what are traditionally conceived as non-epistemic factors, such as the law and rules, procedure, strategy, institutional traditions, policy sensitivities and concerns about social problems, into the study of judicial decision-making. These are some of the considerations which make the practice of judging an extremely important and complex social practice. Indeed, a social practice that is not adequately explained by recourse to legalism, judicial method, rule-following nor institutional and professional norms.

So, the following discussion is intended as a thematic survey. It aims to sensitize the reader to some of the many ways judges have responded to expert evidence, law and procedure, strategy and social order. Rather than conceptualize these as discrete entities, the following account endeavors to illustrate some of the ways in which they are tightly interwoven, even mutually constituting. Judicial practice, as we shall see, draws upon a broad repertoire of institutional, procedural and representational resources which are associated not only with science and expertise but are also conditioned by changing ideas of justice, legitimacy and public accountability.

How to do things with facts (and law, procedure, strategy ... and society)[3]

While this essay predominantly focuses on the representational and persuasive aspects of expertise featured in written judgments, in writing a judgment every judge is simultaneously concerned with a range of considerations which extend beyond *the evidence* (Wootten 2003; Glass 2003). Many of these considerations are quite difficult to examine. For example, in producing a written decision, to varying degrees judges are simultaneously interested in resolving a public dispute plausibly and expeditiously, advancing their career, cultivating the law, establishing a personal reputation, resisting or encouraging review and maintaining the social legitimacy of their institution. These concerns are not experienced consistently across our conspicuously hierarchical judiciary.

In adversarial legal systems judges and (fewer and fewer) juries are routinely confronted with competing cases which incorporate conflicting factual accounts. Many of the narratives are supported by the reports and testimony of experts. In their capacity as fact-finders judges (and juries) are expected to evaluate factual discrepancies. To assist that process fact-finders are provided with a legal 'grid' describing the appropriate standard of proof (or certitude) required to sustain or defend a case (Allen 1991; Campbell, 1985). Ultimately, even where a defendant offers no response to an action, those prosecuting must prove their case on the balance of probabilities (for civil actions) or beyond reasonable doubt (in criminal cases). To sustain findings of (non-) liability and (non-) guilt, the evidence must be considered and evaluated against these deliberately vague vernacular formulations (Note 1995a).

Before a case makes it to court, the relevant parties have to decide whether they can transform their concerns into a legally tractable cause of action. They must ascertain whether they have the inclination and interest (e.g. the victim in a rape accusation) or the resources (e.g. the plaintiffs in tobacco litigation) to go through with prosecuting the case.[4] Evidence only comes to court as part of a claim: a legally recognizable cause of action. To varying degrees, substantive legal doctrine and rules of evidence and procedure regulate the types of cases and therefore the evidence and expertise which enter legal settings. Expertise almost always enters the courtroom as part of a legally acclimatized narrative. Earlier decisions, analogous cases, legal commentary, and extra-legal credibility all influence the flexible parameters around the selection, admission and presentation of expert evidence. The borders around what will count as *relevant* and *reliable* expertise, like the selection, interpretation and application of law, are not always clear and uncontested. Lawyers, parties and judges select, manipulate and combine both law and evidence in ways that tend to be highly purposive.

Unlike the judges in inquisitorial jurisdictions who tend to actively preside over litigation and its preparation—for example in criminal cases judges administer the investigation as well as the trial—judges in adversarial (or accusatorial) systems have traditionally been conceived more as umpires with limited responsibility for the preparation and even the administration of the case (Frankel 1975; Langbein 1985, 2003; Damaska 1997). In adversarial jurisdictions the rhetorical and institutional displacement between the judge and the preparation of cases effectively insulates the judiciary from the consequences of inadequate investigation or poor expert selection and performance. Even if a judge from an adversarial jurisdiction accepts the evidence of a particular expert which is later shown to have been unreliable, the preference can usually be explained in terms of how the evidence was presented *at the trial*.[5] The judge can always attribute responsibility for any *derogation* to the parties or a particular expert. Police and forensic scientists, rather than judges and lawyers, are routinely blamed in miscarriage of justice exposés. In inquisitorial systems, by contrast, the selection of court-appointed experts implicates the judge and sometimes professional organizations more directly in the production of evidence, and the maintenance of professional standing.[6] Court-appointed experts are seldom used in adversarial jurisdictions (Cecil and Willging 1993; Saks 1995; Hooper, Cecil and Willging 2001). That may reflect a judicial reluctance to be involved and aligned but, perhaps more importantly, concern that judicial hands might be constrained—before the case has even been tried—by the very authority that the court confers upon the *independent* expert. The authority invested in court-appointed experts can make it difficult, for the trial judge, to challenge or disregard an expert's opinion, at least on evidentiary grounds.

During a trial the judge is responsible for determining whether the evidence produced by the parties should be heard by the fact-finder. Submissions of expert evidence are often contested on the basis of imputed unreliability and sometimes irrelevance. Questions about the appropriate standard of reliability of expert evidence have, particularly in US federal courts, become extremely important sites for obtaining advantages in litigation. If an opponent's expert(s) can be excluded or have the scope of their evidence restricted on the grounds that the evidence is speculative, or based on *untested* techniques and assumptions, or outside legal constructions of their *appropriate* field of expertise (Gieryn 1998), then an entire case may be adversely affected or quickly disposed of.

Decisions pertaining to the admissibility, relevance and sufficiency of evidence are all typically characterized as *legal* and, therefore, left to the discretion of the trial judge.[7] As a generalization, classifying these determinations as *legal* rather than *factual* opens them to judicial review.[8] Decisions pertaining to admissibility, relevance and sufficiency can be incredibly important in *controlling* the type and volume of litigation able to enter courtrooms. Their implications may extend well beyond a particular case. Jurisprudential trends may deter litigation or encourage plaintiffs and their lawyers to shop around for more conducive legal forums. In making admissibility determinations it is no coincidence that during the last decade federal judges in the United States have been characterized as 'gatekeepers'.[9]

Insulation and exnomination

A brief examination of the jurisprudence around the admission of expert evidence under the US *Federal Rules of Evidence* (1975, hereafter FRE) will provide an indication of some of the legal complexity and the manner in which managerial concerns and social visions are embedded in legal interpretation and practice.

Rule 702 of the FRE governs the admission of expert opinion evidence in US federal courts. Prior to revision in 2000, it stated:

> If scientific, technical, or other specialized knowledge will assist the trier of fact to understand the evidence or to determine a fact in issue, a witness qualified as an expert by knowledge, skill, experience, training, or by education, may testify thereto in the form of an opinion or otherwise.[10]

The US Supreme Court considered the application of Rule 702 several times in the 1990s.[11] Before 1993, most courts adhered to some version of what was known as the *Frye* or 'general acceptance' test as the appropriate standard for admissibility. *Frye v US* (1923), a case which considered the admissibility of an early form of 'lie detector', came to stand for the proposition that expert evidence was admissible if the underlying process or technique had received *general acceptance* in the relevant field.[12] With a few exceptions, versions of the *Frye* test withstood the enactment of the *Federal Rules* in 1975. By 1993, however, inconsistency among the federal circuits over the interpretation of Rule 702 was deemed sufficient to warrant Supreme Court intervention. That Court agreed to hear an appeal concerning the standard for the admissibility of scientific evidence.

In *Daubert v Merrell Dow Pharmaceuticals, Inc.*, the entire Supreme Court decreed that 'general acceptance' was not required under the FRE and, therefore, endeavored to articulate a new admissibility standard consistent with the text of Rule 702.[13] Emphasizing the importance of evidentiary *reliability*, the majority provided alternative criteria which might ordinarily assist the admissibility determinations made by trial judges. Four factors received enumeration, whether the theory or technique: had been tested (referring to falsification and citing Popper and Hempel); had been subjected to peer review and publication; had a known or potential error rate; and, reinvigorating *Frye* in conjunction with these other criteria, whether it had received 'general acceptance' in the relevant field. Justice

Blackmun, the architect of the majority judgment, encouraged federal trial judges to take a close look at the methodology employed by the expert.[14]

Rather than simplify judicial decision-making the *Daubert* majority judgment provided an additional, but non-determinative, set of judicial resources and authority. Given its highly selective appropriation of authority from the philosophy and sociology of science (to which we will return) and the degree of inquiry required of trial judges, some federal judges expressed exasperation at the impending task:

> Our responsibility, then, unless we badly misread the Supreme Court's opinion, is to resolve disputes among respected, well-credentialed scientists about matters squarely within their expertise, in areas where there is no scientific consensus as to what is and what is not "good science," and occasionally to reject such expert testimony because it was not "derived by the scientific method."[15]

Although *Daubert* was widely celebrated as a realization of the 'liberal thrust' intended by the enactment of the FRE in 1975, in practice it provided judges with additional tools for excluding expert evidence on grounds of 'unreliability' (Dixon and Gill 2002; Krafka et al. 2002). Emphasis on 'testing' in conjunction with the three other factors could be particularly onerous upon plaintiffs. The *Daubert* decision, in conjunction with changing judicial responses to expert evidence on the basis of social anxieties caused by publicity associated with litigation 'explosions' (especially mass torts), related insurance crises, and the alleged prevalence of 'junk science', led many judges to take their gatekeeping responsibilities very seriously.[16] Litigant responses—attempting to circumvent this rigor by distinguishing non-scientific expert evidence on the grounds that *Daubert* applied only to scientific evidence—led to further Supreme Court intervention.

Responding to a decision that exempted engineering testimony from the remit of the *Daubert* criteria on the grounds that it was not scientific knowledge, the Supreme Court, in *Kumho Tyre Co. v Carmichael,* extended *Daubert's* emphasis on evidentiary reliability to *all* forms of expert evidence.[17] The entire Court accepted that the *Daubert* factors *may* be applied by the trial judge to all proffers of expert evidence. The Court transformed *Daubert's* gatekeeping responsibility into an obligation and articulated concerns about the prevalence and risks associated with unreliable expertise, especially the need to protect juries.

As a result of *Daubert* and the cases that followed, US federal court judges were provisioned with a more extensive—rather than (just) standardized—set of criteria able to be mobilized in response to all proffers of expertise. In making admissibility decisions trial judges could, at their own discretion, apply any or all of the *Daubert* criteria to both scientific and non-scientific forms of expertise. Significantly, in *General Electric Co. v Joiner*, the Supreme Court reinforced the independence of the trial judge by proclaiming that admissibility decisions were only open to review where there was clear abuse of this discretion.[18] Judicial constructions of testing, peer review, publication and assessments about the extent of acceptance are potential means, and here we are discussing means developed as part of legal procedure, for managing the types of expertise and implicitly the types of litigation that enter the courtroom (Edmond 2000, 2002b). From *Daubert* (1993) through to *Kumho* (1999) the Supreme Court installed a restrictive ethos toward the types of expert evidence able to enter US federal courts. Elaborating a restrictive model of science, purportedly mandated by the FRE, led to a substantial revision of federal admission standards.[19]

Together the *Daubert*, *Joiner* and *Kumho* judgments represent a sustained attempt to reform the reception and treatment of expert evidence in US federal courts.[20] They were judicial responses to the perceived difficulties and dangers posed by purportedly unreliable knowledge entering legal settings.[21] In the context of an assessment of the judicial management of expertise they also provide a felicitous example of how Supreme Court judges selectively appropriated from the history, philosophy and sociology of science to promote their admissibility 'revolution' and how this social science *authority* was subtly exnominated as significant *legal authority* emerged (Barthes 1973: 138–41; Fiske 1987). In this context we will consider how the work and cultural authority of the philosopher Karl Popper which appeared in *Daubert* (1993) disappeared prior to *Kumho* (1999), once 'testing' had become an ostensibly legal category (see also the final essay in this volume).

In *Daubert*, the majority explained that in making admissibility decisions trial judges were required to assess whether the evidence was scientific, that is, constituted genuine scientific knowledge. Only genuine scientific knowledge was admissible. In the provision of factors that might assist the trial judge to identify genuine scientific knowledge the majority explained their first criterion ('testing', above) in the following terms:

> Ordinarily, a key question to be answered in determining whether a theory or technique is scientific knowledge that will assist the trier of fact will be whether it can be (and has been) tested. "Scientific methodology today is based on generating hypotheses and testing them to see if they can be falsified; indeed, this methodology is what distinguishes science from other fields of human inquiry." Green 645. See also C. Hempel, *Philosophy of Natural Science* 49 (1966) ("[T]he statements constituting a scientific explanation must be capable of empirical test"); K. Popper, *Conjectures and Refutations: The Growth of Scientific Knowledge* 37 (5th ed. 1989) ("[T]he criterion of the scientific status of a theory is its falsifiability, or refutability, or testability"). (*Daubert* 1993: 593)

This extract provides a sense of the way Blackmun enrolled Popper and Hempel metonymically—for the authority of the philosophy of science—in order to support the particular model of science and standard of reliability which he was promoting. Of significance, references to Popper and Hempel were derivative: drawn from the work of a legal commentator, tort scholar Michael Green (1992), and several *amicus curiae* briefs.[22] Though not apparent from the text, the philosophy of Popper sits uncomfortably alongside the work of Hempel, as well as the other criteria promoted in the majority judgment. Haack, a prominent philosopher of science, characterized the Supreme Court's offering as 'a little embarrassing' (Haack 2001: 231; Fuller 2003).

The Court drew upon a highly selective vision of science in its attempt to reformulate admissibility standards under the *Federal Rules*. Notwithstanding Popper's extra-legal prominence, prior to his debut in *Daubert* his work on the philosophy of science had appeared in very few judicial discussions of expert evidence.[23] Given that Popper's philosophy of science is not particularly fashionable with contemporary philosophers and even less appealing to historians and sociologists of science, its selection may appear curious. Popper and falsification seem to appear because they purported to offer a rigorous means of demarcating reliable from non-reliable forms of knowledge.[24] Recourse to Popper reinforced the threat posed by unreliable forms of expertise—'junk science' and charlatanism—and appeared to offer judges a potential solution to evidentiary difficulties (Edmond and Mercer 1998a; Gusfield 1981). After *Daubert*, 'testing' became a primary consideration in many admissibility determinations pertaining to expert evidence. In *Kumho* the importance of testing was reiterated, perhaps strengthened. Although Popper was not explicitly named, 'testing' featured as a central tool for assessing the reliability of not only scientific evidence but all expert knowledge.

In *Daubert* a version of Popper's philosophy was translated into federal law. After *Kumho* only a 'folk' version of testing remained. The authority of the philosophy of science was displaced as the Supreme Court drew upon numerous *Daubert*-inspired judicial references to testing. In a relatively brief period the earlier legal apotheosis of Popper, in conjunction with a large number of written judgments, provided the Supreme Court with considerable *legal* authority, enabling the extension of the *Daubert* factors to non-scientific forms of expert evidence in *Kumho*. On the basis of extensive *legal* authority, reference to the philosophy of Popper could be abandoned.[25] Numerous judicial references to *Daubert,* post-*Daubert* judgments and the new doctrine of 'testing', rather than to arcane philosophical foundations, facilitated social legitimation without philosophical engagement. 'Testing' and the other criteria became legal categories, and, in applying them judges could evade specialist criticism on the basis that they were merely applying law—the FRE—in the routine administration of justice.[26] Recourse to 'Popper' *authorized* a more restrictive approach to admissibility decision-making while the conversion of falsification into testing helped to insulate legal institutions from external criticism.

If *Kumho* represents the exnomination of external authority, then *Daubert* and the Australian cases of *March v Stramare* and *Rogers v Whitaker* are more straightforward examples of what might be described as judicial inoculation or insulation in response to external forms of expertise (Barthes 1973: 84, 150). In *Daubert*, Blackmun indicated that even though judges sought reliable knowledge for the resolution of disputes, their quest was not identical to the quest undertaken by others, especially scientists. Drawing upon monolithic images of *law* and *science* (Goldberg 1994; compare Edmond and Mercer 1996), Blackmun explained:

> There are important differences between the quest for truth in the *courtroom* and the quest for truth in the *laboratory*. Scientific conclusions are subject to perpetual

revisions. Law, on the other hand, must resolve disputes *finally and quickly* ... That, nevertheless, is the balance that is struck by Rules of Evidence designed not for the exhaustive search for *cosmic understanding* but for the particularized resolution of legal disputes. (*Daubert* 1993: 485 italics added; Dixon 1965: 43)

In practice Blackmun's qualifications serve to sustain legal legitimacy while mediating potential criticism from outside the legal establishment. Accepting, uncontroversially, the importance of scientific knowledge, Blackmun proceeded to offer an explanation for legal derogation. Blackmun's *cosmological caveat*—that at times courts may arrive at conclusions different to those of scientists—helps to create space for interpretative flexibility in the legal deployment of expert evidence.

In a similar way, judicial expressions of causation tend to be sensitive to levels of consistency with images of causation developed in other domains. These concerns were evident in a leading Australian negligence case, *March v Stramare,* where a 'common sense' approach to legal causation was endorsed by a majority of the High Court:

> It has often been said that the legal concept of causation differs from philosophical and scientific notions of causation. That is because "questions of cause and consequence are not the same for law as for philosophy and science" ... In philosophy and science, the concept of causation has been developed in the context of explaining phenomena by reference to the relationship between conditions and occurrences. In law, on the other hand, problems of causation arise in the context of ascertaining or apportioning legal responsibility for a given occurrence. The law does not accept John Stuart Mill's definition of cause as the sum of the conditions which are jointly sufficient to produce it. Thus, at law, a person may be responsible for damage when his or her wrongful conduct is one of a number of conditions sufficient to produce that damage.[27]

Here, judges explain differences between law and purportedly more pure epistemological domains (such as philosophy and the sciences) in terms of the legal system having a range of constituencies beyond 'truth'. The legal system does not seem concerned exclusively with, nor possessed with the opportunity or resources to reflect upon, refractory epistemological matters. As in the previous example featuring Justice Blackmun, the legal system is sensitive, so we are told, to a range of other, often conflicting, considerations such as the pragmatic and expeditious resolution of disputes, particularization, finality, policy implications, effects of liability, fairness, public acceptance of verdicts and limited resources (Nobles and Schiff 1997; Zuckerman 1994). So, the legal assessment and attribution of causation is deliberately distinguished, and in the process inoculated, from the specific concerns of others, particularly scientists and philosophers.

In *Rogers v Whitaker* the High Court of Australia considered how to determine the appropriate standard of care in relation to a medical negligence action. Ascribing primacy to the legal dimensions of the standard of care, the Court emphatically declared that judges, rather than medical doctors, should determine what constituted medical negligence. Accordingly: 'while evidence of acceptable medical practice is a useful guide for the courts, it is for the courts to adjudicate on what is the appropriate standard of care'.[28] The opinions of medical practitioners, about what was ordinarily done or should be done, might carry considerable weight, but ultimately negligence was a legal category to be determined by judges. This approach was a conspicuous break with the previous jurisprudence, derived from the English decisions of *Bolam v Friern Hospital* (1957) and *Sidaway v Bethlehem Royal Hospital* (1985).[29] In those cases judges had held that: 'It is not enough to show that there is a body of competent professional opinion which considers that there was a wrong decision, if there also exists a body of professional opinion, equally competent, which supports the decision as reasonable in the circumstances' (*Bolam* 1957: 881). In *Rogers* the judges promoted themselves above doctors—law above medicine—in the determination of negligence, but in doing so, insulated themselves from criticism on the grounds that negligence, like reliability and causation, was a legal determination.[30]

The extent to which judges equate legal concerns with extra-legal insights varies considerably. Sometimes emphasis on the similarities between legal and non-legal approaches to fact-finding can strengthen a judgment. On other occasions, emphasizing differences between *law* and *science* can be used to contain anticipated 'epistemological' implications and criticisms. In *Daubert* we observed how the majority developed a (philosophically awkward) model of science, drawing without qualification on the philosophical work and authority of Popper. Yet, in the same judgment the majority explicitly distinguished legal and scientific approaches to knowledge. In their dissent, Chief Justice Rehnquist and Justice Stevens questioned the value of turning trial judges into amateur scientists, or philosophers of science (*Daubert* 1993: 487).

Institutional organization

So far we have considered how judges influence admissibility standards and selectively draw upon (e.g. the appropriation of Popper) or distinguish (e.g. in causation and medical negligence) expert discourses in ways that are presented as distinctively *legal*. In these ways legal practice was insulated from potential exogenous criticism. Now we turn to consider how institutional and organizational arrangements may operate to privilege or protect the perspectives of judges.

In democratic states judges are sensitive to a range of ostensibly non-legal concerns, particularly responsibility to the public at large and the social legitimacy of legal institutions (Hyde 1983). Notwithstanding the purported political commitment to public access and openness flowing from liberal democratic formulations of the 'rule of law', attempts to follow a trial and access legal materials such as exhibits and transcripts can be difficult, fragmentary and expensive.[31] Judgments are often difficult to read and comprehend, even for lawyers.[32] Few academics or journalists have the resources or inclination to review cases in detail.[33] Together, these impediments conspire against observers and strengthen the position of the judge, vis-à-vis the interested parties and more remote publics, in the endeavor to transform the judgment into an official record.

From a distance, and perhaps closer for the winning party, the judgment can become a surrogate for the entire trial (and even the events leading to trial).

The opportunity to observe all of the evidence and hear the legal argument provides the trial judge with an important advantage in the production of a judgment capable of rationalizing the decision.[34] Before having to make a decision the judge usually hears at least two strategically adumbrated, dynamic cases. These conditions afford the judge an unparalleled opportunity to selectively draw from the complex and often fragmentary arrays of evidentiary resources and legal interpretations. The judge has the opportunity and responsibility to produce what frequently becomes the authoritative version.[35] As the authority on law, charged with the responsibility of writing the official 'summary', the perspective of the judge is privileged. The closure produced through the judgment typically exploits many of the tropes and techniques used in creating and sustaining factual representations and reality effects in other contexts (Potter 1996). But the privileged legal perspective of the judge and the institutional procedures associated with trials and appeals offer several strategic advantages in the endeavor to produce a convincing rationalization of decision-making.

As a genre, the judgment endeavors to persuade by carefully integrating law, legal procedure and evidence into a socially sensitive narrative. Consistent with ideals of judicial impartiality, law and evidence appear to compel the judge's decision. The judge, in the capacity of author, however, tends to present the preferred evidence in terms which reinforce its reliability. Usually this involves downplaying, trivializing or selectively presenting the many contingencies explored during cross-examination.[36] Evidence which challenges the judicial narrative is either ignored or apparent problems with it are identified and emphasized.[37] We can observe some of these practices through a form of *legal regression*: by tracing an ordered appellate judgment *back* to the messiness (or contingency) associated with the trial and inquests.[38]

In the *Chamberlain* ('dingo baby') case, where experts could not agree about whether a piece of clothing had been damaged by a blade—suggesting human agency—or the teeth of a dingo, on appeal several judges distinguished between conflicting expert opinions by reference to the different disciplinary origins of the expertise.[39] Preferring the prosecution case, presumably on the basis of the entire evidentiary matrix and the fact that a jury had previously found the accused guilty of murdering her baby daughter, Justice Brennan explained:

> Professor Chaikin's [textile scientist] opinion was that the holes were made either by cutting or by holding the singlet under tension and puncturing it perhaps, but not necessarily, by using a pair of scissors. He was unable to reproduce such holes by mechanically driving a dingo's tooth into the fabric, even if the tooth were driven further than the gum line into the fabric as it lay upon the carcase of a freshly killed rabbit. However, Professor Chaikin *would not exclude the possibility* that an animal could cause damage of the kind observed in the singlet by holding part of the garment in its paws and part in its teeth thereby placing the fabric under tension.
>
> If Professor Chaikin's oral evidence and visual proofs were *accepted by the jury*, the hypothesis that a dingo had caused damage to Azaria's [the victim's] clothing could not be sustained. The *only substantial support* for the hypothesis that a dingo

caused the damage to the clothing came from Dr. H.J. Orams, who teaches the subject of animal dentition and skulls. His qualifications in that field were not challenged, but *he had no expertise in textiles.* (*Chamberlain* 1983-4: 583-4 italics added)

Brennan's treatment of this evidence is asymmetrical. The position of the odontologist (Orams) is devalued on the ground that he had no expertise in textiles.[40] The fact that the textile scientist (Chaikin) had no special knowledge of teeth is elided. Experiments with a single dingo tooth and a singlet wrapped around the carcass of a rabbit are presented as epistemologically remedial. In addition, Brennan alludes to the jury. This criminal appeal is structured around the question of whether the jury's verdict was safe. The judges could have developed the boundaries in other ways and incorporated aspects of Chaikin's cross-examination, developed immediately below, about the limits to his experiment with the tooth.

Unavoidably, judgments are summaries. Emphases, however, like inclusions and omissions, are not arbitrary. The previous extract from Brennan's judgment provides little indication of some of the critical exchanges which occurred during cross-examination at the trial and inquests. During the trial the Chamberlains' barrister, Phillips, vigorously challenged Chaikin's familiarity with teeth:

PHILLIPS: Well, in uttering the opinion that you have, you do it without having seen any of these matters we have just discussed [concerning animal teeth] don't you?
CHAIKIN: Well, I claim that I have some expertise in the interaction between various objects with various properties and fabrics, and fibre assemblies, and I base my opinion and conclusions on that.
PHILLIPS: I will repeat the question ...
CHAIKIN: That's correct.[41]

Under the critical scrutiny of cross-examination (see Lynch and Bogen 1996; Atkinson and Drew 1979), Chaikin reluctantly conceded that he held no experience with animal teeth or knowledge of differences between teeth. During an earlier proceeding, another barrister had questioned Chaikin about his experiment with a single canine tooth.

RICE: Despite the experiment that you conducted on that machine with the canine tooth of a dingo, did you at any time conduct any test whatever using the incisor teeth of a dingo?
CHAIKIN: No.[42]

Rice's question about the significance of a particular tooth, along with concerns about whether a rabbit carcass resembled a baby's body, the pressure exerted by dingo jaws, whether saliva and blood acting as lubricants would make a difference to the damage, the significance of the absence of gums as well as the combined effect of teeth and claws were all directed at compromising the value of Chaikin's experiment and his credibility (Collins 1985; Gooding, Pinch and Schaffer 1989; Shapin 1994). Neither Chaikin's limited experience with animal teeth nor the potential weakness of the experiment were developed in Brennan's judgment. Instead, Chaikin's expertise with textiles, a non-problematic experiment and recognition of the possibility of doubt were all developed in a way that appears to stabilize the jury verdict. However, if a judge sought to overturn the jury verdict we can imagine how they might have supported that choice by: emphasizing the apparent uncertainty—the disagreement between Chaikin and Orams—or corroborating Oram's position with Chaikin's concession 'that he would not exclude the possibility', or raising questions about the value of extrapolations from the experiment—including Chaikin's concessions made during cross-examination—and not conferring evidentiary primacy on the textile evidence. A judge might also have preferred—as another, Justice Murphy, did—the eyewitness testimony to the conflicting opinions of experts. For Brennan, however, none of this constituted 'substantial support'.

Accepting that this example is taken from a more extensive and messier evidentiary matrix, it provides an indication of how the ability to construct the authoritative account introduces considerable interpretative discretion which can enhance it persuasiveness. These discretions are normally protected from ironic contrasts with the trial record because they are displaced from the judgment and public scrutiny. This example also suggests that interpreting and applying rules and procedure and valuing evidence are not simple algorithmic processes. Apart from contexts of use, which are mediated by law, the evidence has no intrinsically stable, or proper, value. In the Chamberlain case, a variety of outcomes between the first inquest, trial, appeals and eventual Morling Royal Commission would seem to support this contention. The transcriptual record provides very fertile materials for privileging and qualifying knowledges, expertise and perspectives— the construction of legal reliability—in the subsequent reconstruction of authoritative judicial accounts.

Following from the previous example, an account of the judicial treatment of expert evidence ought to address the issue of how judges analyze and weigh expert evidence in their judgments. Once admitted, expert evidence forms part of a more complex, legally attuned case. As a generalization, expert evidence will be combined with other types of evidence: frequently lay testimony and sometimes additional expert evidence. During the course of litigation evidence will be strategically elicited and contested through examination-in-chief, cross-examination and re-examination and written reports. These processes tend to produce complex arrays of accepted and controversial facts, claims, opinions and beliefs which, as we have seen, are available to the judge in the endeavor to produce a legally and factually predicated decision as part of their public rationalization. Competent cross-examination, in conjunction with the extent of detail from the trial incorporated into the judgment, can (within limits) make even apparently methodologically rigorous practices appear questionable. Earlier I suggested that it would not have been difficult to represent Chaikin's rabbit experiment in ways that eroded its potential evidentiary value. The ability to provide the official reconstruction of the trial, the procedures and the evidence provides the judge with a considerable, but not insurmountable, rhetorical advantage.

Evidentiary hierarchies

Acknowledging the existence of a large variety of representational practices, the following are a few examples of how judges confronted with competing evidentiary arrays endeavored to persuasively resolve litigation through their evaluation of *evidence*. The examples are taken from product liability and native title litigation and a dissenting judgment in the unsuccessful *Chamberlain* appeal. In each of the examples one or more judges produces an unproblematized *evidentiary hierarchy* as the appropriate means of ordering the epistemic value and legal effects attributed to, but implicitly produced by, the evidence. Rather than reflect the complex relations between law and evidence or the social and policy sensitivities of judges, these judgments tend to reinforce the legal mythology that outcomes are produced ostensibly through the application of non-problematized *fact* to pre-existing *law*.[43]

Litigation over the teratogenic effects of Bendectin began in US courts in the early 1980s. Plaintiffs and their families sued Merrell Dow Pharmaceuticals for a range of birth defects they alleged had been caused through the mother's ingestion of the anti-nausea medication, Bendectin. The scale of Bendectin litigation and the associated evidentiary difficulties were among the factors that led the Supreme Court to hear *Daubert* (1993), an appeal from a Californian Bendectin case.

Before *Daubert*, and in response to an escalating number of Bendectin case filings, the relevant legal standards, and the outcomes of earlier cases, several federal judicial circuits endeavored to disrupt the litigation by imposing a debilitating hierarchy upon the types of evidence that were admissible and sufficient to support any further actions in their jurisdiction. Several federal appellate courts explained that epidemiological studies—preferably those undertaken independent from litigation and published—would be required before plaintiffs could bring any further cases to trial. The Fifth Circuit Court of Appeal explained:

> We expect that our decision here will *have a precedential effect on other cases pending in this circuit* which allege Bendectin as the cause of birth defects. Hopefully, our decision will have the effect of encouraging district judges faced with medical and epidemiologic proof to be *especially vigilant in scrutinizing* the basis, reasoning and conclusiveness of studies presented by both sides. However, we do not wish this case to stand as a bar to future Bendectin cases in the event that *new and statistically significant studies emerge* which would give a jury a firmer basis on which to determine the issues of causation.[44]

Confronted with the logistical problems and resource implications of hundreds of Bendectin cases,[45] in conjunction with a considerable body of evidence, the Court decreed that a particular type of expert evidence—statistically significant epidemiological studies—was the only type of evidence capable of sustaining future Bendectin claims. Unfortunately for the plaintiffs, cases assembled using *in vivo* and *in vitro* studies, chemical structure comparisons, toxicological evidence and unpublished reanalysis and meta-analysis of the large number of predominantly unfavorable published epidemiological studies were, in effect, excluded (deemed inadmissible) or deemed insufficient to sustain legal action. In *Lynch v Merrell-National Laboratories*, the First Circuit Court of Appeal drew support for this approach from Judge Weinstein's *Agent Orange* decision: 'Studies of this sort, singly or in combination, do not have the capability of proving causation in human beings in the absence of any confirmatory epidemiological data'.[46]

By establishing what is presented as an apparently natural evidentiary hierarchy, US federal courts were able to limit the difficulties posed by the many Bendectin suits and other types of potential (mass) tort litigation. Insisting on a demanding evidentiary threshold they were able to prevent civil juries—stipulated under the Seventh Amendment of the US Constitution—from hearing civil cases. The articulation of an evidentiary hierarchy with published epidemiological studies at the apex and other types of evidence located further down the epistemological scale effectively disposed of the plaintiffs' cases as they were unable to establish *legal* causation.

Lest this approach to the evidence be construed as simply proper or natural—as most judges and commentators have implied (Green 1992, 1996; Sanders 1992, 1993, 1998)—a few qualifications are in order. First, throughout the litigation there was disagreement between epidemiologists inside and outside of courts. The debate ranged from how judges should use epidemiological knowledge and professional standards of statistical significance to the value of reanalysis. Second, the epidemiological studies reported levels of association that varied among injuries. Limb deformations, which were most appealing to contingency-fee lawyers, had weaker associations than some of the internal damage attributed to Bendectin. In jury trials, missing limbs were understood as potentially more lucrative than malformed stomachs. So, cases with the strongest epidemiological associations were not always those preferred by lawyers and not necessarily those litigated. Third, scientists, legal commentators and judges all found the evidence to mean different things at different times. Scientists did not agree on whether Bendectin was shown to be a risk, or when and if it had been exonerated. Judges varied markedly in their responses to the plaintiffs' evidence. A few courts admitted the plaintiffs' evidence even as late as the 1990s and the Supreme Court in the *Daubert* (1993) appeal, in contrast to its critical scrutiny of the plaintiffs' evidence in *Kumho*, refrained from analyzing the actual expert evidence. Several eminent epidemiologists submitted *amicus curiae* briefs to the *Daubert* appeal; some criticizing the *Brock* (1989) decision. Fourth, there were differences among judges as to whether the pharmaceutical company's 'chequered history', including an association with Thalidomide and MER-29, was relevant to the Bendectin claims and the reliability of some of its in-house studies. Fifth, some courts heard cases in their entirety. Other courts divided particular elements of the cases, like causation, using trial bifurcation or trifurcation, so they could be heard discretely. Sixth, there was disagreement over how the different types of evidence should be combined and evaluated. It was not clear that privileging epidemiological evidence, as Judge Weinstein had in his *Agent Orange* decision, would be the appropriate response in the Bendectin cases. Weinstein's *Agent Orange* decision did, however, provide a useful cultural (and importantly legal) resource (Schuck 1986). Seventh, some of the courts basically adopted (and naturalized) the trial strategy advocated by the manufacturer Merrell, as the appropriate legal response. Merrell tended to cite the *Agent Orange* decision and advocate rigorous standards of admissibility and evidentiary sufficiency. Eighth, several judges expressed concerns about the logistical implications of so many Bendectin trials. Even if such anxieties did not determine outcomes, they presumably influenced them. Ninth, the evidentiary record was changing as the litigation continued. Litigation actually encouraged further research, in particular additional epidemiological studies. Consequently, other types of scientific study were less likely to be funded. While the number of epidemiological studies finding no statistically significant association increased, this can only be substituted for a lack of proof of causation if, somewhat tautologically, statistically significant epidemiological evidence is privileged (Edmond and Mercer 2000).

The second example of an explicit evidentiary hierarchy is drawn from the dissenting judgment of Justice Murphy in an appeal in the *Chamberlain* case. Considering the various types of evidence produced by both the Crown (prosecution) and the defence, Murphy, the only trained scientist on the bench, explained that in cases where controversial technical evidence was in direct conflict with the unchallenged evidence of independent lay witnesses, preference should be accorded to the lay testimony. For Murphy the case 'illustrates that it is dangerous to convict on "expert" evidence which is inconsistent with the otherwise credible evidence of what witnesses saw or heard'.[47]

The final example also involves the hierarchization of evidence, only this time in the context of an Aboriginal native title claim in the Australian Federal Court. In the controversial *Yorta Yorta* judgment, Justice Olney was, as he explained, confronted with a tremendous volume of different types of evidence, including: anthropological, historical, genealogical and claimant testimony.[48] For Olney, the basic legal question in the *Yorta Yorta* litigation was whether the claimants fulfilled the requirements specified under the *Native Title Act*.[49] That Act emerged as a legislative response to the High Court's recognition (really legal innovation and refinement) of native title in the earlier *Mabo* and *Wik* decisions.[50] On the basis of these decisions the Act was composed so that judges hearing native title applications were particularly sensitive to continuity of *possession* and Aboriginal *tradition* (Strelein 2001; Ray 2003). In order to succeed the claimants had to prove they were *descended* from the original inhabitants and maintained a sufficiently *traditional* link to the land. In his rejection of the Yorta Yorta claim, Olney developed an evidentiary hierarchy where particular types of evidence informed his construction of legal tradition and the possibility of proving descent. Expressing his distrust of what was described as partisan, speculative and controversial anthropological evidence and the mixed motives he attributed to the Aboriginal claimants, especially the younger and more overtly politicized individuals, Olney indicated that he would apply his critical judicial abilities to an avowed preference for *the historical record* in his assessment of the claim.[51]

This historical record was composed primarily of the diaries and writings of nineteenth century farmers, squatters and clergy, official records and an Aboriginal petition to the governor. Emphasizing uncertainty, Olney relied heavily on the contemporaneous accounts left by Curr, Mathews and Robinson.

> The Court has derived little assistance from the testimony of the various experts who have given evidence in this proceeding and this because apart from the recorded observations of Curr and Robinson, much of the evidence was based upon speculation. I say that without in any way meaning to disparage the qualifications, experience or integrity of the witnesses concerned. Obviously, the issues with which the Court is required to grapple in a native title claim were not matters at the forefront of academic thought at the time when it really mattered, namely (in this case) the 1830s and 1840s. (*Yorta Yorta* 1998: para. 54).

And, later:

> There are no objective facts to which the Court can have regard to support a conclusion one way or the other. That being so, if scholars learned in the relevant discipline are unable to provide an authoritative answer, the Court must have resort to such *credible primary evidence* as is available and apply *the normal processes of analysis and reason.* (*Yorta Yorta* 1998: para. 62 italics added)

In the absence of 'objective facts' Olney expressed a preference for 'credible primary evidence'. As a result he accepted the observations of nineteenth century squatters and farmers notwithstanding their lack of formal qualifications and tendency to perpetuate the prejudices of their age. Olney's use of these historical materials was uncritical. He privileged *this* historical record even though the interests of settlers were often in direct conflict with those of the Aboriginal inhabitants. Olney's 'credible' observers held aspirations for land which seem to have been in direct conflict with continuing Aboriginal possession. For example, Curr's 'purchase' of land, on which his sheep were 'already grazing', from an Aboriginal boy for a stick of tobacco is described by Olney as evidence of Curr's 'rights to land' and Aboriginal complicity in its alienation. The missionary Mathews' perspective was accepted, notwithstanding his description as 'the architect of further disruption of aboriginal life'.

On the basis of inconsistencies between the nineteenth century practices drawn from *the historical record* provided by Curr, Mathews and Robinson—which purported to present the *real* Aboriginal tradition—and contemporary Aboriginal practices, Olney determined that the claimants had lost, actually abandoned, their tradition. In addition, the absence of detailed genealogical records meant that it was difficult to prove that the majority of claimants were clearly related to the original inhabitants.

Even without embarking on a detailed critique (or defence) of Olney's pidgin historiography, the case provides an excellent example of how evidentiary preferences are constructed alongside, or simultaneously with, legal, here statutory, standards. Olney's static model of Aboriginal tradition—which seriously constrained the chances of succeeding in a native title application, especially in populated and productive agricultural regions—is not only reinforced but structured by his conservative evidentiary preferences. Presumably, other evidentiary preferences would have sustained more flexible models of 'tradition', recognizing adaptation and change. In an earlier native title claim—significantly, a case concerning land in a more economically marginal area by a remote group of (legally) more *traditional* Aborigines—Olney accepted what he presented as uncontested anthropological and claimant testimony.[52] Notwithstanding these differences which seem to correlate with a political economy which may transcend immediate evidentiary concerns—where recognition of native title in certain places is vulnerable to serious politicization—in *Yorta Yorta* Olney claimed that he was following the dictates of law and refused to engage in social engineering.[53]

The point here is not to advocate preference for a particular hierarchy, although that might be an appropriate response on some occasions, but rather to emphasize that hierarchies are judicial constructions. Evidentiary hierarchies and legal interpretations that support liability, innocence and native title are no less constructed than those leading to non-liability, guilt and *terra nullius*. The *evidence* never speaks for nor arranges itself. This is not to suggest the hierarchies are arbitrary; in each of the examples the particular selection drew upon a variety of pre-existing cultural repertoires and was organized so that, in conjunction with interpretation of the law (or the identified legal principles) and procedure, it produced desired effects (Fish 1989; Goodwin 1994). The persuasiveness of these effects, however, is a matter for the reader (Abercrombie and Longhurst 1998; Dickinson et al. 1998).

Once we remove the primacy of determinations conventionally attributed to evidentiary arrays or particular interpretations of the law we can begin to observe consistency and synergies between elaborations of law and fact. In the Bendectin litigation, the focus upon admissibility and equating epidemiology with legal causation eventually stemmed the litigation. In *Yorta Yorta*, perhaps more clearly, privileging a particular type of historical evidence reinforced Olney's preference for a static model of tradition. That model was intolerant to social change, largely silent about descent and personal relations with the lands and effectively dispossessed the claimants of both their land and 'traditional' culture (Oakeshott 1962: 31; Hobsbawm and Ranger 1983). In the *Chamberlain* appeal, Murphy's confidence in the lay testimony led him, as one of two dissenting judges, to find that the evaluation of the evidence by the jury had been unsafe and required the Court to set the convicted prisoner free. In contrast, the other judges, in an earlier appeal to the Northern Territory Court of Criminal Appeal and a majority in the High Court of Australia—including Brennan—explained how they found the scientific evidence compelling and the conviction sound.

'Freshness' and other evidentiary modulations

Hierarchization is not the only way to understand judicial evaluation of expert evidence. The value of evidence can be modulated and qualified in a great variety of ways (Edmond 2000). Expert evidence can be trivialized or ignored. It can be corroborated and become cumulative. Alternatively, experts with conflicting views can 'cancel each other out'. Controversy or disagreement, even if only apparent, can be substituted for, or equated with, 'uncertainty'. Interests can be apportioned, or motivations examined in ways that threaten the independence, objectivity or reliability of expert knowledge and opinions. Methods can be criticized, derogations from popular norms and established protocols identified and rendered (in)significant (Schuster and Yeo 1986; Mulkay 1980). Previous performances—especially in other legal proceedings—may be considered, perhaps in conjunction with impressions of stubbornness and pliability, alignment or the nature of the opinion. These kinds of evaluations and representations can be considered individually or in combination.

There are numerous ideal images, norms and counter-norms with which to juxtapose expert performances (Lynch 1998; Edmond 1998, 2001, 2004). During the Chamberlain trial, an expert witness was questioned extensively about his relationship with (really independence from) the defence lawyers while they were temporarily based in a small city in Northern Australia for the duration of the trial. The same expert's presentation as a professor (an academic biologist) as opposed to an experienced (or practical) forensic scientist also provided basic outlines that could be selectively infused with contextual significance (Edmond 1999). In *Kumho* the inspection of a tyre in a lawyer's office rather than a laboratory was subsequently used to suggest that something was awry. Locating knowledge in its proper place (consider Shapin and Schaffer 1985; Shapin 1994), like persistent allusions to hired-guns and charlatans, are tropes with considerable lineage in adversarial litigation.[54]

The complexity of litigation, the evidentiary arrays and the local integration of law, procedure, evidence and strategy also insulate judges from a range of potential criticisms. Specific criticisms can often be parried by shifting from one dimension, such as some of the evidence, to multiple dimensions including (the interaction of) law, other evidence, procedures, similar cases and the jury. Reference to length and complexity is a common feature of judgments resulting from large scale litigation where dozens of witnesses are called and thousands of pages of documents and transcript produced in accordance with legal categories and rules of procedure. Judges are legal experts, so even when interpretations of evidence are criticized, it is judges who retain the right to interpret their *legal significance* (Isaacs 1922; Peller 1985). Notably, legal significance *can* be distinguished from evidentiary significance. Tensions around *truth, accuracy, fairness* and *justice* have recently produced considerable anxiety (Huber 1991; Farber 1997; Levitt 1999: 211–30; Park 2000). The metaphysics of the law/fact dichotomy, and the combination of law and fact serves to compromise non-legal assessments of legal decisions.[55]

Notwithstanding the apparent simplicity of the dichotomy, 'law' and 'fact' are continuously and to some extent inextricably intertwined. Questions such as whether the evidence is sufficiently reliable for admission, whether the evidence can support or prove a case, whether the verdict was safe, whether a range of procedures such as cross-examination or summing up were adequate are all classified as ostensibly legal decisions. This classification actually prejudices the way in which non-legal approaches to the facts and procedures are understood and valued. Investing law with primacy over fact privileges the judge's legal expertise and authoritative interpretation of the entire case while qualifying criticisms based exclusively upon evidentiary dimensions of a case. Even where a judge or jury is deemed to have misinterpreted or misunderstood some of the evidence, the legal implications or outcome may remain undisturbed. Once again, this is ostensibly a legal consideration.

Alleged miscarriages of justice provide poignant examples of the potential complexity associated with law/fact relations. In criminal appeals, questions of whether the verdict is *safe* on the basis of the evidence and procedure or whether evidence that was not adduced during the trial is actually new and sufficiently significant to warrant reconsideration are treated as legal issues. In relation to 'fresh' evidence, the legal framing is motivated by judicial concerns about parties withholding evidence to improve their chances of success on appeal, in addition to the very serious implications of having to reverse a criminal conviction. Consequently, appeals concerning the relevance and value of *fresh evidence* actively inquire into the circumstances attending the evidence at the trial: whether the 'fresh' evidence was known or ought to have been known *at that time.* Typically, the negligence or failure of legal advisers and experts ought not to warrant further judicial review. Here we can see how questions of law, such as whether evidence is 'fresh', are in actuality complex aggregations of concerns, including the temporal emergence, potential significance and reliability of evidence; the credibility of experts; the earlier performances of judges and lawyers; the relevant traditions associated with review; and may even extend to institutional implications and the publicity associated with appeals or anticipated from acquittals. The metaphysical shift required to transform guilt to non-guilt can create serious problems of legitimacy for the criminal justice system. Recourse to 'fresh' evidence shifts agency and responsibility from the judges to the evidence and those responsible for (not) adducing it (Eckhoff 1966; Edmond 2002b; Barnes 2000).

In a similar way the judicial treatment of legal causation in the Bendectin litigation was closely linked to concerns about the implications of admissibility; specifically, whether the plaintiffs' cases were capable of proving that Bendectin was a teratogen. Legal images of causation were coterminous with responses to the assortment of evidence. Notwithstanding the ability to express the required standard of legal rather than, say, regulatory versions of causation abstractly, until the standard was infused with the various evidentiary arrays it had no self-evident meaning. Judicial assessments of the value of evidence produced legal effects and the legal framing of the case, as well as earlier tort cases, held evidentiary implications. Earlier, the discussion of admissibility standards provided some illumination of the role of social order, judicial economy, the nature of science and non-science and the value of different types of evidence in judicial constructions of Rule 702.

Finally, an important institutional feature of adversarial systems is the participation of the jury. The historical development of the law of evidence and procedure has been profoundly influenced by judicial concerns about the need to *assist* the jury and *protect* the innocent (Langbein 1977, 2003). Historically, more than any other group, judges in adversarial jurisdictions have tended to support the continued use of lay juries (Kalven and Zeisel 1966; Litan 1993; Special Committee 1989). The jury not only relieves the judge of fact-finding responsibility, but the impenetrability of its sequestered decision-making process and the absence of reasons means that courts of appeal can either endorse jury findings, celebrating the important participatory role of the citizen in the polity, or alternatively, they can override the jury decision through the identification of mistakes at the trial, the production of fresh evidence, the recognition of flawed performances by scientists and police and even by characterizing the jury's decision as inappropriate or perverse. The absence of reasons in jury cases enables appellate courts to re-interpret the evidence *ab initio*.

Conclusion

In the foregoing discussion I have interpreted a number of judgments in ways that were designed to show how judges actively and constructively managed the admission, presentation and implications of a range of expert knowledges. This involved making qualified claims about the indeterminacy of law and of fact, and recognizing complexity in their interaction and mutual constitution. In conclusion, it is my intention to tentatively locate these claims in the context of legal scholarship on decision-making and in doing so return to some of the limitations inherent in using *distortion* as the primary lens through which to understand the multivalent legal responses to expertise.

Examining the jurisprudence around the *Federal Rules of Evidence*, we saw how through the use of relevance, reliability, admissibility, sufficiency and burdens of proof, judges (and others) were able to influence the types of expertise that could enter US federal courts and, once admitted, how that evidence could be used to rationalize decisions. By raising the standard for the admission of expert evidence, thereby requiring more established and mainstream expertise, judges were able to actively manage the legitimacy of certain types of litigation. As a generalization, more onerous admissibility standards and more *reliable* evidence meant that it was easier to represent verdicts by a judge, or jury, as reasonable. Perhaps ironically, in determining what can count as an actionable case judges influence the social credibility of expert knowledges (King and Kaganas 1998: 221–42; Galanter 1983). These influences also work in reverse. Judges are not insensitive to impressions of the social standing and social authority of particular fields, disciplines and experts (Edmond 2001).

Historically, models of judicial reasoning and the assessment of evidence have tended to explain judicial decision-making as the necessary result of applying law to the evidence, or facts.[56] Probably the best known formulation was expressed many decades ago by Jerome Frank as the 'conventional theory':

> For convenience, let us symbolize a legal rule by the letter R, the facts of the case by the letter F, and the court's decision by the letter D. We can then crudely schematize the conventional theory of how courts operate by saying

$$R \times F = D$$

In other words, according to the conventional theory, a decision is a product of an *R* and an *F*. If, as to any lawsuit, you know the *R* and the *F*, you should, then, know what the *D* will be.[57] (Frank 1949: 14)

Responding to the conventional view, Frank recognized several limitations to the use of factual evidence. Because the senses were unreliable and people were motivated, though not always consciously, by personal interests, for Frank like Hume before him, the facts were subjective. Accordingly he thought the equation ought to read *R X SF = D*, where *SF* stands for subjective fact (Frank 1949: 24; Hume 1999: 115–16). While American legal realists and more recently critical legal scholars have been attentive to both rule and fact scepticism, most of their interest seems to have been directed toward the limits of rule-following and the mutability of legal doctrines as part of their critique of legal rhetoric, method and ideology (Kairys 1982, but see Twining 1990). This is true of Kennedy's 'phenomenological' account of judging: *Freedom and Constraint*. In an analysis of the construction of an outcome-oriented judgment, Kennedy basically accepts the facts in his various scenarios and provides only limited indication of the extent of any constraint (Kennedy 1986). More recent, and less sceptical, work by Feeley and Rubin provides a more institutionally sensitive response to judicial decision-making, but again reveals little about fact construction or the constitutive relationships between laws, facts, decisions, procedures and strategy (Feeley and Rubin 1999; Jackson 1991). Notwithstanding the existence of a very substantial critical legal literature spanning almost a century, judges continue to explain their decision-making (*D*) on the basis of applying law (*R*) to the facts (*F*). Typically, expert evidence is considered as a special type of fact (*F*).

In this account I have argued that facts—particularly judicial representations of facts—are, like laws and rules, polysemous and promiscuous. While laws, doctrines, rules and procedures may all be expressed abstractly, in the particular context of the case they are related to specific factual claims, which are often contested (consider Duhem 1906). Attempts to embrace particular facts or interpret rules and apply procedures are not only sensitive to each other but can be mutually constituting. The use of facts to support a case, counter other facts, or to infuse some incarnation of the law—such as tradition or causation—with significance requires judicial attention, namely managerial and representative work. Consequently, decision-making in trials and judgments is a form of *evidentiary bricolage*. The judge, like the parties and witnesses, is unavoidably a bricoleur (Levi Strauss 1966; Frank 1949). This observation is not trivial, because attention to evidence and procedure, as in the native title and Bendectin litigation, can be as effective in determining or delimiting rights as any substantive legal doctrine. In addition, we have seen how the *two* are often intimately intertwined.

Notwithstanding the considerable analytical attention that has been devoted to the judicial interpretation of law, legal indeterminacy and the difficulty of strict rule-following, perhaps the most interesting and controversial conclusion emerging from this analysis is that in many cases the evidence, including expert evidence, is *at least as* pliable as the law. There are several reasons for this conclusion.

Evidence tends to be case-specific.[58] Evidence tends to change from case to case, whereas the law, at least in more abstract versions, may remain stable, often verbatim, over a considerable period of time. Cardozo, an eminent American jurist, wrote that: 'In countless litigations the law is so clear that judges have no discretion' (Cardozo 1921: 160). Legal doctrines are often reviewed. Senior courts and commentators strive to provide standardized formulations. *Daubert*, *Joiner* and *Kumho* were examples of such formulations. Judges are far more conversant with legal doctrines, in their abstract guise, than particular evidentiary arrays. While appellate courts may produce hegemonic interpretations of fact, the interpretations are largely limited to the particular, or *sui generis*, case.[59] In *Yorta Yorta* Olney found the anthropological evidence and claimant testimony insufficient to support a native title claim and yet similar sorts of evidence were adequate in an earlier native title case. For the judge, flexibility in fact construction and interpretation is probably greater than for law. Indeed, these observations find support in the aphorism 'hard cases make bad law', or in the familiar practice of distinguishing cases—really outcomes or the way to apply relevant law—on their facts. Judges can always distinguish cases on their facts where the application of relevant law seems to produce inconsistent or problematic outcomes.[60]

Recognition of the often complex relations between law, procedure, evidence and strategy confers an additional benefit. It can accommodate the possibility, advanced by many theorists, that the desired outcome may actually shape or even determine judicial decisions (e.g. Garfinkel 1967: 114; Wynne 1982: 120–37). These circumstances may have serious implications for our understanding of law and evidence, especially if evidence can be as pliant as law. To some extent these observations resemble Collins' (1985) description of the 'experimenter's regress' in the production of scientific knowledge. For Collins, during periods of controversy the right methods and the identity of Nature remain controversial until particular experimental outcomes are accepted. When the identity of Nature is eventually resolved—socially—the appropriate methods and correct interpretation of the relevant evidence are simultaneously settled. So, too, in legal practice the preferred outcome may structure the selection and integration of law and fact. By recognizing degrees of indeterminacy in law, procedure and evidence, both individually and in combination, we are provided with an additional means of understanding decisions and judicial sensitivities to factors that extend beyond the narrow constraints expressed in Frank's formulation. If judges are sensitive to the results of litigation and their implications, then (some of) the reasons for a decision may lie beyond the court, or the law and evidence, notwithstanding narrow legal and evidentiary rationalization. These concerns may be most conspicuous in high profile or politically sensitive cases. The *Yorta Yorta* decision is comprehensible in terms of outcome. Politically, it may have been controversial and divisive to have recognized Aboriginal native title in an area extensively settled by European Australians. Olney's evidentiary and legal preferences may well have *determined* the outcome, but given the obstacles it seems more plausible to argue that his evidentiary and legal preferences *enabled* him to achieve—what was for him—the politically expedient result. Emphasizing degrees of indeterminacy allows for varying degrees of flexibility, while remaining sensitive to jurisprudential stasis, established traditions, and approaches to particular types of evidence or the cogency of particular evidentiary ensembles.

In combination with the recognition of judicial discretions and freedoms, it has also been my intention to recognize and emphasize degrees of legal constraint. In analyzing judicial decisions we are no more required to become 'outcome dopes' than ascribe proper values to the law and evidence. Professional socialization, legal institutional values, position in the judicial hierarchy, the cases presented and constructions of the relevant law all constrain judicial decision-making. Law and/or evidence may determine or constrain the outcome. Notwithstanding the various constraints, we have seen how law, procedure, strategy, outcome and the way they can be interrelated and extended across society, all provide potential explanatory resources and occasionally pressures which act upon judges (and analysts).

Literature in science studies and the public understanding of science has tended to emphasize the importance of context and experience in understanding diverse responses to scientific knowledge, institutions and individuals (Irwin and Wynne 1996; Gregory and Miller 1998). For example, the significance attributed to an epidemiological study may vary considerably between a research-funding agency, a regulatory body, the court in a negligence case and a pregnant woman. The meanings are context-related and draw upon and reinforce resources and concerns relevant to the individual or institutions in the particular setting. Questions about whether something should count as evidence, as well as its situated meaning(s) can become quite complex, particularly as formidable and differentiated arrays develop and diachronic relations are considered. Notwithstanding a growing range of empirical studies on the public understanding of science, little seems to have been written about how judges actually approach expertise in the courtroom and the judgment. This chapter has endeavored, in a preliminary sort of way, to provide an indication of how judges use their own professional identities and institutional resources to moderate the meaning of expert knowledge in specific contexts. Consequently, we encountered senior appellate courts exerting tremendous influence by altering admissibility standards, re-characterizing trial judges as gatekeepers and provisioning them with a variety of rhetorical tools, all under the guise of statutory interpretation. More locally, in native title and Bendectin litigation, we saw how trial judges differentiated between different types of knowledge through their responses to mixtures of law, procedure and evidence. In the *Chamberlain* case, the distance between the trial (and the transcriptual and evidentiary record) and the appellate judgment assisted in the construction of an authoritative decision—even if it was temporary and controvertible.[61]

Legal institutions have developed elaborate rules and procedures for administering trials, especially the preparation and presentation of evidence. Parties often come to litigation with matters of life and death, liberty, health and property at stake. In these circumstances judges are required to produce important decisions in ways that are socially responsible, credible and often timely. In rationalizing their decisions judges have to attend to the law and evidence and the cogency of their explanations, in conjunction with the social standing of their institutions and any anticipated implications flowing from their decisions.

Consequently, judgments are very special literary creations where particular types of social knowledges are produced. We have seen how judges have developed means of dealing with what are often presented as the necessary epistemological effects of the evidence, particularly expert evidence, both inside and outside of the courtroom. To characterize (some) judgments as distortions without considering the range of institutional concerns and constituencies seems inappropriate (Edmond 2001; Wootten 2003). It perpetuates the conventional view and the reverence for fact parodied by Frank and others over half a century ago. Judges have constituencies and concerns that extend beyond perspectives on evidence. In decision-making they have a range of legal resources and repertoires for explaining their choices which not only shield them from criticism but uphold important and at times contradictory social values. Recourse to, not always consistent, visions of justice, rule-following, procedural fairness, consistency, openness, rights, public accountability and the separation of powers all provide means of differentiating and insulating the practice of law from other social practices and epistemologies.

Many critics and proponents of reform, especially those concerned with legal distortion in the guise of 'junk science' and charlatanism, present technocratic procedures (masquerading as the *rule of fact*) such as court-appointed experts, expert panels, science courts and science-trained judges as viable alternatives to our current practices (Huber 1991; Note 1995b, compare Edmond and Mercer 1998a). Without embarking on a comprehensive defence of adversarial legal institutions and practices, it would appear that technocratic and scientistic solutions are unlikely to function in the ways implied. The resolution of the Bendectin litigation, like the determination of native title and guilt is not entirely reducible to some kind of asocial factual determinations. There are no such facts, no neutral procedures and no non-controversial means of evaluating the evidence—or even determining what should count as evidence. Procedures and standards, such as burdens of proof, statutes of limitations, resource limitations and the need to resolve disputes relatively quickly, all have the potential to influence outcomes. Apparently straightforward procedural dimensions such as allocating responsibility for proof, the time allowed for resolution or the terms of the litigation may assist parties or encourage highly strategic responses (Casper and Wellstone 1982; Martin 1977; Edmond 2003). Earlier we encountered some of the politics associated with establishing admissibility standards, and the implications of hierarchizing evidence. The sciences, as they currently stand, are not homogeneous, do not share universal or transferable values—such as how to approach different kinds of evidence or what kinds of knowledge should count as evidence—and are in no position to credibly resolve complex social disputes unilaterally. For a variety of historical reasons, including the way in which scientists have endeavored to generate and maintain their own cultural authority, legal responsiveness and participatory mechanisms have few scientific equivalents (Barnes 1985).

In contrast, legal institutions allow appeals—albeit sometimes reluctantly—have reforms imposed upon them, stimulate social change, (eventually) respond to changing social circumstances and enable citizens to participate in or initiate change(s). Consequently courts and judges, as political actors, will continue, as they always have, to muddle through (Linblom 1959). They will continue to make policy-sensitive and political decisions which will be explained and defended on the basis of law and evidence. They will also continue to draw upon expertise to make their processes appear socially credible, or at least plausible. In the process they will continue to appropriate expertise in ways that reinforce (shrinking) legal independence from the sciences, occasionally by exploiting slippage in the sciences' own rhetorics and occasionally and idiosyncratically exposing aspects of what will be presented as bad *science*—rather than bad *law*.

In closing, while recognizing the importance of laws, legal values and processes we need to avoid the risk of valorizing or reifying them. At the beginning of the chapter I advocated an agnostic stance toward evidence; now I am advocating a more agnostic stance toward law and the interactions between law and fact. Failure to appreciate the importance of legal traditions, processes and values, notwithstanding degrees of indeterminacy, would be to repeat the error made by those alleging legal distortion of fact. Images of law and fact and their strategic combination, under the guise of legalism, sanitize political decision-making. This, as Wynne has argued, represents a 'degenerate style of political conduct' (Wynne 1982: 137). Neither the scientific method nor the legal method can redeem or fully explain judicial decision-making. Recognizing that *the law* and *the facts* are not always independent and do not always determine outcomes in a straightforward (or algorithmic) fashion, we need to be more attentive to judicial decision-making and rationalization. Through modifying our own theoretical frameworks we are empowered to more actively and, perhaps more realistically, judge the judges.

Acknowledgements

I would like to thank Tony Connolly, Leighton McDonald, Tim Rowse, Robert Nelson, David Turnbull and members of the ECR Reading Group, UNSW, for commenting on earlier versions.

Notes

1   For example, judges have consistently rejected, as heretical, the claim that expert disagreement precludes a firm finding of fact. See *R v Sodo* (1975) 61 Cr.App. R. 131, 133; *Chamberlain v The Queen* (1983–4) 153 CLR 521, 559, 575, 623.
2   The impact of procedure has become increasingly significant in legal scholarship during the last two decades, see Yeazell (1994), Molot (1998), Schwartz (1991), Finley (1999).
3   See Austin (1962) and Twining and Miers (1982).
4   These are only a couple of the considerations. Sometimes litigation, or the threat of litigation, can be used to frighten, intimidate, exhaust resources, induce settlements and so forth. See, for example, Rabin (1992). Others have explained how legal doctrines, formal rights and litigation are not always the preferred means of resolving disputes: Macaulay (1963), Ellickson (1986), Yngvesson (1988).

5   It is not my intention to suggest that images of 'reliability' and 'unreliability' are fixed or ascertained by some simple mechanism(s). Images of (un)reliability are strategic and variable.

6   This may enable the judge to impose closure by limiting the extent of disagreement. Adversarial systems may actually exaggerate the extent of disagreement and inquisitorial systems may structurally foreclose the possibility of encountering contrary views. For some discussion, see Edmond (2000: 242–9).

7   In jury trials once the judge has deemed the evidence relevant and admissible its value is left to the discretion of the jury, in their capacity as fact-finder. If a judge deems a case sufficient to be tried, that is recognizes it as a *prima facie* case, the jury can, quite properly, produce any of a range of verdicts.

8   Compare *General Electric Co. v Joiner* 522 U.S. 136, L.Ed.2d 508, 118 S.Ct. 512 (1997).

9   Considerable debate and academic commentary has emerged around admissibility standards in US federal courts. See for example: Bernstein (1996); Chan (1995) and 'Law and science symposium' (1994) 15 *Cordozo Law Review* 15.

10   Rule 702 now reads: 'If scientific, technical, or other specialized knowledge will assist the trier of fact to understand the evidence or to determine a fact in issue, a witness qualified as an expert by knowledge, skill, experience, training, or education, may testify thereto in the form of an opinion or otherwise, if (1) the testimony is based upon sufficient facts or data, (2) the testimony is the product of reliable principles and methods, and (3) the witness has applied the principles and methods reliably to the facts of the case'. See Brixen and Meis (2000).

11   It is important to note that there had been inconsistent application of Rule 702 since 1975. The decision to hear an appeal, therefore, reflected emergent concerns about the role of expertise in the US federal courts. After the *Daubert* judgment, new inconsistencies quickly emerged as parties sought to modulate the impact of the decision.

12   *US v Frye* 293 F 1013 (D.C.Cir. 1923). *Frye* was often associated with novel proffers of expert evidence.

13   *Daubert v Merrell Dow Pharmaceuticals, Inc.* 509 U.S. 579, 593, 125 L.Ed.2d 469, 483, 113 S.Ct. 2786, 2797 (1993).

14   This was later qualified in *General Electric Co. v Joiner* 522 U.S. 136, 139 L.Ed.2d 508, 519, 118 S.Ct. 512 (1997).

15   *Daubert v Merrell Dow Pharmaceuticals, Inc.* 43 F.3d 1311, 1316 (9th Cir. 1995). This was the *Daubert* case on remand to the Court of Appeals from the Supreme Court.

16   Galanter (1998, 2002) provides a range of reasons for judicial anxieties.

17   *Kumho Tyre Co. v Carmichael* 526 U.S. 137, 143 L.Ed.2d 238, 119 S.Ct. 137 (1999).

18   *General Electric Co. v Joiner* 522 U.S. 136, 139 L.Ed.2d 508, 519, 118 S.Ct. 512 (1997). Compare Silbey (1981).

19   This analysis was confirmed in the case of *Weisgram v Marley* 528 US 440, 120 S.Ct. 1011, 1021, 145 L.Ed.2d 958 (2000) where the Supreme Court explained that: 'Since *Daubert*, moreover, parties relying on expert evidence have had notice of the exacting standards of reliability such evidence must meet'.

20   Elsewhere, Edmond and Mercer (2002a, 2004) have argued that regardless of whether the *Daubert* majority judgment is read charitably—as an initial attempt to liberalize admissibility requirements—in practice it has inaugurated a more onerous judicial response to expert evidence which has been reinforced in subsequent supreme and federal court jurisprudence.

21 These concerns have been actively promoted by conservative think-tanks and commentators. See, for example: Huber (1991) and Foster and Huber (1998).

22 Popper and other philosophers and sociologists were cited in several *amicus curiae* briefs submitted in relation to *Daubert*. Here, I have focused primarily upon Popper because his name appeared in more federal court judgments than Hempel or any of the others, and is more closely associated with the idea of testing as falsification. For two quite distinctive accounts of the use of science studies, compare Jasanoff (1995, 1996a) with the final chapter in this volume.

23 Falsification previously appeared in litigation over the teaching of creation science. Interestingly, in those few cases, judges tended to develop a slightly different, context-influenced, definition of science where naturalistic explanation assumed primary import. See Edmond and Mercer (2002a), Ruse (1988) and *McLean v Arkansas* 529 F.Supp 1255, 1267 (1982).

24 It may be that some of the political implications and philosophy appealed to the judges. Popper's political 'baggage,' including criticisms of sociology, Marxism and psychology, were, however, obscured in the judgment.

25 Even if the inclusion of qualifications was a form of judicial accommodation, subsequently they could be elided and displaced. Of course, Supreme Court judges do not have complete control over the use of their decisions.

26 The discretion invested in trial judges is compromised by the Supreme Court's own rigorous application, in *Kumho*, of all the criteria to the expert opinion evidence of the plaintiff's expert (Carlson) as a very public lesson about the risks associated with 'junk science'.

27 *March v Stramare* (1991) 171 CLR 506, 509. See also *Seltsam Pty Ltd v McGuiness* (2000) 49 NSWLR 262, 286, 293–5. Hart and Honoré (1987) are ubiquitous in the literature. See also Dixon (1965: 9) and Edmond and Mercer (2002b). Though, the discussion of the Bendectin litigation indicates that the judicial treatment of causation, evidentiary sufficiency and admissibility were not always distinguished from the perspectives of extra-legal sources, particularly the work of (some) epidemiologists.

28 *Rogers v Whitaker* (1992) 175 CLR 479, 487. See also *Naxakis v Western General Hospital* (1999) 197 CLR 269: 'a finding of medical negligence may be made even though the conduct of the defendant was in accord with a practice accepted at the time as proper by a responsible body of medical opinion'.

29 *Bolam v Friern Hospital* [1957] 1 WLR 582; [1957] 2 All ER 118; *Sidaway v Bethlehem Royal Hospital* [1985] AC 871.

30 Another prominent example is the rejection, in several jurisdictions, of Bayesian analyses of evidence, especially in cases involving DNA typing: *Adams v The Queen* [1996] 2 Cr App R 467. See Redmayne (2001).

31 Notwithstanding recent developments in information technology, most courts do not record the full range of information, transcripts, submissions, statements and reports on their websites and do not always make it convenient, cheap, and sometimes even possible, to inspect such documents.

32 As part of my work on the public understanding of law I would be reluctant to draw firm lines around an informed legal profession and a legally ignorant public. Further, public ignorance attribution creates problems in many legal models, especially in areas like presumption of knowledge of the law, see Fuller (1964) and Dan-Cohen (1984).

33 Though, a persistent minority have uncovered what might be considered as a surprisingly large number of miscarriages of justice.

34 The architecture of many old courts can make it difficult for the public to see and hear cases and argument. Further, some parts of trials, and even entire trials, are conducted in camera. Juries do not hear legal argument, and so on.

35   Whereas the victor gets to write the history, the judge gets to choose the 'victor' *and* write the official 'history'.

36   The meaning of these contingencies is open to debate. Compare Jasanoff (1995: 211–18) with Edmond (1998: 391–401).

37   These are similar to the constitutive and contingent repertoires (or forums) developed by Gilbert and Mulkay (1984) and Collins and Pinch (1982).

38   The following example draws predominantly on the transcript. There are many aspects of the trial which are not captured by transcript, sound recordings or even video.

39   *Chamberlain v The Queen [No. 2]* (1983–4) 153 CLR 521.

40   While this example is highly simplified, it was not resolved by greater detail. See Campbell (1985). During the Galvin inquest and trial Orams' opinion was challenged by another odontologist (Sims), imported from the United Kingdom, testifying for the Crown.

41   *The Queen and Alice Lynne Chamberlain, Michael Leigh Chamberlain* (1982: 1133) (Trial transcript).

42   *In the matter of An Inquest into the death of missing child Azaria Chantel Loren Chamberlain at Ayers Rock on 17 August 1980* (1981: 529) (Galvin Inquest transcript).

43   There are similarities between the literary construction of the judgment and the scientific paper, see Latour and Woolgar (1979), Myers (1985), Lenoir (1997).

44   *Brock v. Merrell Dow Pharmaceuticals, Inc.* 874 F.2d 307 and 884 F.2d 167 (5th Cir. 1989) (italics added).

45   *In re Richardson-Merrell, Inc., 'Bendectin' Products Liability Litigation. MDL* 624 F.Supp. 1212, 1221 (S.D. Ohio, 1985); *DeLuca v Merrell Dow Pharmaceuticals* 911 F.2d 941, 952 (3rd Cir. 1990).

46   *Lynch v Merrell-National Laboratories* 830 F.2d 1190, 1194 (1st Cir. 1987).

47   *Chamberlain v The Queen [No. 2]* (1983–4) 153 CLR 521, 575. By way of contrast, recent developments in the US criminal justice system, arising from developments in DNA typing, have, in effect, reversed Murphy's admonition to prefer unchallenged lay testimony. The triumph and power of advanced forensic technologies such as DNA typing have been employed to challenge the conviction of the *innocent* (Dwyer, Neufeld and Scheck 2000; Borchrad 1932; Nobles and Schiff 2000: 39–91; Laufer 1995), adding to existing criticism of lay identification evidence (Loftus 1979; Cutler and Penrod 1995). Given the publicity associated with the Innocence Project and similar initiatives, judges (or legislators) will presumably develop means of managing potential conflicts between DNA typing and other forms of evidence as well as the impact upon the legitimacy of the criminal justice system, by altering admissibility standards or assembling sensitive new hierarchies or distinguishing between the expertise proffered by plaintiffs and state forensic science (see Lynch and Cole in this volume).

48   *Members of the Yorta Yorta Aboriginal Community v State of Victoria* [1998] FCA 1606 (hereafter *Yorta Yorta*). See also the appeals: *Members of the Yorta Yorta Aboriginal Community v State of Victoria* [2001] FCA 45, *Members of the Yorta Yorta Aboriginal Community v State of Victoria* [2002] HCA 5. See also Reilly (2000).

49   In 1998 the Act was modified so that it was more closely aligned to the Commonwealth *Evidence Act* (1995) and consequently less receptive to some types of Aboriginal evidence.

50   *Mabo and others v The State of Queensland (No. 2)* (1992) 175 CLR 1; *The Wik Peoples v State of Queensland* (1996) 195 CLR 1. See also *Milirrpum v Nabalco Pty Ltd* (1971) 17 FLR 141.

51 There are some striking parallels with the judgment in the Canadian case of *Delgamuukw v The Queen* 79 DLR 185 (1991). But compare the appeal in *Delgamuukw v British Columbia* 3 SCR 1010 [1997].

52 *Yarmirr v Northern Territory (No. 2)* (1998) 82 FCR 533.

53 *Yorta Yorta* (1998) para. 17. There is a moral economy to legal-expert knowledge construction, compare Thompson (1971).

54 Recourse to partisanship has a long lineage in Anglo–American judgments. See, for example: *Thorn v Worthing Skating Rink Co.* (1877) 6 Ch. D. 415.

55 Wynne (1989b) argues that trial judges often try to protect their decisions from judicial review by incorporating considerable factual detail. This may have some value but, given the prevalence of facts *and* law in judicial review, the use of facts does not entirely restrain the actions of superior courts. Indeed greater attention to detail may provide superior courts with additional means of finding (legal) *mistakes* and *remedying* them.

56 Several scholars developed elaborate schemes for the assessment of evidence. At the forefront of this rationalist tradition are Bentham (1827) and Wigmore (1940). See Twining (1985).

57 The 'conventional theory' is flawed in at least three ways. First, it treats the evidence, law and decision discretely. Second, it puts them in a particular temporal relationship. Third, no agency is credited to the decision-maker, or those presenting cases, or the application of legal procedures.

58 To varying degrees mass torts are an exception. Debates over the extent of similarity and difference between claims have led to concerns around judicial management techniques such as the certification of classes and particular case congregations.

59 Compare Monahan and Walker (1986, 2000). Specialists in law and social science, Walker and Monahan suggest that under certain circumstances 'fact' should be accorded the weight of legal precedent.

60 Some commentators try to do the same, identifying *identical* cases and *identical* law and then ironicizing inconsistency in outcomes. See Huber (1991) and Foster and Huber (1998).

61 Lindy Chamberlain, the mother convicted of murdering her baby daughter, was subsequently exonerated after a Royal Commission (1986–7) and another appellate court hearing (1987). The legal doctrine associated with the Chamberlain appeal to the High Court—which concerned the appropriate use of circumstantial evidence—was revised in *Shepherd v R* (1990) 170 CLR 573. Interestingly, judicial elaborations of legal doctrine tend to be ambivalent about their relationship to evidence or particular cases. Usually, the particular evidence (or circumstances) can be displaced, allowing a purely legal formulation, especially where (similar) cases are distinguished. Before *Shepherd*, *Chamberlain* remained the authoritative *law* in relation to the use of circumstantial evidence—even after the accused had been released and exonerated.

Chapter 9

Narrative Traditions of Space, Time and Trust in Court: *Terra nullius*, 'wandering', the *Yorta Yorta* Native Title Claim, and the Hindmarsh Island Bridge Controversy

David Turnbull

Introduction

This chapter endeavors to show how differing understandings of what constitutes knowledge help explain the apparent failure to reach a common ground of agreement between members of the judiciary, anthropologists and Aboriginal claimants in Australian courts in the Hindmarsh Island Bridge case and the *Yorta Yorta* Native Title claim (see also Turnbull 1998b; 2002; 2005a). What is at stake in these cases is the nature of knowledge, its structure and its movement, which are subsumed by narratives of spatiality and temporality and by protocols governing its authority and credibility. Western scientific and legal conceptions of knowledge represent it as placeless, timeless, authorless and value-free. Knowledge is thus abstract, public, unattached and objective, yet in a profound inversion, when its authenticity is challenged, it reveals its suppressed spatio-temporal narrative structures and reliance on concealed protocols. By contrast Aboriginal knowledge is acknowledged as a commodity of the highest value and as being intimately embedded in place, time and protocol (Elkin 1944; Myers 1986: 149ff; Williams 1986: 24; Mulvaney 1989: 1–2; Palmer 1991). In Aboriginal culture knowledge is inseparable from land or 'country' and can only be spoken of by acknowledged and trusted owners and elders. Knowledge is thus land-based, and restricted in its movement; making it public requires careful examination of the protocols governing its revelation.

The first section of this chapter explores a narratological approach to framing the problem of the multiplicity of knowledges. It considers the ways in which knowledge is structured by spatial and temporal narratives and how these spatio/temporal narratives differ between knowledge traditions. The second section examines the ways in which the spatiality and mobility of knowledge are revealed in the conception of Australia as *terra nullius* and in the conception of Aborigines as 'wanderers'. It then considers the ways narratives of spatiality and temporality produce misunderstandings, conflicts, collisions, and occasional coalescences in examples of the forensic encounter of differing knowledge traditions. In conclusion a resolution is proposed to the problem of conflicting and incommensurable knowledges: that of dialogic 'bothness', of the creative tension of weaving and telling contrasting narratives together rather than trying to render them commensurable or choosing between them.

Lay, indigenous, expert, scientific and legal knowledge traditions

One of the most profound challenges we face in the postmodern world is the multiplicity of knowledges. The modernist dream of one universal form of knowledge—science—and of its unified totality being assembled in one place, and then being redistributed in a seamless, uniform, space–time has reached an impasse. The technical capacity for such assemblage now exists, but the pursuit of the goal of panoptic unity reveals that scientific knowledge itself is not unified or unifiable: it is multiple (Galison and Stump 1996). Not only are there incommensurabilities between such scientific disciplines as physics and biology, but within them. There are, for example, fundamental and unbridgeable differences in approaches to defining such ontologically basic entities as 'genes' and 'species' (on genes see Turnbull 2004; on species see Pigliucci 2003). Attempts to measure biodiversity, for example, are dependent on assembling all the known data on the number and varieties of species, and have struck intractable problems, owing to the incommensurability of information gathered by ecologists on the one hand and by systematicists on the other. In Bowker's (2000) analysis the incommensurability is due to the incompatibility of the ontologies of the differing disciplinary approaches to understanding biodiversity. He concludes that 'integration cannot be smoothly accomplished. Ecological and systematics data cannot be rendered equal just by standardising over a set of weights and measures' because they are dependent on radically differing forms of spatiality and temporality (Bowker 2000).

But, in addition to the emerging cracks in the unified facade of science, we are also faced with the problem of the multiplicity of knowledges and knowledge spaces in the wider social, political, and cultural arenas where local, lay knowledge has always been in tension with expert knowledge, especially in courts of law where differing forms of knowledge are increasingly coming into conflict (Wynne 1996a, 1996b; Tulloch 1999). The standard approach has been to attempt to resolve such tensions and conflicts in various ways; for example by establishing a hierarchy of knowledges. Typically local knowledge has been characterized as opinion or belief, tradition or superstition, and used as a dichotomous foil to scientific or expert knowledge. Alternatively local, lay and indigenous knowledges are being increasingly recognized as a hugely valuable resource and the problems of incommensurability with scientific knowledge are handled through subsumption and the deletion of any local characteristics (Turnbull 2005b).

The approach taken here is to resist the hierarchization and subsumption of knowledges through accepting the tension and dealing with the incommensurabilities by recognizing that *all* knowledges are similarly structured through narratives of spatiality and temporality and are grounded in protocols of trust and authority. Their significant differences lie in the ways that knowledges move and are assembled creating their own forms of spatiality (Turnbull 2000). Knowledge traditions including science result from the activities of particular people, in particular places, using particular techniques, and are necessarily dependent on the deployment of particular practices. In order for knowledge to move beyond the site of its production, traditions develop technical devices and social institutions which serve to link people, practices and places, and in so doing create knowledge spaces. Western science, for example, is notorious for its use of maps in framing the visibility of the environment while simultaneously making invisible a complex web of practices, social relationships and attitudes to land. Scientific maps are technical modes of visual representation that are dependent on a social infrastructure of surveying, measuring and standardization which structure and legitimate the kinds of lived spatiality that characterizes modernity. Such scientific maps have served as instruments of colonization, creating and dividing blank spaces for appropriation and exploitation. Mapping is thus frequently portrayed as a form of spatial practice that is radically incompatible with indigenous knowledge (Deleuze and Guattari 1986; Reilly 2002). But just as there are multiple knowledges, so there are multiple forms of mapping and spatial representation. Encounters between the spatial practices of differing knowledge traditions, especially in cartography and mapping, can produce complex, crumpled and hybrid spatialities, for example, when Australian Aboriginal maps are produced as evidence in courts of law, or when indigenous groups appropriate non-indigenous practices. Not only are there multiple spaces and forms of spatiality, there are multiple ways of conceiving them and producing them, but ultimately they are all embedded in narratives, practices, technologies and bodily movements (Turnbull 1997, 1998a, 1998b, 2002).

Knowledge and narrative

Since the 1980s a huge body of literature has been built around the role of narrative in virtually every discipline including all the sciences, both natural and social, and the law, but there are only a few articulations of the variety of forms, levels and effects of narrative (one of the best overviews is Pluciennik 1999).[1] Here I want to offer a general outline of the narrative nature of knowledge and a topography of its roles in shaping our ways of understanding knowledge claims in differing traditions. While narration is a primary form of making meaning and sense, there are not only differences and incommensurabilities between forms of narrative resulting in conflict in courts and in the wider cultural arena, but there are also other ways of being and knowing including the ludic and the irrational as well as the performative and practice-based that should be held in tension with narrative understandings (Sartwell 2000).

Homo narrans: A story about the origins and epistemological grounds of storytelling as a basic form of human knowing

The palaeontologist Alexander Marshack has found evidence of humans recording lunar and solar cycles as far back as the early Palaeolithic (Marshack 1972). He concludes from his minute examinations of markings on bones and cave walls that we have always been storytellers. Humans were inscribing these 'time-factored' accounts at the very earliest stages of human history, because stories are essential to our capacity to relate to other people, to feed and shelter ourselves, and to order our social and symbolic lives. 'Time-factoring' or the placing of events in order and thereby making them meaningful is an essential characteristic of narrative (Ricoeur 1984; Howard and Hollander 1993). But, narratives, being ultimately based in human agency and action, are also spatial, since space is co-produced with the travel, interaction and movement of bodies.

Alasdair MacIntyre in *After Virtue* and elsewhere claims; 'man is, in his actions and practice, a story telling animal'. 'Conversations and human actions in general are enacted narratives, as are our ways of knowing such as science.' We render the actions of others intelligible narratologically because 'action itself has a basically historical character' (MacIntyre 1977, 1981). For Marshack and MacIntyre human beings are deeply and profoundly storytelling animals leading Dennis Mumby to suggest that *Homo narrans* provides a more illuminating model for ourselves as social agents than the currently dominant Cartesian rational actor (Mumby 1993; McNeil 1996; Pratchett et al. 2003).

Narrativity, spatiality and temporality

There has been considerable discussion and analysis of the nature and role of narrative but there seems to be some general agreement summarized in Lamarque's characterization:

> In the most general terms to narrate is to tell a story ... narration of any kind involves the recounting of events ... narration has an essential temporal dimension ... narrative imposes structure, it connects as well as records ... Finally, for every narrative there is a narrator real or implied or both. Stories don't just exist, they are told, and not just told but told from some perspective or other. Already we have the basic dimensions of all narrative, time, structure, voice and point of view. (Lamarque 1990: 131)

On Pluciennik's account what distinguishes narrative is:

> sequentiality and emplotment—the way in which the story achieves overall coherence, the way in which it unfolds so that the end result or situation can be understood as a logical or at least plausible consequence of previously described situations or conditions. Out of the selective (re)description of objects, elements, events, conditions and characters and the myriad possible relationships between them in space and time and nature, it is the plot, the thread of the story which emphasizes particular paths, possibilities and plausibilities, of the 'characters' and 'events', which draws the text together as a narrative. (Pluciennik 1999: 656)

Telling stories is a primary way of making meaning and creating an identity (de Certeau 1984; Turner 1996). To tell a story is to organize things in space and time and vice versa; to reference or factor events and people temporally and spatially is to construct a narrative. Narrative, space and time have thus developed in complex interactions and co-productions creating what Mikhael Bakhtin calls 'chronotopes' (Bakhtin 1981, 1986; Holloway and Kneale 2000; Joyce 2002; Morson and Emerson 1990). Narratives, in their construction of coherent and persuasive accounts, create ontologies—what sort of things exist, in what kind of causal relationships. They frame the world in a contested field—determining for the moment, in a struggle for authority, what counts as knowledge, what sort of questions can be asked and what counts as an answer (Bourdieu 1975; Rouse 1996: 163–5). A great strength of narrative lies in its capacity for bridging incommensurabilities, in handling gaps and elisions; it creates coherence, continuity and commonality of reference across varieties of local practices, playing a similar but broader role than that of boundary objects (Star and Griesmer 1989). At the same time it makes persuasive and legitimates particular ways of seeing the world and treating evidence.

Irony and intertextuality

The literary theorist Mark Turner claims that small spatial stories and parables— the projection of one story on another—are the root of the human capacities for thinking, knowing, acting and possibly even speaking. Most of our experience, our knowledge, and our thinking is organized as stories. The mental scope of story is magnified by projection—one story helps make sense of another (Turner 1996: v, 15).

Herein lies the source of narrative's polysemic adaptability—the essentially ironic duality or bothness of narrative that Pelton so brilliantly reveals in his account of the African trickster (Pelton 1980). The trickster is the god of irony, the storyteller who enables us to deal with the 'betweenness' or 'bothness' of life, the tension between the contingent and the ordered, between the anomalous and the classified, between the personal and the theoretical, the concrete and the abstract, the essential contradictions of existence, the sublime, the inexpressibility of human existence.

The trickster symbolizes the human imagination in dialogue with all being. The essential irony of narrative comes from the bothness that lies in the recognition that the coherence, the order we impose on the world, derives from our linking things together, and that all stories are told against a background tradition of other stories; while at the same time recognizing that entirely contradictory orderings are equally possible. The trickster figure represents an explicit recognition of the performativity and narrativity of the human imagination (Pelton 1980: 258). The trickster reveals the human world to language and how the human world is storied and performed as we move between contexts and frames, between theatres (Pelton 1980: 270). The trickster is the figure at the heart of MacIntyre's claim that we construct ourselves in stories within a contested tradition.

Narrative multiplicity, contestability: dominance and subversion

Stories are multiple and contested, they are always incomplete, indeterminate and open to interpretive flexibility, but in bridging the gap of incommensurability, in rendering the discontinuous continuous, some stories come to dominate.

Patricia Ewick and Susan Silbey, in their insightful discussion of narrative and the law, show ways that the dominant and the hegemonic can be both sustained and subverted by narratives. They suggest that when narratives 'efface the connection between the particular and the general, they help sustain hegemony. Conversely when narrativity helps bridge particularities and makes connections across individual experiences and subjectivities it can function as a subversive social practice' (Ewick and Silbey 1995: 200). What narratives can do is 'reverse the naturalization of the arbitrary and show the historically contingent process of knowledge movement and assemblage by displaying the connections through narrative of the local and universal that are central to, and have been erased in, the hegemonic account (Turnbull 2004).

Narrative and tradition

The complex tensions of bothness that lie at the heart of narratives are also embedded in an inherent characteristic of law, that of traditionality. According to the Australian legal scholar Patrick Parkinson, 'it is of the essence of law that it is traditional'. Tradition means being able to argue authoritatively in the present on the basis of the past. In the process of precedential reasoning 'the past is not only significant, its authoritatively present' (Parkinson 2001: 9–10). The bothness is implicit in the fashioning of arguments or stories in the present on the basis of other stories from the past whose temporal authority derives jointly from their being based in time immemorial and from their continuous link to the present. This makes law very like the Australian Aboriginal notion of the dreaming; law is not in the ancient past—it is continuously present. But it gives it a different temporality to that of science's continuous reinvention in which it is always dependent on accumulated past achievements, but holds itself in readiness to abandon tradition in favour of the new—the essential tension noted by Kuhn (1977).

Questions of knowledge and tradition are deeply imbricated with differing narratives of temporality and spatiality. The English legal tradition is often defined as worthy of respect, credibility and authority because it is rooted in a tradition described as 'out of time' or 'immemorial', while the same argument can also be reversed in the case of indigenous knowledge to show that precisely because it stretches back so far it is not worthy of belief because it is not capable of change. Indeed English common law has developed precisely through balancing the tension between the unchanging and the innovative (Davies 1994). Similar articulations of the temporal narrative, of either being embedded in a long-scale process and hence traditional and unchanging, or denying a knowledge claim or a cultural production any temporality or ancestry and being of the now, contemporary or modern, are apparent in another aspect of Aboriginal culture—the art world. In the early 1990s the Cologne Art Fair rejected some Aboriginal art works on the grounds that they were traditional and hence not contemporary art. A few years later Aboriginal art was again rejected by Cologne on the grounds of inauthenticity—not being true to its tradition.

Nicholas Blomley argues that in order for the rule of law to appear rational, benign and necessary, that is to say authoritative, it must achieve closure and separation. There must be a legal boundary—closure is achieved at one end of the spectrum by the display of the system as formal rules, and at the other as tradition (Blomley 1994: 8–10; Lawson 2001). So it is in its spatial and temporal marking of narrative reconstruction that the law displays itself as simultaneously bounded and placeless, timeless and contemporary.

We advance narratives to explain and account for ourselves and our actions, we modify them continuously and they are in constant conflict and co-production, we perform them differently in varying dialogic contexts, with the attendant problems of interpretation rampant, yet we mostly experience an apparent seamlessness in our meaning-making. Narratives can be woven at one level from historical myths and at another from the stuff of our lives, our jobs, our families; there are meta-narratives, non-stories, counter-stories, but nonetheless it is through narrative that order, sense and knowledge are accomplished in the face of uncertainty, conflict and ignorance.

All forms of knowledge—lay and expert, theoretical and practical, legal, scientific, anthropological and indigenous—are spatially and temporally constituted in part through narrative. They have geographies and chronologies, spatialities and temporalities, and just as we live with multiple identities in our daily lives, so do we move between multiple and contradictory spatialities and temporalities, in and between knowledge traditions and protocols. It is when traditions are brought together for comparative evaluation or when coordination of commensurability is attempted that possibilities can arise, either for serious conflicts, or for interaction and narrative co-production.

The 'doctrine' of *terra nullius*

The complex interweaving of temporal and spatial narratives of ownership/ sovereignty, continuity/discontinuity, possession/dispossession, presence/absence is clearly apparent in the most notorious of conflicts between differing knowledge traditions in Australia—the supposed 'doctrine' of *terra nullius*.

In the case of *Cooper v Stuart* (1889) before the Privy Council, Lord Justice Watson declared that Australia was a 'colony of settlement' as opposed to a 'colony of conquest' because in 1788 it was a 'tract of territory practically unoccupied without settled inhabitants or settled law'.[2] This was a legal judgment which of course legitimated Britain's appropriation and colonization of Australia, without conquest, negotiation or treaties; but a judgment supposedly based in an empirical claim. The claim was initially promulgated by Joseph Banks in his report to the Committee on Transportation in 1785, based on his observations on the *Endeavour* voyage with Cook where he reported 'this immense tract of land ... is thinly inhabited even to admiration ... We saw indeed only the sea coast: what the immense tract of inland country may produce is totally unknown: we may have liberty to conjecture however they are totally uninhabited' (Reynolds 1996: 16–17, 77).

What is so striking here is that Banks' spatial imaginary enables him to assert that, despite any actual experience of, or evidence about, the interior or the vast bulk of Australia, his failure to see any sign of cultivation on the coast and only small groups of people was evidence that the rest of Australia was practically unoccupied and that this opinion should still be considered warranted 100 years after the first colonists arrived.

The standard story is that the denial or suppression of native title or ownership rights and the assertion of sovereignty through the British annexation of Australia was justified by a supposed legal doctrine—*terra nullius*. That story also holds that the doctrine was famously overthrown in the *Mabo v Queensland [No 2]* (1992) decision, under which the indigenous inhabitants of the Murray Islands were found to have native title rights over their islands and the adjacent sea, though they had no sovereignty (Attwood 1996b).[3] The legal justification has been severely criticized from the indigenous perspective on the grounds that *terra nullius* is a spatio-temporal narrative that makes indigenous people invisible, denying and erasing both their occupancy of the land and their system of law and social organization (Watson 1997). '*Terra nullius* is the creation of an empty space in which indigenous people don't exist' (Smith 1999: 53). Furthermore *Mabo* does not adequately recognize Aboriginal and Torres Strait Islanders' relationship with the land nor their law; it simply turns their land into tradeable, commoditized, property (Kerruish and Purdy 1998: 162).

But, there is also a more complex narrative of temporal and spatial continuity in the legal tradition that is revealed in Ritter's critique of the doctrine's overthrow in the *Mabo* case. Ritter argues there never was a legal doctrine *terra nullius,* there was only a set of self-evident assumptions about distribution, unsettledness and systems of law of indigenous Australians (Ritter 1996). *Terra nullius* was therefore never invoked to justify the British appropriation of Australia.

> When Australia was originally colonised by the Crown, neither *terra nullius* nor any other legal doctrine was used to deny the recognition of traditional rights to land under the common law ... because the indigenous inhabitants of the colony were seen and defined by the colonists as intrinsically barbarous and without any interest in land ... so no doctrine was required for what was axiomatic. (Ritter 1996: 6)

Ritter claims that Justice Brennan, in recognizing the continued existence of native title of the Murray Islanders in the *Mabo* case, was faced with a 'crisis of truth'—a discontinuity in the Australian legal tradition. In order to account for how the legal tradition could now acknowledge native title, which it had previously refused to recognize at all, the judge had to invent a pre-existing legal doctrine—*terra nullius*—which had supposedly denied native title. Thus in a classic piece of narrative reconstruction he called the doctrine into existence only to overthrow it, thereby maintaining a seamless, continuous, legal tradition (Purdy 1999). But, it was not just the temporal continuity of the legal tradition over time that Judge Brennan was concerned to conserve, but also the legal tradition's spatial continuity. 'This court is not free to adopt rules that accord with contemporary notions of justice and human rights if their adoption would fracture the skeleton of principle which gives the body of our law its shape and internal consistency' (cited by Watson 1997: 14).

According to Ritter the concept of *terra nullius* was first invoked in an Australian land rights case in *Coe v Commonwealth* (1978) when the Sydney Aboriginal lawyer Paul Coe tried to show that Australia was already occupied in 1788 and Australia had become a colony by conquest (Coe 1994; Ritter 1996: 17).[4] But Borch's more recent commentary suggests, in an additional ironic twist, that though the concept was not utilized in the original occupancy in 1788, it was incorporated in British law in the 19th century as a result of the establishment of the colony of New South Wales (Borch 2001).

'Wandering' and the spatio-temporal dimensions of rationality and knowledge

In addition to spatial and temporal narratives of the legal tradition and of Aboriginal presence, there are complex spatio-temporal dimensions to the underlying assumptions about a settled existence, land ownership, and systems of law, that speak to the fundamental conceptions of rationality and knowledge.

It was in the narrative process of dialogue with political philosophy about appropriate forms of acquisition, ownership and cultivation of land that English law formulated the chronotopic dimensions of rationality that are implicit in the evocation of the term 'wandering' as the first-order descriptor invoked whenever indigenes are described; as in 'wandering tribes of Indians'—implying a timeless, placeless, and directionless existence—a literal emptiness, no space, no time, no presence, no settlement and hence, no ownership, no systematic laws, no rationality, and no knowledge (Blaut 1993: 15). Land that was empty, desert and uncultivated was land that could simply be taken as belonging to no one. And it was held to be empty if its inhabitants were mere wanderers with no complex organization or laws (Ritter 1996). Wheaton, in *Elements of International Law* (1836), made a distinction between civil society and 'unsettled hordes of wandering savages' (Reynolds 1996) and 'Fidelis' in the Sydney *Gazette* (1824) argued:

> Any doubt, therefore, as to the lawfulness of our assuming the possession of this Island must arise from the opinion that it was the *property* of its original inhabitants. Such opinion, however, would be incorrect; for the very notion of property as applicable to tribal possessions, did not exist among them ... Each tribe wandered about wheresoever inclination prompted without ever supposing any one place belonged to it more than another. They were the *inhabitants* but not the proprietors of the land. (cited in Reynolds 1987: 167)

To Joseph Banks:

> Aborigines seemed "never to make any stay [in their houses] but wandering like the Arabs from place to place set them up wherever they meet with one where sufficient

supplies of food are to be met with, and as soon as these are exhausted remove to another leaving the houses behind, which are farmed with less art or rather less industry than any habitations of human beings probably that the world can shew." (Beaglehole 1963, cited in Frost 1981: 519)

Alexandro Malaspina the Spanish commander similarly reported on the newly established British colony in 1793 that Aborigines are 'a wandering nation, without agriculture and industry, and without any product that would attest their rationality' (King 1990: 84). The crucial premise in the expropriation of indigenous land as untilled or unsettled is vagrancy, 'the premise that a wandering condition dehumanizes or must precede humanization' (Pocock 1992, cited in Patton 2000: 119). Having no place meant no organization, no law, no labor, no cultivation, no property, no boundaries. All of which were essential components of enlightenment rationality and the complete antithesis of wandering, revealing both the profoundly place-based, static and boundaried spatial ontology underpinning modern rationality and epistemology and the profound tensions in which it was constituted.

The colonial and the enlightenment projects were in large part concerned with the establishment of boundaries to determine and delimit sovereignty over territory, and authority over knowledge. 'The bureaucratic nature of state practices' led to the subjugation of the unbounded and establishment of the frontiers of rationality through 'the conversion of messy places into rational spaces' (Taylor 1999: 104). Thus, the tensions inherent in the modern conceptions of objectivity, rationality and knowledge are reflected in their portrayal as despatialized and placeless, as 'the view from nowhere' (Nagel 1986; Olsson 1998).

While at the same time as indigenes are described as wandering placeless and irrational; the trope of the nomad is deployed by postmodernists and the 'wandering grounds' (Soguk and Whitehall 1999) of knowledge are invoked in the effort to establish a spatial narrative based in an essentialized understanding of movement to counter the apparent self-evidence of the dominant modern spatial narrative of the state and the control of movement (Deleuze and Guattari 1986; Kuehls 1996; Cresswell 1997; Shapiro 1997, 1999). The questioning of Aboriginal conceptions of territory, boundary, ownership, rationality and knowledge are now even more bitterly disputed (Attwood and Foster 2003; Manne 2003; McIntyre and Clark 2003; Sandall 2000; Windschuttle 2002). The historian Keith Windschuttle, for example, asserts that 'Aborigines showed no evidence of anything that deserved the name of political skills at all', (cited in Reynolds 2002) and the Tasmanian Aborigines had no sense of ownership of land. But, the evidence produced by Williams and Myers and many other anthropologists shows that Australian Aboriginal groups had a highly articulated understanding of their own territory and kinship and had a well developed form of social organization reflected in boundary practices and protocols governing the ways authority and ownership should be acknowledged, and how permission should be sought and granted. This system of norms and signs that made negotiated boundary-crossing permissions possible reveals a spatialized form of politics and territorial distribution and also provides the conditions for the possibility of trust and the movement of knowledge along networks or 'strings of connectedness' (Keen 1995; Turnbull 2000, 2005a; Mulvaney 1989; Myers 1986).

However, recognition of these tensions and contradictions is perhaps better handled by careful positioning between the extremes of nomadism and the fixity of imperial space and adopting, as Jane Jacobs suggests, 'theories sensitized to movement and studies configured around diverse assemblages of people and place' (Jacobs 1996: 7). That would avoid the beguiling illusion of either extreme, and by telling both accounts together, the varieties of spatial narratives and protocols of trust that are co-produced with knowledge and rationality in both traditions may be revealed.

The *Yorta Yorta* native title claim

The dispute over what counts as knowledge, who gets to decide and in what disciplinary space, has had a variety of names: the 'history wars', the 'culture wars' and the 'science wars'. In Australia the dispute has had multiple loci. In the history of white impact on Aboriginal Australia—was it genocidal or not? In understanding and ameliorating contemporary Aboriginal social problems, deaths in custody, Aboriginal violence against women, alcoholism, petrol sniffing—are they to be explained in terms of the specifics of Aboriginal culture or in terms of the effects of dispossession? In the status of Aboriginal knowledge and land claims—are they genuine or spurious? By what criteria can we decide? What is the role of anthropology and the law? Have they been abetted by activist anthropologists or disadvantaged by assumptions inherent in Western legal conceptions of ownership? All of these controversies are, of course, embedded in furious political debates between left and right, environmentalists and developers, indigenous groups and miners.

So, Australia has for some time been the site of especially problematic and acrimonious struggles over how claims to knowledge from outside the Western legal and anthropological narrative traditions should be treated, over how such narratives can be authorized, legitimated and given credibility. 'Nowhere are the contradictory, complicit, and mutually embedded double binds of relations between indigenous and non-indigenous people and the colonizing power more evident than in a land claim' (Rose 1996: 36). Land claim hearings are theatres in which the complex interactions of indigenous knowledge and Western scientific knowledge traditions are played out.

The first case to be tried under the *Native Title Act* (1993) was the Yorta Yorta claim.[5] The area in question covers both sides of Australia's largest river, the Murray, roughly from Echuca to Mildura, and was claimed as native title by the Aboriginal group now known as the Yorta Yorta. The claim was rejected by Judge Olney who held that 'the tide of history had indeed washed away any real acknowledgment of their traditional laws and any real observance of their traditional customs' (Cockayne 2001; see also Young 2001; Weiner 2002). As Cockayne has pointed out in his astute case notes, what is really at issue here is again the question of tradition (Cockayne 2001 passim). Differing narratives of temporality can be told which either subvert or sustain the concept of a tradition, precisely because the concept of a tradition embraces an essential tension. 'A tradition is always unchanging *and* dynamic' (Cockayne 2001: 794 italics added).

Judge Olney's finding was based in his unwarranted assertion that temporal and spatial continuity from pre-contact days to the present were the formal conditions for the acknowledgement and that they were not met. The judge found that there was no persuasive Aboriginal evidence in favor of continuity, since it was oral. But, there was persuasive evidence for the discontinuity of the indigenous tradition (see Edmond, on evidentiary hierarchies, in this volume). Firstly in the written but amateur anthropological observations of the pastoralist Edward Curr from the 1840s. Curr noted that in his ten years on the Murray the numbers of Aborigines radically decreased from 200 to 80 due to disease, and that:

> the Bangerang gave up in great measure their wholesome and exhilarating practices of hunting and fishing, and took to hanging about our huts in a miserable and objectless frame of mind and underfed condition, begging and doing trifling services of any sort. (Curr 1883: 106–7)

Secondly, in a classic catch-22, the judge found more evidence for discontinuity in the fact that the Yorta Yorta had filed a petition last century asking for their land back saying their way of life and occupancy had been disrupted. The irony of this double bind is strongly reminiscent of the grounds on which Justice Blackburn dismissed the first land claim by the Yolgnu people in Arnhemland saying that the Yolgnu ontology, in which they see the land as owning them, means that they don't own the land (Williams 1983). The crucial issues are the differing narratives of temporality underpinning the concept of tradition. Judge Olney, in the case of the indigenous claimants, took it to be an unattainable criterion of seamless continuity from pre-1788 to now, a condition he did not apply either to the legal or the anthropological knowledge tradition (Weiner 2002). As the Aboriginal lawyer and spokesman, Mick Dodson argues: 'The law must allow Indigenous cultures to create meaning. It must not confine Indigenous expression to the pristine and inaccessible past' (cited in Young 2001: 50).

As the case went to appeal, Monica Morgan, spokeswoman for the Yorta Yorta, invoked a similar spatially situated narrative in her view that the claim was all about recognition of Aboriginal relation to land. 'Our people are one of the lowest rungs on the social strata and we want to be able to have jobs and employment and training but we want to have it land-based. That's really all our people are asking for' (Haslem and Dodd 2002). The appeal was rejected by the High Court of Australia, leaving the United Nations as the last resort (Shiel 2003).

The judge in the *Yorta Yorta* case created a narrative of temporal and spatial discontinuity in the indigenous tradition thereby dismissing indigenous oral evidence and narratives of coherence and identity while simultaneously invoking a temporal narrative of continuity for the legal tradition. Alexander Reilly points out that while historical evidence is presented within the dynamic context of native title trials the law's approach to history is far from dynamic. It 'assumes that the past belongs to another realm of time which is separate from the present, and that consequently ... it is possible to show the past as it really was and to understand it on its own terms'. 'Whereas written histories separate the past and the present, oral histories assume and maintain a conjunction between the past and the present ... oral histories have a different criterion of causation and chronology' (Attwood cited in Reilly 2000: 467–8; see also Choo and Holbach 1998/99). Nonetheless, despite the obduracy of the judge in this case, and the tendency for the legal processes of native title claims to perpetuate the colonialism they were established to ameliorate, as both Alexander Reilly and Deborah Bird Rose have argued, the very process of native title claims can also bring about transformations in what counts as evidence and the blending and co-production of narratives (Rose 1996; see also Turnbull 1998b).

Secret women's business and the Hindmarsh Island Bridge controversy

More than any other case in Australia, the Hindmarsh Island Bridge dispute has profoundly problematized traditional knowledge as well as anthropological and legal knowledge claims (the best overall account is Simons 2003; a representative cross-section includes: Brunton 1999; Clarke 1996; Fergie 1996; Hemming 1997; Rowse 2000; Tonkinson 1997; Wilson 1998; Weiner 1999). The story, in brief, goes like this. The controversy originated with a proposal in 1989 to build a bridge from the mainland to an island at the mouth of the Murray, Australia's largest river, so that the island, previously only reachable by ferry, could be developed as a marina. A group of Ngarrindjeri women, led by Doreen Kartinyeri and assisted by the Adelaide University anthropologist Deane Fergie, objected to the bridge on the grounds that it would interfere with a sacred women's site on the island. Consequently sealed envelopes containing details of the women's business on the Island were handed to the Minister of the Environment and he placed a ban on bridge construction for 25 years. Claims then started to circulate that what was now referred to as 'secret women's business' had been fabricated. A Royal Commission was established in 1995 to determine the truth of the matter. The Commission concluded that the secret women's business had been fabricated as the result of another group of Ngarrindjeri women, led by Dorothy Wilson, claiming they did not know of any secret women's knowledge on the island. The so-called 'dissident women' were supported in this by Phillip Clarke, an anthropologist from the South Australian Museum. Clarke argued that no mention had been made of any secret women's business by earlier anthropologists who had studied the area, including Australia's most renowned anthropological couple, the Berndts, and that furthermore the Berndts found that the Ngarrindjeri, unlike any other Australian Aboriginal group, had made no demarcation between secular and sacred knowledge; nor was there any demarcation between men's and women's knowledge.

After this judgment, it seemed that the reputations of so-called 'feminist anthropology' and Australian Aborigines were irreparably damaged as sources of credible knowledge. Politically it provided very strong ammunition for the right-wing historians and politicians who were able to use the case to support the anti-revisionist, anti-postcolonialist cause in Australia. It seemed to be that a potato too hot to handle was best forgotten. However, the developers who then built the bridge and went on to succeed in a series of libel cases, decided in 1997 to sue Deane Fergie, the former Minister Robert Tickner and his nominated reporter Professor Cheryl Saunders in the Federal Court for $70m in losses due to the delay in the building of the bridge. In the judgment of that case, *Chapman v Luminis* (2001), Justice von Doussa of the Federal Court determined that there was no evidence that the women's business had been fabricated and found against the developers.[6]

A very significant point in his conclusion that neither the anti-bridge Ngarrindjeri women nor Deane Fergie had made the evidence up, was that in his view, the anthropologist Phillip Clarke, who had testified against them, was lacking in objectivity as revealed in his subpoenaed diary.

> On the anthropological evidence, I have serious concerns about the objectivity of Dr Clarke and the opinions he has given in evidence. His personal diaries on which he has been extensively cross-examined disclose that he is, and has been from the time the declaration was made, resistant to considering the possibility that his spontaneous assessment that Dr Fergie's opinion must be wrong might itself be wrong. He formed the opinion *before* he had read the reports of either Dr Fergie or Professor Saunders, and within hours of learning of the declaration. His diaries show that he was the originator of the fabrication theory, and that he thereafter embarked on a course to undermine and discredit Dr Fergie and her opinion. (*Chapman v Luminis Pty Ltd* 2001: 96)

The judge also noted that the Commission had not expressed any doubt about the finding of fabrication despite the fact that the anti-bridge Ngarrindjeri women had not appeared before it, nor had the envelopes containing the evidence been opened.

A key piece of reasoning for the Commission had been that the postulation of 'secret women's business' came forward very late, i.e. *after* the bridge was proposed. It made their claim 'redolent with suspicion of fabrication' but in Judge Doussa's view this is what you would expect of genuine sacred information of importance. It is what you would expect if you take the view that knowledge develops in context. James Weiner (2001: 144) argues that 'the farcical elements of the Hindmarsh Island Royal Commission emerged because the inquiry proceeded on the assumption that there was a version of Ngarrindjeri culture that existed independently of the anthropologist's and the commission's attempts to configure and interpret it, and hence repressed the dialogic properties of encounters of this sort where the nature and extent of culture and knowledge are contested'.

Indeed as Jacobs points out even the dissident pro-bridge women now think of the island as significant because they became engaged in the struggle over who has knowledge of the site (Gelder and Jacobs 1998). Margaret Simons, author of *The Meeting of the Waters: The Hindmarsh Island Affair* (2003), a remarkably comprehensive account of all sides of the controversy, concludes that 'it's about the stories we tell to bind us to the land and what happens when those stories clash'.

What counts as sacred, what are the transformative effects on boundaries between knowledge traditions, between the public and the private in the invocation of secret knowledge? What happens to anthropological expertise once knowledge is seen as growing and evolving rather than as information that can be simply collected and accumulated (Brunton 1995)? What happens when the arena for legal judgments, federal courts, royal commissions and state courts are in radical disagreement over protocols governing who is an expert, what counts as evidence, who can speak, who remains silent, who in the end is to be trusted? There can be no clear resolution of these issues except to recognize that all knowledge claims are embedded in conflicting narratives of space, time and protocols of trust— dimensions whose salience only becomes visible and tractable when they are held in tension.

Many of the issues turn crucially on the characterization of the nature of tradition and innovation and are directly addressed by Diane Bell in her book on the Ngarrindjeri, where she asks 'Can traditions change? Be relearned? Be reasserted? Can there be a tradition of innovation? Are anthropologists part of the "invention of culture"?' (Bell 1998: 13). In her account Ngarrindjeri women often say 'not everyone has to know everything for it to be true' (Bell 1998: 15). Here there are hidden narratives of spatiality as well as temporality. Knowledge is a valued commodity and arguably it's *the* commodity in Aboriginal culture and hence is unevenly distributed (Palmer 1991). As a Kaurna Elder explained to Margaret Simons 'Our culture is all about protocol … isn't like [TV]. People talking everybody's business all the time' (Simons 2003: 129). What is at issue are the protocols of trust which determine its distribution, its spatial and temporal boundaries. The Commission seems to have been arguing that a claim is worthy of the status of knowledge if it's evenly distributed within a predetermined group, i.e. all Ngarrindjeri at least of one gender would have to know it for it to be true. Similar spatial distribution criteria apply in the test of scientificity in forensic evidence. For a knowledge claim to be designated expert it must be trusted and accepted by the relevant community, again not evenly distributed across the whole community, otherwise it is not expert knowledge, yet at the same time distributed within a specific group (Collins 1985: 142ff; Shapin 1994).

Hence there are spatial narratives held in tension and it is that tension and the performative fecundity of bothness that is so nicely captured in the unifying thema of Bell's book—the art of weaving, making and narrating, doing and telling, being forms of bodily movement, practices of connecting (Guss 1989; Rowley 1997; Quilter and Urton 2002).

One of the Ngarrindjeri women, Daisy Rankine, explains: 'When we weave with the rushes, the memories of our loved ones are there, moulded into each stitch. And, when we are weaving, we tell stories. It is not just weaving, but the stories we tell when we are doing it' (Bell, 1998: 43; see also Conroy, with Ellen and Tom Trevorrow 1997). Ellen Trevorrow describes the process of weaving a basket:

> From where we actually start, the centre part of a piece, you're creating loops to weave into, then you move into the circle. You keep going round and round creating the loops and once the children do those stages they're talking, actually having a conversation, just like old people. It's sharing time. And that is where a lot of stories were told. (Bell 1998: 44)

So for Bell narrative and weaving are interconnected:

> To talk about weaving is to talk about family and country in an intimate way. Stories and memories of loved ones sustain and structure the Ngarrindjeri social

world; explain the mysterious; provide a secure haven in an otherwise hostile world; bring order to and confer significance on relationships amongst the living; hold hope for future generations; and open up communications with those who have passed on. The stories of cultural life recall the creation of the land, of the seas, rivers, lakes and lagoons. They tell of the coming into being of fish and fowl, of the birds of the air and the beasts of the fields. They spell out the proper uses of flora and fauna. These are stories of human frailty and triumph, of deception and duty, of rights, responsibilities and obligations, of magical beings, creative heroes and destructive forces. Everything has a story, but not everyone knows every story. Nor does everyone have the right to hear every story, or having heard it, to repeat the words. (Bell 1998: 45)

Weaving and holding differing knowledges in tension

The anthropologist Tim Ingold develops a very important insight on weaving and the performative nature of knowledge. He suggests that making is a form of weaving rather than the other way round.

> To emphasise making is to regard the object as the expression of an idea; to emphasise weaving is to regard it as the embodiment of a rhythmic movement. Therefore to invert making and weaving is also to invert idea and movement, to see the movement as truly generative of the object rather than merely revelatory of an object that is already present, in an ideal, conceptual or virtual form, in advance of the process that discloses it. The more that objects are removed from the contexts of life-activity in which they are produced and used—the more they appear as static objects of disinterested contemplation (as in museums and galleries)—the more too, the process disappears or is hidden behind the product, the finished object. Thus we are inclined to look for the meaning of the object in the idea it expresses rather than in the current of activity to which it properly and originally belongs. (Ingold 2000: 346)

Ingold claims that there are three points about skill which are exemplified in weaving and basketry but which are nevertheless common to the practice of any craft and which have strong analogies with storytelling:

> First the practitioner operates within a field of forces set up through his or her engagement with the material; secondly the work does not merely involve the mechanical application of external force but calls for care, judgement and dexterity; and thirdly the action has quality, in the sense that every movement, like every line in a story, grows rhythmically out of the one before and lays the groundwork for the next. (Ingold 2000: 346–7)

Weaving, making and narrative, from this perspective, are thus about bodily movements and hence the co-production of space and time. And it is to the question of space and place that I want to return in a performative conception of local knowledge. Again Ingold has some useful insights:

Places do not have locations but histories. Bound together by the itineraries of their inhabitants, they exist not in space but as nodes in a matrix of movement. [He calls] this matrix a 'region'. It is the knowledge of the region, 'and with it the ability to situate one's current position within the historical context of journeys previously made—journeys to, from and around places—that distinguishes the countryman from the stranger. Ordinary wayfinding, then, more closely resembles story-telling than map-using. To use a map is to navigate by means of it: that is to plot a course from one location to another in space. Wayfinding by contrast is a matter of moving from one place to another in a region. (Ingold 2000: 219)

I have argued elsewhere that all knowledge is like travelling, like a journey between parts of a matrix while also arguing that all knowledge is local (Turnbull 1991). Ingold gently and persuasively corrects an error in my thinking about this characterization of the local. He points out that knowledge is never in places, rather it is regional, it is to be cultivated by moving along paths that lead around, towards, or away from places, 'we know as we go', so all knowledge, including science, is based on lateral movement, not vertical connection (Ingold 2000: 230).

As de Certeau tells us 'Every story is a travel story—a spatial practice' (de Certeau 1984: 115–16). So, if places are the product of spatial histories, stories of journeys remembered, then the notion of the local as place, and the universal as placeless, are equally deeply and profoundly based in stories of movement either remembered or forgotten. All knowledge, indigenous, legal or scientific is again spatial, temporal, narratological, and performative. Herein lies the fundamental commonality of knowledge and weaving. Weaving and storytelling have a common origin reflected in the Latin verb *texere,* to weave, from which text and textile are both derived. They are dependent on the tension of the warp and the weft, on the bothness of storytelling. The conflicts, similarities and differences of knowledge from and within differing traditions should be explored and celebrated by holding them in the tension of weaving, allowing the fecundity of what the South American postcolonial historian Enrique Dussel aptly calls 'agonistic pluralism'. The fecundity of bothness is akin to Bowker's notion of 'dynamic *un*compromise' and Bakhtin's insistence that truth is dialogical and depends on a plurality of '*unmerged* voices' (Morson and Emerson 1990: 236–7; Dussel 1993; Bowker 2000). Performing stories from the multiple conflicting knowledge spaces and telling them together could help to make visible their concealed narratives of space and time. Naturally this relativistic pluralism raises problems in judicial judgments that of necessity have to choose between alternatives, but it allows the prospect of judgments being more reflexive if they are made in a recognition of the narrative, practice and protocol dimensions of knowledge from varying traditions. 'The real chance to make a difference ... lies in a modest willingness to live, to know and to practice in the complexities of tension' (Law 1999: 12).

Notes

1   See also Bal (1985), Bennett and Feldman (1981), Bochner (1997), Bowker (1995),
     Briggs (1996), Brockmeier and Harré (1997), Brown (1998), Bruner (1990), Crang
     (1994), Deuten and Rip (2000), Edmond (1999), Ewick and Silbey (1995), Finnegan

(1998), Franzosi (1998), Goodrich (1990), Haraway (1989), Hinchman and Hinchman (1997), Kerby (1991), Maclean (1988), Mattingly (1998), Mitchell (1980), Polkinghorne (1991), Roe (1994), Rouse (1996), Sarbin (1986), Schank (1990), Staudenmaier (1985), Vogler (1996), White (1980, 1984, 1987).

2   *Cooper v Stuart* (1899) 14 AC 286.

3   *Mabo and others v The State of Queensland (No. 2)* (1992) 175 CLR 1.

4   *Coe v Commonwealth* (1979) 24 ALR 118.

5   *Members of the Yorta Yorta Aboriginal Community v. State of Victoria* [1998] 1606 FCA, *Members of the Yorta Yorta Aboriginal Community v. State of Victoria* [2001] FCA 45, *Members of the Yorta Yorta Aboriginal Community v. State of Victoria* [2002] HCA 5.

6   *Chapman v Luminis Pty Ltd (No 5)* [2001] FCA 1106. See also Edmond (2004a).

Chapter 10

Ethical Dimensions of Law–Science Relations in US Courtrooms

David S. Caudill

Introduction

Expertise is imported with regularity into legal processes and institutions, but the ethical aspects of that relationship are not at all obvious. In the regulatory or legislative policy context, of course, law might be viewed as imposing ethical constraints on science. Governmental restrictions on stem cell research, or requiring administrative agency analyses of risk with respect to new drugs (prior to their being marketed), provide examples. Perhaps that is why Michel Serres, when he suggests that science without law is inhuman, seems to include law on the ethical 'side' of things, alongside religion and the humanities, *against* science. For Serres, however, this is only a hope or a goal, as law has tended to be in collusion with or subservient to science, which 'has all the power, all the knowledge, all the rationality, all the rights, too, of course, all plausibility or legitimacy' (Serres 1990: 87). That evaluation can be contrasted with Peter Schuck's view that law and politics 'continue to rein in science', therefore science 'will have to make its case at the bars of public opinion and administrative law as well as in the laboratory and the market for technology' (Schuck 1993: 45).

With respect to litigation involving expert scientific testimony in US courtrooms, the dimensions of ethics are more than a little different. While judges and lawyers are bound by ethical rules of professional conduct, and while an expert (by organizational or professional affiliation) may have a code of ethics, questions of scientific admissibility are generally not ethical issues. To the extent that judges in the US are gatekeepers who are supposed to admit only valid science, it would be difficult to characterize their activities as ethical constraints on science. I realize that science is never value-free, not only because of epistemic values but also because science reflects cultural assumptions about what is important, but those 'constraints' are internal to science and are not legal constraints. Indeed, because US judicial standards of scientific validity idealize and mirror science's own self-image, there are virtually no external constraints; those who have proposed pragmatic legal standards of validity (that might, depending on the goals of justice, be different from science's own standards) have not been successful (Resnik 2000: 249–64). Nevertheless in post-

Daubert scholarly discourse in the US, a concern persists over 'junk science' in the courtroom, and sometimes the blame for that phenomenon is placed not on incompetent judges or emotional jurors, but on unethical lawyers and experts.[1] We therefore need ethics, some say, not to constrain science, but to free it from those who get in its way—genuine science is in this view being constrained by unethical behavior, by peddlers of bad science.

The notion of 'junk science,' which has no precise or consistent definition, seems to have functioned (since the late 1980s) as a rallying cry for those who claim that the introduction and admission of unreliable scientific testimony in courtrooms has resulted in a litigation 'explosion' and an insurance 'crisis' (Edmond and Mercer 1998a: 3–6). On examination, however,

> the junk science model ... relies on ... untenable images of efficacy, methods, norms, and motivation as hallmarks of "good science"; inadequate, and sometimes clearly erroneous, views drawn from the history of science; impoverished understandings of the public perception of risk and its influence on the construction of scientific knowledge; and naïve views of the relationship between law and science (Edmond and Mercer 1998a: 5–6).

Nevertheless, judges and legal scholars often base their analyses upon the assumption that 'junk' science is clearly or easily distinguishable from 'genuine' science. In the discussion that follows, therefore, the strategic, polemical, and rhetorical role of the term 'junk science' should be kept in mind.

The ethics of expert testimony

Within the literature of contemporary US judicial opinions, the cure for 'junk science'—whether viewed as a massive epidemic or the odd mishap—is better gatekeeping by judges. A minor ethical dimension is here identifiable, since judges must be impartial and prepared for trial, but their responsibility is to understand the science being proffered—is there sufficient data, a reliable methodology in the abstract, and then a reliable application of that methodology to the facts of the case? Moreover, a recent survey concluded that US judges do not understand science, at least as scientific literacy was defined by the survey authors (as an understanding of 'falsification'), thus they need more *scientific* training to carry out their responsibilities (Gatowski et al. 2001: 444–7, 455).

In US judicial opinions, when an expert's testimony is deemed inadmissible because it is not scientific, there is typically no accusation of unethical attorney conduct. In the spirit of advocacy, we might say, there is no harm in trying. Indeed, as

> an advocate in the adversary system, it is a lawyer's job to make the best possible argument in support of her client. A lawyer will often find herself advancing a position in the hope that it will work, without necessarily believing that the view is correct. (Lubet 1998: 171)

Such indirect language is the norm in the US literature on the ethics of presenting scientific testimony.[2] Even Rule 3.3(a)(3) of the American Bar Association *Model Rules of Professional Conduct*, which clearly *allows* an attorney to offer evidence reasonably believed to be false, actually says that a lawyer, impliedly on strategic grounds, 'may *refuse* to offer evidence ... that the lawyer reasonably believes is false'.[3] In the latest 2002 version of those *Rules*, the earlier Comment (1983) that 'an advocate does not vouch for the evidence submitted' was sanitized by placing 'although' before the clause and adding (after the clause) a duty to ensure that the tribunal is not misled by 'evidence that the lawyer knows to be false'. It is as if US lawyers are in denial, or ashamed, of their discretion to offer evidence they believe (but do not 'know') to be false.

Viewing Rule 3.3(a)(3) as an exhaustive set of categories in which to place expert testimony, three possibilities appear: (i) evidence that is known to be false *cannot* be offered, (ii) evidence that is known *or* believed to be true *can* (obviously) be offered, and (iii) evidence that is *believed* to be false can also be offered.[4] With respect to scientific expertise, the situations in which an attorney *knows* that an expert is wrong would seem to be quite rare. In Virginia, for example, *knowledge* of fraudulent testimony is established by acknowledgment of the fraud by the expert, which of course leaves little doubt on the part of the attorney (Virginia LEO 1650).[5] Short of such an acknowledgment, however, attorneys may often have serious doubts about their expert's testimony but not knowledge of falsity, which seems to relieve attorneys from responsibility for shaky or less-than-credible science.

On the other hand, the rules may not be as generous as they first appear. First, Comment 8 to Rule 3.3, and Rule 1.0 (f), which is cited in that Comment, confirm that knowledge of falsity 'can be inferred from the circumstances', and also that a 'lawyer cannot ignore an obvious falsehood'.[6] This Comment raises the possibility that a lawyer claiming not to know of an expert's falsehoods may be deemed to have actual knowledge of them because they are so obvious to others. This notion is similar to the inference in contract law that a commercial party is familiar with 'trade usage' (i.e. common usage and interpretation of terms in the trade); because a member of a trade *should* know such usage, that understanding will be imposed in spite of a claim that no such understanding existed. Likewise, just as one can be convicted on the basis of circumstantial evidence, a lawyer's claim not to know can be second-guessed. Moreover, some commentators highlight the term *reasonable* in Rule 3.3 and its official commentary—'A lawyer's reasonable belief that evidence is false does not preclude its presentation ...' (see Comment 8, Rule 3.3)—and suggest that the lawyer's uncertainty must be 'genuine *and* reasonable'.[6] That is, if one's belief that a certain expert's testimony is false is so strong that one really has no 'genuine and reasonable' doubt that it is false, and one is only categorizing it as a belief for strategic reasons, the belief may be transformed into knowledge of falsity. Finally, there is the suggestion, in some judicial opinions and legal ethics opinions (discussed below), that knowledge of falsity can be imputed if the lawyer *should have known*, which raises the spectre of a duty to inquire or even to confirm suspicions.

In the cases discussed below, it should be noted that unethical attorneys are typically disciplined—for violations of the applicable rules of professional conduct—by an ethics committee or other non-judicial body that is (i) responsible for enforcement of ethical rules, and (ii) that imposes sanctions such as a public reprimand, suspension, or disbarment. Courts rarely impose sanctions, thus a procedural ruling against an attorney (for example, a judge's refusal to allow introduction of fraudulent testimony by an expert) is often not the end of the matter, because attorney misconduct can be reported to the applicable regulating authority by the judge, opposing counsel, or a party. As to ethical codes for experts, which might exist due to an expert's membership in an organization with such a code, courts typically have no jurisdiction over such matters; the existence of such codes might be revealed in a lawyer's examination of an expert, and perhaps used to bolster credibility or discredit an expert, but enforcement of such codes is not a judicial concern. This regime can be contrasted with recent Australian procedural reforms that include a code of conduct for experts, an explicit obligation to assist the court, and the possibility of being charged with professional misconduct for non-compliance (Edmond 2003: 139–40).

In *Harre v A.H. Robins Co., Inc.*,[7] a Dalkon Shield case in the US federal courts, a doctor serving as an expert for the defendant testified at trial that he had directed certain tests, implying that he had personally conducted the experiments. Shortly thereafter, in another case, the same expert was questioned by the same attorney, and this time testified that he had neither conducted nor supervised such tests. On appeal of the trial verdict in the earlier case, the Court concluded that the expert had testified falsely *and* that defence counsel 'knew *or should have known* of the falsity of the testimony' (*Harre* 1985: 1503).

> [In] view of the fact that Dr. Keith had acted as a consultant/expert for Robins attorneys since 1977, it becomes obvious that Robins' counsel must have been aware [of the contradictory testimony] … This court is deeply disturbed by the fact that a material expert witness, with complicity of counsel, would falsely testify on the ultimate issue of causation. (*Harre* 1985: 1505)

In other words, as soon as an expert's testimony is contradictory, the usual discretion to offer evidence believed to be false—based on the notion that the lawyer does not vouch for her expert's testimony if she does not *know* it is false—is lost. The falsehood is *obvious*, and if the lawyer claims merely to have doubts about the testimony but not knowledge of its falsity, her doubts are not *genuine and reasonable*.

Another recent case from the England and Wales Court of Appeal (Civil Division), *Vernon v Bosley*, is analogous to *Harre*.[8] In *Vernon*, the plaintiff offered expert testimony of a debilitating psychiatric illness sustained when he witnessed the unsuccessful attempts to rescue his two daughters from a car that was driven into a river by the children's nanny. In connection with a later divorce and child custody proceeding, however, Mr. Vernon offered evidence, by the same experts, that he had fully recovered. In reconsidering the plaintiff's favorable tort judgment, the Court of

Appeals opined that if the trial judge

> had appreciated that the prognosis given by [the psychiatrist and the psychologist] would be so swiftly falsified and the significance which they attached to the ... deterioration so soon discounted as being a temporary phenomenon, not even worth mentioning [in the family proceedings], he might have wished to reconsider his findings. (*Vernon* 1997: 345)

Worse yet, the experts provided additional, new evidence (contrary to the evidence of full recovery in the family proceedings) to the Court of Appeals on reconsideration of the earlier, generous tort judgment:

> It comes as no great surprise that following ... further consultation ... both witnesses report a deterioration in the plaintiff's position. [This] demonstrated quite clearly, if any further demonstration was needed, their lack of objectivity. (*Vernon* 1997: 346)

The Court of Appeals reminded plaintiff's counsel of his duty to avoid misleading the Court, and concluded that even though counsel *knew* that the experts' testimony early in the tort case was no longer true, he neither advised the plaintiff to reveal the fraud nor withdrew (*Vernon* 1997).[9] While counsel in *Harre* knew of false testimony as to a fact—whether the doctor had supervised or conducted experiments—counsel in *Vernon* knew of two different opinions—both of which may have been true at the time due to the plaintiff's initial deterioration and apparent recovery—and allowed the Court to rely on an outdated, and therefore known-to-be-false, prognosis. Again, the current falsity of the earlier prognosis in *Vernon* was obvious (in light of the newer prognosis from the same experts), such that the plaintiff's attorney could no longer claim a merely genuine and reasonable doubt about its falsity—he now *knew* it was false.

A third recent US federal court case with similar facts, *McNeil v the Atchison, Topeka and Santa Fe Railway Company*, involved an employee who won a verdict (based on expert testimony by his treating physicians) for a permanent disability.[10] Eight days later, the employee tried to return to his former position, and when his employer refused he filed a discrimination suit claiming he had been rehabilitated. The Court, 'astonished by the audacity of the Plaintiff', remarked that

> absent a representation of outright Divine Intervention ... the Court is left with an uncomfortable inference of outright fraud
> ...
> Given the egregious conduct of Plaintiff and the apparent willing complicity of his counsel, this Court is not at all surprised by the current public outcry for tort reform ... (*McNeil* 1995: 990–91)

Here, instead of contradictory or new testimony alerting counsel to falsity, the second claim was inconsistent with the expert testimony in the first. The circumstances suggested an obvious falsehood, arguably leaving the attorney without any genuine and reasonable doubt as to the falsity of his client's claim.

These cases together suggest expansions of the category of *known* falsities that cannot be offered, as well as corresponding contractions of the category of evidence 'reasonably believed to be false' that can be offered. Actual knowledge can be inferred from circumstances, and even constructive knowledge (e.g. *Harre's* 'known or should have known' phrase) of an obvious falsehood places limits on claims of 'genuine and reasonable doubt but not knowledge'. Whether there is an additional duty of due diligence and reasonable inquiry to confirm doubts (about an expert's testimony) is not clear, but a recent Virginia legal ethics opinion is apposite. The opinion concerned a lawyer who suspected fraud on the part of his client, prior to representation, to obtain a benefit from the Immigration and Naturalization Service (Virginia LEO 1687). Ordinarily, in Virginia, a fraud must be *clearly established* by acknowledgment (in this case, by the client) before a duty to reveal arises, and even then the duty only arises with respect to a fraud occurring during the course of the attorney–client relationship. No duty to inquire about or reveal the fraud was raised under the facts, because the fraud preceded representation, but the committee did observe that it

> is not improper for an attorney to accept at face value that the representation of [a] client is bona fide unless the attorney knows or, in the exercise of due diligence upon reasonable inquiry ..., the attorney should know information to the contrary. (Virginia LEO 1687)

Moreover, 'if an attorney never receives an "admission" or "confession" from his client which would clearly establish the fraud suspected, but nevertheless believes that the fraud is obvious', the attorney should withdraw (Virginia LEO 1687). Even though this analysis was in the context of client fraud, and did not concern an expert witness, the notion that the lawyer has a duty to confirm suspicions could arguably be extended to expert witnesses, since Rule 3.3(a)(3) does not distinguish between 'a lawyer, the lawyer's client, or a witness'.[11] In other words, when a lawyer reasonably believes, but does not know, that her expert will testify falsely, her genuine and reasonable doubt could be treated as knowledge of falsity if, 'in the exercise of due diligence upon reasonable inquiry', the attorney *should know* it to be false (Virginia LEO 1687).

That position has been suggested by one commentator on Rule 3.4, which prohibits falsifying evidence, who asserted that Rule 3.4 'forbids an attorney to permit an expert to testify as an expert in an area that is not scientifically valid' (Murphy 2000: 230). Such an interpretation implies that an attorney should or could determine the scientific validity of an expert's opinion; significantly, this interpretation is not qualified by the attorney's knowledge of scientific validity, as in Rule 3.3, but rather sets up scientific validity as a standard for what we *know* or *should know* to be true or false. This, I think, is an extreme view that is not warranted by the rules of professional conduct. Even as I identify bases for more responsibility on the part of attorneys with respect to their experts, I think that there is a risk, evident in the literature on law and science, of idealizing science as an unproblematic standard for truth. Even scientists disagree about the validity of many hypotheses, thus it hardly makes sense to require that lawyers make evaluations of scientific validity, or even to assume that lawyers know when a hypothesis is 'true'.

'Junk science': who's to blame?

> When all else fails—when neither improved pretrial procedures nor strengthened ethical codes succeed in terminating litigation in which one party's position is grounded solely on specious expert testimony—it may be the task of the judge to do what the adversarial process and professional ethics have failed to do. (Weinstein 1986: 491)

That statement by Chief Judge Weinstein in 1986 impliedly recognized the 'safe haven' (in the rules of professional conduct) that allows lawyers to present expert testimony that is reasonably believed to be false. Indeed, Judge Weinstein's article was full of suggestions to eliminate frivolous and obfuscating expert testimony—including revised procedural rules and rules of evidence, control of experts by outside agencies, substantive law reform, using neutral experts, stronger controls by courts, and scientific enlightenment of judges—but lawyers were not direct targets of his critique (Weinstein 1986). Arguably in response to concerns over 'junk science' in the courtroom, the US Supreme Court in *Daubert* reinforced the gatekeeping role of judges and offered a legal standard for scientific validity.[12] Shortly thereafter, the federal rules of evidence were amended to confirm that admissible scientific testimony must be 'based upon sufficient facts or data' and be 'the product of reliable principles and methods' that have been applied 'reliably to the facts of the case' (FRE 702). Viewed as a cure for 'junk science', the new federal jurisprudence of law–science relations places the responsibility on trial judges and evidentiary rules, not on lawyers. Lawyers are advocates, and when you read an appellate opinion reversing a trial judge's admissibility determination, the trial judge may well be admonished for letting 'junk science' in or for failing to be a gatekeeper; but trial lawyers are rarely blamed for their efforts.[13]

Other examples of US proposals for reform which do not place the responsibility (for supposedly junk science) on lawyers include the use of 'neutral' scientific experts (in addition to those called by the parties), advisory juries (in non-jury trials) consisting entirely of experts, appointment of special 'masters', and science panels (of scientists) or science courts (with judges who are scientists) to hear and decide scientific issues (Murphy 2000: 236–9). Such solutions, however,

> are unlikely to be embraced because they inevitably undercut the adversary process that is the foundation of the American legal system. By tradition and widely accepted theory, justice is believed to be served best when the parties control the development and presentation of their cases. (Saks 1987; Johnston 1987)

Perhaps, in the alternative, we could put the burden on experts themselves to know the rules of evidence and to follow their own profession's (or professional organizations') ethical guidelines.

They should know the rules of the game into which they usually wander naively, not be introduced to them by a lawyer who has no incentive to educate and every incentive to control ... They should learn to stand up to lawyers who try to lure them [farther] than they should go. And they should learn to give accurate, two-sided presentations in court, recognizing that they are witnesses, not advocates.[14]

Experts, that is, should regulate themselves to ensure independence, confidentiality, no conflicts of interest, reasonable fees, and appropriate conduct during trials and depositions (Lubet 1999). Even when commentators blame unethical lawyers for their part in the production of 'illusory science', alongside bad experts (e.g. 'professional experts' who become advocates, or who are poorly trained or use inadequate procedures), they often propose reliance on 'neutral court-called experts' (Thames 1995). That is, instead of arguing for ethical attorneys, they eliminate the problem by taking the expertise away from the influence of lawyers.

Some, however, do claim that lawyers have an ethical obligation to keep 'junk science' out of the courtroom. For example, Dick Thornburgh, former US Attorney General, boldly asserts that 'it is unethical lawyers who are largely to blame' for 'junk science' (Thornburgh 1998: 449).

It is clear that the lawyer does have a duty to determine whether he believes expert testimony will be admissible before trying to introduce such evidence in court. ... To be an effective advocate, the lawyer must ... test the accuracy and reliability of ... expert testimony ... he wishes to introduce. (Thornburgh 1998: 462)

Thornburgh bases this argument on the duty in Rule 3.1 to bring only meritorious (i.e., not frivolous) claims and contentions, which he interprets as requiring that, prior to introducing an expert, lawyers ensure 'that there is a good faith basis to believe that [the proffered testimony] is reliable scientific evidence' (Thornburgh 1998: 463). Thornburgh even suggests that court-imposed sanctions against the offending attorney (e.g. a fine) would be appropriate if 'it is discovered before the conclusion of the proceedings that certain evidence presented was, in fact, junk science' (Thornburgh 1998: 467).

It is simply not clear whether Thornburgh is arguing for law reform or claiming that the current rules of professional conduct already make lawyers ethically responsible to police 'junk science'. He concedes that 'an attorney's ethical obligations would not be enough to present the admission of junk science', since lawyers are allowed to proffer expert testimony they reasonably believe is false, but then he refers to 'the full recognition of the lawyer's professional obligation to carefully scrutinize the integrity of his own expert's proposed testimony ...' (Thornburgh 1998: 467, 469). To the extent that he bases this latter ethical obligation on the duty to bring only meritorious claims and contentions, I see at least three problems with his analysis. First, after he claims the 'ethical rules ... require that a lawyer must ensure there is a good faith basis for the admissibility of evidence', he concedes that '"shaky" scientific evidence could still be admissible' under *Daubert*, and that lawyers 'have no clear guidelines on what will, or will not, be deemed admissible scientific expert testimony' (Thornburgh 1998: 463–4). Second, any ethical obligation to ensure *reliable* testimony would be inconsistent with the discretion to present expert testimony reasonably believed (but not *known*) to be false. Thornburgh, uniquely I think, views the introduction of expert testimony as a claim or contention of law (as to admissibility) and fact (as to reliability) on behalf of a client, but the rule against bringing frivolous claims does not require that the lawyer believe his client's position will ultimately prevail or even that the facts be fully substantiated.

This brings me to my third, and most important, concern—Thornburgh's frustrated attempt to find some basis for the ethical responsibility of lawyers for 'junk science' is coupled with an idealized view of science. His preferred solution for the problem of 'junk science', a 'court-appointed board of experts or advisory panel', signifies his confidence in science itself as neutral and disinterested (Thornburgh 1998: 468). Indeed, the examples of cases and controversies that Thornburgh offers to conceptualize his discussion of the ethical responsibilities of lawyers (Bendectin, Norplant, breast implants) are presented as involving two opposing kinds of evidence: 'genuine' science and 'junk' science (Thornburgh 1998: 449). That tendency to see 'good' versus 'junk' science in law, rather than scientific *theories* in *conflict*, is indicative of a particular view of science as a field that is far removed and different from law.[15] Law is, in that view, unstable, adversarial, rhetorical, institutional, and value-laden, while science is characterized by universal standards, rigorous methodologies and testing, and consensus. Given that picture, it is not surprising that commentators like Thornburgh both (i) recommend neutral science panels to stabilize legal disputes and (ii) criticize attorneys for their ethical shortcomings—why don't attorneys just, in Thornburgh's words, 'test the reliability and accuracy' of their experts' testimony and reject experts who lack 'integrity'? (Thornburgh 1998: 462, 469). The very question presumes that in any scientific dispute in court, it is obvious that one expert is wrong and the other is right—and that a lawyer who presents the 'junk' expert is unethical and knows it.

As I have argued elsewhere, this idealized view of science pervades contemporary literature on law–science relations, and leads to an oversimplified view of scientific expertise (Caudill 2002). This is not to say that all scientific 'experts' are revered in law—judges do identify *bad* experts who peddle *junk* science—but that law is generally not critical of science and its pretensions. For example, the search for bias, interest, or motivation on the part of experts (in depositions or in cross-examinations) is usually associated with the effort to discredit a witness, as if a genuine expert would be neutral, disinterested, and objective. Little attention is paid in law nowadays to the inevitable, not anomalous, features of science as a human activity and social enterprise, including its rhetorical, discursive, and consensus-building strategies, its institutional characteristics (including training, professionalization, and credentialing processes), its methodological variations and experimental *conventions*, its theoretical biases, its funding sources, and its values (including standards as to what is worth researching). These inevitable characteristics do not, in themselves, signal 'junk' science, but rather constitute a realistic, albeit modest, account of the scientific enterprise. Indeed, while many judges continue to idealize science, some seem to have adopted a 'pragmatist view of the scientific enterprise—naturalistic but not a perfect mirror, rigorous but approximate, both social and empirical, evidence-based but probabilistic' (LaRue and Caudill 2001–2: 344). In such a perspective, science is (like law) a contested field; the evidence on each side of a scientific controversy may be based on methodological inquiry and therefore be properly admissible.

Idealized and other accounts of the scientific enterprise

The image of science in post-*Daubert* jurisprudence, including the revisions to the federal rules of evidence (and commentary) following *Daubert*, is idealized in the sense that science is defined as or characterized by its core activities: hypothesis, data collection, careful testing, and conclusions. That is, science is not defined as or characterized by its social, institutional or rhetorical aspects. The discourse of law–science relations, especially in judicial opinions but even in treatises and law journals, mirrors traditional or internal accounts of the scientific enterprise. Social, institutional, and rhetorical aspects are classified as either (i) external influences—including fraud, rhetoric, political and economic interests, and errors—or (ii) internal *supports*—including professionalization, values, methodological conventions, and scientific language—and in either event are viewed as contingent and, if not dispensable, at least irrelevant to determinations of scientific validity.

Other accounts of science, including those associated with science and technology studies, the sociology of scientific knowledge, ethnographic studies of scientific practices, and cultural studies of science, tend to characterize social, institutional, and rhetorical aspects of science as inevitable and constitutive. Such accounts are generally not viewed as useful in courtroom law–science relations, for several reasons. First, law needs stable scientific knowledge, so any suggestion that science is unstable, or 'socially constructed,' or merely a narrative, is seemingly out of place in the discourse of law–science relations. Significantly, every judge and legal scholar knows that scientific knowledge is uncertain and subject to revision, due, for example, to limitations in measurement technologies, probability analyses, and changing models. Moreover, everybody knows that science is not immune from fraud, theoretical or funding bias, poor experimental techniques, and public and governmental pressures, but these are not generally acknowledged as typical features of science; instead, they all become examples of 'junk science'. It is rare, for example, for legal scholars to concede that theoretical bias and financial opportunism 'provide powerful motors for many fields of contemporary science' (Edmond and Mercer 1998a: 11). Finally, even if the social, institutional, and rhetorical aspects of science are acknowledged—of course scientists use language, persuade one another, and belong to institutions—these are rarely considered relevant in the courtroom, where attorneys try to establish that their experts are better than the opposing side's experts. The point is to reveal the bias, interest, and motivation of the other side's scientists, and to show that one's own experts are relatively objective.

For example, we now see the term 'evidence-based medicine', or EBM, used to designate the clinical strategy of using current research findings, the best evidence available, to make medical treatment decisions. Personal clinical experience, and the judgment and intuition that follows, arguably should be subordinated to systematic reviews of randomized controlled trials, the results of individual controlled clinical trials, and observational studies (Noah 2002). While this sounds good, critics have identified the shortcomings of the peer review process, the problems of information overload, and biases and conflicts of interest in funding and in the publication process. In addition, some attorneys are concerned that medical expertise will be limited to EBM, and that medical opinion testimony will be excluded if it does not have statistical and epidemiological support. That is, some attorneys are concerned that their expert physicians, testifying with only consensual, not statistical, support, about a matter that has not yet been subjected to epidemiological study, will be considered 'junk' scientists. And they are concerned that studies funded and controlled by pharmaceutical companies will become the gold standard of scientific testimony (Peters 2002: 74–9).

In one recent case, *Cooper v Carl Nelson & Co.*, an injured worker brought a suit and offered the testimony of medical experts who relied on the plaintiff's statements as the basis for their diagnosis.[16] The trial judge rejected the testimony as unscientific, but an appellate panel thought the trial judge was an 'overly aggressive ... gatekeeper'. Conscientious clinicians, that is, often rely on physical examinations and self-reported medical histories, which are acceptable diagnostic tools. In another case, *Walter v Soo Line Railroad Co.*, the trial judge disallowed medical testimony that relied on the work of fellow team members, especially since the testifying expert did not agree with her team members' conclusions; an appellate panel rejected that argument, since medical professionals often rely on other medical professionals, and there can be contradictory conclusions among qualified, reliable experts.[17] Finally, in a veterinary malpractice case, *Jahn v Equine Services*, a trial judge viewed the uncertainty of an expert's opinion as to the cause of death of a racehorse as unscientific and inadmissible, but an appellate panel disagreed, since the methodology was sound given the lack of reliable data.[18] In all three of these cases, the trial judge rejected what he viewed as 'junk' science, which judicial action reflected an idealization of science as based on objective measurement techniques, consensus among scientists, and certainty. Such idealizations are common in scholarly legal discourse nowadays; attacks on forensic science and the techniques of fingerprint analysis, hair sample identification, and ballistic studies are on the increase (see Cole and Lynch, in this volume). While I am sympathetic to critical re-evaluations of legally sanctioned science, my concern is that they emanate from a belief that genuine, rigorous science rises above social structures, institutional frameworks, and rhetorical strategies. That idealized discourse concerning science, which proposes disinterested science panels and chides judges for failing to consult or appoint neutral experts, is also the usual source of both (i) hysterical warnings about the 'junk science' epidemic, and (ii) the condemnation of unethical attorneys, who should be sanctioned for presenting 'junk science'.

Some judges, however, seem to have a more modest assessment of the scientific enterprise—science is pragmatic, approximate, probabilistic. And some attorneys, especially plaintiffs' counsel in tort cases, are concerned with the bias, interest, and motivation of industry-sponsored research. These perspectives are commensurate with alternative accounts of science—all science—as social, institutional, and rhetorical. In briefest terms, soft science is not as 'junky,' and hard science is 'junkier,' than those who idealize science would have us think.

The presumption that 'junk science' is easily identifiable leads not only to the simplistic notion that ethical attorneys will become gatekeepers, but similarly leads some to suggest that an explicit duty (to the court) on the part of experts will result in more reliable science. The difficulties with that optimism—including the facts that experts have always been under oath, that scientific controversies exist outside the legal forum, and that certain types of parties will be advantaged by more circumspection and uncertainty—have recently been explored (Edmond 2003: 148–62).

Conclusion

The implication of the foregoing analysis for the ethics of presenting scientific testimony is that proposals to make attorneys 'a kind of gatekeeper' are not so troubling once those proposals are disengaged from idealizations of science. That is, attorneys should feel comfortable constructing the best case they can, and comfortable in challenging their opponent's seemingly superior scientific experts. At the same time, attorneys who genuinely and reasonably doubt that their experts have anything scientific to offer should not, under the ideology of advocacy or the cynical notion that one never really 'knows' anything, feel comfortable in their zeal and ignorance. A duty to inquire about and investigate their experts' claims is consistent with the public expectation that advocates will not include fraud in their arsenal of trial tactics. On the other hand, simplistic conceptions of scientific expertise that fail to acknowledge the possibility of conflicting, admissible science, and that too quickly characterize one side as 'junk' and one side as 'genuine' in any scientific controversy, seem to me to confuse ethical consciousness with scientism. In short, I would be in favor of increased ethical responsibilities as long as there is a corresponding increase in our understanding of how science actually works—socially, institutionally, and rhetorically, as well as methodologically and empirically.

Notes

1 See *Daubert v Merrell Dow Pharmaceuticals, Inc.* 509 US 579 (1993).

2 That is, 'without necessarily believing the view is correct' is seemingly preferred to 'even if she believes that the view is false'.

3 See, Comment 9 to Rule 3.3(a)(3). 'Offering such proof may reflect adversely on the lawyer's ability to discriminate in the quality of evidence and thus impair the lawyer's effectiveness as an advocate.'

4 See Rule 3.3(a)(3), American Bar Association *Model Rules of Professional Conduct*

(2002): 'A lawyer shall not knowingly … offer evidence that the lawyer knows to be false … A lawyer may refuse to offer evidence … that the lawyer reasonably believes is false.'

5   Comment 8, Rule 3.3. See also Rule 1.0(f): 'A person's knowledge can be inferred from circumstances'.

6   See Hazard and Hodes (1990: §3.3:401): 'If the lawyer's uncertainty is genuine and reasonable, he can present the evidence without risk of violating Rule 3.3'.

7   *Harre v AH Robins Co., Inc.* 750 F.2d 1501 (11th Cir. 1985), recons'd at 866 F.2d 1303 (11th Cir. 1989).

8   *Vernon v Bosley (No. 2)* [1997] 1 PIQR 326.

9   A similar analysis can be found in Virginia LEO 1477 (24 August 1992), wherein the issue was whether a lawyer could remain silent during settlement negations concerning an inaccuracy in his client's answers to interrogatories. The inaccuracy was not noticed by the lawyer when the answers were given to opposing counsel, but had been noticed by the lawyer just before settlement negotiations. The committee opined that silence would amount to assistance in fraud.

10   *McNeil v the Atchison, Topeka and Santa Fe Railway Company* 878 F. Supp. 986 (S.D.Tex 1995).

11   See Rule 3.3(a)(3). Note that there is an exception for testimony of a defendant in a criminal matter, *id.*, which is not relevant to the present analysis.

12   *Daubert* 1993: 593–4. In *Kumho Tire v Carmichael*, 526 US 136, 152 (1999), the Court confirmed the flexibility of the four-part *Daubert* test—any number of the features might be emphasized.

13   See *Goebel v Denver and Rio Grande Western Railroad Co.* 215 F.3d 1083, 1086–8 (10th Cir. 2000).

14   The Federal Court of Australia, interestingly, has developed an innovative procedure called the 'hot tub' for dealing with experts—a reference to a casual interchange between friends. See Heerey (2000: 166–70): 'The procedure involves the parties' experts giving evidence at the same time … in the witness box … They do not literally sit in a hot tub … [The] plaintiff's expert will give a brief exposition, [then] the defendant's expert will ask the plaintiff's expert questions … without the intervention of counsel. Then the process is reversed. In effect, a brief colloquium takes place … In my experience … the physical removal of the witness from his party's camp into the proximity of a (usually) respected professional colleague tends to reduce the level of partisanship'.

15   See generally Caudill and Redding (2000: 720–24) and Jasanoff (2001: 45): '[J]udges confronted with expert conflict need to resist the extreme labels of both "pure science" and "junk science", neither of which well characterizes the scientific foundations of evidence, while remaining open to all available knowledge that meets the threshold tests of relevance and reliability … They must strive to develop a sixth sense … for ways in which bias can creep into even well-intentioned forms of scientific inquiry, as well as for the differences between legitimately divergent viewpoints and truly marginal claims of expertise'.

16   *Cooper v Carl Nelson & Co.* 211 F.3d 1008 (7th Cir. 2000).

17   *Walter v Soo Line Railroad Co.* 208 F.3d 581 (7th Cir. 2000).

18   *Jahn v Equine Services* 233 F.3d 382 (6th Cir. 2000).

Chapter 11

The Invisible Branch: The *Authority* of Science Studies in Expert Evidence Jurisprudence

Gary Edmond and David Mercer

Metascience and US federal jurisprudence

This chapter analyses references to science and technology studies (STS) literature in US federal court judgments. We endeavor to reconsider the role played by STS in the seminal *Daubert v Merrell Dow Pharmaceuticals, Inc.* (1993) decision and post-*Daubert* jurisprudence using Jasanoff's concept of *accommodation* as a framing device.[1] Initially our analysis will examine the appearance of Jasanoff's *The Fifth Branch* (1990) in the *Daubert* judgment. Then we compare this citation with references to falsification drawn from Karl Popper's *Conjectures and Refutations*. In order to provide a wider indication of the uses of the sociology of science, broadly conceived, our analysis will also consider judicial recourse to the work of Merton, Latour and Woolgar. At this point analysis will shift away from references to STS and focus on judicial citations of prominent, non-constructivist, law and science commentator Peter Huber and his popularization of the concept 'junk science'.

In summary, our research suggests that STS literature is rarely cited and even more rarely used in ways that appear to accord with its more conventional specialized deployments. In contrast, ideas promoted by the (sometime) polemicist Huber appear to have exerted an identifiable influence on judicial representations of science and expertise. These findings lead us to question the value of *legal accommodation* as an analytical heuristic for understanding Jasanoff's *appearance* in *Daubert* or the role currently played by STS in federal jurisprudence more generally. In its place we offer a more contextually sensitive account of federal jurisprudence where images of science are deployed and actively contested because of the manner in which they mediate access to the federal courts—via rules of evidence and procedure and substantive legal doctrine such as negligence and product liability—as well as broader perceptions about the operation of the legal system—including the existence of litigation explosions or the extent of jury (in)competence. Rather than *accommodation*, the very limited role played by STS is probably better characterized by strategic, but qualified, appropriation: where judges may be ignorant of, indifferent to, or even hostile to specialized interpretations drawn from the work of science studies scholars.[2] The prevalence of Huber's work and ideas offers an important and influential alternative for reflecting upon the impact, and possible limitations, of explicitly *accommodating* STS in legal practice.

Daubert v Merrell Dow Pharmaceuticals, Inc. *(1993) and STS*

Daubert is the most important US judgment addressing the legal use of expert evidence. In *Daubert*, the US Supreme Court declared the standard for the admissibility of scientific evidence in US federal courts. The *Daubert* decision followed decades of judicial inconsistency in the definition of admissibility standards. Interest in admissibility standards intensified in the 1980s with the proliferation of mass torts and considerable socio-political commentary.[3] Because of the close relationship between the admissibility of expert evidence and the scope of tort liability, admissibility standards continue to be controversial.

Confronted with a range of different approaches to the admission of expert opinion evidence among the federal circuits, in *Daubert* the US Supreme Court granted *certiorari* to hear an appeal about the standard of admissibility for scientific evidence under Rule 702 of the *Federal Rules of Evidence* (FRE). While ostensibly the appeal examined the admissibility of expert evidence in a proceeding concerned with the etiology of birth defects, in its judgment the Supreme Court was most interested in more general issues surrounding the admissibility of scientific evidence and the role of the trial judge. The Court declined to decide the specific case before it, confining itself to pressing issues in evidence jurisprudence: the status of the *general acceptance* test and the meaning of Rule 702 (FRE).

The general acceptance test is conventionally attributed to the case of *US v Frye* (1923).[4] In *Frye* the trial judge ruled that a novel scientific technique was inadmissible because it was not sufficiently well established to have gained general acceptance among the relevant community of scientists. This became known as the 'general acceptance' or *Frye* test. During the seventy years between 1923 and the *Daubert* decision, state and federal courts had used, modified and departed from the *Frye* test in a variety of ways. The introduction of the FRE in 1975 did not produce standardization in admissibility jurisprudence across the federal circuits.[5] In hearing the *Daubert* appeal, the Supreme Court was endeavoring to reduce inconsistency by authoritatively determining the status of the *Frye* test in relation to Rule 702 (FRE). Before its recent revision Rule 702 read:

> If scientific, technical, or other specialized knowledge will assist the trier of fact to understand the evidence or to determine a fact in issue, a witness qualified as an expert by knowledge, skill, experience, training, or education, may testify thereto in the form of an opinion or otherwise.[6]

In addition to submissions from the parties, in reviewing the admissibility standard required by Rule 702, the Supreme Court was presented with a large number of *amicus curiae* (friends of the court) briefs. These briefs, relatively common in socially significant appeals, represented the concerns and aspirations of a broad cross-section of stakeholders proffering their preferred standard(s) to the Court in the guise of 'advice'.[7] *Amicus curiae* briefs are not binding.

For STS scholars, as well as historians and philosophers of science, the *Daubert* judgment is important because the highest US court defined *science* for the purpose of admissibility decision-making. *Daubert* is also significant because in defining science for legal purposes the Supreme Court made reference to the work of several eminent STS and history and philosophy of science (HPS) scholars. The majority judgment cited Carl Hempel, Karl Popper, Sheila Jasanoff and John Ziman. Several more STS/HPS scholars were cited in *amicus* briefs or contributed to the production of briefs submitted in the appeal.[8] The appearance of these scholars has stimulated considerable interest among legal academics, historians, philosophers and sociologists of science. Some of that interest has focused on the suitability and representativeness of these writers and the extent to which their ideas have been understood and embraced by judges. It is in this context that comments by Sheila Jasanoff, about her citation in the *Daubert* judgment, provide a pretext for a more general reassessment of science and technology studies in US federal jurisprudence.

Inoculating against Jasanoff (and STS) and exnominating Popper

This section provides a summary of Jasanoff's interpretation of *Daubert* which is particularly attentive to claims about her purported *accommodation* in the Supreme Court decision. In considerable detail, we document how Jasanoff and her constructivist insights fare in both *Daubert* and its aftermath. For comparative purposes we offer an account of the treatment of Popper and falsification and reflect on the absence of social science *authority* in a subsequent Supreme Court decision also concerned with the admissibility of expert opinion evidence.

Jasanoff and Popper in the Daubert *decision*

In *Daubert* the entire Supreme Court agreed that as an independent standard the general acceptance (or *Frye*) test had not survived the enactment of the FRE in 1975.[9] The majority replaced the general acceptance test with an emphasis on evidentiary reliability and the expectation that, acting in their capacity as *gatekeepers*, trial judges would undertake an assessment of proffered expert evidence drawing upon the features of 'good science' and 'the scientific method' (*Daubert* 1993: 590, 593). The majority explained that in making admissibility decisions trial judges were required to determine whether the evidence was properly scientific, that is, constituted genuine scientific knowledge (*Daubert* 1993: 592–3).

The majority, through Justice Blackmun's written judgment, provided four *indicative* criteria—effectively a judicial tool kit—to assist with admissibility determinations. For the purposes of our analysis we are most interested in the first two criteria, which incorporate references to Popper and Jasanoff.

[1]   Ordinarily, a key question to be answered in determining whether a theory or technique is scientific knowledge that will assist the trier of fact will be whether it can be (and has been) tested. "Scientific methodology today is based on generating hypotheses and testing them to see if they can be falsified; indeed, this methodology is what distinguishes science from other fields of human inquiry." **Green** 645. See also **C. Hempel**, *Philosophy of Natural Science* 49 (1966) ("[T]he statements constituting a scientific explanation must be capable of empirical test"); **K. Popper**, *Conjectures and Refutations: The Growth of Scientific Knowledge* 37 (5th ed. 1989) ("[T]he criterion of the scientific status of a theory is its falsifiability, or refutability, or testability") (emphasis deleted).

[2]   Another pertinent consideration is whether the theory or technique has been subjected to peer review and publication. Publication (which is but one element of peer review) is not a *sine qua non* of admissibility; it does not necessarily correlate with reliability, see **S. Jasanoff**, *The Fifth Branch: Science Advisors as Policymakers* 61–76 (1990), and in some instances well-grounded but innovative theories will not have been published, see **Horrobin**, *The Philosophical Basis of Peer Review and the Suppression of Innovation*, 263 JAMA 1438 (1990). Some propositions, moreover, are too particular, too new, or of too limited interest to be published. But submission to the scrutiny of the scientific community is a component of "good science," in part because it increases the likelihood that substantive flaws in methodology will be detected. See **J. Ziman**, *Reliable Knowledge: An Exploration of the Grounds for Belief in Science* 130–133 (1978); **Relman & Angell**, *How Good Is Peer Review?*, 321 New Eng.J.Med. 827 (1989). The fact of publication (or lack thereof) in a peer reviewed journal thus will be a relevant, though not dispositive, consideration in assessing the scientific validity of a particular technique or methodology on which an opinion is premised.[10]

In addition to falsification, peer review and publication, the *Daubert* majority indicated that the known or potential rate of error of a scientific technique [3] and whether it had been 'generally accepted' (reintroducing *Frye*) in the relevant scientific community [4] could also have a bearing on admissibility decision-making (*Daubert* 1993: 594).

In the extract above, the first two criteria—'testing' and 'peer review and publication'—are interspersed with extra-legal—that is, philosophical, medical and sociological—support.[11] Popper and Hempel enter Supreme Court jurisprudence via reference to a legal academic, tort scholar Michael Green (1992). Jasanoff, Horrobin, Ziman, Relman and Angell (as well as Popper and Hempel) all appeared in *amicus curiae* briefs submitted to the Court in support of a variety of propositions and images of science. The third [3] and fourth [4] criteria do not draw upon secondary (by which we mean non-legal literary) support. Instead, they refer to earlier appeals and influential legal texts.[12] Of the four criteria, in this particular guise, the first two were the most novel, even though judges had previously drawn upon publication and peer review in their assessment of admissibility and evidentiary sufficiency, and falsification had featured in attempts to demarcate science from creation science in First Amendment litigation.[13]

Jasanoff and 'legal accommodation'

In published commentaries on the *Daubert* judgment Jasanoff has described how the Supreme Court referred to extra-legal sources, including her own book *The Fifth Branch,* in its attempt to define science (albeit for legal purposes). In these discussions Jasanoff (1996a: 403) devotes repeated attention to the manner in which her constructivist interpretations of science were included in the decision adjacent to non-constructivist views of science, such as Popper's method doctrine of falsificationism.

According to Jasanoff, Justice Blackmun displayed agility and catholicism in responding to the different approaches to science presented in the briefs. Blackmun, we are told, apparently endorsed (or *accommodated*) a variety of perspectives and traditions. For example, Jasanoff (1996a: 408–9) suggests that: 'Scientism and skepticism both found support, as the *Daubert* court paired a rhetorical deference to the universality of science with a tolerance of multiple viewpoints about how science works'.[14] *Daubert* seems to capture 'a middle course between deference and distrust' (Jasanoff 1995: 213), between 'scientism and skepticism' as the Supreme Court exemplified the 'common law's genius by muddling through' (Jasanoff 1995: 63). This majority decision was an example of the judge's 'faculty for normative and epistemological co-production' (Jasanoff 1996a: 406). This reading is subsequently reinforced:

> Tellingly, the Court managed to weave into its rehearsal of evaluative criteria markedly different conceptions about the nature of scientific knowledge. The late Karl Popper's largely discredited notion of science as progressing through clear falsifications of erroneous claims appeared side-by-side with the view of constructivist sociologists of science that knowledge accumulates through negotiation and consensus among members of the scientific community. (Jasanoff 1995: 63, 1996a: 406–8)

The *Daubert* decision conferred considerable discretion upon 'lay' trial judges because, according to Jasanoff (1996a: 408), of the ambiguity flowing from the Supreme Court's 'choice to *accommodate* rather than adjudicate between the positivist and the constructivist accounts of science presented by the parties'. Jasanoff's observations about the accommodation of STS are not restricted to the *Daubert* judgment. Several influential amici, such as the Carnegie Commission on Science, Technology, and Government, referred to a small body of work in the social studies of science, in Jasanoff's words, 'to illustrate the sociological understanding of scientific facts and to make the claim that peer review offers only "presumptive proof" that a hypothesis has been tested' (Jasanoff 1996a: 408, compare Edmond and Mercer 1998b; Caudill and Redding 2000).

These comments on the reception of Jasanoff's work are drawn from *Science at the Bar* and a separate discussion of the politics of engagement which suggests that because the sociology of scientific knowledge (SSK) is inherently political, analysts should not be surprised when 'their scholarship [is] appropriated in unexpected ways' (Jasanoff 1996a: 400). The second source, the article 'Beyond

Epistemology', is a self-styled 'manifesto against reductionist story-telling' (Jasanoff 1996a: 413). For Jasanoff (1996a: 412), SSK is distinctive because it has the potential to 'destabilize the dominant stories'. As examples of unwitting engagement Jasanoff discusses the *accommodation* of her work in *Daubert* and the *appropriation* of her work in debates about environmental regulation. In the environmental context Jasanoff's earlier scholarly endeavours were used in ways which she contends were inconsistent with her project:

> Here was a sobering lesson for the reflexive SSK analyst. Unbeknownst to me, I was being enrolled in a struggle to define and maintain the boundaries of 'science' in accordance with the very patterns of American politics that my article was trying to elucidate. (Jasanoff 1996a: 403)

Interestingly, the tenor of 'Beyond Epistemology' suggests that those appropriating (this) Jasanoff (and her work) 'evidently ... misunderstood the point of the article' (Jasanoff 1996a: 416 n29). This use is conspicuously different to (or her explanation more reflexive than) the manner in which Blackmun supposedly embraced Jasanoff, and by association STS, in the *Daubert* decision. *Accommodation* involves a more *consistent* use or *recognition* of the author's background and purposes, or so it would seem.

Accepting that *Daubert* brings together a very eclectic assortment of authorities, we believe that the decision provides little evidence of accommodation and makes no attempt to reconcile the very different approaches juxtaposed there. On average, members of the federal judiciary do not appear to be (particularly) attentive to the history, philosophy and sociology of science. Nevertheless the images and criteria elaborated in *Daubert* are not arbitrary. While it might be argued that the decision reflects the Supreme Court's lack of philosophical sophistication, we suggest that in the context of intense debate over admissibility standards and judicial attempts to manage the parameters of civil liability *Daubert* offers a set of practical tools or resources for judicial gatekeeping. From this vantage, the Supreme Court's common law or pragmatic genius may have been to provide a malleable, though philosophically incoherent, description of science that could be mobilized against the perceived threat posed by unreliable evidence while simultaneously acknowledging a range of qualifications to models of science (including those from Jasanoff's writings) which could be routinely ignored. This reading is consistent with the apparent lack of judicial interest with, in Jasanoff's terms, 'distrust' and 'skepticism', to which we would add 'constructivism'.

While it appears that Jasanoff is not advancing a comprehensive thesis about the way science studies are *put to work* in judicial settings, her accounts provide an enduring image of the *Daubert* judgment and the Supreme Court's attitude to science more generally. As a synonym for appropriation, her claims for legal accommodation raise few problems. However, where accommodation is used to suggest some additional level of comprehension, heightened understanding or engagement, as in Jasanoff's *Daubert* example, then we think that the term misrepresents the *Daubert* judgment, Supreme Court jurisprudence and is misleading in the context of the contest over admissibility standards in US federal courts. The use of accommodation dulls the potential for a more overtly political analysis of the exclusionary (and epistemological) trajectory consolidated by the *Daubert* judgment.

Extending this analysis to some of Jasanoff's (1995: 63, 67; 1996a: 408) other comments on the *Daubert* decision, we would suggest that the judgment was not in any simple terms a 'shared' victory, even if both defendants and plaintiffs subsequently (and somewhat ritualistically) claimed success.[15] We read *Daubert* as a straightforward victory. From our perspective, the articulation of specific and potentially quite onerous admissibility criteria was a dividend for civil defendants. Those dividends were manifested in the provision of a very favorable, though non-deterministic, array of strategic resources, including testing, peer review, publication and the gatekeeping metaphor. Since *Daubert*, the initial *success* has been strategically consolidated and expanded.[16]

In the following discussion we question the Supreme Court's purported accommodation of social constructivist perspectives. Our findings suggest that rather than accommodating distinctive STS perspectives, the *Daubert* decision and the judgments which have followed it, are more usefully characterized as part of an identifiable trajectory geared to restricting the admissibility of expert evidence. Notwithstanding references to STS authorities in *Daubert* and a few other cases, this unfolding trajectory has drawn primarily from legal authority bolstered by occasional alignment with positivist-orientated philosophy of science and non-constructivist metascience commentary.

Non-constructivist dimensions of Daubert

Jasanoff's contention that the *Daubert* decision constitutes the legal accommodation of a range of approaches to the sciences, including some of those associated with STS, seems to be seriously compromised if the *Daubert* decision is examined holistically or its use and application monitored. In this subsection, it is our intention to begin by assessing Jasanoff's claims focusing exclusively on the *Daubert* decision.

Notwithstanding Jasanoff's (1996a: 408; 1995: 213) characterization of the *Daubert* judgment as an example of a 'choice to accommodate rather than adjudicate', to steer a 'middle course between deference and distrust', several features of the judgment are very difficult to reconcile with what we might describe as STS perspectives. Indeed, some of the central features of the *Daubert* judgment would seem to immediately compromise accommodation as an adequate heuristic. Some of these include:

1. Jasanoff is cited for qualifications to peer review which, in this particular iteration, do not require (or imply) constructivist readings of the processes of publication and peer review, let alone scientific knowledge and practice more generally. There is nothing intrinsically constructivist about this: 'Publication (which is but one element of peer review) is not a *sine qua non* of admissibility; it does not necessarily correlate with reliability'.

This assessment is supported by considering the propositions that the non-constructivist authors adjacent to Jasanoff are associated. In the extract above [2],

Horrobin, Ziman, Relman and Angell are all credited with qualifications to peer review and publication which appear to resemble those attributed to Jasanoff. The only way they are distinguished in the text is by their source. The fact that Jasanoff (1995: 50–51; 1998a: 97–9) is a social constructivist and has elsewhere criticized some of these authors or distinguished their work from her own passes without comment. In the absence of additional context, explanation or sensitivity to Jasanoff's work, it might not be unreasonable to attribute her *Daubert* contribution to a realist or positivist model of science.[17] The Supreme Court may have only intended to *accommodate* realist-inspired (or realist-reconciliable) observations about limits to peer review and publication. In contrast to Jasanoff's own reading, it could be argued that had the more constructivist dimensions of her work been recognized it is quite possible that the citation might not have appeared. We will return to the question of whether constructivist orientations are suited to judicial decision-making and rationalization in our conclusion.

2. The majority decision in *Daubert* (1993: 590) advances what appears, at times, to be a very simple model of science: 'But, in order to qualify as "scientific knowledge", an inference or assertion must be derived by the scientific method'. More than one philosopher of science has described the Court's description as embarrassing (Haack 2001; Laudan 1982). Initially, Justice Blackmun was so confident about the value of falsification/testing [1] that he dispelled the need to worry about an expert's conclusions, providing the methodology was reliable: 'The focus, of course, must be solely on principles and methodology, not on the conclusions they generate' (*Daubert* 1993: 595).[18] Assumptions and practical complications underlying the rather ambitious method/conclusion dichotomization were subsequently read down by the same Court four years later in *General Electric Co. v Joiner*.[19]

The concern with method, the *Daubert* criteria and emphasis on reliability are all for the purposes of identifying an unproblematized image of 'good science'. None of these images requires, or makes explicit concession to, STS perspectives or more sceptical (or empirically predicated) images of scientific practice.

3. References in *Daubert* to scientific uncertainty and temporal contingency— like limits associated with peer review and publication in example 1—do not require constructivist or relativist interpretations. References such as 'arguably there are no certainties in science' are linked to *amicus* briefs submitted on behalf of institutions with limited sympathy for STS perspectives.[20] The previous quote, for example, is credited to briefs submitted by the American Association for the Advancement of Science (AAAS) and Nobel laureates (*Daubert* 1993: 590).[21]

4. Blackmun, in the majority decision, draws clear distinctions between law and science. Accordingly, we are told that the *Rules of Evidence* were not designed for 'cosmic understanding but for the particularized resolution of legal disputes' (*Daubert* 1993: 597). Such a clear law/science dichotomy is at odds with Jasanoff's (1996a: 397–8) notion of co-production and more sociologically oriented accounts of law–science relations.

5. The dissent by Chief Justice Rehnquist and Justice Stevens makes no reference to constructivists or constructivism. Rather, they express concern at the use of Popper 'and other secondary sources'. For Rehnquist and Stevens 'the

unusual subject matter' and the variety of non-legal authority 'should cause us to proceed with great caution in deciding more than we have to, because our reach can so easily exceed our grasp' (*Daubert* 1993: 599). The dissentients were at a loss to understand what was meant by: 'the scientific status of a theory depends on its "falsifiability"' (*Daubert* 1993: 600) and even wondered, and this offers a glimpse of judicial pragmatism rather than purely philosophical sensitivity, whether the *Daubert* criteria should also apply to 'technical, or other specialized knowledge' (Rule 702). This question would have to await the appeal in *Kumho Tire Co. Ltd. v Carmichael* (1999). Nevertheless, their judgment seems to imply (or accept) that the *Daubert* criteria are genuine indicia of science. Reserving some gatekeeping functions for the trial judge, the dissentients explained that Rule 702 does not impose 'on them either the obligation or the authority to become amateur scientists in order to perform that role'. These judges were concerned by the perceived need for trial judges to become amateur scientists, rather than amateur sociologists or philosophers.

6. In suggesting that STS were accommodated, Jasanoff seems to operate metonymically for the entire field of STS. While Jasanoff's work may have been a good choice, why were other authors who had also studied peer review and publication, such as Chubin, Hackett, Nelkin and LaFollete, omitted? This selection also raises questions, adopting her own nomenclature, about whether it was Jasanoff herself, her work or the field of STS that was accommodated in the actual judgment. We might ask whether Jasanoff (1996a: 394) knew the judges— from her occasional forays 'into the closed worlds of Washington'[22]—or whether her (*low*) level of engagement, in comparison to say Chubin, Hackett and Nelkin, who all contributed to a brief, may have enabled her work to be cast in a more favorable (that is *independent*) light.[23]

7. Jasanoff's accounts merely gloss over the unwieldy combination of very different images of science in the judgment. She describes this as 'the fine disregard for a philosophically coherent decision rule' (Jasanoff 1995: 63). Conventionally, proponents tend to suggest that falsification transcends sociologically orientated factors involved in the confirmation of theories, such as peer review and other philosophical criteria such as probabilistic analysis or the determination of error rates.[24] From such a perspective, the diverse models of science and assortment of authorities associated with the *Daubert* criteria are revealing. These concerns are reflected in Susan Haack's reaction to the conjunction of Popper and Hempel:

> In fact, it is hard to think of a philosophy of science less congenial than Popper's to the relevance-and-reliability approach … And if the reference to Popper is a *faux pas*, running Popper with Hempel—a pioneer of the logic of confirmation, an enterprise the legitimacy of which Popper always staunchly denied—is a *faux pas de deux*. (Haack 2001: 219)

Similarly, juxtaposing Popper and Jasanoff must be considered curious at the very least. According to Jasanoff, this kind of combination reflects the Supreme Court's 'common law genius' in accommodating rather than adjudicating 'between the positivist and the constructivist accounts of science'. However, as Haack intimates, it is difficult to describe the positions of the philosophers, sociologists, physicians and scientists cited in *Daubert* as consistent or even reconcilable.[25] Having described the *Daubert* decision as a skillfully crafted synoptic accommodation of various theoretical positions, Jasanoff provides little sense of the appropriateness or possibility of combining these various tests and perspectives. If strict versions of falsification were designed to be independent of other, more sociological criteria, how do STS perspectives (assuming, for the moment, they are manifest in *Daubert*) accord with the emphasis on the 'largely discredited notion' of testability? This point is compounded when we consider the numerous studies demonstrating the complexity and difficulties associated with falsification, replication and experimentation more generally (Collins 1985).

Overall, the fact that *Daubert* does not problematize 'evidentiary reliability' or 'good science' and emphasizes the importance of the scientific method—to the point that methods are more important than conclusions—suggests that the judges are either inattentive to science studies and/or unwilling to countenance or refer explicitly to its many insights in their written judgments. We would contend that *Daubert* makes no explicit concessions to constructivists and no attempt to *accommodate* STS. In *Daubert*, reference to Jasanoff is superficial. All that seems to have been accommodated were relatively prosaic qualifications to peer review and publication. This interpretation of *Daubert*, which might be characterized as the dominant reading, is consistent with those adopted by an overwhelming majority of legal commentators and judges (Edmond and Mercer 1998b; Abercrombie et al. 1980). We note that few non-constructivist commentators, even those critical of the *Daubert* decision, have identified its alleged constructivist implications or, what is even more disconcerting, understood Jasanoff's work in this way.[26]

Alternatively, if judges are using STS (or HPS) materials and assumptions covertly then their failure to make those choices explicit raises problems for judicial legitimacy and possibly sociological engagement. However, a simpler explanation for the virtual invisibility of constructivist approaches to the sciences will emerge when we consider judicial practice and the strategic intervention by commentators from other traditions.

References to Jasanoff after Daubert

Accepting that our interpretation of the influence of Jasanoff's work and the accommodation of constructivism is open to challenge, our interpretation of *Daubert* is supported by the way the federal judiciary have understood and applied the decision. For, if Jasanoff, operating metonymically for STS, was accommodated in the Supreme Court we might have expected to observe some indication or support for constructivist insights as the *Daubert* judgment was operationalized among the federal circuits. In this subsection we aim to illustrate how, in judicial practice, the influence of constructivist contributions seems to be highly circumscribed after *Daubert*.

Since *Daubert* Jasanoff has been cited in federal court judgments on only four occasions. Three of those citations were produced by the same district court judge (Eisele) as part of a large indiscriminate extract from *Daubert*.[27] Those verbatim quotations, an even longer version of the extract we reproduced earlier as [1] and [2], provide little indication of an attempt to engage with questions pertaining to publication and peer review or more general features of Jasanoff's (or *the* STS) oeuvre.[28]

The closest that any jurist approaches to recognizing aspects of Jasanoff's constructivist position is in the remaining citation. In a patent infringement case, *Markman v Westview Instruments, Inc.*, another of Jasanoff's essays was cited by a judicial dissentient. Judge Newman wrote:[29]

> "The community of trial lawyers knows perhaps better than any other professional group just how unruly science often is in practice." Sheila Jasanoff, *What Judges Should Know About the Sociology of Science*, 77 Judicature 77, 80 (1993) (discussing the "social dimension [that] gives legitimacy to particular scientific 'facts'").[30]

This claim, that the practice of science can be unruly and that social dimensions may influence the legitimation of scientific facts, is the most explicit example of *recognition* of the social dimensions of science using authority from the STS corpus that we could locate. The reference to Jasanoff, from this dissenting judgment, is not drawn from *Daubert*. In this *en banc* appeal Judge Newman disagreed with the opinions of ten other federal judges, including the Chief Judge of the Circuit. Furthermore, in Newman's judgment, reference to Jasanoff's writing is presented as consistent with *Daubert* (which assures 'the adequacy of the methodology upon which the evidence is based') even though it is used to question the majority's demarcation between law and fact in the uncertainty endemic to patent litigation. The extent to which Newman accepts or endorses constructivist images of science, how these images conform to her other judgments and the conflicting majority perspectives do not suggest sustained engagement, consistent use or clearly convey the extent of comprehension.

These few references to Jasanoff represent a considerable proportion of citations to the STS corpus in federal jurisprudence. Jasanoff is seldomly cited and, with one exception, never in relation to an evidentiary proposition relevant to the particular case. Consequently, if judges have accommodated perspectives from STS then they have done so informally, perhaps discretely. In the virtual absence of formal citations we will now turn to consider this possibility.

*Jasanoff's 'invisible hand': Qualifications to peer review in post-*Daubert *jurisprudence*

Leaving aside the question of whether reference to Jasanoff in *Daubert* reveals much about STS or the social construction of scientific knowledge, we ought to consider how Jasanoff's (1995: 99) qualifications to peer review and publication were understood and applied by the federal judiciary after *Daubert,* even in her ostensive absence. In this section it is our intention to provide a sense of how the qualifications to peer review and publication *associated* with Jasanoff in *Daubert*—namely, 'Publication (which is but one element of peer review) is not a *sine qua non* of admissibility; it does not necessarily correlate with reliability'— were subsequently understood and/or used by the federal judiciary.[31] This undertaking will help us to determine whether the constructivist origins of Jasanoff's qualifications to peer review and publication are recognized or their implications embraced.

After *Daubert*, thirty-four cases make verbatim reference to the 'qualifying phrase' in the context of evidentiary jurisprudence. Notwithstanding reference to the express qualifications to the value of peer review and publication, in twenty of twenty-nine civil cases the plaintiffs' expert evidence was either excluded (as inadmissible) or considered insufficient to sustain a verdict or even a case to answer (the case was thrown out).[32] In the criminal justice system, where the state's burden is to prove its case beyond reasonable doubt, the qualification phrase was cited on five occasions: three cases in which the state's DNA typing evidence was admitted and two cases where the accused's *exonerating* polygraph evidence was considered—one judge admitting it and the other excluding it.[33]

Significantly, in post-*Daubert* jurisprudence, even around the subject of peer review and publication, references to Jasanoff and her constructivist commitments are conspicuously absent. Where qualifications to the value of peer review and publication do appear the plaintiffs' evidence is nonetheless often excluded. Typically judgments take the form expressed in *Heller v Shaw*:

> Although publication is not the *sine qua non* of admissibility, ""'submission to the scrutiny of the scientific community is a component of 'good science,' in part because it increases the likelihood that substantive flaws in methodology will be detected."[34]

Potential limitations to peer review and publication are skillfully elided. Notwithstanding the potential limitations articulated in *Daubert*, in federal court jurisprudence publication and peer review are frequently transformed into substantive indicia of 'good science' which, in conjunction with testing, facilitate the detection of methodological flaws. This is consistent with the dominant reading of Blackmun's judgment. Further, the act of acknowledging limitations to idealized versions of publication and peer review does not prevent judges excluding plaintiffs' expert evidence where no peer review or relevant publication is undertaken. In *Heller* (1997: 11), expert evidence linking the plaintiffs' respiratory problems to chemicals emitted by their new carpets was excluded, in part because the expert's 'theories have not been published and subjected to peer review'.[35] Having qualified the value of publication and peer review, the majority of trial and appellate judges undertake their assessments as if the qualifications had never been expressed. Failure to produce published and peer-reviewed evidence often proves decisive.

This situation is commonly reversed in decisions pertaining to evidence and forensic techniques deployed by the state in criminal prosecutions. The tendency to operationalize *Daubert* differentially in criminal trials is exemplified in *US v Bonds*. In an appeal focused on the reliability of the state's DNA typing evidence, the Sixth Circuit Court of Appeals admitted the evidence. The Court explained:

> As the *Daubert* Court noted, publication is but one element of peer review, is not a *sine qua non* of admissibility ... and is not a prerequisite to a finding of scientific validity ... Any shortcomings in the peer review of the FBI's procedures are not sufficient to overcome the other strong evidence that the FBI's principles and procedures were both *generally accepted* and *scientifically valid*.[36]

The *Daubert* criteria and *Daubert*'s commitment to 'good science' are routinely invoked, traded and hierarchized in ways that enable judges to account for evidence and practically manage preferred outcomes. Evidence, which is frequently part of a more complex matrix, is combined and judges use other factors—especially testing, general acceptance and the credibility of the source—to assist with the rationalization of admissibility decision-making. In *Bonds*, general acceptance and scientific validity override potential limits to the state's evidence introduced through imperfect processes of peer review and publication.[37]

Typically, concerns about the reliability of the plaintiffs' expert evidence and the absence of publication and peer review are not extended, even in criminal proceedings, to expert evidence produced by the state. In effect, the qualifications associated with peer review and publication, which Jasanoff equates with the accommodation of constructivist insights, do not seem to have the effects we might anticipate. Reference to *Daubert* and limits to peer review and publication are frequently cited where expert evidence is excluded in civil cases and where the state's, occasionally unpublished or unreviewed, evidence is included in criminal prosecutions and appeals. None of these citations or their practical implications discloses any sensitivity or sympathy to STS, SSK or constructivist approaches to science and technology.

Popper and 'testing' after Daubert

It might not be surprising to find that in the wake of *Daubert* federal courts have adopted a variety of responses to expert opinion evidence and the authority of sociologists, physicians and philosophers purportedly supporting it. Of all the secondary authors referred to in the annunciation of the *Daubert* criteria, Popper is the most frequently cited. Most of the judgments citing Popper seem to serve the purpose of rehearsing the standard to be used by judges in making admissibility decisions after *Daubert*. Superficially, Popper's experience in the federal courts after *Daubert* resembles the treatment of Jasanoff. Although more numerous, explicit references to Popper also gradually taper off.

A major difference, however, lies in the way the propositions associated with their names are subsequently used.[38] The extract, reproduced above as [1], indicates that in *Daubert* Popper was quoted in support of the importance of falsification or testability. No qualifications to testing were advanced and no attempt was made to distinguish Popper from Hempel. In post-*Daubert* litigation 'testing' has become a central, sometimes acrimonious, aspect of admissibility decision-making and discussions of evidentiary reliability more generally. The emphasis on the need to have actually tested theories and techniques is frequently used, particularly in civil litigation, as a means of excluding plaintiffs' evidence from the courtroom. The exclusionary impact of (judicial approaches to) testing, after *Daubert*, encouraged plaintiffs' lawyers to attempt to circumvent the strict application of the *Daubert* criteria and this led to another appeal to the Supreme Court—in *Kumho*. In the criminal justice system, by contrast, defence lawyers tend to contest the state's evidence and prosecutors try to exclude or impugn defence expert evidence on the basis of strict application of what is now the *legal* doctrine of testing.

Following *Daubert* most explicit references to Popper were produced by judges endeavoring to identify and describe the admissibility standards authoritatively enunciated by the Supreme Court in *Daubert*. Burdened by enhanced judicial sensitivity to their gatekeeping responsibilities, plaintiffs and criminal defendants found that *Daubert* could raise the admissibility standards for their expert evidence. The examples below provide an indication of the emergent practice around 'testing' in the federal courts.

In *Cummins v Lyle* the plaintiff (Cummins) lost three fingers while operating a trim press.[39] She brought a product liability action against the manufacturer (Lyle) alleging defective design and inadequate warnings. The district court excluded the testimony of Cummins's expert witness. On appeal, the Court of Appeals, explained:

> the Supreme Court has articulated several nonexclusive guideposts to assist the district courts in determining whether expert testimony fairly can be characterized as scientific opinion: (1) whether the proffered conclusion lends itself to verification by the scientific method through testing ... The first and most significant *Daubert* factor is whether the proffered opinion has been subjected to the scientific method. (*Cummins* 1996: 368)[40]

Here, a version of testing is portrayed as the most significant of the *Daubert* criteria. Notwithstanding the attempt to demonstrate that Lyle's product could have been rendered safer with a few readily available inexpensive design alterations, the expert's failure to actually (build and) test his alternative designs was rendered fatal.

> Dr. Carpenter did not conduct any testing to substantiate his opinion that the alternative test designs feasibly could have been incorporated into the Lyle trim press ...[He] agreed that testing is a necessary part of the design process. He acknowledged, however, that he had not tested any of the machinery at issue in this case. (*Cummins* 1996: 369)

On the basis of these observations, in conjunction with Carpenter's failure to publish—once again, none of the qualifications are mentioned—or specify an error rate, the Court of Appeals concluded that the district court had not abused its discretion when it excluded Carpenter's evidence on the basis that it was not 'derived from the scientific method' (*Cummins* 1996: 370).

The case of *US v Starzecpyzel* provides an example from the field of criminal law. Defendants sought to have the prosecution's forensic document examination evidence excluded because it did not meet the *Daubert* criteria—especially the rigors of falsification. The trial judge resisted the application on the basis of a restricted reading of *Daubert* where falsification applied only to scientific evidence.[41]

> The *Daubert* Court derives the gatekeeping task of the trial judge from a reevaluation of *Frye* (itself *limited to scientific testimony*) and from consideration of the word "scientific" in Rule 702. The essence of *Daubert's* "reliability" standard lies within the Court's citation to *philosopher of science* Karl Popper's statement that "the criterion of the *scientific status* of a theory is its falsifiability, or refutability, or testability." —U.S.— at—, 113 S.Ct. at 2797 (quoting Karl Popper, *Conjectures and Refutations: The Growth of Scientific Knowledge* 37 (5th ed. 1989).[42]

For Judge McKenna, the *Daubert* criteria did not apply to 'technical, or other specialized knowledge' (from Rule 702). The judgment provides some indication of the active judicial construction of legal reliability through the demarcation of science from non-science.[43] By characterizing document examination as non-scientific, but not *pseudo-* or *junk* science, McKenna was able to admit the state's evidence without applying the *Daubert* criteria. Similar distinctions were raised in *Moore v Ashland Chemical, Inc.*, this time a civil action, where the exclusion of a medical expert's opinion was reversed and remanded on appeal because the appellate court determined that *Daubert* applied only to hard science and not to medical testimony: 'The methodology of hard or Newtonian science is what distinguishes it from other fields of human inquiry'.[44] The examples of *Starzecpyzel* and *Moore* provide some indication of the contest around the application of *Daubert* prior to the appeal in *Kumho Tire Co. Ltd. v Carmichael* (1999).[45] The doctrine of testing enabled (rather than required) trial judges to exclude plaintiffs' expert evidence on the basis that if untested it was not authentic science and therefore insufficiently reliable (under Rule 702).[46] The applicability of *falsification* (usually in the guise of testing) to non-scientific evidence and the active attempts to demarcate the boundaries around what constitutes *reliable* science were emerging areas of resistance and judicial inconsistency.

Manufacturing legal authority

Inconsistency in the application of *Daubert* to non-scientific and technical evidence led the Supreme Court to give leave to hear a further appeal. In terms of the analysis to follow, it is important to refer to *Kumho Tire Co. Ltd. v Carmichael*, even though it makes no direct reference to the philosophical, medical or sociological literature relied upon in *Daubert*. The issue to be resolved in *Kumho*— as in *Starzecpyzel* and *Moore*—was: Do the *Daubert* criteria apply to expert opinion evidence of a non-scientific nature?[47] The *Kumho* appeal was concerned with the admissibility of the expert testimony of an engineer. In *Kumho*, the Court explained that when making Rule 702 admissibility determinations the trial judge *may* apply the *Daubert* criteria to any type of expert opinion evidence. Within a decade of *Daubert*, the gatekeeping role of the trial judge was authoritatively reinforced. Whereas the *Daubert* court had remanded the actual application of the new criteria in the specific case to a lower court, in *Kumho* the majority decision actually exemplified the application of the criteria to the evidence before it.[48] Notwithstanding the flexibility attributed to *Daubert* and reiterated in the *Kumho* judgment, in *Kumho* the Court applied *all* of the criteria seriatim to exclude the engineer's opinion evidence and simultaneously the plaintiffs' case (Edmond 2002c).

Since *Daubert* a Popperian-inspired image of testing has dominated the field of admissibility decision-making. Despite the decrease in references to Popper the centrality of testing as a demarcation criterion has stubbornly persisted. In *Kumho*, the importance of testing was powerfully reiterated through the Supreme Court's own example. *Kumho* features few of *Daubert's* qualifications.[49] Referencing *Daubert*, Breyer's majority opinion explained that two of the factors that may bear upon the trial judge's evidentiary gatekeeping determination include testing, and publication and peer review. We reproduce his words exactly:

> —Whether a "theory or technique ... can be (and has been) tested";
> Whether it 'has been subjected to peer review and publication' ...[50]

There are no references, in *Kumho*, to limitations to testing and, more conspicuously, peer review and publication.[51]

The legal careers of Popper and Jasanoff

The model of science developed by Popper (and others who appeared in the *Daubert* judgment such as Hempel and Jasanoff et al.) was not in any simple way determinative of the images of science ultimately promoted in the judgments that cited it. Indeed Popper's philosophy of science was invariably described (or summarized) in a most cursory and rudimentary manner: typically it was equated with testing. The continued reliance on testing in conjunction with the disappearance of direct references to Popper represents his legal *exnomination* (Barthes 1973: 138). Rather than describe the sudden appearance of Popper and Jasanoff (and the others) as an attempt to engage with or accommodate the history, philosophy and sociology of science, judicial reference to such work seemed to operate as synecdoche: for an implicitly *proper* and *comprehensive* representation of science and its processes in a decision where important evidentiary principles were being authoritatively re-interpreted. In this way STS/HPS was appropriated as a legitimatory resource (Mody 2002). Invoking Popper and others in order to articulate a new vision of (what is consistently presented as *good*) science for legal settings seems to have been intended to help manage expertise and to some extent restrict the volume of civil litigation rather than provide an informed philosophical exposition.[52]

It is our contention that, through the quite deliberate emphasis on testing, the Supreme Court sought to inaugurate a more predictable and more onerous approach to admissibility decision-making among federal courts. *Daubert* represents a deliberate response to anxieties about the prevalence of questionable expertise, gratuitous lawsuits and jury competence in US courts.[53] The new desire for rigor encouraged by *Daubert* established the 'gatekeeping' metaphor—thereby supplanting 'screening' and other more passive images—as the appropriate means of conceptualizing admissibility decision-making.

In *Daubert*, Jasanoff (though not in her capacity as the doyen of the STS community) makes a cameo appearance. Her work stands for the proposition that publication and peer review are not definitive indicia of evidentiary reliability. After *Daubert*, Jasanoff effectively disappears from federal jurisprudence. Nowhere, perhaps with the exception of a dissenting opinion in *Markham*, are Jasanoff or constructivist insights expressly developed in a federal court decision. Jasanoff, links to constructivism and to some extent the limits to peer review and publication are effectively *inoculated* (Barthes 1973: 150).

Two of the most conspicuous features of the post-*Daubert* litigation landscape are the limited judicial criticism or provision of alternatives to Popper's philosophy of science and inconsistency in the legal use of testing. In their citations of Popper and applications of testing only a handful of judges have referred to the existence of other traditions and alternative approaches to expertise. Where judges do refer to social science and humanities literatures to inform their understanding of science they are just as likely to cite perspectives which are not closely associated with STS. Judge Zagel, as one example, provides an indication of the diversity of perspectives and, prior to *Daubert* (1993), the virtual invisibility of Popper and testing (and Jasanoff). In 1991, rather than invoking falsification Zagel drew upon the work of Quine, Gadamer, Geertz, Kuhn and Wildavsky to support his contention that 'validation ... is today the accepted method for deciding what is science'.[54] After *Daubert*, in deference to the Supreme Court, Zagel referred to the work of Popper. Judge Zagel, however, is atypical in his use of secondary authority and in counterposing Kuhn to Popper, even if, in his post-*Daubert* footnote discussion, he prefers Popper 'despite his flaws'.[55]

In *Daubert* versions of Popper's *philosophy* and Jasanoff's *sociology* were transformed into law. After *Kumho* only Popper's (legal) ghost remains to haunt plaintiffs and criminal defendants—and to a lesser extent crime enforcement agencies. In a relatively brief period the earlier legal apotheosis of Popper and a large number of written judgments enabled the Supreme Court to draw upon considerable *legal* authority for its extension of the *Daubert* criteria to non-scientific forms of expert evidence in *Kumho*. In that case, reference to Popper, Jasanoff, and the other secondary commentators—especially those associated with qualifications to peer review and publication—could be dropped.[56] Numerous references to *Daubert* and the new doctrine of testing, rather than recourse to arcane philosophical and sociological foundations, facilitated judicial legitimation without unnecessary philosophical engagement. Testing and the other criteria were transformed into legal categories, and, as we have seen, in applying them judges could evade criticism of their epistemological (in)adequacy.

More legal transients: Putting Merton, Latour and Woolgar to work

Judicial references to prominent sociologists of science, apart from Jasanoff, suggest further limitations to *accommodation*.[57] These examples, which capture most of the remaining STS citations in federal judgments, also suggest that recourse to science studies is both rare and opportunistic. Where STS scholars are cited, typically some small section of a text or proposition is extracted and used as a resource in the specific litigation, often divorced from its theoretical context. Newman's reference to Jasanoff was an example of this tendency. In this section we encounter the work of Robert Merton used in a variety of apparently inconsistent capacities and then consider how incredibly mundane perspectives on laboratory practice were drawn from the work of Latour and Woolgar in copyright infringement litigation.

The first example, *Kewanee Oil Company v Bicron Corporation*, was an appeal to the US Supreme Court.[58] On the question of whether state trade secret law was pre-empted by the federal patent laws a majority of the Court indicated that as long as it did not trespass on the purpose of the constitutionally-based legislative scheme enacted by Congress, the state law could co-exist. Outlining the reasons for these protections, Chief Justice Burger explained that trade secret law protected individuals and companies that had expended efforts in domains that were not patentable. Patenting was designed to encourage investment and industry while providing years of protection to the patent owner. In the words of Thomas Jefferson, some things 'are worth to the public the embarrassment of an exclusive patent' (*Kewanee* 1974: 1890). Patents encourage the public dissemination of ideas, while protecting the interests and efforts of the owner. Whereas patent protection tends to act as a barrier to prevent people using the technique, procedure or process, the trade secret law protects items that would not be proper subjects for consideration for patent protection and operates more like a sieve. Trade secret law tends to provide far weaker protection than patent law. So the fact that some might prefer the more limited protection afforded by trade secrets law to patent was not considered sufficiently significant to interfere with the state's legislative initiative. Chief Justice Burger acknowledged that the more limited protections provided by the trade secrecy laws allowed—actually could stimulate—competitors to attempt to copy or approximate through 'fair and honest means' such as reverse engineering.

It was in this context that Burger, writing for the majority, drew on the work of Merton and others to support his contention that conferring secrecy on a limited selection of techniques would not significantly retard industry and national development.

> Nor does society face much risk that scientific or technological progress will be impeded by the rare inventor with a patentable invention who chooses trade secret

protection over patent protection. The ripeness-of-time concept of invention, developed from the study of the many independent multiple discoveries in history predicts that if a particular individual had not made a particular discovery others would have, and in probably a relatively short period of time. If something is to be discovered at all very likely it will be discovered by more than one person. *Singletons and Multiples in Science* (1961), in R Merton, *The Sociology of Science* 343 (1973); J Cole and S Cole, *Social Stratification in Science* 12–13, 229–30 (1973); Ogburn and Thomas, *Are Inventions Inevitable?*, 37 Pol.Sci.Q. 83 (1922).[19]

FN19. See J Watson, *The Double Helix* (1968). If Watson and Crick had not discovered the structure of DNA it is likely that Linus Pauling would have made the discovery soon. Other examples of multiple discovery are listed in the Ogburn and Thomas article.[59]

For Burger, the trade secret law offered many beneficial effects. It might be considered ironic that Merton, perhaps best known for his discussion of scientific norms, including the norms of openness and communalism, would be cited in support of the proposition that keeping some knowledges secret in order to reward research efforts and to stimulate industry might not retard scientific progress.[60]

A more conventional approach to the work of Merton is evident in *Forsham v Califano*.[61] *Forsham* was a case that concerned access to raw data from federally sponsored scientific research under the *Freedom of Information Act* (FOIA). Bazelon's dissent refers to Merton's normative scientific ethos in order to criticize the majority judgment. Bazelon drew on both the purpose of the FOIA and the standards of the scientific community, espoused by Merton, to support his position:

> The essence of the scientific community, I had thought, is the commitment to the advancement of scientific truth by subjecting findings and conclusions to the "exacting scrutiny of fellow experts."[25] Moreover, where scientific data bear the earmarks of agency "records" subject to FOIA, it would be the height of irony to deny disclosure on the ground that it could expose errors or frauds and thereby discourage those who do the work of the Government. FOIA was enacted in part to end the practice of withholding information "only to cover up embarrassing mistakes or irregularities …"

FN25. R. Merton, The Sociology of Science 275 (1973); *see also* B. Barber, Science and the Social Order 89 (1952).[62]

The third case, *Joel Blaz v Michael Reese Hospital Foundation*, involved a motion to dismiss a civil action on the basis of the reach of the duty of care owed by a hospital-based research scientist studying the effects on former patients of radiation treatment in a Chicago hospital.[63] In undertaking the study and applying for research funding from the National Institutes for Health, a research scientist responsible for the Thyroid Follow-Up Program indicated that a study based on the program showed 'strong evidence' between the earlier treatment and various sorts of tumor. Attempts to survey and inform patients, however, were more circumspect. A questionnaire sent to former patients indicated that it was merely part of a follow-up study 'to determine the possible associated risks' (*Joel Blaz*

1999: 804). The question for determination was whether the hospital and the research scientist, who was not the treating physician, owed a duty of care to warn the hospital's former patients about the risk of future tumors on the basis of the research results.

Acknowledging a responsibility, consistent with Illinois law, to interpret the extent of any duty carefully, District Judge Bucklo, suggested that he could identify few reasons to exclude the researcher from a duty. Bucklo found that even though the research scientist was not the treating physician, relative to the plaintiff he was in a special position to acquire relevant information and that hospitals and doctors maintained obligations to former patients. In his assessment of whether there were any policy reasons for limiting the extent of duty Judge Bucklo considered whether constructing such a duty would inhibit research into the effects of medical treatment by non-treating physicians. He continued:

> But this does not strike me as a real worry. First, the duty would be discharged by a mere warning which, as explained, would here have been neither costly nor burdensome to give. The more costly and burdensome the warning would be to give, of course, the less likely there would be a finding of duty. Second, the medical researchers' legitimate desire for professional prestige and honor due to new discoveries, *see generally* Robert K. Merton, *The Sociology of Science* (1973), would counteract any such inhibition; as of course would the concern for the well-being of its former patients which any self-respecting hospitals would have.[64]

In each of these examples, quite different views of the role of secrecy and open communication of scientific findings are being bolstered by citing Merton's characterizations of the ethos and structure of the scientific community. Like the uses of Jasanoff and Popper identified earlier, it is not our contention that this merely displays judicial ignorance or inadequate understanding of the meaning of secondary (non-legal) sources. Rather it implies a different kind of understanding: an appreciation of the value of such citations as strategic resources to help support a variety of different images of science depending on the demands of decision-making in the specific situation.

Now we move to consider the legal life of *Laboratory Life. American Geophysical Union v Texaco Inc.*, was an appeal in a copyright infringement action against Texaco.[65] The publishers of scientific journals alleged that unauthorized reproduction of copyright-protected articles by Texaco scientists and engineers was inconsistent with 'fair use'. We are most concerned with the dissenting judgment of Judge Jacobs. Unlike the majority, Jacobs thought that the photocopying of articles by Texaco employees in order to assemble a personal 'archive' was within the realm of 'fair use'. In a forceful dissenting judgment, it is perhaps not surprising to find Jacobs supplementing the opinion by drawing on (non-legal) work by sociologists and historians of science. Expressing a preference for a broad model of research Jacobs suggested that the practice of science extended beyond the laboratory experiment.[66]

> The scientific method, properly conceived, is much more than a system of repeated laboratory experimentation. Rather, it is a dynamic process of "planned cooperation

of scientists, each of whom uses and continues the investigations of his predecessors
..." Edgar Zilsel, "The Sociological Roots of Science," in Hugh F. Kearney, ed.
Origins of the Scientific Revolution, 97 (1968).[67]

Jacobs referred to the work of Latour and Woolgar to support the preferred image
of research and to emphasize the importance of photocopying to the practice of
science.

> The anthropologist Bruno Latour spent two years studying scientists at the Salk
> Institute for Biological Sciences. During the course of his study, he conducted
> anthropological observations of a neurobiologist working on an article for a journal.
> This scientist's desk was littered with copies of journal articles authored by other
> scientists:
>> Xeroxed copies of articles, with words underlined and exclamation marks in the
>> margins, are everywhere. Drafts of articles in preparation intermingle with
>> diagrams scribbled on scrap paper, letters from colleagues and reams of paper
>> spewed out by the computer in the next room; pages cut from articles are glued
>> to other pages; excerpts from draft paragraphs change hands between colleagues
>> while more advanced drafts pass from office to office being altered constantly,
>> retyped, recorrected, and eventually crushed into the format of this or that
>> journal.
> Bruno Latour and Steve Woolgar, *Laboratory Life: The Social Construction of
> Scientific Facts*, 49 (1979). One essential step toward this drafting process is the
> accumulation over time of the journal articles that reflect the current state of
> knowledge that the journal author seeks to advance. Latour confirms that the
> photocopying of journal articles, and the use of them, is customary and integral to
> the creative process of science.[68]

For legal purposes, one of the most influential texts from the science studies corpus
was *reduced* to the proposition that 'the photocopying of journal articles, and the
use of them, is customary and integral to the creative process of science'.

In conjunction with his construction of the copyright statute, Jacobs drew on
the history of science to support the contention that strict application would stifle
progress and that professional considerations aside from profit—'in order to gain
distinction, appointment, resources, tenure'[69]—motivate authors to read and
produce the scientific literature. Referring again to Zilsel, in conjunction with Sir
Francis Bacon, *Philosophical Transactions*, William Eamon, A Rupert Hall and
Merton's earlier historical work, Jacobs insisted that the primary objective of
copyright is to 'promote the Progress of Science and useful Arts' and that these
objectives are coterminous with the scientific project (*American Geophysical* 1994:
941).

> The incentives for scientific publication have been in place since the project of
> science began to be perceived as a cooperative venture more than three centuries
> ago.[70]

Even after the Supreme Court's seminal *Daubert* judgment, in the realm of
copyright law, Jacobs drew on the work of sociologists of science who had

undertaken ethnographic work, rather than the images of science developed by Popper or even those linked to Jasanoff. On the basis of these additional examples, it would seem that different contexts, orientations and needs seem to encourage the production of different images of science.

As with the appearance of Jasanoff, these examples raise the question of whether we should consider the work of Merton, Latour and Woolgar accommodated and what that might mean in each of these instances. Before moving to discuss these questions, one final example focused on the legal reception of an explicitly STS-antagonist will provide another useful comparator for our assessment of the influence of STS and the extent of its judicial accommodation.

Capturing the courts: Huber (and Foster) and 'junk science'

This section examines the prevalence and influence of Peter Huber and 'junk science'. Judicial references to the work of Huber, a legally trained engineer and senior fellow of the politically conservative Manhattan Institute, provide a sobering foil to claims about the legal accommodation of STS.

Huber is often credited with coining the term 'junk science' through his popular book *Galileo's Revenge* (1991).[71] This text features a number of polemical reviews of tort congregations, such as those associated with Bendectin, which Huber argues can be best explained by the collusion between charlatan scientists and the plaintiff bar. *Galileo's Revenge* was published, perhaps not coincidentally, shortly before the *Daubert* appeal to the Supreme Court. After *Daubert*, with Kenneth Foster, Huber produced another book concerned with admissibility decision-making. That book, *Judging Science* (1998), purports to provide a definitive reading of the implications of *Daubert* and is designed to serve as a judicial guide for the legal interpretation of the reliability of scientific evidence. Much of Huber's work adopts perspectives which are quite hostile to science studies and its proponents.[72]

For the purposes of this chapter, we intend to show that Huber's written work has featured in federal court judgments far more often than citations of STS literatures, and that many of Huber's central ideas appear to be explicitly endorsed by the federal judiciary. Indeed, the decade of reforms to admissibility standards in the Supreme Court from *Daubert* (1993) to the present seem to mirror Huber's attempts to publicize and ameliorate the social problems he attributes to lax admission standards and 'junk science'. In contrast to Jasanoff, Merton, Latour and Woolgar—altogether cited in eleven cases—we identified twenty-eight explicit references to Huber and his work. Huber's apparent influence among the federal circuits is even more remarkable once we realize that *Galileo's Revenge* has never been cited by the US Supreme Court.

Initially, it is our intention to provide some examples of the variety of ways in which the work of Huber and his collaborators (particularly Kenneth Foster) has been applied in federal court judgments.

'Good science' and 'junk science'

Many of the judges who cite Huber's work seem to share his conviction that 'junk science' is ubiquitous and readily identifiable. Perhaps more conspicuous is their belief that 'junk science' is a serious social problem posing a serious threat to productivity, social relations and the ability for legal institutions to effectively resolve disputes. *Berry v City of Detroit* is typical in this regard:

> The problem of "junk science" has not gone unnoticed.[5]
>
> FN5. See, e.g., PETER W. HUBER, GALILEO'S REVENGE, JUNK SCIENCE IN THE COURTROOM (1991); KENNETH R. FOSTER ET AL., PHANTOM RISK, SCIENTIFIC INFERENCE AND THE LAW (1993).[73]

Concerns about the prevalence of unreliable expertise—manifested as 'junk science'—seem to have motivated *Daubert* and informed post-*Daubert* jurisprudence, particularly the need for judicial gatekeeping and the critical assessment of expertise. Consequently, since the *Daubert* decision, several circuits have drawn upon *Galileo's Revenge* and the more recent *Judging Science* to augment and operationalize the *Daubert* decision. Perhaps the most conspicuous appropriation from Huber's work is the idea that expert evidence prepared for the courtroom—commonly depreciated as 'science for litigation'—is a debased and suspect form of knowledge.

Considering the actual specifics of the *Daubert* case on remand—after the Supreme Court had sent it back to be reconsidered on the basis on the new *Daubert* standard—the Ninth Circuit Court of Appeals embraced some of Huber's ideas.[74] Endeavoring to rationalize its unflattering assessment of the plaintiffs' evidence, the Court explained:

> ... we may not ignore the fact that a scientist's normal workplace is the lab or the field, not the courtroom or the lawyer's office.
>
> That an expert testifies based on research he has conducted independent of the litigation provides important, objective proof that the research comports with the dictates of good science. See Peter W. Huber, *Galileo's Revenge: Junk Science in the Courtroom* 206–209 (1991) (describing how the prevalent practice of expert shopping leads to bad science).[75]

While the Ninth Circuit accepted that the *Daubert* criteria provided useful means of identifying 'good science', they incorporated supplementary considerations, such as the purpose of inquiry and the motivations of expert witnesses, to assist with their practical determination. In terms which are consistent with the legal institutional hierarchy, the Supreme Court's *Daubert* decision provided the general framework for the Court of Appeals' analysis, though none of the secondary authors (such as Popper, Hempel and Jasanoff) were cited in the decision. Only Huber's polemical text *Galileo's Revenge* was quoted in support of these particular images of science.

In the same case, the Court of Appeals also drew upon *Galileo's Revenge* to inform its understanding of the significance of peer review and publication. Discussing the value of the plaintiffs' expert evidence the Court explained:

> *Lynch, Richardson* and *Brock* [earlier Bendectin appeals] reflect a well-founded skepticism of the scientific value of the reanalysis methodology employed by plaintiffs' experts; they recognize that "[t]he best test of certainty we have is good science—the science of publication, replication, and verification, the science of consensus and peer review." P. Huber, *Galileo's Revenge: Junk Science in the Courtroom* 228 (1991).[76]

Despite the express qualifications to the value of peer review and publication in *Daubert*, in practice (particularly in civil litigation) many judges—including the Supreme Court in *Kumho*—apply peer review and publication as a fairly inflexible demarcation criterion. This approach resonates with the perspective of Huber (1991: 206–9) quoted above, and a discussion in a section of *Galileo's Revenge* entitled 'Publish and be Damned'. Once again these perspectives were endorsed in the Ninth Circuit Court of Appeals:

> One means of showing this is by proof that the research and analysis supporting the proffered conclusions have been subjected to normal scientific scrutiny through peer review and publication. [FN6] Huber, Galileo's Revenge at 209 (suggesting that "[t]he ultimate test of [a scientific expert's] integrity is her readiness to publish and be damned").[77]

In *Hollander v Sandoz Pharmaceuticals Corporation* the Tenth Circuit Court of Appeals cited *Judging Science*—and not *The Fifth Branch* or *Science at the Bar*—for the proposition that peer review in regulatory decision-making is viewed 'typically as "far more careful and systematic" than the peer review employed by scientific journals'.[78] Even after *Daubert*, Huber's work is cited more often than Jasanoff's for observations about the importance of peer review, limits to peer review and in making comparisons between peer review for legal and regulatory decision-making.

Given the Supreme Court's *Daubert warrant*, recourse to the work of Huber rather than Jasanoff, Angell, Horrobin or Ziman suggests that simplistic notions of precedent and being bound by superior courts are not as analytically powerful as we might initially suppose. Notwithstanding Jasanoff's claims about having been accommodated in the Supreme Court, lower courts—especially those endeavoring to explain the exclusion of expert evidence—have tended to cite the work of Huber and concerns about 'junk science', rather than STS-based sensitivities to the complexities of peer review and publication. In practice courts have favored the more affirmative (or dominant) reading of *Daubert*, reflected in the popular writings of Huber (and Foster).

Explicating and exemplifying Daubert

Whereas reference to the work of Popper has been exnominated and Jasanoff (and STS) inoculated—effectively written-out of post-*Daubert* jurisprudence—Huber's ideas seem to have been *incorporated*—that is, written-in. Concerns about socio-legal problems allegedly caused by 'junk science' and the need for rigorous judicial *gatekeeping* based on simplistic and restrictive models of scientific practice link the work of Huber with federal court practice and jurisprudence. In our analysis this seems to have been one of Huber's goals—to *capture* the courts.[79]

In this way *Galileo's Revenge* (1991) operates as a social problem identifier (and accentuator). The Supreme Court's decision to hear the *Daubert* (1993) appeal in relation to the admissibility standard in the federal courts represents a response to judicial inconsistency in the circuits and perceived problems with the reliability of expert evidence—particularly those attributed to 'junk science'.

In the wake of *Daubert*, Huber, with Foster, produced *Judging Science* (1998), which endeavored to explicate *Daubert* in terms consistent with their political agenda. As a response to, what they described as, the very real risks posed by 'junk science', *Daubert* is presented as a solution which, for Foster and Huber, requires courts to insist upon *mainstream* science—now defined in terms which reflect rigorous application of all the *Daubert* criteria and intense suspicion of plaintiffs' experts and 'science for litigation'. The following examples capture some of these exclusionary orientations manifested in both attempts to understand and apply *Daubert* and the relevant *Federal Rules of Evidence*.

For many judges the works by Huber (and Foster) inform their interpretation of rules and practice. In *Bartley* a judge referred to both *Daubert* and *Judging Science* when discussing the treatment of scientific evidence:

> *Daubert v. Merrell Dow Pharms., Inc.*, 43 F.3d 1311, 1321 n. 17, 1320–22 (9th Cir. 1995) ("Federal judges must therefore exclude proffered scientific evidence under Rules 702 and 403 unless they are convinced that it speaks clearly to an issue in dispute in the case, and that it will not mislead the jury."); Kenneth R. Foster & Peter W. Huber, *Judging Science: Scientific Knowledge and the Federal Courts* 34-36 (1997);[80]

Elsewhere, attempts by Foster and Huber to promote the aspects of *Daubert* conceived as most useful—such as strict application of 'testability'—find expression in the federal court. Endeavoring to understand and apply the first of the *Daubert* criteria, the *Brumley* Court drew support from *Judging Science*:

> The "testability" requirement is a threshold requirement aimed at excluding pseudoscience from the courtroom. *A theory that is untestable is unfalsifiable and of no practical value in the courtroom.* See Foster, Kenneth R. and Peter W. Huber, *Judging Science; Scientific Knowledge and the Federal Courts* Ch. 3 (MIT Press 1997).[81]

Both examples are from judgments where plaintiffs' expert evidence received unsympathetic treatment. In a dissenting judgment in *Bartley*, Circuit Judge

DeMoss found the evidence insufficient to sustain the plaintiffs' case and in *Brumley* District Judge Jack excluded the plaintiffs' evidence as insufficiently reliable. Consistent with the aspirations of Foster and Huber, in *Brumley* testing has been promoted to the stage where it acts as an effective test of evidentiary value. Of interest, the majority judgment in *Bartley,* which affirmed a jury's pro-plaintiff findings, made no reference to Huber or 'junk science'.

Another instructive, if slightly cryptic, example of the relationship between *Daubert* and the work of Huber is suggested in the following extract from *Carter v Great American Ins.*[82] Here *Daubert* and *Galileo's Revenge* are not only collocated but cited in support of the same proposition. Finding that the evidence of the plaintiffs' expert witness would not assist the jury, District Judge Livaudis explained:

> The Court has read Mr. Gallardo's [plaintiff's safety expert] ... report. It is obviously not scientific nor does it impress the Court as being one of technical or specialized knowledge which would assist the fact finder as Rule 702 requires. It falls clearly within the ambit of Rule 403. The matters at issue are within the common knowledge of jurors. *Peters v. Five Star Marine Serv. ... Daubert ...* (1993); *Galileo's Revenge—Junk Science in the Courtroom,* Peter W. Huber 1991, Basic Books division Harper Collins Publishers.[83]

Here, Livaudis directly equates Huber's work with *Daubert*. In its judicial manifestations, Huber's work is not restricted to images of pathological science or stark dichotomies between so-called good and junk science. Both the polemical *Galileo's Revenge* and the ostensibly more exegetical *Judging Science* are used by judges (and defence lawyers) to explicate the *Daubert* decision.

Evidentiary support

Throughout his legal writings Huber provides an abundance of examples of purportedly spurious litigation where the limited technical abilities of judges, the gullibility of jurors and the greed of plaintiffs and their lawyers are exploited. To varying degrees *Galileo's Revenge, Phantom Risk* and *Judging Science* are all critical of a number of specific civil actions and provide overwhelmingly positivistic analyses of evidentiary issues in those cases. The numerous controversies include: Bendectin, obstetrics, sudden acceleration, traumatic cancer, paternity suits and witch trials.

Discussing the plaintiffs' chemical sensitivity evidence in *Summers,* the Tenth Circuit Court of Appeals referred to the writings of Huber:

> See *Bradley v. Brown, 42 F.3d 434, 438–39 (7th Cir. 1994);* see generally, Kenneth R. Foster & Peter W. Huber, *Judging Science: Scientific Knowledge and the Federal Courts* 59 (1997) ("Chemical ecologists have failed to provide criteria that allow a doctor to decide when somebody does not suffer from MCS which is one of the main reasons why MCS is regarded skeptically by mainstream medicine.")[84]

Notwithstanding that both Jasanoff (1995: 131–4) and Huber have written about multiple chemical sensitivity (MCS) and clinical ecology, we find that Huber alone is cited and credited with substantial contributions.

On the subject of sudden acceleration, Huber's work is again cited to discredit the plaintiffs' claims:

> FN3. This slippery theory [sudden acceleration] with its various permutations has come under fire. See Peter W. Huber, *Galileo's Revenge: Junk Science in the Courtroom* 57–74 (1991).[85]

In both instances the plaintiffs were unsuccessful. Other judgments refer to Huber's work in relation to the misuse of statistics, how courts should assess causal relationships and the epidemiological position on the relationship between tobacco and cancer.[86] In providing exemplars of 'junk science' Huber goes beyond merely identifying a preferred model of science but also provides instances where his 'reforms' are required. This can be contrasted with Jasanoff's more politically detached register.

Exceptions

In the vast majority of cases, the work of Huber is cited to support the exclusion of expert evidence or where evidence is deemed insufficient to sustain a cause of action. In this section, it is our intention to provide an indication of how Huber's work has, on occasion, been deployed more creatively.

The first example illustrates how boundaries around 'junk science' can be mobilized not only to exclude evidence but also to justify the admission of evidence. Invoking the pejorative characteristics associated with 'junk science' enables lawyers and judges to represent (arguably) contentious evidence as 'good science'.

> Accordingly, the diagnosis which Dr. Grove was prepared to offer was based on a well-established mental disorder and represented neither "junk science"[4] nor scientific speculation "beyond the boundaries of current knowledge."
>
> FN4. ...*Galileo's Revenge* ... quoted in *Daubert* ... (9th Cir. 1991).[87]

In this case the judge accepts the existence of 'junk science'—in line with *Galileo's Revenge* and the Ninth Circuit's *Daubert* (1991) decision—but locates the boundaries in a way that exempts Dr. Grove's evidence from its compass. Implicitly, Dr. Grove's testimony is not 'junk science' but 'good science', and therefore admissible according to *Daubert*.

A more creative and informative use of 'junk science' was made by the lawyers acting for the estate of persons killed and injured by an automobile being chased by US Border Patrol agents. In *Stuart v US*, the district court found that the US Government was immune from liability for the plaintiffs' injuries or, that in the alternative, its agents had not been negligent in 'pursuing a suspected illegal alien smuggler'.[88] On appeal, the plaintiff (Stuart) contended that the trial judge had been biased in favor of the government, had been rude and had disparagingly excluded his expert evidence. Part of Stuart's appeal concerned the trial judge's favorable reference to 'extrajudicial sources':

> Apparently attempting to fit his appeal into the policy against judicial decisions being founded on extrajudicial sources, Stuart contends that the judge had been influenced by an extrajudicial source: *Galileo's Revenge: Junk Science in the Courtroom* (1991). The book, written by Peter W. Huber, condemns the plaintiffs' personal injury bar for their use of expert witnesses, who he characterizes as "junk scientists." Huber argues that such experts often have dubious credentials and offer farfetched theories of liability. In court, the judge mentioned the book and spoke disparagingly of "junk science."
>
> ...
>
> While the judge "made no secret of his skepticism of appellants' position" it does not necessarily follow that the judge's ultimate fact findings were erroneous. ... Intemperate bench behavior does not require reversal merely to chastise a judge if the judgment appealed from was one supported by the law and the facts.[89]

This example illustrates how judges are potentially vulnerable where they rely on non-legal forms of authority.[90] Earlier we suggested this as one of the reasons motivating the exnomination of Popper and inoculation of Jasanoff, and why few busy judges take Popperian falsification, as opposed to folk versions of testing, seriously.

Prevalence of 'junk science'

If, in a manner consistent with our earlier interpretive charity, where we analyzed citations of Jasanoff's 'invisible hand'—the statement qualifying peer review—we now consider the prevalence of citations to Huber's trade-mark phrase 'junk science' then the influence on the federal courts of his assumptions about the nature of science appear even more striking. A search for 'junk science' returned references to 135 judgments.[91] Few judges offered criticism of the concept. Accepting that the majority of these citations make no reference to Huber or his work—again evidence of legal exnomination—significantly, many of the references equate *Daubert* with the attempt to exclude 'junk science' from the courtroom. Two examples taken from appeals to the Supreme Court after *Daubert* suggest explicit judicial linkages between *Daubert* and 'junk science'. Commenting on the plaintiffs' expert evidence in the *Joiner* appeal, Justice Breyer (concurring) indicated that: 'this is not the sort of "junk science" with which *Daubert* was concerned'.[92] In *Kumho*, the opinion of Justices Scalia, O'Connor and Thomas (also concurring) explained that the discretion invested in the trial judge to choose 'the manner of testing expert reliability' is a 'discretion to choose among reasonable means of excluding expertise that is *fausse* and science that is junky'.[93]

Unlike references to Jasanoff, in the judgments where Huber and/or 'junk science' appear, significant aspects of Huber's conceptual apparatus are embraced and frequently mobilized. 'Junk science' is routinely construed as a social problem and, even when judges do not refer to Huber, restrictive (that is, the dominant) readings of the nature of science from *Daubert, Joiner* and *Kumho* are typically conceived as the appropriate tools for judicial practice.

Conclusion: Lodging with Procrustes

In order to offer a tentative explanation for the relatively successful promotion of Huber's vision of science among the federal judiciary (and beyond), and reasons for the relative invisibility of STS and SSK perspectives, in this final section we intend to outline several working hypotheses. Provisionally, we offer three main explanations: (i) active political (and media) lobbying in favor of the 'junk science' message, its attendant ideologies and reform implications; (ii) the manner in which scientism and legalism provide barriers to the legal reception of science studies (but not 'junk science'); and, (iii) the possibility that science studies is not well suited to the implicit legal demand, permeating *Daubert* and its progeny, for simple operational demarcation criteria capable of distinguishing between science, unreliable science and non-science.

Political lobbying and the 'junk science' message

Ideas do not 'speak for themselves'. The 'junk science' polemic is part of a broader social problem discourse accompanied by substantial interest group funding, media sensitivity and political and legal lobbying (Edmond and Mercer 1998a, 2004). STS and SSK perspectives have not received the same kind of overt political promotion.[94]

Huber, by way of example, is a senior fellow in the 'Center for Legal Policy' which forms part of a right-wing think-tank: the Manhattan Institute. The Manhattan Institute appears to have drawn inspiration from the efforts of British economist Antony Fisher. During the 1970s Fisher established a conservative think-tank in Britain which is often credited with aiding Margaret Thatcher's ascendancy to Prime Minister. The Manhattan Institute's first chairman, William Casey, later became head of the CIA.[95] Besides Huber, other members of the Manhattan Institute, like co-fellow Walter Olson (1991, 2003), are trenchant critics of the US tort system. Olson is also an Atlantic Legal Foundation (ALF) advisory council member.[96] The ALF is a politically conservative tort and law reform lobby group closely related to the Manhattan Institute. In its promotional materials, the ALF describes itself as 'a non-profit public interest law firm advocating traditional American values in the courts'.[97] Huber's sometime co-author Kenneth Foster, another prominent critic of 'junk science', is also associated with the ALF. Both the Manhattan Institute and the ALF have consistently and strategically advocated the need for more rigorous standards for the admission of scientific evidence into courts of law.[98] The list of benefactors, members, award recipients and endorsees of the ALF and the Manhattan Institute reads like a rollcall for peak trade organizations, insurers, major manufacturing and pharmaceutical corporations.[99] These are the type of organizations widely perceived to obtain economic benefits from stricter admissibility thresholds and less civil litigation (Calabresi 1970; Bogus 2001).

In addition, the ALF lists the endorsement of several Nobel laureates and eminent semiretired 'visible scientists'. Harvard University and the physical sciences are particularly well represented. One example is Harvard University physicist Richard Wilson. As we were writing this chapter Wilson was convening an ALF website: 'Sound science in the courtroom'.[100] The site is devoted to demonstrating how the identification of *mainstream* science, aided by the *Daubert* criteria, can be applied to prevent the proliferation of 'junk science' in American courts. Wilson's enthusiasm for the ALF is attested by his participation as signatory in many of the ALF's *amicus* briefs. Participation in briefs and litigation, for many of the eminent scientists including Wilson, does not always seem to follow their scientific specialization.

The ALF participated in the production of an *amicus* brief in the *Daubert* appeal and submitted briefs in many of the major admissibility cases that followed, most notably *Joiner* and *Kumho*. Many of these *amicus* briefs are formulaic. Usually they provide strategic exemplifications of the *Daubert* criteria, often incorporating liberal references to Popper, the *Daubert* judgment and scientific and technical evidence. The ALF has also submitted *amicus* briefs in response to specific types of product liability and tort litigation, such as claims associated with the health effects of EMF (electric and magnetic fields), with the expressed intention of preventing these *controversies* from developing into massive toxic torts (Slesin 1995).[101]

The Manhattan Institute and the ALF carefully market their *successful* interventions.[102] According to ALF sources, its activities contributed to the elaboration of the exclusionary regime inaugurated by *Daubert*.[103] The ALF claims credit for its leadership 'in advocating against the admission of poorly reasoned "junk" scientific (and technical) expert testimony into evidence' (Lewis 1999: 1– 3). The Manhattan Institute is equally strident in advancing its own involvement in the *Daubert* reforms:

> Manhattan Institute Senior Fellow Peter Huber (*Galileo's Revenge, Judging Science*) originated the term 'junk science' and is as responsible as any one individual for the fact that all federal and most state judges now have a mandate to act as gatekeepers of scientific evidence: to admit good science and reject poor science through making an independent assessment of the evidence brought before the court. New refinements on the landmark *Daubert* decision at the Supreme Court and in lower courts are making this time an unprecedented progress toward the goal of providing fact finders with scientific evidence that is reliable and sound.[104]

We accept that these claims may represent examples of institutional self-promotion and bravado, but the association of a more exclusionary ethos with post-*Daubert* evidence jurisprudence is consistent with our more qualitative empirical findings.

Aside from the issue of the attribution of credit for the emergent 'exclusionary ethos', other commentaries and studies provide support for an association between the *Daubert* decision and less favorable outcomes for plaintiffs in US federal courts. One comprehensive study prepared by the Rand Corporation concluded that in the aftermath of *Daubert* expert evidence was more regularly contested and more commonly excluded by judges in civil litigation (Dixon and Gill 2001; Bernstein 2001).

Having endeavored to provide some sensitivity to the extra-legal contestation around federal evidence and tort law, we now wish to conclude this subsection by returning to more recent commentary on the state of mass tort litigation by Jasanoff (2002) in 'Science and the Statistical Victim'. According to Jasanoff (borrowing from JC Scott), in response to the challenges posed by mass torts, judges have been under increasing pressure to 'see like a regulatory state':

> [T]he rise of managerial judging meant the replacement of particularistic inquiries into individual case histories with vastly more simplified criteria of inclusion and exclusion defining the groups to be compensated. It meant the transformations of the trial court's passionately personal gaze into the dispassionate processing routines of an administrative agency that puts efficiency of risk mitigation for all above the classic 'day in court' for each. (Jasanoff 2002: 51)

At the same time, in the wake of *Daubert* and its progeny (*Joiner* and *Kumho*), judges have also been expected to 'think like scientists'. Jasanoff (2002: 51) does not seem to mean 'think like scientists' literally, instead referring to the growing need for judges to legitimate their reasoning by adding the *Daubert* indicia to their traditional markers of objectivity. Notwithstanding these constraints, Jasanoff (2002: 63) believes that judges have exercised autonomy and used their own 'experientially informed sense of rationality' to decide on what they believe is persuasive.

This account would appear to have 'moved on' from Jasanoff's earlier contention that the *Daubert* judgment provides evidence for the *legal accommodation* of science studies. Nevertheless, her analysis of the post-*Daubert* context—where judges 'thinking like scientists' wrestle for individual autonomy while constrained to 'see like a state'—misses part of the trajectory identified in our discussion.

Given that some of the evidentiary ideas adopted or endorsed by federal judges appear to have originated, or received their most influential articulation, in corporate-sponsored think-tanks we might suggest that rather than 'seeing like a state' or 'thinking like a scientist', since *Daubert* judges have exhibited a more marked tendency to *see like corporations* or, more precisely, to *see like corporate-sponsored polemicists* when confronted with the scientific evidence of plaintiffs.

Scientistic and legalistic barriers to the reception of science studies

Another explanation for the apparently cool reception afforded STS by the federal judiciary may be drawn from considering the ideologies of legalism and scientism and recognizing certain affinities between them.[105]

In public arenas judges and scientists often employ similar professional rhetorical repertoires to represent their activities and knowledge claims (Wynne

1982: 120–58; Mulkay 1979). Accepting that judging is shaped by temporal pressures, institutional and professional values and, in adversarial systems, party-led case development, nevertheless in rationalizing decisions and explaining procedural choices a significant measure of judicial authority continues to rely on positivist tropes similar to those conventionally associated with the ideology of science.[106] For example, just as scientific practice purportedly relies on the application of a universal scientific method to identify objective facts, in its more idealized versions—what we might describe as law-in-general—judicial practice is supposed to exemplify the objective application of rules in an environment where facts and values are capable of being meaningfully and consistently distinguished (see Edmond in this volume). Similarly, in practice both law and the sciences exploit claims about objectivity, independence and forms of professional review (Edmond 2003). While it is not uncommon for judges to acknowledge epistemic and institutional differences between law and science, particularly in relation to burdens of proof, models of causation and temporal constraints (some of Blackmun's statements from *Daubert* come to mind), nevertheless, such reflections and qualifications are normally more epistemologically superficial than might be required to convincingly demonstrate that judging is sensitive, let alone receptive, to STS perspectives.

The occasional judicial reference to the epistemological status of law and science rarely involves the rejection of longstanding and profound commitments to scientism or legalism. Instead judicial commentary on scientific evidence is usually the by-product of strategic differentiation of law and the sciences in relation to specific points of contest or friction in a particular litigation context. Notorious miscarriages of justice often provide good examples of some of these difficulties. In such circumstances judges are required to carefully manage the authority of legal institutions, legal processes and, at least, some types of scientific practice and knowledge. Similarly, attempts by advocates, experts or judges to strategically *deconstruct* scientific and legal claims should not automatically be assumed to imply a more general sensitivity to epistemic reflexivity in relation to either science or law (Lynch and Jasanoff 1998: 685 n3; Lynch 1998; Fuchs and Ward 1994). In practice, processes of legal deconstruction—the exposure of some of the contingency associated with the production of scientific knowledge—tend to be strategic and highly selective (and usually asymmetrical). This also applies to interpreting the effects of deconstruction resulting from vigorous cross-examination. For example, judges are often more receptive to defendants' attempts to deconstruct plaintiffs' evidence in civil litigation than to criminal defendants' attempts to deconstruct evidence from the state's institutionalized forensic sciences. Instrumental goals related to the case and the subsequent need to credibly reconstruct evidence in any judicial rationalization militates against consistent exposure of the social contingency of scientific evidence and limits the potential for *civic education* through adversarial litigation.[107] In explaining their decisions it is uncommon for judges to adopt models of the sciences displaced from traditional positivist images (Edmond 2000, 2001). These contentions, reinforced by our study of citations, gain support from more general studies of law and science.

Brian Wynne identified some of these processes in his study of the *Windscale Inquiry*. The inquiry proceeded under the assumption that its main purpose was to apply legal discipline to establishing the (scientific) facts about the safety of nuclear power. This legalistic/scientistic framing effectively excluded issues, such as the trustworthiness of institutions involved, the relevance of energy policy, choices about alternative technological futures and the significance of scientific uncertainties, from legitimate consideration.

> Scientific knowledge is a fragile, shifting network of interpretive and theoretical activity, but this goes unrecognised by the legal mind. Accepting the incomplete nature of all scientific facts would be tantamount to its acceptance for legal knowledge too, given the law's growing use of scientific expertise and its cultivation of authority by reference to empiricist models of natural science. (Wynne 1982: 129, 1996c)

Wynne's critique would also appear to elucidate an important dimension of Huber's work. Accompanying Huber's denunciation of 'junk science' in *Galileo's Revenge* is a legalistic insistence that good judging be grounded in positivist epistemology:

> With or without a philosophically certain demarcation between science and pseudoscience, courts are still going to issue certain judgments. *Judging is the ultimate exercise in positivism*, a faith in facts strong enough to justify transferring fortunes, ruining reputations, and putting people to death. Anyone who does *that* for a living has a moral obligation to maintain faith in external, discoverable truth. Those who can't should practice their uncontained credulity elsewhere. (Huber 1991: 223)

It may be that the frame (or register) in which legal discourse usually operates makes it difficult, in circumstances where law and science are brought together, for non-positivistic justifications to appear persuasive.

On the basis of these insights the legal accommodation of STS may require the development of more flexible and reflexive institutions where judges and regulators may not feel the need to link their professional identity and authority as closely to legalistic and positivist images of practice.[108]

The (in)ability of science studies to provide operational demarcation criteria

Returning to the question which has motivated our paper—that is, the amenability of science studies to legal accommodation—in this final subsection we intend to consider whether science studies can be translated into forms which are capable of meaningfully satisfying judicial demands. Previously we described how the legal discourse generated around and beyond *Daubert* has led senior appellate courts to seek answers to questions such as: What is the scientific method? and What uniquely demarcates science from other forms of knowledge? Science studies may be well positioned, on the basis of empirical, historical and theoretical studies, to inform us about the nature of the sciences and perhaps to problematize, as philosophically naive or inconsistent, such questions and some of the images presented in *Daubert*. However, the multidisciplinary origins and variety of hermeneutic approaches underlying STS and SSK perspectives may deter the promotion of simple prescriptive answers to questions of method and demarcation.[109]

Some of these issues have been rehearsed suggestively, but rather inconclusively, by philosophers of science in relation to how their work was and should be put to work in the context of litigation over the teaching of creation science in public schools. The crux of this discussion can be located in the exchanges between Michael Ruse, Phillip Quinn and Larry Laudan in the wake of the *McLean v Arkansas* (1982) trial which focused on whether creation science was science or religion for the purposes of the First Amendment of the US Constitution (Laudan 1982, 1988a, 1988b; Ruse 1988; Quinn 1984). Briefly, a district court judge found that creation science was not scientific, in part, because it lacked naturalistic explanations and was unfalsifiable. As part of a religion, rather than one of the sciences, creation science could not legally be taught in public schools.

After the trial the philosopher Ruse made a number of rather triumphal comments about his role as an expert witness and the judicial embrace of his definition of science in the judgment. A key ingredient of Ruse's definition of science included reference to Popperian falsification. Subsequently, Quinn and Laudan, also philosophers of science, subjected Ruse's performance and claims to critique. They accused Ruse of promoting an inadequate model of scientific method which misrepresented the views held by many philosophers of science. In response Ruse conceded that falsification was not necessarily the best ideal characterization of science. Nevertheless, he defended his actions on the basis that the image of science he promoted was able to expose fundamental weaknesses in the style of arguments underpinning creation science. For Ruse, philosophers of science were not required to provide a unanimous view of the field when they appeared as expert witnesses.[110] Aside from his specific criticisms of Ruse's performance, Quinn wondered whether acting as an expert witness in creation science litigation might be an occasion when it was morally defensible to present the 'effective bad argument'. For Quinn providing creation science with some kind of legal purchase may present itself as a greater evil to philosophers than strategically (mis)representing their discipline.

Perhaps, following Quinn, the cost of accommodating STS within the current frame of US federal jurisprudence might be to put more effort into the production of 'STS for litigation' and the generation of 'effective bad arguments'. If STS perspectives were to be repackaged in this way we might observe a form of Huber's revenge: *junk* STS in the courtroom (Kroll-Smith 1996).

These observations should not be understood to imply that various branches of science studies are unable to offer valuable insights into the way science and expertise may enter and intersect with legal processes. Rather, they suggest that the style of metanarrative (especially metascience) sought by the legal system, particularly after *Daubert*, may not be compatible with much of the work produced under the rubric of science studies. The idea that the sciences are susceptible to description in terms capable of being operationalized for legal contexts while accommodating the breadth of perspectives and philosophical preoccupations of science studies (and other) literatures may be naive. Indeed, the ways in which the *Daubert* judgment blends competing and contradictory philosophies of science suggests both the dilemma as well as judicial disinterest in its more abstract implications.

It is difficult to definitively ascertain whether judges (personally) accept or endorse the writings and political commitments we have attributed to Huber. But, given the ways in which Huber's writings have been mobilized—predominantly as a means of rationalizing the exclusion of evidence, offering the possibility of easy demarcation between *good* and *bad* science and defining the essential nature of science more generally—it seems that many of Huber's ideas have taken root and propagated across the federal judicial circuits. On the basis of the foregoing examples, the appropriations of Huber's ideas would, as a generalization, seem to be consistent with the original context of use and his expressed aspirations. Many of Huber's ideas would appear to have been accommodated. It would be difficult to make similar claims about the work of Jasanoff or other sociologists of science and technology. Non-STS approaches are routinely used to address problems of demarcation, reliability, uncertainty and to represent the nature of scientific knowledge and practice in US federal courts. Our contention, contra that of Jasanoff, is that all of the Supreme Court decisions from *Daubert* onwards, and the majority of federal courts, have promoted an exclusionary orientation to expert opinion evidence. Perhaps ironically, the exclusionary approach would seem to extend to Jasanoff's own claims and, more significantly, the field of STS more generally.

Acknowledgements

The authors would like to thank several referees for commenting on a draft of this paper. Earlier versions were presented at the annual conference of the Society for the Social Study of Science (4S) in Milwaukee, Washington and Lee University and Virginia Tech.

Notes

1   *Daubert v Merrell Dow Pharmaceuticals, Inc.* 509 U.S. 579, 125 L.Ed.2d 469, 113 S.Ct. 2786 (1993).

2   An interesting example of judicial antagonism to science studies, or a proponent of science studies, can be found in a recent case in the Supreme Court of New York: *The People of the State of New York v James Hyatt* (10 October 2001: 5). In a pre-trial *Frye* hearing Justice Michael Brennan considered whether the Court would permit STS scholar Simon Cole to testify as an expert witness for the defence in relation to the reliability of fingerprinting evidence. Cole had recently published a book discussing the social contingency of fingerprint identification (Cole 2001). Brennan dismissed the application in rather sarcastic terms. First, he rejected Cole's approach because it was not generally accepted in the relevant scientific community: that of fingerprint

examiners. After a lengthy quote from the *Skeptical Inquirer* he suggested that Cole's evidence would have also been rejected as 'junk science' had the *Daubert* standard applied to the court: 'Even applying the Federal Court's *Daubert* standard what Dr Cole has offered here is "junk science" ... To take the crown away from the heavy weight champ you must decisively out score or knock him out. Going twelve (12) rounds will just not do. What Dr Cole has offered here is interesting but too lacking in scientific method to even bloody the field of fingerprint analysis as a generally accepted scientific discipline'.

3   Compare the approaches in the following circuits: *US v Alexander* 526 F.2d 161, 163–4 (8th Cir. 1975); *US v Smith* 776 F.2d 892, 898 (10th Cir. 1985); *US v Metzger* 778 F.2d 1195, 1203 (6th Cir. 1985); *US v Shorter* 809 F.2d 54, 59–60 (D.C. Cir. 1987); *US v Smith* 869 F.2d 348, 351 (7th Cir. 1989); *Christophersen v Allied Signal Corp.* 939 F.2d 1106, 1110–11, 1115–16 (5th Cir. 1991) (en banc); *Daubert v Merrell Dow Pharmaceuticals, Inc.* 951 F.2d 1128, 1129–30 (9th Cir. 1991); *US v Baller* 519 F.2d 463, 465–6 (4th Cir. 1975); *US v Downing* 753 F.2d 1224, 1237–40 (3rd Cir. 1985); *US v Piccinonna* 885 F.2d 1529, 1536–7 (11th Cir. 1989); *US v Jokobetz* 955 F.2d 786, 793–7 (2nd Cir. 1992).

4   *Frye v US* 293 F 1013 (1923). In *Daubert* (1993: 585), Blackmun commented on the absence of citations in the *Frye* judgment: 'The *Frye* test has its origin in a short and citation-free 1923 decision concerning the admissibility of evidence derived from a systolic blood pressure deception test, a crude precursor to the polygraph machine'.

5   This sits oddly with some of the discussion concerning the liberality frequently associated with *Frye* and the FRE. We acknowledge that the majority *Daubert* judgment explicitly claims that it continues the liberalization of admissibility laws (apparently) anticipated in the enactment and text of the FRE in 1975. While the Court might have been disingenuous in its account there are alternative explanations considered by, or consistent with, this chapter. In some courts *Frye* had been used to actively exclude evidence so that other admissibility tests may have been conceived as more liberal. Another possibility is that the judges—acting as naïve realists—were interested in the model of science, championed by authoritative *amici* such as the National Academy of Sciences (NAS) and AAAS, as relevant and useful criteria for identifying genuine and implicitly reliable knowledge.

We should also indicate that we are not making teleological and anachronistic claims about the Supreme Court's designs. To some extent, the meaning of the *Daubert* decision developed diachronically as the exclusionary ethos seems to have been intensified in the later cases of *General Electric Co. v Joiner* 522 U.S. 136, 148–50 L.Ed.2d 508, 520–21 (1997), *Kumho Tire Co. Ltd. v Carmichael* 143 L.Ed.2d 238 (1999), and *Weisgram v Marley,* 528 US 440, 120 S.Ct. 1011, 145 L.Ed.2d 958 (2000). The preference for Popper and testing, however, should not be construed as arbitrary.

6   The text of Rule 702 now reads: 'If scientific, technical, or other specialized knowledge will assist the trier of fact to understand the evidence or to determine a fact in issue, a witness qualified as an expert by knowledge, skill, experience, training, or education, may testify thereto in the form of an opinion or otherwise, if (1) the testimony is based upon sufficient facts or data, (2) the testimony is the product of reliable principles and methods, and (3) the witness has applied the principles and methods reliably to the facts of the case'. The new rule came into effect on 1 December 2000.

7   Some of the organizations that submitted briefs to the Supreme Court in the *Daubert* appeal include: Pharmaceutical Manufacturers Association, National Association of Manufacturers, Business Roundtable, Chemical Manufacturers Association, Association of Trial Lawyers of America, American Tort Reform Association, the

Chamber of Commerce of the United States of America, American Insurance Association, Nobel Laureates, NAS, AAAS, AMA, New England Journal of Medicine, the US Solicitor General and a group of law professors.

8   They include: Dorothy Nelkin, Daryl Chubin, Edward Hackett, Stephen J Gould. They are found in: Brief Amici Curiae of Physicians, Scientists and Historians of Science in support of petitioners and Brief Amici Curiae of Darryl E Chubin, Ph.D., Edward J Hackett, Ph.D., David Michael Ozonoff, M.D., M.P.H., Richard W Clapp, Sc.D., M.P.H., in Support of Petitioners. (The plaintiffs were the petitioners.)

9   The legal metaphysics may be of interest. Notwithstanding that Rule 702 had been used in federal courts since its enactment in 1975, in *Daubert* the Supreme Court provided an authoritative interpretation. This interpretation was, implicitly, always the meaning of the rule, though interim decisions—those between 1975 and 1993—which were inconsistent with the Supreme Court's interpretation in 1993 were not thereby rendered invalid.

10   *Daubert v Merrell Dow Pharmaceuticals, Inc.* 509 U.S. 579, 593, 125 L.Ed.2d 469, 483, 113 S.Ct. 2786, 2797 (1993). (emphasis added)

11   An early and influential account of legal authority is Merryman (1954). For a more recent account consider Mody (2002). For a curious and seemingly impractical proposal consider: Monahan and Walker (2000: 801–33). Conventionally, the use of social science authority in US courts is traced back to a brief prepared by Louis Brandeis (as counsel for the State of Oregon) in *Muller v Oregon* 208 US 412 (1907). See also Monahan and Walker (1985).

12   Such as the cases of *US v Smith* 869 F.2d 348 (7th Cir. 1989), *US v Williams* 583 F.2d 1194 (2nd Cir. 1978), *US v Downing* 753 F.2d 1224 (3rd Cir. 1985) and Jack Weinstein and Margaret Berger's textbook, *Weinstein's Federal Evidence*.

13   One example is the earlier Bendectin appeal in *Brock v Merrell Dow Pharmaceuticals, Inc.* 874 F.2d 307 (5th Cir. 1989). For First Amendment litigation, see: *McLean v Arkansas Board of Education* 529 F.Supp. 1255 (D.C. Ark. 1982); *Edwards v Aguillard* 482 US 578, 107 S.Ct. 2573 (1987).

14   The quote continues: 'and with an institutional declaration that, when in doubt, lay judges should decide whose viewpoint should be given controlling authority'.

15   Jasanoff (1995) indicated that: 'Altering any component of the current system for using expert evidence would change the balance of interests that have become engaged in constructing and deconstructing scientific facts in the legal arena'.

16   We note that these developments have a diachronic dimension. Subsequent litigation and the arguments presented in *amicus* briefs suggests that defendants sought to retain and even expand the advantages (or *successes*) they had previously obtained. Some of these arguments are recounted in Edmond (2002c: 377–82). Many of the briefs in *Kumho,* submitted on behalf of petitioners *and* respondents, characterize *Daubert* as the inauguration of a more rigorous admissibility regime.

17   Even those authors who claim to have read the writings of Jasanoff often produce very different interpretations to our own. It would be interesting if Jasanoff would be willing to *excuse* these authors if they claimed to be *accommodating* her. For a prominent example of this tendency—that is, Jasanoff's contructivist ideas being inoculated in legal discourse—see Dobbin et al. (1999: 29–31). The *Deskbook* was structured around a survey of approximately 400 state trial judges. In Chapter 3, 'An Introduction to the Philosophy of Science', there are brief accounts of social constructivism, Kuhn, Popper, inductivism and even a few lines on Feyerabend. Despite the variety of perspectives the *Deskbook* is underpinned by the implicit assumption that *Daubert's* Popperian-inspired call for falsification accurately captures the essence of science. For example, the *Deskbook* devotes attention to surveys of

judicial understanding of Popperian falsification. (Similar surveys of judicial understandings of 'alternative' philosophies of science were not undertaken.) The results of the surveys are used to suggest that notwithstanding the apparent commitment to the utility of falsification, among state trial judges (38 per cent of judges indicated that falsification was 'very useful' and 50 per cent indicated 'somewhat useful') a *correct* understanding of the concept could only be inferred in 5 per cent of the responses.

18   Compare: *Claar v Burlington Northern R. Co.* 29 F.3d 499, 501 (9th Cir. 1994); *Hopkins v Dow Corning Corp.* 33 F.3d 1116, 1124 (9th Cir. 1994); *In re Paoli R.R. Yard P.C.B. Litigation* 35 F.3d 717, 743–5, 746 (3rd Cir. 1994); *Hall v Baxter Healthcare Corp.* 947 F.Supp. 1387, 1399, 1411 (D. Or. 1996).

19   522 U.S. 136, 139 L.Ed.2d 508, 519, 118 S.Ct. 512 (1997). See Jasanoff (1998a, 1998b 2002).

20   Jasanoff (1996a: 408). We would also contend that constructivist sociologists might want to make larger claims than 'knowledge accumulates through negotiation and consensus among members of the scientific community'.

21   The Nobel laureates' brief was produced with the assistance of the politically conservative Atlantic Legal Foundation, which will be discussed in our conclusion. It was submitted as the Brief of *Amicus Curiae* of Nicolas Bloembergen et al. and was cited in the *Daubert* judgment in relation to peer review. The brief concluded: 'Publication, peer review and replication are the practices of the scientists outside the courtroom as they proceed with their task of corroborating or falsifying scientific theories and conclusions. This is the method the lower courts insisted on as a prerequisite to admissibility of scientific evidence'. The comprehensive, eclectic and inconsistent epistemological mix is similar to that found in many subsequent judgments.

22   In a rather personal attack Norman Levitt (1999: 226) presents an account of Jasanoff's involvement in US law and science policy debates through her contributions in the AAAS. Levitt juxtaposes Jasanoff's approach, which he derides, with Peter Huber's, which is celebrated. Curiously, he quotes from Jasanoff's (1996a) article 'Beyond Epistemology' to make the following point: 'Her disdain for *Daubert*, however, arises not from its incoherence, but from its very coherent and very sensible view that mainstream science ought generally be accorded serious respect. This is what Jasanoff finds insupportable'. Levitt appears to have missed Jasanoff's claims about accommodation. We will discuss the work of Peter Huber in subsequent sections.

23   Jasanoff (1996a: 404): 'My work was drawn into the resolution of the second problem [operationalization of the standard for admissibility of scientific evidence], again with no active intervention by me.'

24   Popper's popularity may be, in part, attributable to his willingness to explicitly link his ideals of scientific method to normative and quite prescriptive accounts of the nature of science. Some of the normative orientation, associated with his early career, can be linked to his Cold War political views, and in his later career to fears that the images of science promoted by Kuhn and others represented a dangerous scepticism towards the scientific enterprise. See discussions in Oldroyd (1986: 297–317), Horgan (1998: 32–41), Magee (1974), Albury (1983: 18–33), 'Symposium' in *Radical Philosophy* (1995: 2–6), Lakatos and Musgrave (1974) and especially Fuller (2003).

25   Blackmun also employs the terms 'validity' and 'validation' (*Daubert* 1993: 590, 593, 594, 597). For a succinct discussion of Popper and Hempel, set against broader traditions in the philosophy of science, see Losee (2001: 143–76).

26 Few legal commentators convey a critical appreciation of the work of Jasanoff or the history and philosophy of science more generally. Three exceptions are Leiter (1997), Schwartz (1997), Farrell (1994).

27 *National Bank of Commerce (of El Dorado, Arkansas) v Dow Chemical Co.* 965 F.Supp. 1490, 1494 (E.D. Ark. 1996); *National Bank of Commerce (of El Dorado, Arkansas) v Associated Milk Producers, Inc.* 22 F.Supp.2d 942, 947–8 (E.D. Ark. 1998); *Savage v Union Pacific Railroad Company* 67 F.Supp.2d 1021, 1025 (E.D. Ark. 1998).

28 This is similar to our experience on the few occasions we have been cited in the Federal Court of Australia or discussed in oral argument before the High Court of Australia.

29 *Markman v Westview Instruments, Inc.* 52 F.3d 967 (CA Fed. (Pa.) 1995).

30 52 F.3d 967, 1005 (1995).

31 This sample does not represent all occasions where *Daubert* is discussed in relation to peer review, publication and admissibility. It does, however, provide some sense of how Jasanoff's *work*, particularly the qualifications to peer review and publication associated with her in *Daubert*, are understood and used in practice.

32 In civil litigation, the plaintiff is required to prove their case on the preponderance of the evidence or the balance of probabilities.

33 In order: *US v Bonds* 12 F.3d 540, 564 (6th Cir. 1993); *US v Martinez* 3 F.3d 1191, 1196 (8th Cir. 1993); *US v Lowe* 954 F.Supp. 401, 410, 414 (D.Mass. 1996); *US v Galbreth* 908 F.Supp. 877, 880 (D.N.M. 1995); *US v Varoudakis* 1998 WL 151238 (D.Mass. 1998).

34 *Heller v Shaw Industries, Inc.* 1997 WL 535163 11 (E.D. Pa.). There are numerous examples of this approach, especially from judges dealing with claims under the National Vaccine Injury Compensation Act. See, for example: *Rogers v Secretary of Health and Human Services* 2000 WL 1337185; *Zimmer v Secretary of Health and Human Services* 1999 WL 1246937; *Ashe-Robinson v Secretary of Health and Human Services* 1998 WL 994191.

35 Another reason was that 'Todd [the expert] nor any other researcher had tested Todd's subtraction and back-extrapolation methodologies to see whether the given results are reproducible'.

36 *US v Bonds* 12 F.3d 540, 564 (6th Cir. 1993) (italics added). See also *Daubert v Merrell Dow Pharmaceuticals, Inc.* 43 F.3d 1311, 1317 n.5 (9th Cir. 1995).

37 These particular aspects of the evidence were contested because of the way the admissibility standard was articulated in *Daubert*.

38 Interestingly, Hempel has basically disappeared. Even in secondary work Hempel is rarely cited or discussed.

39 *Cummins v Lyle* 93 F.3d 362, 368 (7th Cir. 1996).

40 See also *Bradley v Brown* 42 F.3d 434, 438 (7th Cir. 1994).

41 *US v Starzecpyzel* 880 F.Supp. 1027 (S.D.N.Y. 1995).

42 880 F.Supp. 1027, 1040 (1995) (italics added). See also *Freeman v Case Corp.* 924 F.Supp. 1456, 1466 (W.D.Va. 1996).

43 This is a form of legal boundary work. For a discussion of the contestation and negotiation around the construction of scientific boundaries, consider Gieryn (1998); Bowker and Star (1999).

44 *Moore v Ashland Chemical, Inc.* 126 F.3d 679, 685 (5th Cir. 1997). Citing Green (1992), Popper and Faigman (1989), Judge Dennis distinguished between 'hard' or 'Newtonian' science and 'knowledge outside the realm of hard science'. In this context, 'Newtonian' stems from the work of the eminent evidence scholar

Imwinkelried (1994) and appears to be based on a very casual analysis of the history and philosophy of science. Judge Dennis also cited the case of *Starzecpyzel*.

45   *Kumho Tire Co. Ltd. v Carmichael* 143 L.Ed.2d 238 (1999).

46   Note the tautological loop. The selection of falsification as the scientific method and the appropriate means of identifying scientific knowledge in effect determines what is scientific and, therefore, to be considered (legally) *reliable*.

47   This was one of the questions raised in *City of Tuscaloosa, Starzecpyzel* and *Moore*.

48   In the application of the *Daubert* criteria to the facts, Justice Stevens dissented in both *Joiner* and *Kumho*.

49   *Peabody Coal Co. v McCandless* 255 F.3d 465, 486 (7th Cir. 2001): 'Yet the Court held in *Kumho* that junk science cannot be rescued by some principle such as a doctrine that courts must receive the views of any expert who does hands-on work. Bad science is bad science, even if offered by the first expert to express a view.'

50   *Kumho* (1999: 250). This is a verbatim quotation. Breyer has deleted the qualifications and references to non-legal authority.

51   The only possible exception might be *Kumho* (1999: 252). Here the failure to publish might be explained by a lack of previous interest in an area rather than other types of influence. According to Breyer: 'It might not be surprising in a particular case, for example, that a claim made by a scientific witness has never been the subject of peer review, for the particular application at issue may never previously have interested any scientist'. There is, however, an implicit expectation that *reliable* work will be reviewed or published in some form.

52   The Supreme Court, or particular judges, may have thought that their version of Popper accurately represented the nature of scientific practice. Though, the references to the other, supplementary criteria, suggests either: (i) they were not entirely convinced by Popper, and/or (ii) were not completely attentive to the philosophical detail of his work.

53   See *General Electric Co. v Joiner* 522 U.S. 136, 148–50 L.Ed.2d 508, 520–21 (1997) and *Weisgram v Marley* 528 US 440, 120 S.Ct. 1011, 145 L.Ed.2d 958 (2000).

54   *Mercado v Ahmed* 756 F.Supp. 1097, 1101 (N.D.Ill. 1991).

55   *US v Director of Illinois Dept. of Corrections* 963 F.Supp. 1473, 1489–90 (N.D.Ill. 1997). See also *US v Hines* 55 F.Supp.2d 62, 65 (D.Mass. 1999).

56   Of course, Supreme Court judges do not have complete control over the use of their decisions. *Stare decisis* does not always operate in the manner we might expect.

57   This section is adapted from Edmond and Mercer (2002a: 327–9).

58   *Kewanee Oil Company v Bicron Corporation* 94 S.Ct. 1879 (1974). See also: *Lotus Dev Corp. v Paperback Software Intern.* 740 F.Supp. 37, 77–9 (D.Mass. 1990).

59   94 S.Ct 1879, 1890 (1974).

60   These claims are more consistent with the work of Mitroff (1974) and Mulkay (1980). For some recent studies which provide overviews of the shaping of the reward system, normative ethos and professional ideologies of science by commercial, state and public interests, see Etzkowitz and Webster (1995: 480–505); Nowotny et al. (2001); Jasanoff (1996b).

61   *Forsham v Califano* 587 F.2d 1128 (D.C. Cir. 1978).

62   587 F.2d 1128, 1147–8 (1978).

63   *Joel Blaz v Michael Reese Hospital Foundation* 74 F.Supp.2d 803 (N.D.Ill. 1999).

64   74 F.Supp.2d 803, 807 (1999).

65   *American Geophysical Union v Texaco Inc.* 60 F.3d 911, 913 (2nd Cir. 1994).

66   Compare the rhetorical importance of the (Peter Huber-inspired) laboratory-centered and generally more restrictive models of science elaborated by the Court of Appeals in

the remand from the Supreme Court: *Daubert v Merrell Pharmaceuticals, Inc.* 43 F.3d 1311, 1317 n.5 (9th Cir. 1995).

67 60 F.3d 913, 933 (1994). Zilsel's paper was recently reprinted (Zilsel 2000).

68 60 F.3d 913, 934–5 (1994).

69 Legal support for this proposition is drawn from: *Weissmann v Freeman*, 868 F.2d 1313, 1324 (2nd Cir. 1989). Judges often seem to prefer legal authority to other sources of authority, even when confronted with non-legal specialized knowledges. This tendency was conspicuous in early judicial descriptions of DNA typing technology, where prior judgments were as common as scientific texts, both as authority for admission and use as well as descriptions of appropriate practice and the limitations associated with the technology.

70 60 F.3d 913, 940–41 (1994).

71 See also Foster et al. (1993). Though, there are earlier references to 'junk science' in US federal court judgments. For example, *Brock v Merrell Dow Pharmaceuticals, Inc.* 884 F.2d 167 (5th Cir. 1989); *Carroll v Otis Elevator Co.* 896 F.2d 216 (7th Cir. 1990); *Krist v Eli Lilly and Co.* 897 F.2d 293 (7th Cir. 1990).

72 The practice of acknowledging a variety of history, philosophy and sociology of science perspectives which are subsequently ignored or trivialized in favor of simplistic interpretations of testing or peer review is widespread among legal commentators and judges. The tendency to 'inoculate'—admit a little evil to prevent a greater one—is a pronounced feature of Foster and Huber's influential text: *Judging Science* (1998). Notwithstanding some eclectic recognition of limits to the work of Popper and others, ultimately falsification is presented as the best legal solution to admissibility and sufficiency *problems* on the highly contentious basis that it provides the closest approximation to actual scientific practice. Faigman's text, discussed in Chapter 1, also provides a range of historical and philosophical sources which do not appear to be integrated into the analysis.

For purposes of symmetry, references to the work of Huber and 'junk science' appear in Jasanoff (1995: 5, 51, 131, 229–30 n.9; 1998b: 722; 1992). See also Edge (1995: 3–23, 19 n21).

73 *Berry v City of Detroit* 25 F.3d 1342, 1349 (6th Cir. 1994). See also *Hodges v Secretary of the Department of Health and Human Services* 9 F.3d 958, 962 (Fed. Cir. 1993); *Kay v First Continental Trading, Inc.* 1997 WL 614394 2 (N.D.Ill. 1997); *US v Starzecpyzel* 880 F.Supp. 1027, 1029 (S.D.N.Y. 1995).

74 In this appeal from a Bendectin case *Galileo's Revenge* is cited for ideas pertaining to images of science, yet nothing is said about the chapter where Huber critically comments on the entire Bendectin congregation. See Edmond and Mercer (2000).

75 *Daubert* (1995: 1317, 1318). *Daubert* and *Huber* are both quoted in: *National Bank of Commerce (of El Dorado, Arkansas) v Dow Chemical Co.* 965 F.Supp. 1490, 1516 (E.D.Ark. 1996); *Lauzon v Senco Products, Inc.* 270 F.3d 681, 692–3 (8th Cir. 2001). In *Kumho*, the fact that the plaintiffs' expert first inspected the tyre in a lawyer's office rather than a laboratory was used to impugn the expert's performance and credibility.

76 *Daubert v Merrell Dow Pharmaceuticals, Inc.*, 951 F.2d 1128, 1131 (1991). Before *Daubert* went to the Supreme Court in 1993, Huber was cited for descriptions of science which were not necessarily consistent with the falsificationist model frequently associated with the *Daubert* decision.

77 *Daubert v Merrell Dow Pharmaceuticals, Inc.* 43 F.3d 1311, 1318 (9th Cir. 1995).

78 *Hollander v Sandoz Pharmaceuticals Corporation* 2002 WL 963423 (10th Cir. 2002).

79 Here *capture* may mean to represent some of the ideologies maintained by judges and/or to have convinced judges to approach evidentiary *problems* in a particular way.

80 *Bartley v Euclid, Inc.*, 158 F.3d 261, 288 (5th Cir. 1998).

81 *Brumley v Pfizer, Inc.*, 200 FRD 596, 602 (S.D.Tex. 2001) (emphasis added).
82 *Carter v Great American Insurance* 1994 WL 374283 (E.D.La. 1994).
83 1994 WL 374283 1 (1994).
84 *Summers v Missouri Pacific Railroad System*, 132 F.3d 599, 603–4 (10th Cir. 1997). Also quoted in *Coffin v Orkin Exterminating Co. Inc.*, 20 F.Supp.2d 107, 110 (D.Me. 1998).
85 *Antevski v Volkswagenwerk Aktiengesellschaft* 4 F.3d 537, 541 (1993). See also *Blue Cross and Blue Shield of New Jersey v Phillip Morris, Incorporated*, 113 F.Supp.2d 345, 356 (2000).
86 *Bartley v Euclid, Inc.*, 158 F.3d 261, 287 (5th Cir. 1998); *Treadwell v Dow-United Technologies*, 970 F.Supp. 974, 985 (M.D.Ala. 1997).
87 *US v DiDomenico*, 985 F.2d 1159, 1167 (1st Cir. 1993). The reference to *Daubert* (1991) concerns an appeal to the Court of Appeals (9th Circuit) before the issue was heard by the US Supreme Court. See also *Safrani v Werner Co.* 1997 WL 729110 (S.D.N.Y. 1997); *Lauzon v Senco Products, Inc.* 270 F.3d 681, 692–3 (2001); *Lust By and Through Lust v Merrell Dow Pharmaceuticals, Inc.* 89 F.3d 594, 597 (9th Cir. 1996).
88 *Stuart v US*, 23 F.3d 1483, 1485 (9th Cir. 1994).
89 23 F.3d 1483, 1486 (1994). See also *Stuart v US* 797 F.Supp. 800, 802 (C.D.Cal. 1992).
90 Previously we recounted how Rehnquist and Stevens were concerned about the majority's use of these sources in their *Daubert* (1993) dissent. This example, however, also shows how judges can deflect and manage criticism through the exigencies of legal practice and classification.
91 We concede that these figures represent only a modest proportion of the cases referring to *Daubert* or dealing with evidentiary issues more generally. They are, however, greater by an order of magnitude than references to science studies or sociologists of science.
92 *Joiner* (1997: 522). Some of the multitude of cases which link *Daubert* and *Kumho* to the exclusion of 'junk science' include: *Peabody Coal Co. v McCandless* 255 F.3d 465, 468 (7th Cir. 2001); *Tuf Racing products, Inc. v American Suzuki Motor Corp.* 223 F.3d 585, 591 (7th Cir. 2000); *Terran ex rel. Terran v Secretary of Health and Human Services* 195 F.3d 1302, 1316 (Fed.Cir. 1999); *Skidmore v Precision Printing and Pkg., Inc.* 188 F.3d 606, 618 (5th Cir. 1999).
93 *Kumho* (1999). Once again the emphasis is placed on the exclusion of evidence. The concept 'junk science' appears to be particularly appealing to Posner, Chief Justice of the Seventh Circuit.
94 Further, many of Huber's ideas seem to align with some of the dominant public (or popular) images of science, what Michael (1992) describes as science-in-general, more easily than many of the STS and more critical Public Understanding of Science (PUS) perspectives might, especially in media discourses.
95 See the Manhattan Institute website, <http://www.manhattan-institute.org/html/about_mi.htm>; Fred Kaplan, 'Conservatives plant seed in NYC' *Boston Sunday Globe* (22 February 1998); Janny Scott, 'Turning Intellect Into Influence' *New York Times* (12 May 1997). For commentary on the Manhattan Institute and its links with the Bush Administration and 'right wing' political causes see essays by Robert Lederman, including: 'GW Bush, Jesus and the Manhattan Institute', <robert.lederman@worldnet.att.net>. Lederman contends that the Manhattan Institute's main sources of funding are the JP Morgan/Chase Bank and the pharmaceutical companies Pfizer and Lilly. According to Norman Solomon from the Institute for Public Accuracy, the Manhattan Institute has managed to sustain an

annual budget of five million dollars since the early 1990s. Solomon outlines strategies used by the Manhattan Institute to promote conservative authors and their publications through generous financial advances and promotional schemes. See the discussion in 'The Manhattan Institute: Launch Pad for Conservative Authors' IPA Articles (1998): <http:www.accuracy.org/articles/manhat.htm>.

96   Olson's work is cited in *Jansen v Packing Corp. of America* 123 F.3d 490, 541 (7th Cir. 1997).

97   See, for example, Atlantic Legal Foundation, *Science in the Courtroom Review* (1999: 1).

98   For example, the Manhattan Institute published a commentary by Foster and Huber, 'Science in the Courts', which summarized the main themes of their book *Judging Science*. See Center for Legal Policy, *Civil Memo No. 33* (1997), <http://www.manhattan-institute.org/html/cjm_33.htm>.

99   For example, the recipient of the ALF's most recent annual award (26 June 2002) was Henry McKinnell Jr., Chairman and Chief Executive Officer for Pfizer (according to the ALF, the worlds largest research-based pharmaceutical company). Previous annual award honorees include current and retired CEOs from Du Pont, Citicorp, Sprint Corporation, General Mills, Lockheed Martin, Forbes Inc., the former Mayor of New York City, Rudolph Giuliani, and Donald Rumsfeld—the current US Secretary of Defense. See *Atlantic Legal Foundation Report* (2002: 1, 5).

100 Wilson (2000) has also criticized Jasanoff in the correspondence pages of *Nature*. In an essay published in *Nature,* Jasanoff (1999) called for a 'conversation between science and society'. Wilson suggests that such 'calls' are 'peculiar' because the real source of technological problems and scientific controversy can be traced to the failure of some nonscientists, especially politicians and managers, to accept scientific advice. He cites the *Daubert, Joiner*, and *Kumho* trilogy, as an example of an important attempt to clarify the role of experts in legal settings.
     See <http://phys4.harvard.edu/~wilson/soundscience/ALF_Science.html>.

101 The ALF submitted *amicus* briefs in two important EMF cases: *San Diego Gas and Electric Co. v Coval* 55 Cal.Rptr.2d 724 (1996) (Brief of Amici Curiae Robert K Adair, Nicolaas Bloembergen, David Bodansky, Alan Cormack, Walter Gilbert, Sheldon Lee Glashow, David Hafemeister, James H Merritt, John E Moulder, Robert L Park, Robert V Pound, Glenn T Seaborg, Rosalyn Yallow, and Richard Wilson in support of petitioners San Diego Gas and Electric Company) and *Ford v Pacific Gas and Electricity Co.* 70 Cal.Rptr.2d 359 (1997) (Brief of Amici Curiae Eleanor R Adair, Robert K Adair, Leo L Beranek, Nicolaas Bloembergen, Patricia Buffler, Alan Cormack, Robert L Park, Robert V Pound and Glenn T Seaborg in support of Defendant-Respondent Pacific Gas and Electric Company, Inc.). Prominent 'science wars' crusader Robert Park is one of the ALF's 'regular' amici. Park's text, *Voodoo Science* (2000: 162–71), employs a failed attempt to litigate in relation to EMF as an example of the exclusionary potential of *Daubert's* reform.

102 They interpret many of the appeal outcomes as successes. The italics are used to problematize their causal assertions. We suggest that there may be genuine links but this needs further investigation.

103 These claims continue at the time of writing. In its 2002 annual report the ALF records the alleged impact of its *amicus* brief filed in the Court of Appeals for the Ninth Circuit in *Kennedy v Southern California Edison Company and Combustion Engineering* 219 F.3d 988 (9th Cir. 2000) (Brief of Amici Curiae Robert K Adair, Bruce N Ames, D Allan Bromley, Patricia A Buffler, Bernhard Cohen, Bernard Gittelman, Sheldon Lee Glashow, Michael Gough, Ronald Hart, Dudley Herschbach, Lawrence Litt, A Alan Moghissi, Rodney W Nichols, Robert V Pound, Norman

Ramsey, Joseph P Ring, Frederick Seitz, Edward Thorndike, Lynn H Verhey and James D Watson in support of defendants–appellees' motion for rehearing en banc.) This case considered claims that exposure to 'fuel fleas' caused fatal cancer to the wife of a nuclear power station worker. The *Atlantic Legal Foundation Annual Report* (2002: 3), explains that their brief: 'was cited by the appellate court in its stunning reversal of its own earlier opinion ... In their petition for *certiorari* to the United States Supreme Court, the unsuccessful plaintiffs attributed the Ninth Circuit's about face [in 2001] to the brief "of a so called think tank called the Atlantic Legal Foundation", once again demonstrating ALF's effectiveness in promoting sound science'.

104 Manhattan Institute website: 'The Center for Legal Policy',
     <http://www.manhattan-institute.org/html/clp.htm>.

105 We should also note that, even in their most polemical works, Huber, Foster and Olson are explicitly writing for a legal and policy-sensitized audience. Fewer STS scholars working on law and science are actively promoting a range of explicit policy implications. Further, it may be that many of the policy implications are more explicit and more explicitly political in the work of Huber and his associates, though we acknowledge that most STS perspectives on law and science tend to be pro-plaintiff or question the direction and rationale for reform. The *Daubert amicus curiae* briefs by Chubin, Hackett and Nelkin were all submitted in support of the petitioners (plaintiffs).

106 In adversarial jurisdictions the judge is generally limited in her ability to draw upon factual material (or evidence) additional to that adduced by the parties. Though, in recent decades judges in most common law jurisdictions have, for various reasons, become more active in the preparation and conduct of trials and appeals. One of the better recent accounts endeavoring to deal empirically and theoretically with judicial policy-making is by Feeley and Rubin (1999).

107 Jasanoff (1995: 215–17). For critical commentary of the scope of the legal deconstruction of science, see Edmond and Mercer (1996), Edmond (1998). Not infrequently, tactical decisions may mitigate the significance of evidence and the possibilities for forms of deconstruction. Technical legal issues and strategies which do not involve specific forms of evidence may be invoked to make the evidence, in a particular case, largely irrelevant. For example, if a case is not filed within the requisite period of time a judge may decline to hear the case, regardless of the quality of the expert evidence. Similarly, in many cases the evidence may be accepted by all the parties, but the applicable law controversial—awaiting judicial *clarification*.

108 Precautionary principles, where they attempt to approach uncertainties and social values with transparency, may represent some kind of movement in this direction. Perhaps unsurprisingly, precautionary principles are now encountering criticisms from 'junk science' critics such as Huber and Foster. For an example of arguments against precautionary principles, see Foster et al. (2000: 979–81), Huber (1999). For general discussion of ideas of how institutional changes may be needed to avoid traditional scientistic tendencies, see Irwin (1995).

109 A recent discussion paper by Collins and Evans (2002) examines the potential for science studies to determine the appropriate political role for expertise in technical decision-making (see Irwin in this volume). Collins and Evans suggest that the 'second wave' of science studies, 'social constructivism' which has run from the early 1970s to the present, has not been well suited to developing a 'normative theory of expertise'. 'Second wave' studies have predominantly focused on *describing* the social processes involved in attributing the label *expert*, rather than identifying what forms of expertise *should* be granted legitimacy over others (2002: 239). Collins and Evans (2002: 249–65) advocate the development of a so-called 'third wave' of science studies which,

they suggest, should attempt to classify and assess different types of expertise according to various categories of expert experience and the proximity of particular experts to relevant knowledge-making contexts. This exercise could then be used to guide decisions about which experts should, or should not, be allowed to participate in technical decision-making. In an extended 'Appendix' Collins and Evans refer to Jasanoff's studies of expertise in law and science. They appear to draw inspiration from Jasanoff's 'second wave' studies, in particular, the contention that adversarial legal proceedings have exposed divergent understandings of technical expertise and assisted in disclosing the underlying normative commitments of experts (2002: 276). The authors' concern with the possibility of drawing a 'normative theory of expertise' from 'second wave' science studies resonates with our identification of difficulties in 'exporting' concepts and ideas from science studies to legal and judicial audiences. Our study suggests, in contrast to the position adopted by Collins and Evans (and Jasanoff), that there is little evidence that the adversarial orientation of US law provides a vehicle for the legal deconstruction of science or encourages 'civic education'. The naïve, indeed technocratic, images of science and expertise that seem to have dominated the exclusionary post-*Daubert* jurisprudence suggest that attempts to develop a 'third wave' of science studies, capable of influencing policy and practical decision-making, may require a more sophisticated analysis of the politics of policy-sensitive arenas like law and regulation.

110 This was one of the difficulties encountered with the application of the *Frye* test. In addition to determining the *relevant* community it was always difficult to determine the extent of acceptance within such specialist *communities*.

Appendix: Methodology

In searching for references to prominent scholars (more than 100) from the history, philosophy and sociology of science we have relied on the WESTLAW database as our primary research tool. Our analysis is not strictly quantitative—we could only locate a handful of relevant citations—but rather qualitative. Our primary goal was to provide some context and perspective to the judicial uses of STS. Consequently, the significance and meaning of citations is assessed against the backdrop of wider socio-legal debates and judicial uses of *Daubert*. We have devoted special attention to those scholars featured in *Daubert* (Popper, Jasanoff and to a lesser extent Hempel) and other prominent sociologists of science cited in Supreme Court decisions (Merton) and recent cases (Latour and Woolgar) in an attempt to monitor judicial appropriation of the social sciences and to analyze how their ideas were used to support particular propositions and conformed with larger jurisprudential trends. For comparative purposes we also examined the prevalence of a non-constructivist commentator (Huber) and his promotion of the concept of 'junk science'. (The primary research was performed in 2002.)

Bibliography

Abadee, A. (2000), 'The Expert Witness in the New Millennium',
     <http://www.lawlink.nsw.gov.au/sc\sc.nsf/pages/abadee_expertw>.
Abbott, A. (1988), *The System of Professions: An Essay on the Division of Expert Labor*,
     Chicago, University of Chicago Press.
Abercrombie, N., S. Hill and B.S. Turner (1980), *The dominant ideology thesis*, London,
     George Allen & Unwin.
Abercrombie, N. and B. Longhurst (1998), *Audiences*, London, Sage.
Abraham, J. (1995), *Science, politics and the pharmaceutical industry: Controversy and
     bias in drug regulation*, London, UCL Press/Taylor & Francis.
Abraham, J. and G. Lewis (2000), *Regulating medicines in Europe: Competition, expertise
     and public health*, London, Routledge.
Abraham, J. and T. Reed (2002), 'Progress, innovation and regulatory science in drug
     development', 32 *Social Studies of Science*, 337–69.
Abraham, J. and H. Lawton Smith eds (2003), *Regulation of the pharmaceutical Industry*,
     Basingstoke, Palgrave Macmillan.
Agriculture and Environment Biotechnology Commission (AEBC) (September 2001),
     Crops on Trial, <www.aebc.gov.uk>.
Albury, R. (1983), *The Politics of Objectivity*, Melbourne, Deakin University Press.
Allen, R. (1991), 'The Nature of Juridical Proof', 13 *Cardozo Law Review*, 373–422.
Anderson, T.L. and D.R. Leal (2001), *Free Market Environmentalism*, New York, Palgrave.
Ashbaugh, D.R. (1999), *Quantitative–Qualitative Friction Ridge Analysis: An Introduction
     to Basic and Advanced Ridgeology*, Boca Raton FL, CRC Press.
Ashbaugh, D. (6 June 2002), 'Ridgeology—Science and Law', Toronto, Annual
     Professional Learning Conference of the Canadian Identification Society.
Atkinson, J. and P. Drew (1979), *Order in Court: The organisation of verbal interactions in
     judicial settings*, London, Macmillan.
Atlantic Legal Foundation (1999), *Science in the Courtroom Review*, New York, Atlantic
     Legal Foundation.
Atlantic Legal Foundation (2002), *Annual Report*, New York, Atlantic Legal Foundation.
Attwood, B. (1996a), 'Introduction. The Past as Future: Aborigines, Australia and the
     (Dis)course of History' in B. Attwood ed., *In the Age of Mabo: History, Aborigines
     and Australia*, St Leonards, Allen & Unwin, vii–xxxviii.
Attwood, B. (1996b), 'Mabo, Australia and the End of History' in B. Attwood ed., *In the
     Age of Mabo: History, Aborigines and Australia*, St Leonards, Allen & Unwin, 100–
     106.
Attwood, B. and S. Foster eds (2003), *Frontier Conflict: The Australian Experience*,
     Canberra, National Museum of Australia.
Ault, A. (1997), 'FDA Advisers find no Major Halcion Danger', (1997) 350 *Lancet*, 1760.
Austin, J. (1962), *How to do things with words*, Oxford, Oxford University Press.
Bailis, D. and R. MacCoun (1996), 'Estimating liability risks with the media as your guide:
     A content analysis of media coverage of civil litigation', 20 *Law & Human
     Behavior*, 419–29.
Bakhtin, M. (1981), *The Dialogic Imagination: Four Essays*, Austin, University of Texas
     Press.

Bakhtin, M. (1986), *Speech Genres and Other Late Essays*, Austin, University of Texas Press.

Bal, M. (1985), *Narratology: Introduction to the Theory of Narrative*, Toronto, University of Toronto Press.

Barnes, B. (1985), *About Science*, Oxford, Basil Blackwell.

Barnes, B. (2000), *Understanding Agency: Social theory and responsible action*, London, Sage.

Barnes, B. and D. Bloor (1982), 'Relativism, rationalism and the sociology of knowledge' in M. Hollis and S. Kukes eds, *Rationality and Relativism*, Oxford, Blackwell, 21–47.

Barnes, B. and D. Edge eds (1982), *Science in Context*, Milton Keynes, Open University Press.

Barthes, R. (1973), *Mythologies*, London, Paladin.

Baumgartner, F.R. and B.D. Jones (1993), *Agendas and Instability in American Politics*, Chicago, University of Chicago Press.

Beaglehole, J.C., ed. (1963), *The 'Endeavour' Journal of Joseph Banks*, Sydney, Angus & Robertson.

Beavan, C. (2001), *Fingerprints: The Origins of Crime Detection and the Murder Case that Launched Forensic Science*, New York, Hyperion.

Beck, U. (1992), *Risk society: Towards a new modernity*, London, Sage.

Bell, D. (1973), *The coming of post–industrial society*, New York, Basic Books.

Bell, D. (1998), *Ngarrindjeri Wurruwarrin: A World that Is, Was, and Will Be*, Melbourne, Spinifex Press.

Belper, Lord, F.A. Bosanquet, A. De Rutzen, C.S. Murdoch and C.E. Troup (1901), *Minutes of Evidence taken before the Departmental Committee on Identification of Criminals*, London, Wyman & Sons.

Bennett, W.L. and M.S. Feldman (1981), *Reconstructing Reality in the Courtroom: Justice and Judgment in American Culture*, New Brunswick, Rutgers University Press.

Bensel, R.F. (1987), *Sectionalism and American Political Development, 1880–1980*, Madison, University of Wisconsin Press.

Bentham, J. (1827), *Rationale of Judicial Evidence*, London, Hunt & Clarke.

Berger, M. (2001), 'Upsetting the balance between adverse interests: The impact of the Supreme Court's trilogy on expert testimony in toxic tort litigation', 64 *Law & Contemporary Problems*, 289–326.

Bernstein, D. (1996), 'Junk science in the United States and the Commonwealth', 21 *Yale Journal of International Law*, 123–82.

Bernstein, D. (2001), '*Frye, Frye*, Again: The Past Present, and Future of the General Acceptance Test' *George Mason University School of Law: Law and Economics Research Paper Series*, Paper No. 01–07, Social Science Research Network, Electronic Paper Collection, <http://papers.ssrn.com/paper.taf?abstract_id=262034>.

Bernstein, M.H. (1955), *Regulating Business by Independent Commission*, Princeton, Princeton University Press.

Biró, P.P. (2003), 'Teri's Find: A Forensic Study in Authentication', <http://www.birofineartrestoration.com/Pollock/Pollack.htm>.

Blackman, A., J. Boyd, A. Krupnick and J. Mazurek (2001), *The Economics of Tailored Regulation and the Implications for Project XL*, Washington DC, Resources for the Future.

Blaut, J.M. (1993), *The Colonizer's Model of the World: Geographical Diffusionism and Eurocentric History*, New York, Guilford Press.

Blomley, N. (1994), *Law, Space, and the Geographies of Power*, New York, Guilford Press.

Bloor, D. (1976, 1991), *Knowledge and social imagery*, Chicago, Chicago University Press.

Blumberg, J., A. Korsvold and G. Blum (1996), *Environmental Performance and Shareholder Value*, Geneva, World Business Council on Sustainable Development.

Bochner, A. (1997), 'It's About Time: Narrative and the Divided Self', 3 *Qualitative Inquiry*, 418–39.

Bode, G. (1996), 'Carcinogenicity Testing: Panel Discussion' in P.F. D'Arcy and D.W.G. Harron eds, *Proceedings of the Third International Conference on Harmonisation*, Belfast, IFPMA, 295–302.

Bogus, C. (2001), *Why lawsuits are good for America*, New York, New York University Press.

Borch, M. (2001), 'Rethinking the Origins of *Terra Nullius*', 117 *Australian Historical Studies*, 222–39.

Borchard, E. (1932), *Convicting the Innocent: Errors in Criminal Justice*, New Haven, Institute of Human Relations.

Bourdieu, P. (1975), 'The Specificity of the Scientific Field and the Social Conditions of the Progress of Reason', 14 *Social Science Information*, 19–47.

Bowker, G. (1995), 'Second Nature Once Removed: Time, Space and Representation', 4 *Time & Society*, 47–66.

Bowker, G. (2000), 'Mapping Biodiversity', 14 *International Journal of GIS*, 739–54.

Bowker, G. and S. Star (1999), *Sorting things out: Classification and its consequences*, Cambridge MA, MIT Press.

Brickman, R., T. Ilgen and S. Jasanoff (1985), *Controlling chemicals: The politics of regulation in Europe and the United States*, Ithaca NY, Cornell University Press.

Briggs, C., ed. (1996), *Disorderly Discourse: Narrative, Conflict and Inequality*, New York, Oxford University Press.

Brixen, C. and C. Meis (2000), 'Codifying the *Daubert* Trilogy: The Amendment to Federal Rule of Evidence 702', 40 *Jurimetrics Journal*, 527–36.

Brockmeier, J. and R. Harré (1997), 'Narrative: Problems and Promises of an Alternative Paradigm', 30 *Research on Language and Social Interaction*, 263–83.

Brodeur, P. (1989), *Currents of Death*, New York, Simon and Schuster.

Brown, P.G. (1998), 'Private Matters', 38 *The Sciences*, 2.

Brown, R.H. (1998), *Toward a Democratic Science: Scientific Narration and Civic Communication*, New Haven, Yale University Press.

Bruner, J. (1990), *Acts of Meaning*, Cambridge MA, Harvard University Press.

Brunton, R. (1995), *Blocking Business: An Anthropological Assessment of the Hindmarsh Island Dispute*, Melbourne, Tasman Institute.

Brunton, R. (1999), 'Hindmarsh Island and the Hoaxing of Australian Anthropology', 43 *Quadrant*, 11–20.

Buchanan, J.M., R.D. Tollison and G. Tullock (1980), *Toward a Theory of the Rent Seeking Society*, College Station, Texas A&M Press.

Budowle, B., R. Chakraborty, G. Carmody and K. Monson, (2000), 'Source Attribution of a Forensic DNA Profile', 2 *Forensic Science Communications*, <http://www.fbi.gov/hq/lab/fsc/backissu/july2000/source.htm>.

Burke, K. (1969), *A Rhetoric of Motives*, Berkeley, University of California Press.

Burtraw, D. (2000), 'Innovation Under the Tradable Sulfur Dioxide Emission Permits Program in the U.S. Electricity Sector' in *Resources for the Future Discussion Paper 00-38*, Washington DC, Resources for the Future.

Burtraw, D. and E. Mansur (1999), 'The Effects of Trading and Banking in the SO_2 Allowance Market' in *Resources for the Future Discussion Paper 99-25*, Washington DC, Resources for the Future.

Calabresi, G. (1970), *The costs of accidents: a legal and economic analysis*, New Haven, Yale University Press.

Calow, P. (1998), 'Standards, Science and the Politics of Chemical Risk' in R. Bal and W. Halffman eds, *The Politics of Chemical Risk*, Dordrecht, Kluwer, 251–63.

Cambrosio, A., P. Keating and M. MacKenzie (1990), 'Scientific Practice in the Courtroom: The Construction of Sociotechnical Identities in a Biotechnology Patent Dispute', 37 *Social Problems*, 272–93.

Campbell, B. (1985), 'Uncertainty as symbolic action in disputes among experts', 15 *Social Studies of Science*, 429–53.

Cardozo, B. (1921), *The Nature of the Judicial Process*, New Haven, Yale University Press.

Casper, B. and P. Wellstone (1982), 'Science court on trial in Minnesota' in B. Barnes and D. Edge eds, *Science in context: Readings in the sociology of science*, Cambridge MA, MIT Press, 282–9.

Caudill, D. (2002), 'Ethnography and the Idealized Accounts of Science in Law', 39 *San Diego Law Review*, 269–305.

Caudill, D. and R. Redding (2000), 'Junk Philosophy of Science? The Paradox of Expertise and Interdisciplinarity in Federal Courts', 57 *Washington & Lee Law Review*, 685–766.

Cecil, J. and T. Willging (1993), *Court-Appointed Experts: Defining the Role of Experts Appointed under the Federal Rule of Evidence 706*, Washington DC, Federal Judicial Center.

Chakraborty, R. and K. Kidd (1991), 'The Utility of DNA Typing in Forensic Work', 254 *Science*, 1735–9.

Champod, C. (1995), 'Edmond Locard – Numerical Standards and `Probable' Identifications', 45 *Journal of Forensic Identification*, 136–63.

Champod, C. (24-26 October 1999), 'The inference of identity of source: Theory and practice', London, First International Conference on Forensic Human identification in The Millennium.

Champod, C., C. Lennard and P. Margot (1993), 'Alphonse Bertillon and Dactyloscopy', 43 *Journal of Forensic Identification*, 604–25.

Champod, C. and I.W. Evett (2001a), 'A Probabilistic Approach to Fingerprint Evidence', 51 *Journal of Forensic Identification*, 101–22.

Champod, C. and I. Evett (2001b), 'A Probabilistic Approach to Fingerprint Evidence', 27 *Fingerprint Whorld*, 95–107.

Chan, E. (1995), 'The "Brave New World" of *Daubert*: True peer review, editorial peer review and scientific validity', 70 *New York University Law Review*, 100–134.

Chase, O. (1995), 'Helping jurors determine pain and suffering awards', 23 *Hofstra Law Review*, 763–90.

Cho, A. (2002), 'Fingerprinting Doesn't Hold Up as a Science in Court', 295 *Science*, 418.

Choo, C. and S. Holbach (1998/1999), 'The Role of the Historian in Native Title Litigation', 4 *Indigenous Law Bulletin*, 7–8.

Clarke, P. (1996), 'Response to "Secret Women's Business": The Hindmarsh Island Affair', 50/51 *Journal of Australian Studies*, 141–49.

Clinton, B. and A. Gore (1995), 'Reinventing Environmental Regulation', <http://govinfo.library.unt.edu/npr/library/rsreport/251a.html>.

Coase, R. (1960), 'The Problem of Social Cost', 3 *Journal of Law and Economics*, 1–44.

Cockayne, J. (2001), '*Members of the Yorta Yorta Aboriginal Community v. Victoria*: Indigenous and Colonial Traditions in Native Title', 25 *Melbourne University Law Review*, 786–810.

Coe, P. (1994), 'The Struggle for Aboriginal Sovereignty', 13 *Social Alternatives*, 10–13.

Cole, S. (1998), 'Witnessing Identification: Latent Fingerprint Evidence and Expert Knowledge', 28 *Social Studies of Science*, 687–712.

Cole, S. (1999), 'What Counts for Identity? The Historical Origins of the Methodology of Latent Fingerprint Identification', 12 *Science in Context*, 139–72.

Cole, S. (2001), *Suspect Identities: A History of Fingerprinting and Criminal Identification*, Cambridge MA, Harvard University Press.

Cole, S. (2004), 'Grandfathering Evidence: Fingerprint Admissibility Ruling from Jennings to *Llera Plaza* and Back Again', 41 *American Criminal Law Review*, (forthcoming).

Collins, H. (1985, 1992), *Changing Order: Replication and Induction in Scientific Practice*, Chicago, University of Chicago Press.

Collins, H. (1999), 'Tantalus and the Aliens: Publications, audiences and the search for gravitational waves', 29 *Social Studies of Science* 163-97.

Collins, H. and T. Pinch (1982), *Frames of meaning*, London, Routledge & Kegan Paul.

Collins, H. and T. Pinch (1993), *The Golem: What everyone should know about science*, Cambridge, Cambridge University Press.

Collins, H. and R. Evans (2002), 'The Third Wave of Science Studies: Studies of expertise and experience', 32 *Social Studies of Science,* 235–96.

Collins, H. and R. Evans (2003), 'King Canute meets the Beach Boys: Responses to the third wave', 33 *Social Studies of Science,* 435–52.

Connolly, T. (2003), 'Legal facts and humanist stories: The humanist as expert witness' in I. McCalman and A. McGrath eds, *Proof and Truth*, Canberra, Australian Academy of the Humanities, 135–44.

Conroy, D.W. with E. and T. Trevorrow (1997), 'Both Ways: Yolgnu and Ngarrindjeri Weaving in Australian Arts Practice' in S. Rowley ed., *Craft and Contemporary Theory*, St Leonards, Allen & Unwin, 155–70.

Contrera, J.F. (1996), 'FDA Science Symposium: Developing Alternative *in vivo* Approaches for the Assessment of Carcinogenicity: Background and Objectives', 24 *Toxicologic Pathology*, 514.

Contrera, J.F., A.C. Jacobs and J.J. DeGeorge (1997), 'Carcinogenicity Testing and the Evaluation of Regulatory Requirements for Pharmaceuticals', 25 *Regulatory Toxicology & Pharmacology,* 130–45.

Cooper Dreyfuss, R. (1995), 'Is science a special case? The admissibility of scientific evidence after *Daubert v. Merrell Dow*', 73 *Texas Law Review,* 1779–1804.

Crang, M. (1994), 'Spacing Times, Telling Times and Narrating the Past', 3 *Time & Society,* 29–45.

Cranor, C.F. and D.A. Eastmond (2001), 'Scientific Ignorance and Reliable Patterns of Evidence in Toxic Tort Causation: Is There a Need for Liability Reform?', 64 *Law & Contemporary Problems,* 5–48.

Cresswell, T. (1997), 'Imagining The Nomad: Mobility and The Postmodern Primitive' in G. Benko and U. Strohmayer eds, *Space and Social Theory: Interpreting Modernity and Postmodernity*, Oxford, Blackwells, 360–79.

Cropper, M.L. and W.E. Oates (1992), 'Environmental Economics: A Survey', 30 *Journal of Economic Literature,* 675–740.

Curr, E. (1883, 1965), *Recollections of Squatting in Victoria then called the Port Phillip District (From 1841 to 1851)*, Melbourne, Melbourne University Press.

Cutler, B. and S. Penrod (1995), *Mistaken identity: The eyewitness, psychology and the law*, Cambridge, Cambridge University Press.

Damaska, M. (1997), *Evidence law adrift*, New Haven, Yale University Press.

Dan-Cohen, M. (1984), 'Decision rules and conduct rules on acoustic separation in criminal trials', 97 *Harvard Law Review,* 625–77.

Daston, L. and P. Galison (1992), 'The image of objectivity', 40 *Representations,* 81–128.

Davies, M. (1994), *Asking The Law Question*, Sydney, Law Book Company.

Davis, J. (July 2003), 'Is This a Real Jackson Pollock?', 11 *Wired* 7.

Dawkins, R. (1998), 'Arresting Evidence: DNA Fingerprinting: Public Servant or Public Menace?', 38 *The Sciences,* 20–25.

Dear, P. (1995), *Discipline and Experience*, Chicago, University of Chicago Press.

de Certeau, M. (1984), *The Practice of Everyday Life*, Berkeley, University of California Press.

DeGeorge, J. (1996a), 'Carcinogenicity Testing: Panel Discussion' in P.F. D'Arcy and D.W.G. Harron eds, *Proceedings of the Third International Conference on Harmonisation*, Belfast, IFPMA, 295–302.

DeGeorge, J. (1996b), 'A Regulatory Perspective on the Guidance on the Utility of Two Rodent Species' in P.F. D'Arcy and D.W.G. Harron eds, *Proceedings of the Third International Conference on Harmonisation*, Belfast, IFPMA, 274–77.

DeGeorge, J. (1998), 'Carcinogenicity Testing: A New Approach' in P.F. D'Arcy and D.W.G. Harron eds, *Proceedings of the Fourth International Conference on Harmonisation*, Belfast, IFPMA, 261–63.

Deleuze, G. and F. Guattari (1986), *Nomadology: The War Machine*, New York, Semiotext(e) Columbia University.

Denbeaux, Mark and D. Michael Risinger (2003), '*Kumho Tire* and Expert Reliability: How the Question You ask Gives the Answer You Get', 34 *Seton Hall Law Review*, 15–70.

Derthick, M. and P.J. Quirk (1985), *The Politics of Deregulation*, Washington DC, The Brookings Institution.

DeSimone, L.D. and F. Popoff (1997), *Eco-Efficiency: The Business Link to Sustainable Development*, Cambridge MA, The MIT Press.

Depew, M.C. (1994), 'Challenging the Fields: The Case for Electromagnetic Field Tort Remedies Against Utilities', 56 *University of Pittsburgh Law Review*, 441–82.

De Tullio, P.L., D.M. Kirking, D.K. Zacardellie and P. Kwee (1989), 'Evaluation of Long-term Triazolam Use in an Ambulatory Veterans Administration Medical Center Population', 23 *Annals of Pharmacotherapy*, 290–94.

Deuten, J.J. and A. Rip (2000), 'Narrative Infrastructure in Product Creation Processes', 7 *Organization*, 69–93.

Dickinson, R., R. Harindranath and O. Linne eds (1998), *Approaches to Audiences: A Reader*, London, Arnold.

DiMaggio, P.J. and W.W. Powell (1983), 'The Iron Cage Revisited: Institutional Isomorphism and Collective Rationality in Organizational Fields', 48 *American Sociological Review*, 147–60.

Dixon, L. and B. Gill (2001), *Changes in the Standard for Admitting Expert Evidence in Federal Civil Cases Since the Daubert Decision*, Santa Monica, Rand Institute for Civil Justice.

Dixon, L. and B. Gill (2002), 'Changes in the Standard for Admitting Expert Evidence in Federal Civil Cases Since the *Daubert* Decision', 8 *Psychology, Public Policy & Law*, 251–308.

Dixon, O. (1965), *Jesting Pilate*, Melbourne, Law Book Company.

Dobbin, S.A., S.I. Gatowski, J.T. Richardson and G.P. Ginsburg (1999), *A Judge's Deskbook on the Basic Philosophies and Methods of Science*, Reno, University of Nevada/State Justice Institute.

Duffy, S.P. (2002), 'Experts May No Longer Testify That Fingerprints "Match"', *The Legal Intelligencer*, <http://www.law.com>.

Duhem, P. (1906, 1954), *Aim and Structure of Physical Theory*, Princeton, Princeton University Press.

Dussel, E. (1993), 'Eurocentrism and Modernity', 2 *boundary*, 65–76.

Dwyer, J., P. Neufeld and B. Scheck (2000), *Actual Innocence: Five Days to Execution and other Dispatches from the Wrongly Convicted*, New York, Doubleday.

Eckhoff, T. (1966), 'The mediator, the judge and the administrator in conflict-resolution', 10 *Acta Sociologica*, 158–66.

The Economist (4 January 1986), 'Genetic Fingerprints: Cherchez la gene', 68–9.

Edge, D. (1995), 'Reinventing the wheel' in S. Jasanoff, G. Markle, J. Petersen and T. Pinch eds, *Handbook of Science and Technology Studies,* Thousand Oaks, Sage, 3–23.

Edmond, G. (1998), 'Science in court: Negotiating the meaning of a "scientific" experiment during a murder trial and some limits to legal deconstruction for the public understanding of law and science', 20 *Sydney Law Review,* 361–401.

Edmond, G. (1999), 'Law, Science and Narrative: Helping the "facts" to speak for themselves', 23 *Southern Illinois University Law Journal,* 555–83.

Edmond, G. (2000), 'Judicial Representations of Scientific Evidence', 63 *Modern Law Review,* 216–51.

Edmond, G. (2001), 'The Law-Set: The legal-scientific production of medical propriety', 26 *Science, Technology & Human Values,* 191–226.

Edmond, G. (2002a), 'Whigs in Court: Historiographical problems with expert evidence', 14 *Yale Journal of Law & the Humanities,* 123–75.

Edmond, G. (2002b), 'Misunderstanding the Uses of Scientific Evidence in High Profile Criminal Appeals: The Social Construction of Miscarriages of Justice', 22 *Oxford Journal of Legal Studies,* 53–89.

Edmond, G. (2002c), 'Engineering Knowledge: Contested Representations of Law, Science (and non-Science) and Society', 32 *Social Studies of Science,* 371–412.

Edmond, G. (2003), 'After objectivity: Expert evidence and procedural reform', 25 *Sydney Law Review,* 131–64.

Edmond, G. (2004a), 'Thick decisions: Expertise, advocacy and reasonableness in the Federal Court of Australia', 74 *Oceania,* (forthcoming).

Edmond, G. (2004b), 'Judging Surveys: Empirical evidence, experts and social problems', (unpublished manuscript).

Edmond, G. and D. Mercer (1996), *'Manifest Destiny: Law and Science in America',* 10 *Metascience,* 361–406.

Edmond, G. and D. Mercer (1997a), 'Keeping "junk" history, philosophy and sociology of science out of the courtroom: Problems with the reception of *Daubert v Merrell Dow Pharmaceuticals Inc.',* 20 *University of New South Wales Law Journal,* 48–100.

Edmond, G. and D. Mercer (1997b), 'Scientific literacy and the jury: reconsidering jury "competence"', 6 *Public Understanding of Science,* 327–59.

Edmond, G. and D. Mercer (1998a), 'Trashing "junk" science', *Stanford Technology Law Review,* <http://stlr.stanford.edu/STLR/Core_Page/index.html>.

Edmond, G. and D. Mercer (1998b), 'Representing the sociology of scientific knowledge and law', 19 *Science Communication,* 307–27.

Edmond, G. and D. Mercer (1999), 'Juggling Science: From Polemic to Pastiche', 13 *Social Epistemology,* 215–34.

Edmond, G. and D. Mercer (2000), 'Litigation Life: Law–Science Knowledge Construction in (Bendectin) Mass Toxic Tort Litigation', 30 *Social Studies of Science,* 265–316.

Edmond, G. and D. Mercer (2002a), 'Conjectures and Exhumations: Citations of history, philosophy and sociology of science in US federal courts', 14 *Law & Literature,* 309–66.

Edmond, G. and D. Mercer (2002b), 'Rebels without *a* cause: Judges, scientific evidence and the uses of causation' in I. Freckelton and D. Mendelson eds, *Science, Medicine and Causation,* Aldershot, Ashgate, 83–121.

Edmond, G. and D. Mercer (2004), *'Daubert* and the exclusionary ethos: The convergence of *corporate* and *judicial* attitudes towards the admissibility of expert evidence in tort litigation', 26 *Law & Policy,* (forthcoming).

Eisner, M.A. (1991), *Antitrust and the Triumph of Economics: Institutions, Expertise, and Policy Change*, Chapel Hill, University of North Carolina Press.

Eisner, M.A. (2000), *Regulatory Politics in Transition* 2nd ed., Baltimore, Johns Hopkins University Press.

Eisner, M.A., J. Worsham and E.J. Ringquist (2000), *Contemporary Regulatory Policy*, Boulder CO, Lynne Rienner.

Elkin, A.P. (1944), *Aboriginal Men of High Degree*, Sydney, Australasian Publishing Co.

Elkington, J. (1998), *Cannibals with Forks: The Triple Bottom Line of 21st Century Business,* Gabriola Island BC, New Society Publishers.

Elkins, J. (1985), 'On the Emergence of Narrative Jurisprudence: The Humanistic Perspective Finds a Path', 9 *Legal Studies Forum,* 123–55.

Ellickson, R. (1986), 'Of Coase and Cattle: Dispute Resolution Among Neighbours in Shasta County', 38 *Stanford Law Review,* 623–87.

Elliot, D. and R. Elliot (1976), *The Control of Technology*, London, Wykeham Publications.

Emmerson, J.L. (1992), 'High Dose Selection in the Design of Studies to Evaluate the Carcinogenic Potential of Pharmaceuticals: Industry Perspectives' in P.F. D'Arcy and D.W.G. Harron eds, *Proceedings of the First International Conference on Harmonisation*, Belfast, IFPMA, 202–08.

Environmental Defense (2000), *From Obstacle to Opportunity: How Acid Rain Emissions Trading is Delivering Cleaner Air,* New York, Environmental Defense.

Environmental Protection Agency (1987), *EPA's Use of Benefit–Cost Analysis, 1981–1986*, EPA-230-05-87-028.

Environmental Protection Agency (2001a), *National Performance Track Program Guide*, EPA-240-F-01-002.

Environmental Protection Agency (2001b), *The United States Experience with Economic Incentives for Protecting the Environment*, EPA-204-R-01-001.

Environmental Protection Agency (11 February 2002), *Environmental News*.

Epstein, S. (1996), *Impure Science: Aids Activism and the Politics of Knowledge,* Berkeley, University of California Press.

Etzkowitz, H. and A. Webster (1995), 'Science as Intellectual Property' in S. Jasanoff, G. Markle, J. Petersen and T. Pinch eds, *Handbook of Science and Technology Studies,* Thousand Oaks, Sage, 480–505.

European Commission (2002), *Science and Society Action Plan*, Luxembourg, Office for Official Publications of the European Communities.

Evett, I.W. and R.L. Williams (1996), 'A Review of the Sixteen Points Fingerprint Standard in England and Wales', 46 *Journal of Forensic Identification,* 49–73.

Ewick, P. and S. Silbey (1995), 'Subversive Stories and Hegemonic Tales: Towards a Sociology of Narrative', 29 *Law and Society Review,* 197–226.

Ezrahi, Y. (1990), *The descent of Icarus: Science and the transformation of contemporary democracy*, Cambridge MA, Harvard University Press.

Faigman, D. (1989), 'To Have and Have Not: Assessing the Value of Social Science to the Law as Science and Policy', 38 *Emory Law Journal,* 1005–1095.

Faigman, D. (1999), *Legal Alchemy: The use and misuse of science in the law*, New York, WH Freeman and Co.

Faigman, D.L. (2002), 'Is Science Different for Lawyers?', 297 *Science,* 339–40.

Faigman, D.L., D.H. Kaye, M.J. Saks and J. Sanders (2000), 'How Good is Good Enough? Expert Evidence under *Daubert* and *Kumho*', 50 *Case Western Reserve Law Review,* 645–67.

Farber, D. (1997), *Beyond all reason: The radical assault on truth in American law*, New York, Oxford University Press.

Farrell, M. (1994), '*Daubert v. Merrell Dow Pharmaceuticals, Inc.*: Epistemiology and legal process', 15 *Cardozo Law Review*, 2183–217.

Faulds, H. (1905), *Guide to Finger-Print Identification*, Hanley, Wood Mitchell.

Feeley, M. and E. Rubin (1999), *Judicial Policy Making and the Modern State: How the courts reformed America's prisons*, Cambridge, Cambridge University Press.

Fergie, D. (1996), 'Secret Envelopes and Inferential Tautologies', 48 *Journal of Australian Studies*, 13–39.

Finley, L. (1999), 'Guarding the gate to the courthouse: How trial judges are using their evidentiary screening role to remake tort causation rules', 49 *DePaul Law Review*, 335–76.

Finnegan, R. (1998), *Tales of the City: A Study of Narrative and Urban Life*, Cambridge, Cambridge University Press.

Fiorino, D.J. (1996), 'Toward a New System of Environmental Regulation: The case for an Industry Sector Approach', 26 *Environmental Law*, 457–88.

Fish, S. (1989), *Doing what comes naturally: Change, rhetoric and the practice of theory in literary and legal studies*, Oxford, Clarendon Press.

Fiske, J. (1987), *Television Culture*, London, Metheun.

Fist, S. (2004), 'Michael Repacholi—Resume', <http:/www.electric-words.com/cell/industry/repacholi/reppapers.html>.

Ford, S. and W.C. Thompson (1990), 'A question of identity: Some reasonable doubts about DNA "fingerprints"', 30 *The Sciences* 36–43.

Forrester, J. (1996), 'If *p*, then what? Thinking in Cases', 9 *History of the Human Sciences*, 1–25.

Foster, K. (2004), 'Kenneth R. Foster' (home page), <http://www.seas.upenn.edu/~kfoster/kfoster.htm>.

Foster, K., D. Bernstein and P. Huber eds (1993), *Phantom Risk: Scientific inference and the law*, Cambridge MA, MIT Press.

Foster, K. and P. Huber (1998), *Judging science: Scientific knowledge and the federal courts*, Cambridge MA, MIT Press.

Foster, K., M. Repacholi and P. Veccia (2000), 'Science and the Precautionary Principle', 288 *Science*, 979–81.

Foster, K. and P. Veccia eds (2002/2003), 'Special Issue on the Precautionary Principle', 22 *IEEE Technology and Society*.

Frank, J. (1949), *Courts on trial: Myth and reality in American justice*, Princeton, Princeton University Press.

Frankel, C. (1998), *In Earth's Company: Business, Environment and the Challenge of Sustainability*, Gabriola Island BC, New Society Publishers.

Frankel, M. (1975), 'The search for truth: An umpireal view', 123 *University of Pennsylvania Law Review*, 1031–1082.

Franzosi, R. (1998), 'Narrative Analysis—Or Why (and How) Sociologists Should be Interested in Narrative', 24 *Annual Review of Sociology*, 517–55.

Freckelton, I. (1994), 'Contemporary comment: When plight makes right—The forensic abuse syndrome', 18 *Criminal Law Journal*, 29–49.

Freckelton, I., P. Reddy and H. Selby (1999), *Australian judicial perspectives on expert evidence: An empirical study*, Melbourne, Australian Institute of Judicial Administration.

Freeman III, A.M. (2003), 'Economics, Incentives, and Environmental Policy' in N. Vig and M. Kraft eds, *Environmental Policy* 5th ed., Washington DC, CQ Press, 201–23.

Freeman, M. and H. Reece eds (1998), *Science in Court*, Aldershot, Dartmouth.

Frost, A. (1981), 'New South Wales as *Terra Nullius*: The British Denial of Aboriginal Land Rights', 19 *Historical Studies*, 513–23.

Fuchs, S. and S. Ward (1994), 'What is Deconstruction, and Where and When Does It Take Place? Making Facts in Science, Building Cases in Law', 59 *American Sociological Review*, 481–500.

Fuller, L. (1964), *The Morality of Law*, New Haven, Yale University Press.

Fuller, S. (2003), *Popper vs Kuhn: The struggle for the soul of science*, Duxford, Icon Books.

Funtowicz, S. and J. Ravetz (1993), 'Science for the post-normal age', 25 *Futures*, 735–55.

Fussler, C. (1996), *Driving Eco Innovation: A Breakthrough Discipline for Innovation and Sustainability*, London, Pitman Publishing.

Galanter, M. (1974), 'Why the "haves" come out ahead: Speculations on the limits of legal change', 9 *Law & Society Review*, 95–160.

Galanter, M. (1983), 'The radiating effects of courts' in K. Boyum and L. Mather eds, *Empirical Theories about Courts*, New York, Longman, 117–42.

Galanter, M. (1998), 'An oil strike in Hell: Contemporary legends about the civil justice system', 40 *Arizona Law Review*, 717–52

Galanter, M. (2002), 'The turn against law: The recoil against expanding accountability', 81 *Texas Law Review*, 285–304.

Galbraith, J.K. (1967), *The New Industrial State*, London, Hamish Hamilton.

Galison, P. and D. Stump eds (1996), *The Disunity of Science: Boundaries, Contexts and Power*, Stanford, Stanford University Press.

Galton, F. (1893), 'Decipherment of Blurred Finger Prints' in *Finger Prints*, London, Macmillan.

Garber, S. (1998), 'Product liability, punitive damages, business decisions and economic outcomes', *Wisconsin Law Review*, 237–95.

Garfinkel, H. (1967), *Studies in Ethnomethodology*, Englewood Cliffs, Prentice Hall.

Gatowski, S., S.A. Dobbin, J.T. Richardson, G.P. Ginsburg, M.L. Merlino and V. Dahir (2001), 'A National Survey of Judges on Judging Expert Evidence in a Post–Daubert World', 25 *Law & Human Behavior*, 433–58.

Gelder, K. and J. Jacobs (1998), *Uncanny Australia: Sacredness and Identity in a Postcolonial Nation*, Melbourne, Melbourne University Press.

Gerjuoy, E. (1994), 'Electromagnetic Fields: Physics, Biology and Law', 35 *Jurimetrics*, 55–75.

Gianelli, P. (1980), 'The admissibility of novel scientific evidence: *Frye v United States*, a half century later', 80 *Columbia Law Review*, 1197–250.

Gieryn, T. (1998), *Cultural boundaries of science: Credibility on the line*, Chicago, University of Chicago Press.

Gieryn, T., G. Bevins and S. Zehr (1985), 'Professionalization of American Scientists: Public Science in the Creation/Evolution Trials', 50 *American Sociological Review*, 392–409.

Gilbert, N. and M. Mulkay (1984), *Opening Pandora's Box: A Sociological Analysis of Scientists' Discourse*, Cambridge, Cambridge University Press.

Gillespie, B., D. Eva and R. Johnston (1979), 'Carcinogenic risk assessment in the USA and UK: The case of Aldrin/Dieldrin', 9 *Social Studies of Science*, 265–301.

Ginzburg, C. (1983), 'Morelli, Freud and Sherlock Holmes: Clues and Scientific Method' in U. Eco and T.A. Sebeok eds, *The Sign of Three: Dupin, Holmes, Peirce*, Bloomington, Indiana University Press, 81–118.

Glass, A. (2003), 'Making the facts speak' in I. McCalman and A. McGrath eds, *Proof and Truth*, Canberra, Australian Academy of the Humanities, 123–34.

GM Nation? (2003), *The findings of the public debate*, <http://www.gmpublicdebate.org.uk>.

Goffman, E. (1959), *The presentation of self in everyday life*, New York, Anchor Books.

Golan, T. (2004), *Laws of men and laws of nature: The history of scientific expert testimony in England and America*, Cambridge MA, Harvard University Press.

Golan, T. and S. Gissis eds (1999), 'Science and Law', 12 *Science in Context,* 3–243

Goldberg, S. (1994), *Culture Clash: Law and Science in America*, New York, New York University Press.

Gooding, D., T. Pinch and S. Schaffer eds (1989), *The uses of experiment*, Cambridge, Cambridge University Press.

Goodnow, F.J (1900), *Politics and Administration*, New York, Macmillan.

Goodrich, P. (1990), *Languages of Law: From Logics of Memory to Nomadic Masks*, London, Weidenfeld and Nicolson.

Goodwin, C. (1994), 'Professional vision', 96 *American Anthropology,* 606–33.

Graham, D.J. (8 May 1992), 'Halcion comparison with temazepam', Internal FDA memo.

Graham, M.H. (2000), 'The Expert Witness Predicament: Determining "Reliable" Under the Gatekeeping Test of *Daubert, Kumho,* and Proposed Amended Rule 702 of the Federal Rules of Evidence', 54 *University of Miami Law Review,* 317–57.

Graham-Rowe, D. (2003), 'Special Report: Mobile Phone Safety', 179 *New Scientist,* 12–13.

Grasso, L. (1998), 'Cellular Telephones and the Potential hazards of Rf Radiation: Responses to the Fear and Controversy', 3 *Virginia Journal of Law and Technology,* <http://vjolt.student.virginia.edu>.

Green, M. (1992), 'Expert witnesses and sufficiency of evidence in toxic substances litigation: The legacy of Agent Orange and Bendectin litigation', 86 *Northwestern University Law Journal,* 643–99.

Green, M. (1996), *Bendectin and Birth Defects: The Challenges of Mass Toxic Substances Litigation,* Philadelphia, University of Pennsylvania Press.

Greenpeace (n.d.), *GM on Trial*, London, Greenpeace.

Gregory, J. and S. Miller (1998), *Science in Public: Communication, culture and credibility*, London, Plenum Trade.

Gribben, A.A. (1919), 'How the Finger Print Expert Presents His Case in Court', 12 *Finger Print and Identification Magazine,* 10–14.

Gross, P. and N. Levitt (1997), *Higher superstition: The academic left and its quarrels with science,* Baltimore, Johns Hopkins University Press.

Grove-White, R., P. Macnaghten, S. Mayer and B. Wynne (1997), *Uncertain World: Genetically modified organisms, food and public attitudes in Britain,* Lancaster, Lancaster University.

Gunningham, N. and D. Sinclair (1999), 'Regulatory Pluralism: Designing Policy Mixes for Environmental Protection', 21 *Law & Policy,* 49–76.

Gusfield, J. (1981), *The culture of public problems: drinking–driving and the symbolic order*, Chicago, University of Chicago Press.

Guss, D. (1989), *To Weave and Sing: Art, Symbol and Narrative in the South American Rain Forest*, Berkeley, University of California Press.

Haack, S. (2001), 'An Epistemologist in the Bramble-Bush: At the Supreme Court with Mr. Joiner', 26 *Journal of Health Politics, Policy & Law,* 217–48.

Habermas, J. (1971), *Toward a rational society* (trans. J. Shapiro), London, Heinemann.

Hacking, I. (1992), 'Multiple Personality Disorder and Its Hosts', 5 *History of the Human Sciences,* 3–31.

Haflon, S. (1998), 'Collecting, testing and convincing: DNA experts in the courts', 28 *Social Studies of Science,* 801–28.

Halfmann, J. (1998), 'Citizenship, Universalism, Migration and the Risks of Exclusion', 49 *British Journal of Sociology,* 313–33.

Hand, L. (1901), 'Historical and practical considerations regarding expert testimony', 15 *Harvard Law Review*, 40–58.

Haraway, D. (1989), *Primate Visions: Gender, Race and Nature in the World of Modern Science*, New York, Routledge.

Harris, R.A. and S.M. Milkis (1996), *The Politics of Regulatory Change: A Tale of Two Agencies* 2nd ed., New York, Oxford University.

Hart, H. and T. Honoré (1987), *Causation in the law*, Oxford, Clarendon Press.

Haslem, B. and A. Dodd (23 May 2002), 'History Weighs Against Yorta Yorta Claim', *The Australian* 4.

Hayashi, Y. (1994), 'Utility of Two Rodent Species: Current Regulatory Perspectives' in P.F. D'Arcy and D.W.G. Harron eds, *Proceedings of the Second International Conference on Harmonisation*, Belfast, IFPMA, 291–3.

Hazard, G.C. and W.W. Hodes (1990), *The law of lawyering: A handbook on the model rules of professional conduct* 2nd ed., Englewood Cliffs, Prentice Hall Law & Business.

Heerey, P. (January/February 2002), 'Expert Evidence: The Australian Experience', *Bar Review*, 166–70.

Heidegger, M. (1967), *Being and Time*, Oxford, Basil Blackwell.

Hemming, S. (1997), 'Not the Slightest Shred of Evidence: A Reply to Philip Clarke's "Response to Secret Women's Business"', 53 *Journal of Australian Studies*, 130–46.

Hensler, D. (1989), 'Resolving mass toxic torts: Myths and realities', *University of Illinois Law Review*, 89–104.

Hensler, D. (1998), 'The real world of tort litigation' in A. Sarat, M. Constable, D. Engel, V. Hans and S. Lawrence eds, *Everyday practices and trouble cases*, Evanston ILL, Northwestern University Press, 155–76.

Hilgartner, S. (1990), 'The Dominant View of Popularization: Conceptual Problems, Political Uses', 20 *Social Studies of Science*, 519–39.

Hilgartner, S. (2000), *Science on Stage: Expert advice as public drama*, Stanford, Stanford University Press.

Hinchman, L. and S. Hinchman eds (1997), *Memory, Identity, Community: The Idea of Narrative in the Human Sciences*, Albany, State University of New York Press.

Hobsbawm, E. and T. Ranger eds (1983), *The invention of tradition*, New York, Cambridge University Press.

Holloway, J. and J. Kneale (2000), 'Mikhail Bakhtin: Dialogics of Space' in M. Crang, and N. Thrift eds, *Thinking Space*, London, Routledge, 71–88.

Hooper, L., J. Cecil and T. Willging (2001), 'Assessing causation in breast implant litigation: The role of science panels', 64 *Law & Contemporary Problems*, 139–89.

Horgan, J. (1998), *The End of Science: Facing the Limits of Knowledge in the Twilight of the Scientific Age*, London, Abacus.

House of Commons, Environment, Food and Rural Affairs Committee (November 2003), *Conduct of the GM Public Debate*, Session 2002–03, 18th Report, London, The Stationery Office.

House of Lords, Select Committee on Science and Technology (February 2000), *Science and Society*, Session 1999–2000, 3rd Report, London, The Stationery Office.

Howard, J. and J. Hollander (1993), 'Marking Time', 63 *Sociological Inquiry*, 425–43.

Huber, P. (1991), *Galileo's Revenge: Junk science in the courtroom*, New York, Basic Books.

Huber, P. (1999), *Hard Green: Saving the Environment from the Environmentalists: A Conservative Manifesto*, Basic Books, New York.

Hume, D. (1999), *An Enquiry Concerning Human Understanding*, Oxford, Oxford University Press.

Hyde, A. (1983), 'The concept of legitimation in the sociology of law', *Wisconsin Law Review*, 379–426.

ICH EWG on Safety (1996), 'Carcinogenicity Studies: Background to the Discussions' in P.F. D'Arcy and D.W.G. Harron eds, *Proceedings of the Third International Conference on Harmonisation*, Belfast: IFPMA, 257–60.

Illich, I. (1973), *Tools for Conviviality*, London, Calder and Boyers.

Imwinkelried, E. (1994), 'The Next Step After *Daubert*: Developing a Similarly Epistemological Approach to Ensuring the Reliability of Nonscientific Expert Testimony', 15 *Cardozo Law Review*, 2271–94.

Imwinkelried, E.J. (1999), 'Should the courts incorporate a best evidence rule into the standard determining the admissibility of scientific testimony? Enough is enough when it is not the best', 50 *Case Western Reserve Law Review*, 19–51.

Ingold, T. (2000), *The Perception of the Environment: Essays in Livelihood, Dwelling and Skill*, London, Routledge.

Inman, K. and N. Rudin (2001), *Principles and Practice of Criminalistics: The Profession of Forensic Science*, Boca Raton FL, CRC Press.

Institute of Medicine (Iom) (1997), *Halcion: an independent assessment of safety and efficacy data*, Washington DC, National Academy Press.

International Organization for Standardization (2003), *The ISO Survey of ISO 9000 and ISO 14000 Certificates, Twelfth Cycle*, Geneva, International Organization for Standardization.

Irwin, A. (1995), *Citizen Science*, London, Routledge.

Irwin, A. (2001), *Sociology and the Environment*, Cambridge, Polity.

Irwin, A. and B. Wynne eds (1996), *Misunderstanding Science: The Public Reconstruction of Science and Technology*, Cambridge, Cambridge University Press.

Irwin, A., P. Simmons and G. Walker (1999), 'Faulty environments and risk reasoning: the local understanding of industrial hazards', 31 *Environment and Planning A*, 1311–26.

Irwin, A. and M. Michael (2003), *Science, Social Theory and Public Knowledge*, Maidenhead, Open University Press.

Isaacs, N. (1922), 'The Law and the Facts', 22 *Columbia Law Review*, 1–13.

Jackson, B. (1991), *Law, Fact and Narrative Coherence*, Liverpool, Deborah Charles Publications.

Jacobs, J. (1996), *Edge of Empire: Postcolonialism and the City*, London, Routledge.

Jasanoff, S. (1990), *The fifth branch: Science advisers as policy-makers*, Cambridge MA, Harvard University Press.

Jasanoff, S. (1992), 'What Judges Should Know About the Sociology of Science', 32 *Jurimetrics Journal*, 345–59.

Jasanoff, S. (1995), *Science at the Bar: Law, Science and Technology in America*, Cambridge MA, Harvard University Press.

Jasanoff, S. (1996a), 'Beyond Epistemology: Relativism and Engagement in the Politics of Science', 26 *Social Studies of Science*, 393–418.

Jasanoff, S. (1996b), 'Research Subpoenas and the sociology of knowledge', 59 *Law & Contemporary Problems*, 95–118.

Jasanoff, S. (1998a), 'Expert Games in Silicone Breast Implant Litigation' in M. Freeman and H. Reece eds, *Science in Court*, Aldershot, Ashgate/Dartmouth, 83–108.

Jasanoff, S. (1998b), 'The eye of everyman: Witnessing DNA in the Simpson Trial', 28 *Social Studies of Science*, 713–40.

Jasanoff, S. (1999), 'Knowledge elites and class war', 401 *Nature*, 531.

Jasanoff, S. (2001), 'Hidden Experts: Judging Science After *Daubert*' in V. Weil ed., *Trying times: Science and responsibilities after Daubert*, Chicago: Illinois Institute of Technology), 30–47.

Jasanoff, S. (2002), 'Science and the Statistical Victim: Modernizing Knowledge in Breast Implant Litigation', 32 *Social Studies of Science,* 37–69.

Jasanoff, S. (2003), 'Breaking the waves in science studies', 33 *Social Studies of Science,* 389–400.

Jeffreys, A.J., V. Wilson and S.L. Thein (1985), 'Individual-Specific "Fingerprints" of Human DNA', 316 *Nature,* 76–8.

Jofre, S. (9 July 2001), 'Falsely Fingered', *The Guardian.*

Johnston, P.L. (1987), 'Court-appointed Scientific Expert Witnesses: Unfettering Expertise', 2 *Berkeley High Technology Law Journal,* 249–80.

Jones, C. (1994), *Expert witnesses: science, medicine and the practice of law,* Oxford, Clarendon Press.

Jordan, K. and M. Lynch (1992), 'The Sociology of a Genetic Engineering Technique: Ritual and Rationality in the Performance of the Plasmid Prep' in A. Clarke and J. Fujimura eds, *The Right Tools For the Job: At Work in Twentieth-Century Life Science,* Princeton, Princeton University Press, 77–114.

Jordan, K. and M. Lynch (1993), 'The Mainstreaming of a Molecular Biological Tool: A Case Study of a New Technique' in G. Button ed., *Technology in Working Order: Studies in Work, Interaction and Technology,* London and New York, Routledge, 160–80.

Jordan, K. and M. Lynch (1998), 'The Dissemination, Standardization, and Routinization of a Molecular Biological Technique', 28 *Social Studies of Science,* 773–800.

Joseph, A. (2001), 'Anthropometry, the Police Expert, and the Deptford Murders: The Contested Introduction of Fingerprinting for the Identification of Criminals in Late Victorian and Edwardian Britain' in J. Torpey and J. Caplan eds, *Documenting Individual Identity: The Development of State Practices since the French Revolution,* Princeton, Princeton University Press.

Joyce, R. (2002), *The Languages of Archaeology: Dialogue, Narrative and Writing,* Oxford, Blackwell Publishing.

Kagan, R.A. and L. Axelrad eds (1982), *Regulatory Encounters: Multinational Corporations and American Adversarial Legalism,* Berkeley, University of California Press.

Kairys, D., ed. (1982), *The politics of law: A progressive critique,* New York, Pantheon.

Kalven, Harry and Hans Zeisel (1966), *The American jury,* Boston, Little, Brown and Company.

Keen, I. (1995), 'Metaphor and the Meta-Language: "Groups" in Northeast Arnhemland', 22 *American Ethnologist,* 502–27.

Kennedy, D. (1986), 'Freedom and constraint in adjudication: A critical phenomenology', 36 *Journal of Legal Education,* 518–62.

Kerby, A. (1991), *Narrative and the Self,* Bloomington, Indiana University Press.

Kerruish, V. and J. Purdy (1998), 'He "Look" Honest—Big White Thief', 4 *Law/Text/Culture,* 146–71.

Khana, R. and S. McVicker (10 March 2003), 'New DNA Test Casts Doubt on Man's 1999 Rape Conviction' *Houston Chronicle,* <http://www.truthinjustice.org/sutton.htm>.

King, M. (2002), 'An autopoietic approach to "Parental Alienation Syndrome"', 13 *Journal of Forensic Psychiatry,* 609–35.

King, M. and F. Kaganas (1998), 'The Risk and Dangers of Experts in Court' in H. Reece ed., *Law and Science: Current Legal Issues,* Oxford, Oxford University Press, 221–42.

King, R. (1990), *The Secret History of the Convict Colony: Alexandro Malaspina's Report on the British Settlement of New South Wales,* Sydney, Allen & Unwin.

Klassen, R.D. and D. Clay Whybark (1999), 'The Impact of Environmental Technologies on Manufacturing Performance', 42 *Academy of Management Journal,* 599–615.

Kolko, G. (1963), *The Triumph of Conservatism: A Reinterpretation of American History, 1900–1916*, New York, Free Press.

Kolko, G. (1965), *Railroads and Regulation, 1877–1916*, Princeton, Princeton University Press.

Krafka, C., M.A. Dunn, M. Treadway Johnson, J.S. Cecil, and D. Miletich (2002), 'Judge and attorney experiences, practices and concerns regarding expert testimony in federal civil trials', 8 *Psychology, Public Policy & Law*, 309–32.

Kroll-Smith, S. and P. Jenkins (1996), 'Old Stories, New Audiences: Sociological knowledge in courts' in P. Jenkins and S. Kroll-Smith eds, *Witnessing for sociology: Sociologists in court*, Westport, Praeger, 1–15.

Kuehls, T. (1996), *Beyond Sovereign Territory: The Space of Ecopolitics*, Minneapolis, University of Minnesota Press.

Kuhn, T. (1962), *The Structure of Scientific Revolutions*, Chicago, University of Chicago Press, Chicago.

Kuhn, T. (1977), *The Essential Tension*, Chicago, University of Chicago Press.

Kuhne, F. (1917), *The Finger Print Instructor*, New York, Munn.

Lakatos I. and A. Musgrave (1974), *Criticism and the Growth of Knowledge*, Cambridge, Cambridge University Press.

Lamarque, P. (1990), 'Narrative and Invention: The Limits of Fictionality' in C. Nash ed., *Narrative in Culture: The Uses of Storytelling in the Sciences, Philosophy and Literature*, London, Routledge, 131–53.

Lander, E. (1989), 'DNA Fingerprinting on Trial', 339 *Nature*, 501–05.

Lander, E. (1992), 'DNA fingerprinting: Science, law, and the ultimate identifier' in D.J. Kevles and L. Hood eds, *The Code of Codes: Scientific and Social Issues in the Human Genome Project*, Cambridge MA, Harvard University Press, 191-210.

Lander, E. and B. Budowle (1994), 'DNA Fingerprint Dispute Laid to Rest', 371 *Nature*, 735–8.

Landy, M. and L. Cass (1997), 'U.S. Environmental Regulation in a Competitive World' in P. Nivola ed., *Comparative Disadvantages: Social Regulation and the Global Economy*, Washington DC, The Brookings Institution, 203–31.

Langbein, (1977), *Torture and the law of proof: Europe and England in the Ancien Regime*, Chicago, University of Chicago Press.

Langbein, J. (1985), 'The German advantage in civil procedure', 52 *University of Chicago Law Review*, 823–66.

Langbein, J. (2003), *The origins of adversary criminal trial*, Oxford University Press.

LaRue, L. and D. Caudill (2001), 'Post-*Trilogy* Science in the Courtroom: What are the Judges Doing?', 13 *Journal of Civil Litigation*, 341–57.

Latour, B. (1983a), *The Pasteurization of France*, Cambridge MA, Harvard University Press.

Latour, B. (1983b), 'Give me a laboratory and I will raise the world' in K. Knorr-Cetina and M. Mulkay eds, *Science Observed*, Beverly Hills, Sage, 140–70.

Latour, B. (1987), *Science in Action*, Cambridge MA, Harvard University Press.

Latour, B. (1995), 'The 'Pédofil' of Boa Vista: A Photo-Philosophical Montage', 4 *Common Knowledge*, 144–87.

Latour, B. and S. Woolgar (1979), *Laboratory Life: The social construction of scientific facts*, Beverly Hills, Sage.

Laudan, L. (1982), 'Commentary: Science at the Bar—Causes for Concern', 7 *Science Technology and Human Values*, 16–19.

Laudan, L. (1988a), 'The demise of the demarcation problem' in M. Ruse ed., *But is it science? The philosophical question in the creation/evolution controversy*, Buffalo, Prometheus Books, 337–50.

Laudan, L. (1988b), 'More on creationism' in M. Ruse ed., *But is it science? The philosophical question in the creation/evolution controversy*, Buffalo, Prometheus Books, 363–66.

Laufer, W. (1995), 'The rhetoric of innocence', 70 *Washington Law Review,* 329–421.

Law, J. (1987), 'Technology and Heterogenous Engineering: The case of Portuguese expansion' in W. Bijker, T. Hughes and T. Pinch eds, *The Social Construction of Technological Systems: New Directions in the Sociology and History of Technology*, Cambridge MA, MIT Press, 111–34.

Law, J. (1999), 'After ANT: Complexity, Naming and Topology' in J. Law and J. Hassard eds, *Actor Network Theory and After*, Oxford, Blackwell, 1–14.

Lawson, H. (2001), *Closure: A Story of Everything*, London, Routledge.

Lawton Smith, H., ed. (2002), *The regulation of science and technology*, Basingstoke, Palgrave Macmillan.

Layzer, J.A. (2002), *The Environmental Case: Translating Values into Policy*, Washington DC, CQ Press.

Leiter, B. (1997), 'The epistemology of admissibility: Why even good philosophy of science would not make for good philosophy of evidence', *Brigham Young University Law Review*, 803–19.

Lenoir, T. (1997), *Instituting Science: The cultural production of scientific disciplines*, Stanford, Stanford University Press.

Levi Strauss, C. (1966), *The Savage Mind*, Chicago, Chicago University Press.

Levitt, N. (1999), *Prometheus Bedevilled: Science and the contradictions of contemporary culture,* New Brunswick, Rutgers University Press.

Lewis, E.L. (Summer 1999), *Science in the Courtroom Review: To advocate the proper use of scientific, technical and other expert testimony in the courts*, New York, Atlantic Legal Foundation.

Lewontin, R.C. and D.L. Hartl (1991), 'Population Genetics in Forensic DNA Typing', 254 *Science*, 1745–50.

Lindblom, C. (1959), 'The science of muddling through', 19 *Public Administration Review,* 79–88.

Litan, R., ed. (1993), *Verdict Assessing the Civil Jury System*, Washington DC, The Brookings Institution.

Loftus, E. (1979), *Eyewitness Testimony*, Cambridge MA, Harvard University Press.

London Centre for Governance, Innovation and Science (LCGIS) and The Genetics Forum (March 1998), *Citizen Foresight: a tool to enhance democratic policy-making 1: The future of food and agriculture*, London, The Genetics Forum.

Losee, J. (2001), *A Historical Introduction to the Philosophy of Science* 4th ed., Oxford, Oxford University Press.

Lowi, T.J. (1969), *The End of Liberalism: Ideology, Policy, and the Crisis of Public Authority*, New York, W.W. Norton.

Lubet, S. (1998), *Expert Testimony: A Guide for Expert Witnesses and the Lawyers Who Examine Them*, South Bend, National Institute for Trial Advocacy.

Lubet, S. (1999), 'Expert Witnesses: Ethics and Professionalism', 12 *Georgetown Journal of Legal Ethics,* 465–88.

Lynch, M. (1998), 'The Discursive Production of Uncertainty: The OJ Simpson "Dream Team" and the Sociology of Knowledge Machine', 28 *Social Studies of Science,* 829–68.

Lynch, M. and D. Bogen (1996), *The spectacle of history: Speech, text and memory at the Iran-Contra hearings,* Durham NC, Duke University Press.

Lynch M. and S. Jasanoff (1998), 'Contested Identities: Science, law and forensic practice', 28 *Social Studies of Science,* 675–86,

Lynch, M. and R. McNally (1999a), 'Science, Common Sense, and Common Law: Courtroom Inquiries, and the Public Understanding of Science', 13 *Social Epistemology*, 183–96.

Lynch, M. and R. McNally (1999b), 'Aprisionando um monstro: a producao de representacoes num campo impuro' [Enchaining a Monster: The Production of Representations in an Impure Field] in F. Gil ed., *a Ciencia tal qua se faz*, Lisbon, Portugal, Ministry of Science & Technology/Edicoes Joao Sa da Costa, Lda, 159–86.

Lynch, M. and R. McNally (2003), '"Science", "Common Sense", and DNA Evidence: A Legal Controversy about the Public Understanding of Science', 12 *Public Understanding of Science*, 83–105.

Lynch, M. and S. Cole (2004), 'STS on Trial: Dilemmas of Expertise', 34 *Social Studies of Science*, (forthcoming).

Macaulay, S. (1963), 'Non-contractual relations in Business: A preliminary study', 28 *American Sociological Review*, 55–69.

MacIntyre, A. (1977), 'Epistemological Crises, Dramatic Narrative and the Philosophy of Science', 60 *Monist*, 453–72.

MacIntyre, A. (1981), *After Virtue: A Study in Moral Theory*, Notre Dame, University of Notre Dame Press.

Maclean, M. (1988), *Narrative as Performance: the Baudelairean Experiment*, London, Routledge.

McGarity, T.O. (1991), *Reinventing Rationality: The Role of Regulatory Analysis in the Federal Bureaucracy*, Cambridge, Cambridge University Press.

McIntyre, S. and A. Clark (2003), *The History Wars*, Melbourne, Melbourne University Press.

McLeod, N. (1991), 'English DNA Evidence Held Inadmissible', *The Criminal Law Review*, 583–90.

McNeil, L. (1996), 'Homo Inventans: The Evolution of Narrativity', 16 *Language and Communication*, 331–60.

Magee, B. (1974), *Popper*, London, Woburn Press.

Mairs, G.T. (1945), 'Can two identical ridge patterns actually occur—either on different persons or on the same person', 27 *Finger Print Magazine*. (Reprinted in (1994) 10 *The Print* 3–7)

Mann, M. (1987), 'Ruling Class Strategies and Citizenship', 21 *Sociology*, 339–54.

Manne, R., ed. (2003), *Whitewash: On Keith Windschuttle's Fabrication of Aboriginal History*, Melbourne, Black Ink Agenda.

March, J.G. and J.P. Olsen (1989), *Rediscovering Institutions: The Organizational Basis of Politics*, New York, The Free Press.

Marshack, A. (1972), *The Roots of Civilization: The Cognitive Beginnings of Man's First Art, Symbol and Notation*, New York, McGraw Hill.

Marshall, T.H. (1981), *The right to welfare and other essays*, London, Heinemann.

Martin, J. (1977), 'The proposed "science court"', 75 *Michigan Law Review*, 1058–91.

Marx, J.L. (1988), 'DNA fingerprinting takes the witness stand', 240 *Science*, 1616–18.

Mattingly, C. (1998), 'Time, Narrative and Cultural Action', 100 *American Anthropologist*, 184–6.

Maugh, T.H. (1978), 'Chemical Carcinogens: The Scientific Basis for Regulation', 201 *Science*, 1200–05.

Mayer, S. and G. Clegg (1998), 'The Risk Assessment/Risk Management Boundary: Myth making and its Implications in the UK' in R. Bal and W. Halffman eds, *The Politics of Chemical Risk*, Dordrecht, Kluwer, 13–26.

Mazur, A. (1981), *The Dynamics of Technical Controversy*, Washington DC, Communications Press.

Melnick, R.S. (1983), *Regulation and the Courts: The Case of the Clean Air Act*, Washington DC, The Brookings Institution.

Mercer, D. (2001), 'Overcoming Regulatory Fear of Public Perceptions of Mobile Phone Health Risks', 18 *Radiation Protection in Australasia*, 84–94.

Mercer, D. (2002), 'Scientific Method Discourses in the Construction of EMF Science', 32 *Social Studies of Science*, 205–33.

Merleau-Ponty, M. (1962), *Phenomenology of Perception*, London, Routledge & Kegan Paul.

Merryman, J.H. (1954), 'The Authority of Authority: What the California Supreme Court Cited in 1950', 6 *Stanford Law Review*, 613–73.

Michael, M. (1992), 'Lay Discourses of science: Science-in-general, science-in-particular, and self', 17 *Science, Technology and Human Values*, 313–33.

Michael, M. (1998), 'Between citizen and consumer: multiplying the meanings of the "public understanding of science"', 7 *Public Understanding of Science*, 313–27.

Miller, C. (2004), 'Novelty and heresy in the debate on non-thermal effects of electromagnetic fields', *Rhetoric and Incommensurability*, <www.incommensurability.com>.

Miller III, J.C. (1977), 'Lessons of the Economic Impact Statement Program', 1 *Regulation*, 16–18.

Mirowski, P. and E. Sent eds (2002), *Science Bought and Sold: Essays in the Economics of Science*, Chicago, Chicago University Press.

Mitchell, W.J.T., ed. (1980), *On Narrative*, Chicago, University of Chicago Press.

Mitroff, I. (1974), 'Norms and Counter-norms in a select group of the Apollo Moon Scientists: A Case Study in the Ambivalence of Scientists', 39 *American Sociological Review*, 579–95.

Mitsumori, K. (1998), 'Evaluation of New Models: Initiation and Promotion Models and the Hras2 Mouse Model' in P.F. D'Arcy and D.W.G. Harron eds, *Proceedings of the Fourth International Conference on Harmonisation*, Belfast, IFPMA, 263–72.

Mnookin, J. (1998), 'The image of truth: Photographic evidence and the power of analogy', 10 *Yale Journal of Law & the Humanities*, 1–74.

Mnookin, J. (2001), 'Fingerprint Evidence in an Age of DNA Profiling', 67 *Brooklyn Law Review*, 13–70.

Mody, S. (2002), '*Brown* footnote eleven in historical context: Social science and the supreme court's quest for legitimacy', 54 *Stanford Law Review*, 793–829.

Moe, T.M. (1989), 'The Politics of Bureaucratic Structure' in J. Chubb and P. Peterson eds, *Can the Government Govern?*, Washington DC, The Brookings Institution, 267–329.

Moe, T.M. (1997), 'The Positive Theory of Public Bureaucracy' in D. Mueller ed., *Perspectives on Public Choice: A Handbook*, Cambridge, Cambridge University Press, 455–80.

Molot, J. (1998), 'How changes in the legal profession reflect changes in civil procedure', 84 *Virginia Law Review*, 955–1051.

Monahan, J. and L. Walker (1985), *Social Science in Law: Cases and Materials*, New York, The Foundation Press.

Monahan, J. and L. Walker (1986), 'Social Authority: Obtaining, Evaluating, and establishing social science in law', 134 *University of Pennsylvania Law Review*, 477–517.

Mone L. (2002), 'Philanthropy Roundtable Forum: How Think Tanks Achieve Public Policy Breakthrough', <http://www.manhattan-institute.org/html/lm_pr_address.htm>

Monro, A. (1996), 'Testing for Carcinogenic Potential: Rapporteur's Report' in P.F. D'Arcy and D.W.G. Harron eds, *Proceedings of the Third International Conference on Harmonisation*, Belfast, IFPMA, 266–68.

MORI (1999), *The Public Consultation on Developments in the Biosciences: December 1998–April 1999*, London, Department of Trade and Industry.

Morson, G. and C. Emerson (1990), *Mikhail Bakhtin: Creation of a Prosaics*, Stanford, Stanford University Press.

Mulkay, M. (1979), 'Norms and Ideology in Science', 4–5 *Social Sciences Information*, 637–56.

Mulkay, M. (1980), 'Interpretation and the use of rules: The case of the Norms of Science' in T. Gieryn ed., *Science and Social Structure (A Festschrift for RK Merton)*, New York, New York Academy of Sciences, 111–25.

Mulkay, M. (1991), *Sociology of Science: a sociological pilgrimage*, Milton Keynes, Open University Press.

Mulkay, M. and N. Gilbert (1981), 'Putting Philosophy to Work: Karl Popper's Influence on Scientific Practice', 11 *Philosophy of the Social Sciences*, 389–407.

Mulvaney, D.J. (1989), *Encounters in Place: Outsiders and Aboriginal Australians 1606–1985*, Brisbane, University of Queensland Press.

Mumby, D. (1993), 'Introduction: Narrative and Social Control' in D. Mumby ed., *Narrative and Social Control: Critical Perspectives*, London, Sage, 1–12.

Murphy, J. (2000), 'Expert Witnesses at Trial: Where are the Ethics?', 14 *Georgetown Journal of Legal Ethics*, 217–93.

Myers, F.R. (1986), *Pintupi Country, Pintupi Self: Sentiment, Place and Politics among Western Desert Aborigines*, Washington and Canberra, Smithsonian Institution Press and Australian Institute of Aboriginal Studies.

Myers, G. (1985), 'Texts as knowledge claims: The social construction of two biology articles', 15 *Social Studies of Science*, 593–630.

Nagel, T. (1986), *The View From Nowhere*, Oxford, Oxford University Press.

Nakajima, H. (1996), 'The ICH Programme: Accomplishments and Impact on World Health' in P.F. D'Arcy and D.W.G. Harron eds, *Proceedings of the Third International Conference on Harmonisation*, Belfast, IFPMA, 32.

National Research Council (1992), *DNA Technology in Forensic Science*, Washington DC, National Academy Press.

National Research Council (1996), *The Evaluation of Forensic DNA Evidence*, Washington DC, National Academy Press.

National Science Foundation (1991), 'Attitudes toward science and technology' in *Science and Engineering Indicators 1991*, Washington DC, Government Printing Office, 166–91.

Nelken, D. (1998), 'A just measure of science' in M. Freeman and H. Reece eds, *Science in Court*, Aldershot, Dartmouth, 11–36.

Nelkin, D. (1975), 'The political impact of technical expertise', 5 *Social Studies of Science*, 35–54.

Nelkin, D., ed. (1979), *Controversy: Politics of technical decisions*, Beverly Hills, Sage.

Neufeld, P. and N. Colman (1990), 'When Science Takes the Witness Stand', 262 *Scientific American*, 18–25.

Neutra, R., V. Delpizo and G. Lee (2002), *An evaluation of the possible risks from Electric and Magnetic Fields (EMF) from Powerlines, Internal Wiring, Electrical Occupations, and Appliances: Final Report California EMF program*, Oakland, California Public Utilities Commission and California Department of Health Services.

Niskanen, W.A. (1971), *Bureaucracy and Representative Government*, Chicago, Aldine-Atherton.

Noah, L. (2002), 'Medicine's Epistemology: Mapping the Haphazard Diffusion of Knowledge in the Biomedical Community', 44 *Arizona Law Review*, 373–466.

Nobles, R. and D. Schiff (1997), 'The never ending story: Disguising tragic choices in criminal justice', 60 *Modern Law Review*, 293–304

Nobles, R. and D. Schiff (2000), *Understanding Miscarriages of Justice: Law, the Media, and the Inevitability of Crisis*, Oxford, Oxford University Press.

Nohria, N. and R. Gulati (1994), 'Firms and their Environments' in N. Smelser and R. Swedberg eds, *The Handbook of Economic Sociology*, Princeton, Princeton University Press.

Note (1995a), 'Reasonable doubt: An argument against definition', 108 *Harvard Law Review*, 1955–72.

Note (1995b), 'Confronting the New Challenges of Scientific Evidence', 108 *Harvard Law Review*, 1481–605.

Nowotny, H., P. Scott and M. Gibbons (2001), *Rethinking Science: Knowledge and the Public in an Age of Uncertainty*, Cambridge, Polity Press.

Oakeshott, M. (1962), *Rationalism in politics and other essays*, London, Metheun.

Odgers, S. and J. Richardson (1995), 'Keeping bad science out of the courtroom – Changes in American and Australian expert evidence law', 18 *University of New South Wales Law Journal*, 108–29.

Oldroyd, D. (1986), *The Arch of Knowledge*, Kensington, New South Wales Press.

Olson, W. (1991), *The Litigation Explosion: What happened when America unleashed the lawsuit*, New York, Dutton.

Olson, W. (2003), *The Rule of Lawyers: How The New Litigation Elite Threatens America's Rule of Law*, New York, Truman Tally Books/St. Martins Press,

Olsson, G. (1998), 'Towards a Critique of Cartographical Reason', 1 *Ethics, Place and Environment*, 145–55.

Organisation for Economic Co-operation and Development (1999), *Report by the Environmental Policy Committee on Implementation for the 1996 Recommendation on Improving the Environmental Performance of Governments*, Paris, OECD.

Osborne, L. (15 December 2002), 'The "C.S.I" Myth', *New York Times Magazine* 78.

Oteri, J. S., M.G. Weinberg and M.S. Pinales (1982), 'Cross-Examination in Drug Cases' in B. Barnes and D. Edge eds, *Science in Context: Readings in the Sociology of Science*, Milton Keynes, Open University Press, 250–59.

Palmer, K. (1991), 'Knowledge As a Commodity in Aboriginal Australia' in D. Turnbull ed., *Knowledge, Land and Australian Aboriginal Experience*, Geelong, Deakin University Press, 6–10.

Park, R. (2000), *Voodoo Science: The road from foolishness to fraud*, Oxford, Oxford University Press.

Parkinson, P. (2001), *Tradition and Change in Australian Law* 2nd ed., Sydney, LBC Information Services.

Patton, P. (2000), *Deleuze and the Political*, London, Routledge.

Peller, G. (1985), 'The metaphysics of American law', 73 *California Law Review*, 1151–290.

Pelton, R. (1980), *The Trickster in West Africa: A Study of Mythic Irony and Sacred Delight*, Berkeley, University of California Press.

Perrow, C. (1984), *Normal Accidents*, New York, Basic Books.

Peters, J.D. (July 2002), 'Evidence-based Medicine in Court', *Trial*, 74–79.

Pfiffer, J. and G.R. Salancik (1978), *The External Control of Organizations*, New York, Harper & Row.

Phillips, F. (24 September 2003), 'Science Stressed on Death Penalty', *Boston Globe*, <http://www.boston.com/news/local/articles/2003/09/24/science_stressed_on_death _penalty/>.

Phillips, Lord, J. Bridgeman and M. Ferguson-Smith (2000), *The BSE Inquiry: The Report*, London, The Stationery Office.

Pigliucci, M. (2003), 'Species As Family Resemblance', 25 *BioEssays*, 596–602.

Pluciennik, M. (1999), 'Archaeological Narratives and Other Ways of Telling (1)', 40 *Current Anthropology*, 653–94.

Pocock, J.G.A. (1992), 'Tangata Whenua and Enlightenment Anthropology', 26 *New Zealand Journal of History*, 28–53.

Policy Ethics and Life Sciences Research Institute (PEALS) (2003), *The People's Report on GM*, <http://www.gmjury.org>.

Polkinghorne, D. (1991), *Narrative Knowing in the Human Sciences*, Albany, State University of New York Press.

Popper, K. (1959), *The Logic of Scientific Discovery*, New York, Harper.

Popper, K. (1963), *Conjectures and Refutations*, New York, Harper.

Porter, T. (1995), *Trust in Numbers: The Pursuit of Objectivity in Science and Public Life*, Princeton, Princeton University Press.

Porter, M.E. and C. van der Linde (1995a), 'Green and Competitive: Ending the Stalemate', 73 *Harvard Business Review*, 120–36.

Porter, M.E. and C. van der Linde (1995b), 'Toward a New Conception of the Environment–Competitiveness Relationship', 9 *Journal of Economic Perspectives*, 97–119.

Potter, J. (1996), *Representing Reality: Discourse, rhetoric and social construction*, London, Sage.

Pound, R. (1908), 'Mechanical jurisprudence', 8 *Columbia Law Review*, 605–23.

Prakash, A. (2000), *Greening the Firm: The Politics of Corporate Environmentalism*, Cambridge, Cambridge University Press.

Pratchett, T., I. Stewart, and J. Cohen (2003), *The Science of Discworld II: The Globe*, London, Ebury Press.

Psychopharmacological Drugs Advisory Committee (PDAC) (18 May 1992), *Transcript of Psychopharmacological Drugs Advisory Committee Meeting*, FDA Headquarters.

Purdy, J. (1999), 'Postcolonialism: The Emperor's New Clothes?' in E. Darian-Smith and P. Fitzpatrick eds, *Laws of the Postcolonial*, Ann Arbor, University of Michigan Press, 203–32.

Quilter, J. and G. Urton eds (2002), *Narrative Threads: Accounting and Recounting in Andean Khipu*, Austin, University of Texas Press.

Quinn, P. (1984), 'The philosopher of science as expert witness' in J. Cushing, C.F. Delaney and G.M. Gutting eds, *Science and reality*, Notre Dame, University of Notre Dame Press, 367–86.

Rabin, R. (1992), 'A sociolegal history of the tobacco tort litigation', 44 *Stanford Law Review*, 853–78.

Rauch, J. (1999), *Government's End: Why Washington Stopped Working*, New York: Public Affairs.

Ravetz, J. (1971), *Scientific knowledge and its problems*, Oxford, Oxford University Press.

Ray, A.J. (2003), 'Expertise in Aboriginal title claims: Litigation in Australia and North America, 1946–2002' in I. McCalman and A. McGrath eds, *Proof and Truth*, Canberra, Australian Academy of the Humanities, 97–119.

Redmayne, M. (2001), *Expert Evidence and Criminal Justice*, Oxford, Oxford University Press.

Reece, H., ed. (1998), *Law and science*, Oxford, Oxford University Press.

Reed, C. (27 July 2003), 'Trucker's Arty Joke Could Fetch $20m', *The Observer.*

Reilly, A. (2000), 'The Ghost of Truganini: Use of Historical Evidence as Proof of Native Title', 28 *Federal Law Review,* 453–75.

Reilly, A. (2002), 'Cartography and Native Title', presented at Sharing the Space Conference, Flinders University, Australia.

Resnik, D. (2000), 'A Pragmatic Approach to the Demarcation Problem', 31 *Studies in the History and Philosophy of Science,* 249–67.

Resnik, J. (1982), 'Managerial judges', 96 *Harvard Law Review,* 364–448.

Reynolds, H. (1987), *Frontier: Aborigines, Settlers and Land,* Sydney, Allen & Unwin.

Reynolds, H. (1996), *Aboriginal Sovereignty: Reflections on Race State and Nation,* St Leonards, Allen & Unwin.

Reynolds, H. (13 December 2002), 'Historians at War', *Weekend Australian,* R 12–13.

Richardson, D. (1998), 'Sexuality and Citizenship', 32 *Sociology,* 83–100.

Ricoeur, P. (1984), *Time and Narrative: Vol 1,* Chicago, University of Chicago Press.

Rip, A. (2003), 'Constructing expertise: in a third wave of science studies?', 33 *Social Studies of Science,* 419–34.

Risinger, D.M., M.J. Saks, W.C. Thompson and R. Rosenthal (2002), 'The *Daubert/Kumho* Implications of Observer Effects in Forensic Science: Hidden Problems of Expectation and Suggestion', 90 *California Law Review,* 1–56.

Ritter, D. (1996), 'The "Rejection of Terra Nullius" in *Mabo*: A Critical Analysis', 18 *Sydney Law Review,* 5–33.

Robbins, D. and R. Johnston (1976), 'The role of cognitive and occupational differentiation in scientific controversies', 6 *Social Studies of Science,* 349–68.

Roberts, L. (1991), 'Fight Erupts Over DNA Fingerprinting', 254 *Science,* 1721–3.

Roberts, L. (1992), 'Science in Court: A Culture Clash', 257 *Science,* 732–6.

Rodgers, K.E. (1996), 'The ISO Environmental Standards Initiative', 5 *New York University Environmental Law Journal,* 182–276.

Roe, E. (1994), *Narrative Policy Analysis: Theory and Practice,* Durham NC, Duke University Press.

Rose, D. (1996), 'Histories and Rituals: Land Claims in the Territory' in B. Attwood ed., *In the Age of Mabo: History, Aborigines and Australia,* St Leonards, Allen & Unwin, 35–53.

Rose, N. (1999), *Powers of Freedom: reframing political thought,* Cambridge, Cambridge University Press.

Rosenbaum, W.A. (1998), *Environmental Politics and Policy* 4th ed., Washington DC, CQ Press.

Rosenbaum, W.A. (2000), 'Escaping the "Battered Agency Syndrome": EPA's Gamble with Regulatory Reinvention' in N. Vig and M. Kraft eds, *Environmental Policy* 4th ed., Washington DC, CQ Press, 165–89.

Rouse, J. (1996), *Engaging Science: How To Understand Its Practices Philosophically,* Ithaca NY, Cornell University Press.

Rowley, S. (1997), '"There Once Lived ... "; Craft and Narrative Traditions' in S. Rowley ed., *Craft and Contemporary Theory,* St Leonards, Allen & Unwin, 76–84.

Rowse, T. (2000), 'Hindmarsh Revisited: Review Article', 70 *Oceania,* 252–62.

Royal Commission on Environmental Pollution (1998), *Setting Environmental Standards* 21st Report, London, The Stationery Office.

Rudwick, M. (1985), *The great Devonian controversy: The shaping of scientific knowledge among gentlemanly specialists,* Chicago, University of Chicago Press.

Ruse, M. (1988), 'Pro judice' in M. Ruse ed., *But is it science? The philosophical question in the creation/evolution controversy,* Buffalo, Prometheus Books, 356–62.

Russo, M. and P. Fouts (1997), 'A Resource-Based Perspective on Corporate Environmental Performance and Profitability', 40 *Academy of Management Journal*, 534–59.

Saks, M. (August/September 1987), 'Accuracy v. Advocacy: Expert Testimony Before the Bench', *Technology Review*, 43–49.

Saks, M. (1992), 'Do we really know anything about the behavior of the tort litigation system—and why not?', 140 *University of Pennsylvania Law Review*, 1147–291.

Saks, M. (1995), 'The phantom of the courthouse', 35 *Jurimetrics*, 233–42.

Saks, M. (1998), 'Merlin and Solomon: Lessons from the Law's Formative Encounters with Forensic Identification Science', 49 *Hastings Law Journal*, 1069–141.

Sandall, R. (2000), *The Culture Cult: Designer Tribalism and Other Essays*, Boulder, Westview Press.

Sanders, E. (1987), 'The Regulatory Surge of the 1970s in Historical Perspective' in E. Bailey ed., *Public Regulation: Perspectives on Institutions and Politics*, Cambridge MA, MIT Press.

Sanders, J. (1992), 'The Bendectin litigation: A case study in life cycles of mass torts', 43 *Hastings Law Journal*, 301–418.

Sanders, J. (1993), From science to evidence: The testimony on causation in the Bendectin cases', 46 *Stanford Law Review*, 1–86.

Sanders, J. (1998), *Bendectin on Trial: A Study of Mass Tort Litigation*, Anne Arbor, University of Michigan Press.

Sarbin, T., ed. (1986), *Narrative Psychology: The Storied Nature of Human Conduct*, New York, Praeger.

Sartwell, C. (2000), *End of Story: Toward an Annihilation of Language and History*, New York, State University of New York Press.

Sauerwein, K. (3 October 2003), 'Artists Now Claim Disputed "Ugly" Painting', *Los Angeles Times,* B4.

Schank, R. (1990, 1998), *Tell Me a Story: Narrative and Intelligence*, Evanston, Northwestern University Press.

Schmid-Schönbein, O. and A. Braunschweig (2000), *EPI–Finance 2000: Environmental Performance Indicators for the Financial Industry*, <http://www.epifinance.com>.

Schuck, P. (1986), *Agent Orange on trial: Mass toxic disasters in the courts*, Cambridge MA, Harvard University Press.

Schuck, P. (1993), 'Multi-Culturalism Redux: Science, Law, and Politics', 11 *Yale Law & Policy Review,* 1–46.

Schuster, J. and R. Yeo eds (1986), *The Politics and Rhetoric of Scientific Method*, Dordrecht, Reidel.

Schwartz, A. (1997), 'A "dogma of empiricism" revisited: *Daubert v. Merrell Dow Pharmaceuticals, Inc.* and the need to resurrect the philosophical insight of *Frye v United States*', 10 *Harvard Journal of Law & Technology*, 149–237.

Schwartz, T.M. (1991), 'Product liability reform by the judiciary', 27 *Gonzaga Law Review*, 303–334.

Sclove, R. (1995), *Democracy and Technology*, New York, Guildford Press.

Serres, M. with B. Latour (1990), *Conversations on Science, Culture, and Time* (trans. R. Lapidus), Ann Arbor, University of Michigan Press.

Shapin, S. (1994), *A social history of truth: Civility and science in seventeenth-century England*, Chicago, University of Chicago Press.

Shapin, S. (1995), 'Cordelia's Love: Credibility and the social studies of science', 3 *Perspectives on Science*, 255–75.

Shapin, S. and S. Schaffer (1985), *Leviathan and the Air Pump: Hobbes, Boyle and the experimental life*, Princeton, Princeton University Press.

Shapiro, M. (1997), *Violent Cartographies: Mapping Cultures of War*, Minneapolis, University of Minnesota Press.

Shapiro, M. (1999), 'Triumphalist Geographies' in M. Featherstone and S. Lash eds, *Spaces of Culture: City, Nation, World*, Thousand Oaks, Sage, 159–74.

Shiel, F. (13 September 2003), 'Yorta Yorta to Take Title Case to UN', *The Age*, 12.

Shinn, T. and R. Whitley eds (1985), *Expository Science: Forms and Functions of Popularisation*, Dordrecht, Reidel.

Silbey, S. (1981), 'Making sense of the lower courts', 6 *Justice System Journal*, 13–27.

Simons, M. (26 August 2000), 'A Bridge to the Heart of the Nation', *The Age*, 1, 6.

Simons, M. (2003), *The Meeting of the Waters: The Hindmarsh Island Affair*, Sydney, Hodder.

Sinclair, D. (1997), 'Self-Regulation versus Command and Control? Beyond False Dichotomies', 19 *Law & Policy*, 529–60.

Slesin, L. (November–December 1995), 'Atlantic Legal Foundation: New Player On The EMF Scene', 15 *Microwave News*, 3.

Slesin, L. (1996), 'The Covalt decision and the state of the science', 16 *Microwave News*, 4.

Smith, L.T. (1999), *Decolonizing Methodologies: Research and Indigenous Peoples*, London, Zed Books.

Smith, R. and B. Wynne eds (1989), *Expert Evidence: Interpreting Science in the Law*, Routledge, London.

Soguk, N. and G. Whitehall (1999), 'Wandering Grounds: Transversality, Identity, Territoriality, and Movement', 28 *Millennium: Journal of International Studies*, 675–700.

Solomon, S. and E. Hackett (1996), 'Setting Boundaries Between Science and Law: Lessons from *Daubert v. Merrell Dow Pharmaceuticals, Inc.*', 21 *Science, Technology & Human Values*, 131–56.

Special Committee (1989), *Jury Comprehension in Complex Cases*, Washington DC, American Bar Association.

Specter, M. (27 May 2002), 'Do Fingerprints Lie?', *The New Yorker*, 96–105.

Speer, T.L. (1997), 'Growing the Green Market', 19 *American Demographics*, 45–49.

Star, S.L. and J. Griesmer (1989), 'Institutional Ecology, "Translations" and Boundary Objects: Amateurs and Professionals in Berkeley's Museum of Vertebrate Zoology, 1907–39', 19 *Social Studies of Science*, 387–420.

Staudenmaier, J. (1985), *Technology's Storytellers: Reweaving the Human Fabric*, Cambridge MA, MIT Press.

Stavins, R.N. (2000), 'Experience with Market-Based Environmental Policy Instruments', *Resources for the Future Discussion Paper 00–09*, Washington DC, Resources for the Future.

Stewart, R.B. (1975), 'The Reformation of American Administrative Law', 88 *Harvard Law Review*, 1667–1813.

Stewart, W. (2000), *Independent Expert Group on Mobile Phones (IEGMP) Mobile Phones and Health*, UK, National Radiation Protection Board.

Stigler, G.J. (1971), 'The Theory of Economic Regulation', 2 *Bell Journal of Economics and Management Science*, 3–21.

Stoney, D.A. (2001), 'Measurement of Fingerprint Individuality' in H.C. Lee and R.E. Gaensslen eds, *Advances in Fingerprint Technology*, Boca Raton FL, CRC Press, 327–87

Stove, D.C. (1984), *Popper and After: Four Modern Irrationalists*, New York, Pergamon.

Strelein, L. (2001), 'Conceptualising Native Title', 23 *Sydney Law Review*, 95–124.

Taylor, P. (1999), *Modernities: A Geohistorical Interpretation*, Cambridge, Polity Press.

Thames, J. (1995), 'It's Not Bad Law—It's Bad Science', 18 *American Journal of Trial Advocacy,* 545–63.

Thompson, E.P. (1971), 'The moral economy of the English crowd in the eighteenth century', 50 *Past & Present,* 76–136.

Thornburgh, D. (1998), 'Junk Science—The Lawyer's Ethical Responsibility', 25 *Fordham Urban Law Journal,* 449–69.

Timmermans, S. and M. Berg (2003), *The gold standard: The challenge of evidence-based medicine and standardization in health care,* Philadelphia, Temple University Press.

Tokar, B. (1997), *Earth for Sale: Reclaiming Ecology in the Age of Corporate Greenwash,* Boston, South End Press.

Tonkinson, R. (1997), 'Anthropology and Aboriginal Tradition: The Hindmarsh Island Bridge Affair and the Politics of Interpretation', 68 *Oceania,* 1–27.

Tsong, Y. (1992), 'Statistical comparison of ADE reporting rates between triazolam and temazepam', Internal FDA memo to Chief of Epidemiology Branch, Office of Epidemiology.

Tulloch, J. (1999), *Performing Culture: Stories of Expertise and the Everyday,* Sage, London.

Tunstall, J. (1986), *Communications Deregulation: The Unleashing of America's Communication Industry,* Oxford, Basil Blackwell.

Turnbull, D. (1991), *Mapping The World in the Mind: An Investigation of the Unwritten Knowledge of the Micronesian Navigators,* Geelong, Deakin University Press.

Turnbull, D. (1997), 'Maps and Mapmaking of the Australian Aboriginal People' in H. Selin ed., *Encyclopedia of the History of Science, Technology and Medicine in Non-western Cultures,* Dordrecht, Kluwer Academic Publishers, 560–62.

Turnbull, D. (1998a), 'Cook and Tupaia, a Tale of Cartographic *Méconnaissance?*' in M. Lincoln ed., *Science and Exploration in the Pacific: European Voyages to the Southern Oceans in the Eighteenth Century,* London, Boydell Press/National Maritime Museum, 117–32.

Turnbull, D. (1998b), 'Mapping Encounters and (En)countering Maps: A Critical Examination of Cartographic Resistance' in S. Gorenstein ed., *Research in Science and Technology Studies: Knowledge Systems. Knowledge and Society,* Stanford, JAI Press, 15–44.

Turnbull, D. (2000), *Masons, Tricksters and Cartographers: Comparative Studies in the Sociology of Scientific and Indigenous Knowledge,* Amsterdam, Harwood Academic Publishers.

Turnbull, D. (2002), 'Travelling Knowledge: Narratives, Assemblage and Encounters' in M. Bourget, C. Licoppe, and H.O. Sibum eds, *Instruments, Travel and Science: Itineraries of Precision from the Seventeenth to the Twentieth Century,* London, Routledge, 273–94.

Turnbull, D. (2004), 'Genetic Mapping: Approaches to the Spatial Topography of Genetics' in H. Rheinberger and J. Gaudilliere eds, *Mapping Cultures of Twentieth Century Genetics,* London, Taylor and Francis, (forthcoming).

Turnbull, D. (2005a), 'Locating, Negotiating, and Crossing Boundaries: A Western Desert Land Claim, The Tordesillas Line and The West Australian Border', *Environment and Planning D: Society and Space,* (forthcoming).

Turnbull, D. (2005b), 'Knowledge, Space and Movement: A Post Colonial Approach to the Problem of Assembling Knowledge from Different Traditions', *Science as Culture,* (forthcoming).

Turner, B. (1990), 'Outline of a Theory of Citizenship', 24 *Sociology,* 189–217.

Turner, M. (1996), *The Literary Mind,* New York, Oxford University Press.

Turner, S. (2001), 'What is the problem with experts', 31 *Social Studies of Science,* 123–50.

Twining, W. (1985), *Theories of evidence: Bentham and Wigmore*, Stanford, Stanford University Press.

Twining, W. (1990), *Rethinking Evidence: Exploratory Essays*, Oxford, Basil Blackwell.

Twining, W. and D. Miers (1982), *How to do things with rules: A primer of interpretation*, London, Weidenfeld and Nicolson.

Usui, T., S.A. Griffiths and C.E. Lumley (1996), 'Industry Viewpoint: The Utility of the Mouse for the Assessment of the Carcinogenic Potential of Pharmaceuticals' in P.F. D'Arcy and D.W.G. Harron eds, *Proceedings of the Third International Conference on Harmonisation*, Belfast, IFPMA, 279–84.

Valverde, M. (2003), *Law's Dream of a Common Knowledge*, Princeton, Princeton University Press.

Van der Lann, J.W. (1996), 'Regulatory Viewpoint' in P.F. D'Arcy and D.W.G. Harron eds, *Proceedings of the Third International Conference on Harmonisation*, Belfast, IFPMA, 269–73.

Van Oosterhout, J.P.J., J.W. Van der Laan, E.J. Waal, K. Olejniczak, M. Hilgenfeld, V. Schmidt and R. Bass (1997), 'The Utility of Two Rodent Species in Carcinogenic Risk Assessment of Pharmaceuticals in Europe', 25 *Regulatory Toxicology and Pharmacology*, 6–17.

Van Zwanenberg, P. and E. Millstone (2000), 'Beyond Skeptical Relativism: Evaluating the Social Constructions of Expert Risk Assessments', 25 *Science, Technology & Human Values*, 259–82.

Varnedoe, K. (1998), *Jackson Pollock*, New York, Harry N. Abrams.

Vidal, J. (8 January 2004), 'GM crops linked to rise in pesticide use', *The Guardian*, 5.

Vig, N.J. (2003), 'Presidential Leadership and the Environment' in N. Vig and M. Kraft eds, *Environmental Policy* 5th ed., Washington DC, CQ Press, 103–26.

Vogel, D. (1986), *National Styles of Regulation: Environmental Policy in Great Britain and the United States*, Ithaca NY, Cornell University Press.

Vogel, D. (1989), *Fluctuating Fortunes: The Political Power of Business in America*, New York, Basic Books.

Vogler, C. (1996), *The Writer's Journey: Mythic Structure for Storytellers and Screenwriters*, London, Boxtree.

von Moltke, K. and O. Kuik (1997), *Global Product Chains: Northern Consumers, Southern Producers, and Sustainability*, Amsterdam, Institute for Environmental Studies Vrije Universiteit.

Walby, S. (1994), 'Is Citizenship Gendered?', 28 *Sociology*, 379–95.

Walker, L. and J. Monahan (2000), 'Scientific authority: The breast implant litigation and beyond', 86 *Virginia Law Review*, 801–833.

Walley, N. and B. Whitehead (1994), 'It's Not Easy Being Green', 72 *Harvard Business Review*, 46–52.

Walsh, W.J., R. Wilson and M.S. Kauffman (1997), 'Electric and Magnetic Fields: Policy Science and Litigation' in *Briefly: Perspectives on Legislation, Regulation, and Litigation* No.8, Washington DC, National Center for the Public Interest.

Wambaugh, J. (1989), *The Blooding*, New York, Morrow.

Watson, I. (1997), 'Indigenous People's Law-ways: Survival Against the Colonial State', 8 *Australian Feminist Law Journal*, 39–58.

Weaver, R.K. and B.A. Rockman eds (1993), *Do Institutions Matter? Government Capabilities in the United States and Abroad*, Washington DC, The Brooking Institution.

Weiner, J. (1999), 'Culture in a Sealed Envelope: The Concealment of Australian Aboriginal Heritage and Tradition in the Hindmarsh Island Bridge Affair', 5 *Journal of the Royal Anthropological Institute*, 193–209.

Weiner, J. (2001), 'Strangelove's Dilemma: Or, What Kind of Secrecy Do the Ngarrindjeri Practice?' in A. Rumsey and J. Weiner eds, *Emplaced Myth: Space, Narrative and Knowledge in Aboriginal Australia and Papua New Guinea*, Honolulu, University of Hawaii Press, 139–60.

Weiner, J. (2002), 'Diaspora, Materialism, Tradition: Anthropological Issues in the Recent High Court Appeal', 2 *Land, Rights, Laws: Issues of Native Title*, 1–12.

Weinstein, J. (1986), 'Improving Expert Testimony', 20 *University of Richmond Law Review*, 473–97.

Welsh, I. (2001), *Mobilizing Modernity: the nuclear moment*, London, Routledge.

Wertheim, P.A. (1990), 'Qualifying as an Expert Fingerprint Witness: Designing a Set of Questions to Assist in Court Testimony', 40 *Journal of Forensic Identification*, 60–8.

Wheaton, H. (1836), *Elements of International Law*, London, B. Fellowes.

White, H. (1980), 'The Value of Narrativity in the Representation of Reality' in W.J.T. Mitchell ed., *On Narrative*, Chicago, University of Chicago Press, 1–23.

White, H. (1987), *The Content of the Form: Narrative Discourse and Historical Representation*, Baltimore, Johns Hopkins University Press.

White, J. (1984), *When Words Lose Their Meaning: Constitutions and Reconstitutions of Language, Character and Community*, Chicago, University of Chicago Press.

Wigmore, J.H. (1940), *A Treatise on the Anglo–American System of Evidence in Trials at Common Law* 3rd ed., Boston, Little, Brown & Co.

Wildavsky, A. (1995), *But is it true: A citizen's guide to environmental health and safety issues*, Cambridge MA, Harvard University Press.

Williams, N. (1983), 'Yolngu Concepts of Land Ownership' in N. Peterson and M. Langton eds, *Aborigines, Land and Land Rights*, Canberra, Australian Institute of Aboriginal Studies, 94–109.

Williams, N. (1986), *The Yolngu and Their Land: A System of Land Tenure and the Fight for its Recognition*, Canberra, Australian Institute of Aboriginal Studies.

Wilson, D. (1998), *The Cost of Crossing Bridges*, Mitcham, Small Poppies.

Wilson, R. (2000), 'Technology failures were caused by managers not listening to engineers', 404 *Nature*, 701.

Wilson, R. (2004), 'Science and the Law: Sound Science in the Courtroom', <http://phys4.harvard.edu/%7Wilson/soundscience/ALF_Science.html#EMF>.

Wilson, W. (1887), 'The Study of Administration', 2 *Political Science Quarterly*, 197–222.

Windschuttle, K. (2002), *The Fabrication of Aboriginal History. Vol 1 Van Dieman's Land 1803–47*, Paddington NSW, Macleay Press.

Wood, S., R. Jones and A. Geldart (2003), *The Social and Economic Challenges of Nanotechnology*, Swindon, Economic and Social Research Council.

Woodhouse, E., D. Hess, S. Breyman and B. Martin (2002), 'Science studies and activism: Possibilities and problems for reconstructivist agendas', 32 *Social Studies of Science* 297-319.

Woolf, H. (1996), *Access to Justice: Final Report*, London, The Stationery Office.

Wootten, H. (2003), 'Conflicting imperatives: Pursuing truth in the courts' in I. McCalman and A. McGrath eds, *Proof and Truth*, Canberra, Australian Academy of the Humanities, 15–50.

World Health Organization (1969), 'Principles for the Testing and Evaluation of Drugs for Carcinogenicity', *Technical Report Series* No. 426, Geneva, WHO.

World Health Organization (1974), 'Assessment for the Carcinogenicity and Mutagenicity of Chemicals', *Technical Report Series* No. 546, Geneva, WHO.

Wynne, B. (1982), *Rationality and Ritual: The Windscale Inquiry and Nuclear Decisions in Britain*, Chalfont St Giles, British Society for the History of Science.

Wynne, B. (1989a), 'Establishing the rules of law' in R. Smith and B. Wynne eds, *Expert Evidence: Interpreting Science in the Law*, Routledge, London, 23–55.

Wynne, B. (1989b), 'Frameworks of rationality in risk management: towards the testing of naïve sociology' in J. Brown ed., *Environmental Threats: perception, analysis and management*, London and New York, Belhaven Press, 33–47.

Wynne, B. (1991), 'Knowledges in Context' 16 *Science, Technology & Human Values*, 111–21.

Wynne, B. (1995), 'Public Understanding of Science' in S. Jasanoff, G. Markle, J. Petersen and T. Pinch eds, *Handbook of Science and Technology Studies*, Thousand Oaks, Sage, 361–88.

Wynne, B. (1996a), 'May The Sheep Safely Graze? A Reflexive View of the Expert–Lay Knowledge Divide' in S. Lash, B. Szerszynski and B. Wynne eds, *Risk, Environment and Modernity: Towards a New Ecology*, London, Sage, 44–83.

Wynne, B. (1996b), 'Misunderstood Misunderstandings: Social Identities and Public Uptake of Science' in A. Irwin and B. Wynne eds, *Misunderstanding Science: The Public Reconstruction of Science and Technology*, Cambridge, Cambridge University Press.

Wynne, B. (1996c), 'SSK's Identity Parade: Signing-Up, Off-and-On', 26 *Social Studies of Science*, 357–92.

Wynne, B. (2003), 'Seasick on the Third Wave? Subverting the hegemony of propositionalism', 33 *Social Studies of Science*, 401–17.

Yandle, B. (1983), 'Bootleggers and Baptists: The Education of a Regulatory Economist', 7 *Regulation*, 12–16.

Yandle, B. (1999), 'Grasping For the Heavens: 3-D Property Rights and the Global Commons', 10 *Duke Environmental Law & Policy Forum*, 14–44.

Yandle, B. (2000), 'Public Choice and the Environment' in T. Anderson ed., *Political Environmentalism: Going Behind the Green Curtain*, Stanford, Hoover Institution Press, 31–60.

Yearley, S. (1989), 'Bog Standards: Science and Conservation at a Public Inquiry', 19 *Social Studies of Science*, 421–38.

Yeazell, S. (1994), 'The misunderstood consequences of modern civil procedure', *Wisconsin Law Review*, 631–78.

Yngvesson, B. (1988), 'Making law at the doorway: The clerk, the court, and the construction of community in a New England Town', 22 *Law & Society Review*, 409–48.

Young, S. (2001), 'The Trouble with "Tradition": Native Title and the *Yorta Yorta* Decision', 30 *University of Western Australia Law Review*, 28–50.

Zilsel, E. (2000), 'The sociological roots of science', 30 *Social Studies of Science*, 935–49.

Zuckerman, A. (1994), 'Quality and economy in civil procedure: The case for commuting correct judgments for timely judgments', 14 *Oxford Journal of Legal Studies*, 353–87.

Index